4

GANGSTA:CURSED.
EP_MARCO ADRIANO

Story by KOHSKE   **Art by SYUHEI KAMO**

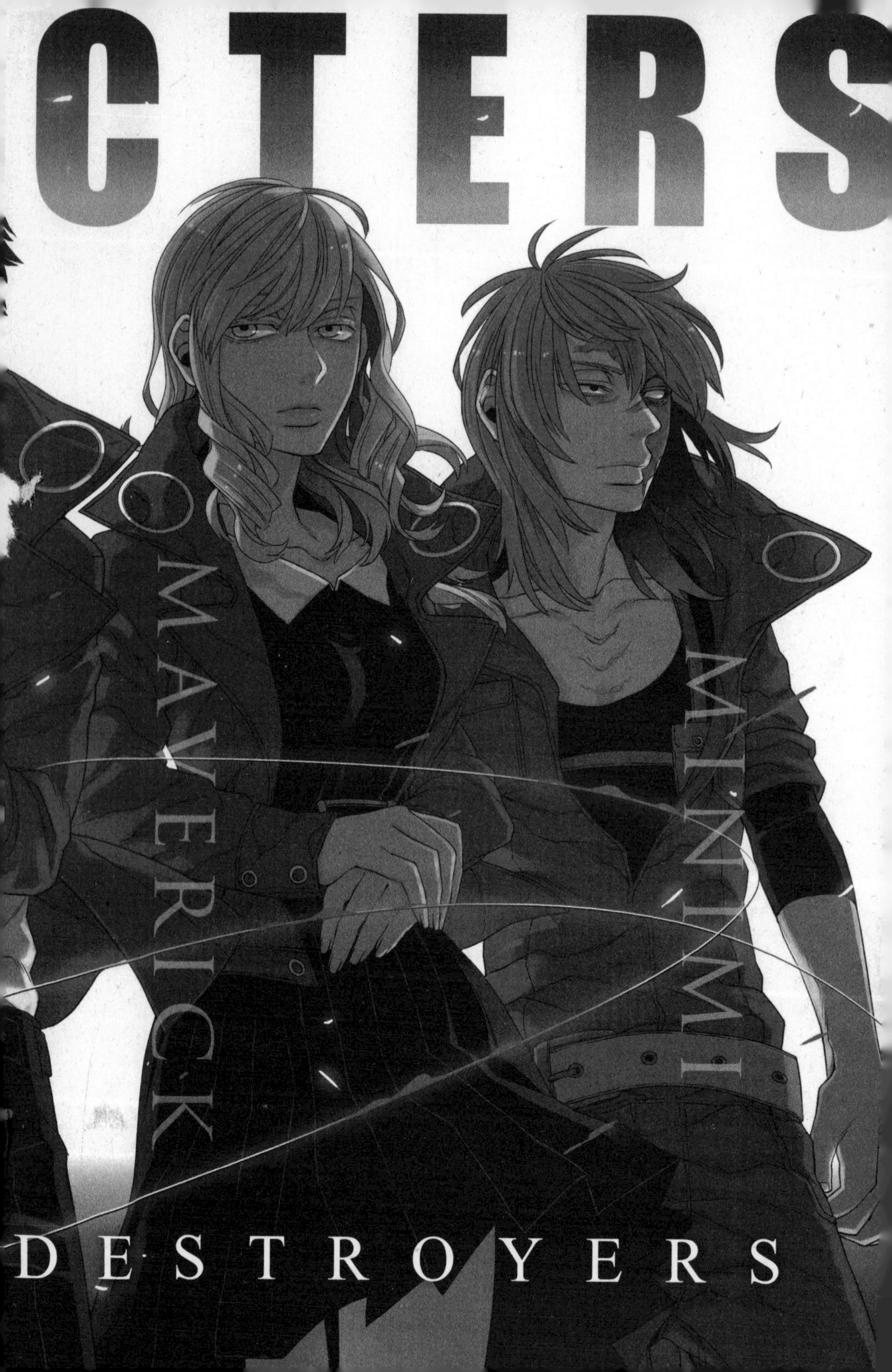
CTERS
MAVERICK
MIMI
DESTROYERS

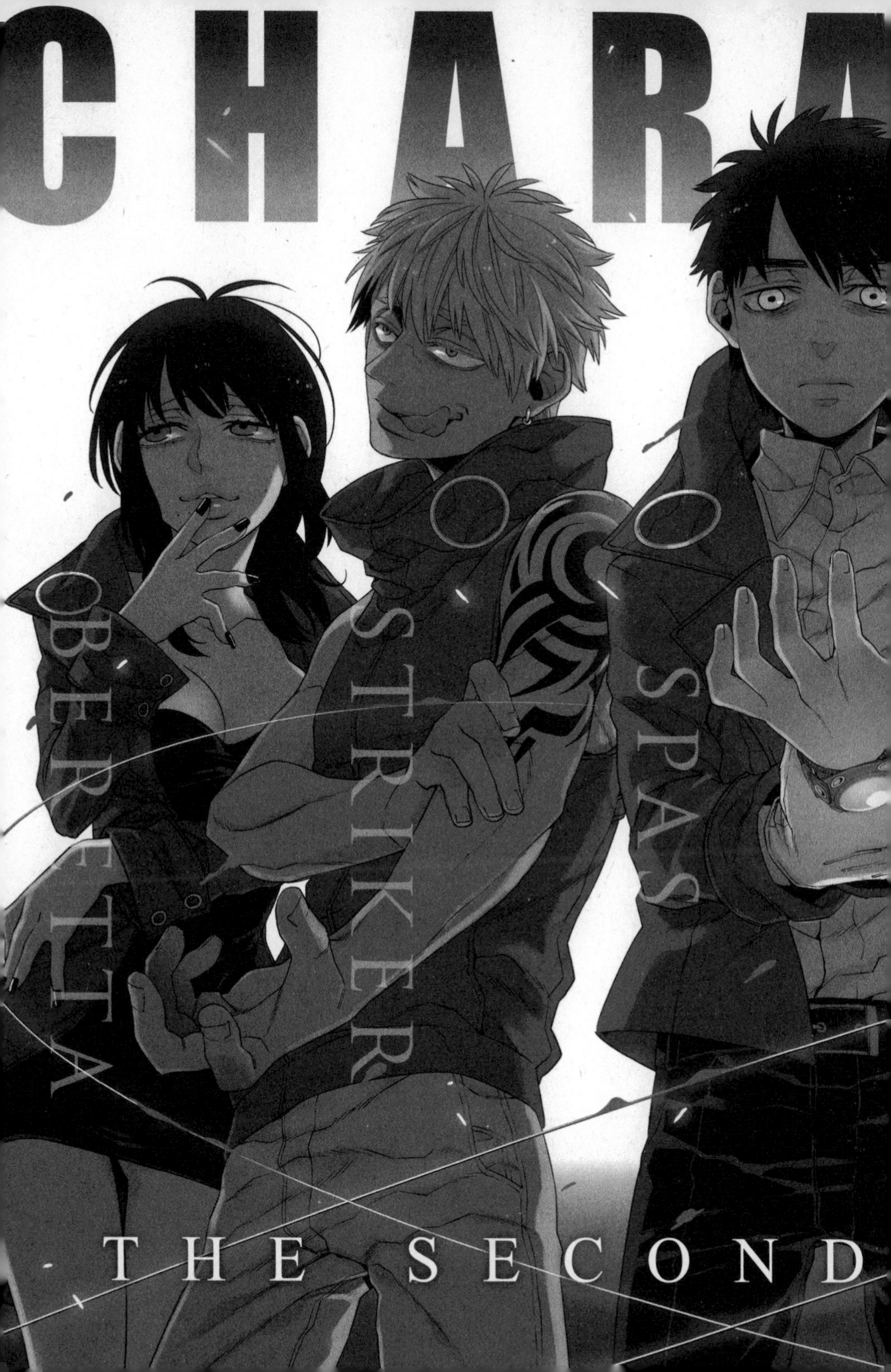
CHARA
BERETTA
STRIKER
SPAS
THE SECOND

CONTENTS

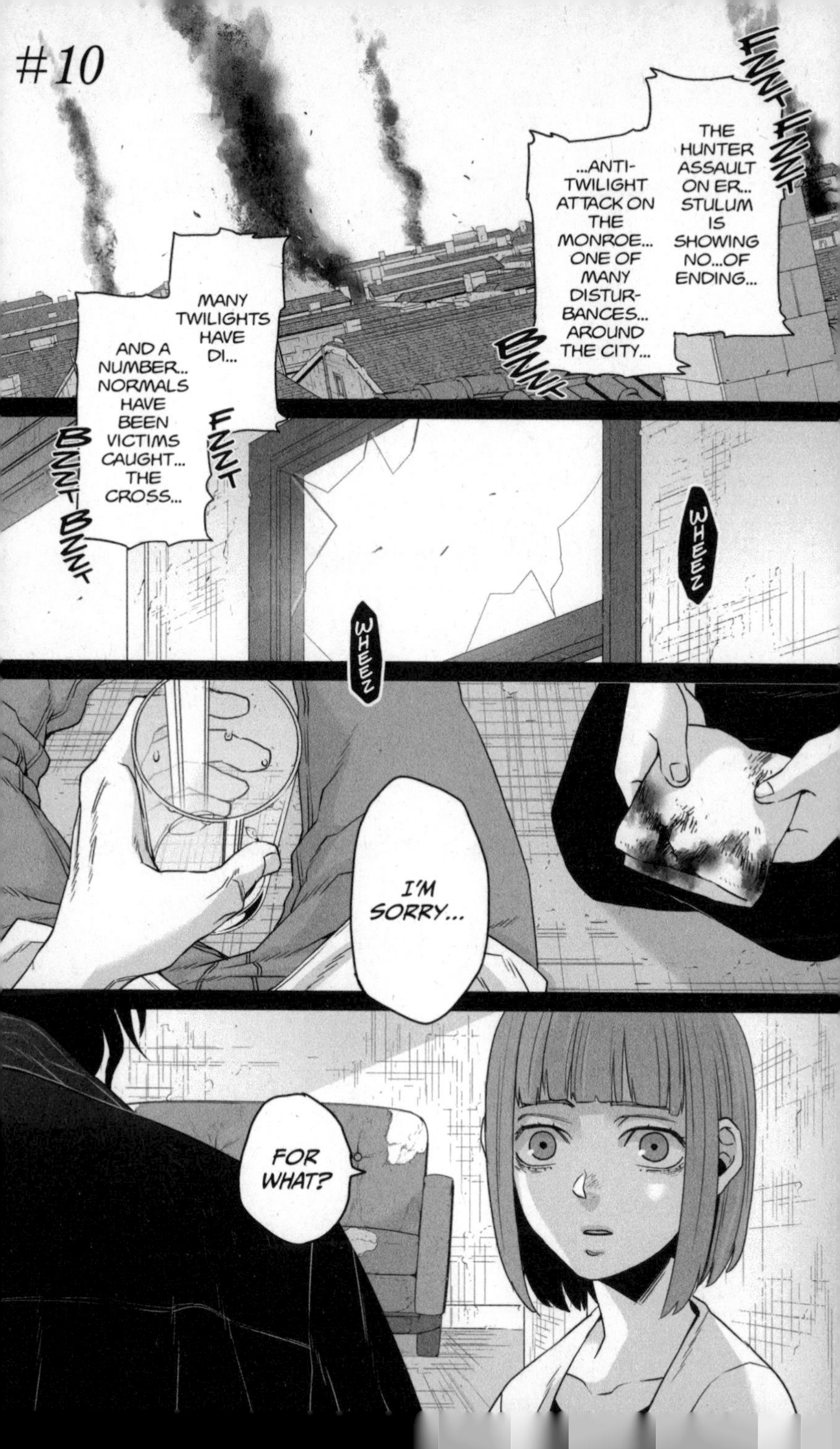
#10
FZZZT FZZZT
THE HUNTER ASSAULT ON ER... STULUM IS SHOWING NO...OF ENDING...
...ANTI-TWILIGHT ATTACK ON THE MONROE... ONE OF MANY DISTURBANCES... AROUND THE CITY...
BZZZT
MANY TWILIGHTS HAVE DI...
AND A NUMBER... NORMALS HAVE BEEN VICTIMS CAUGHT... THE CROSS...
FZZZT
BZZZT BZZZT
WHEEZ
WHEEZ
I'M SORRY...
FOR WHAT?

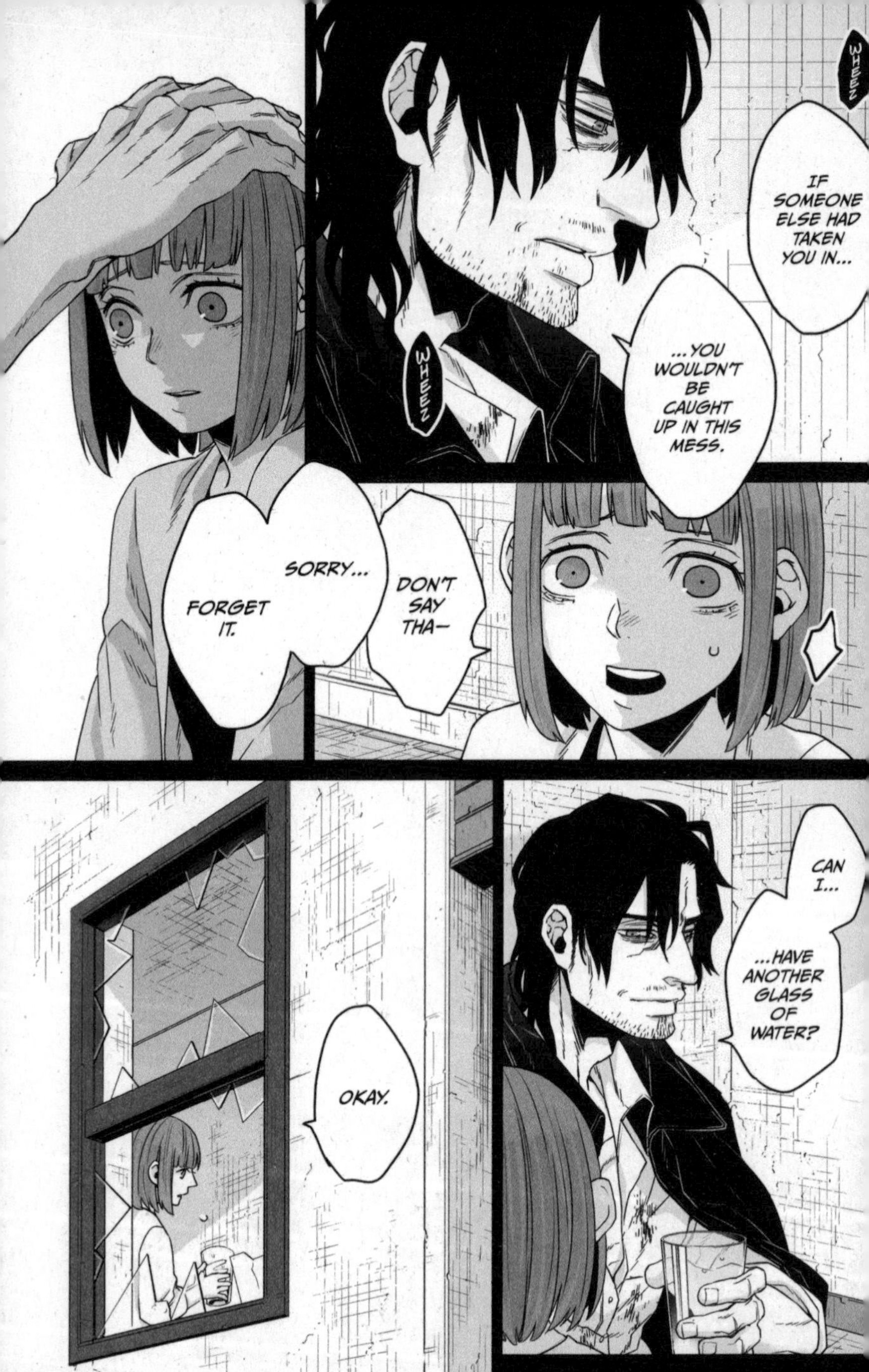
WHEEZ
IF SOMEONE ELSE HAD TAKEN YOU IN...
WHEEZ
...YOU WOULDN'T BE CAUGHT UP IN THIS MESS.
DON'T SAY THA—
SORRY...
FORGET IT.
CAN I...
...HAVE ANOTHER GLASS OF WATER?
OKAY.

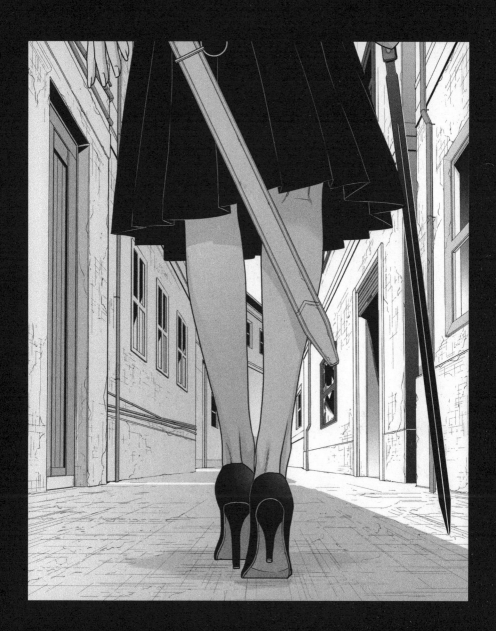

#10

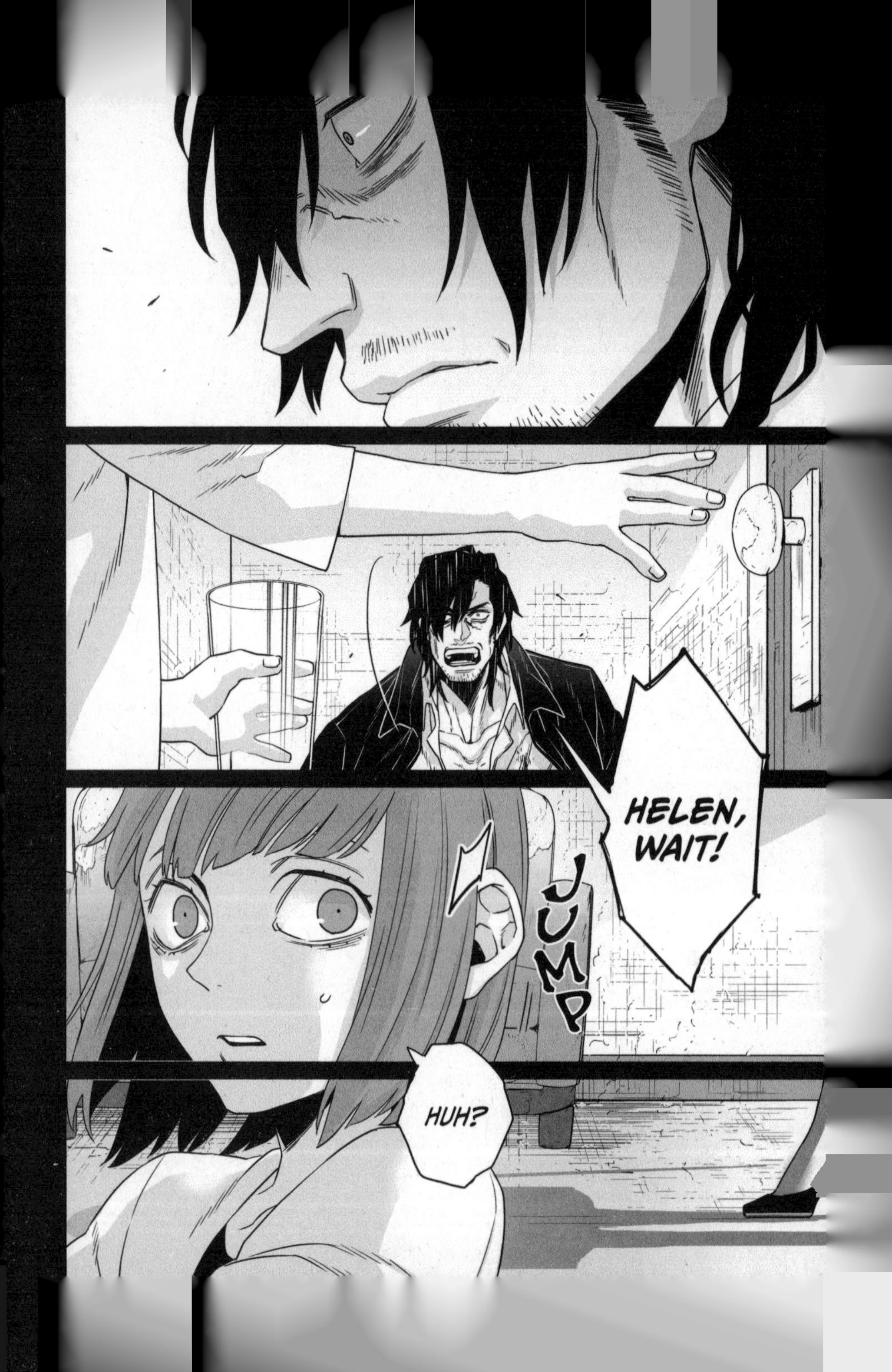
HELEN, WAIT!
JUMP
HUH?

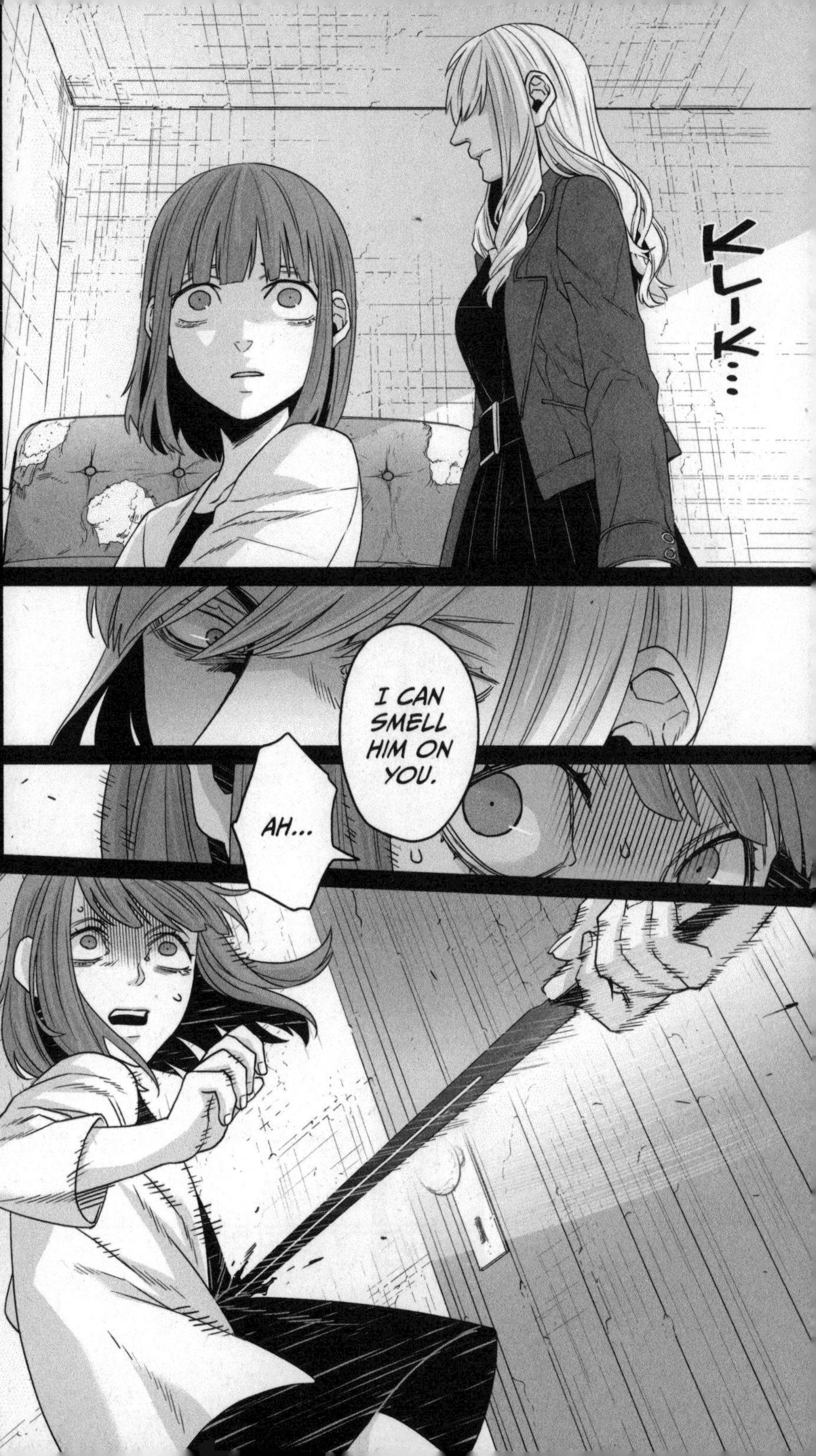
KLUNK...
I CAN SMELL HIM ON YOU.
AH...

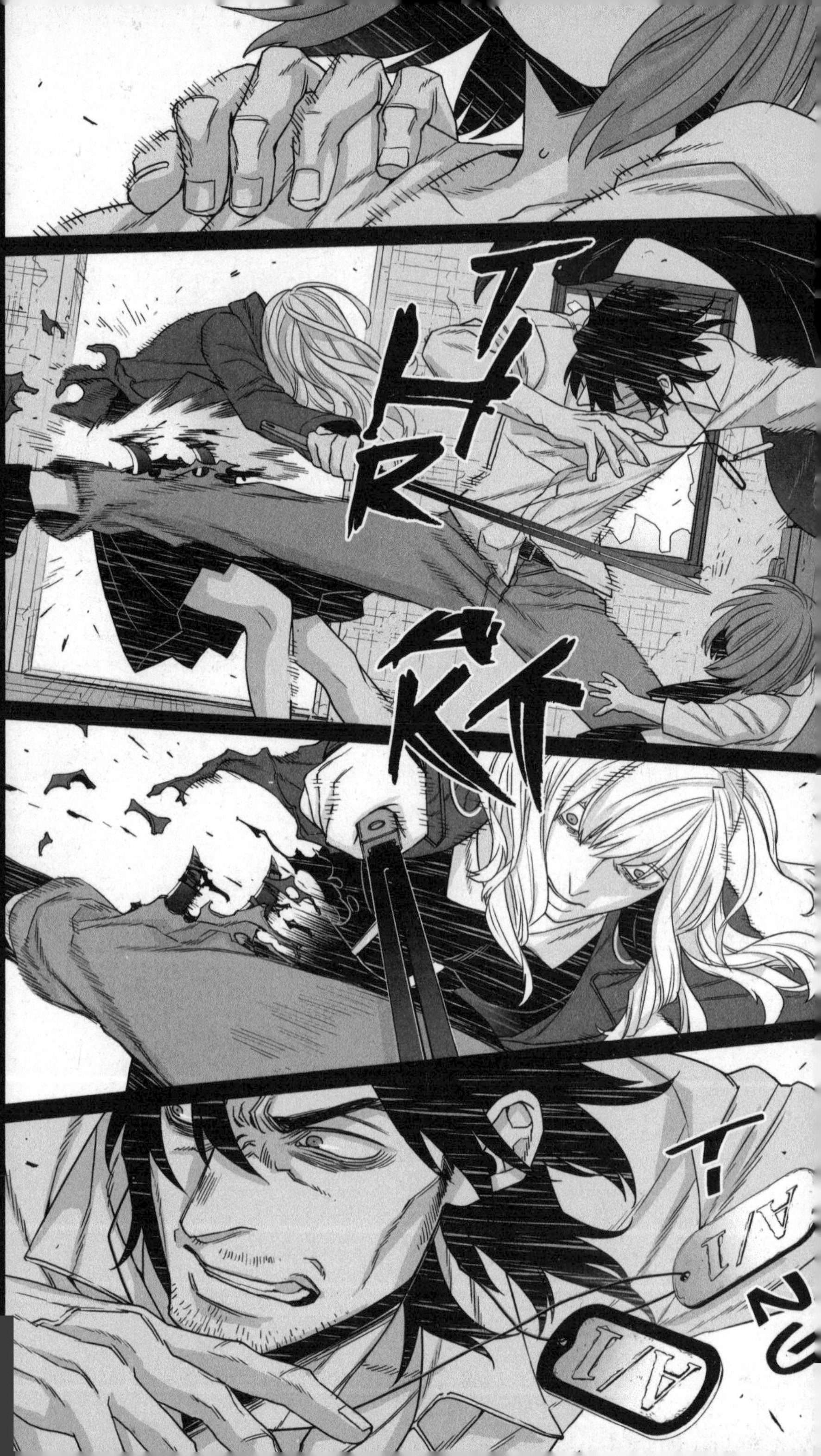

THRAKK
!!

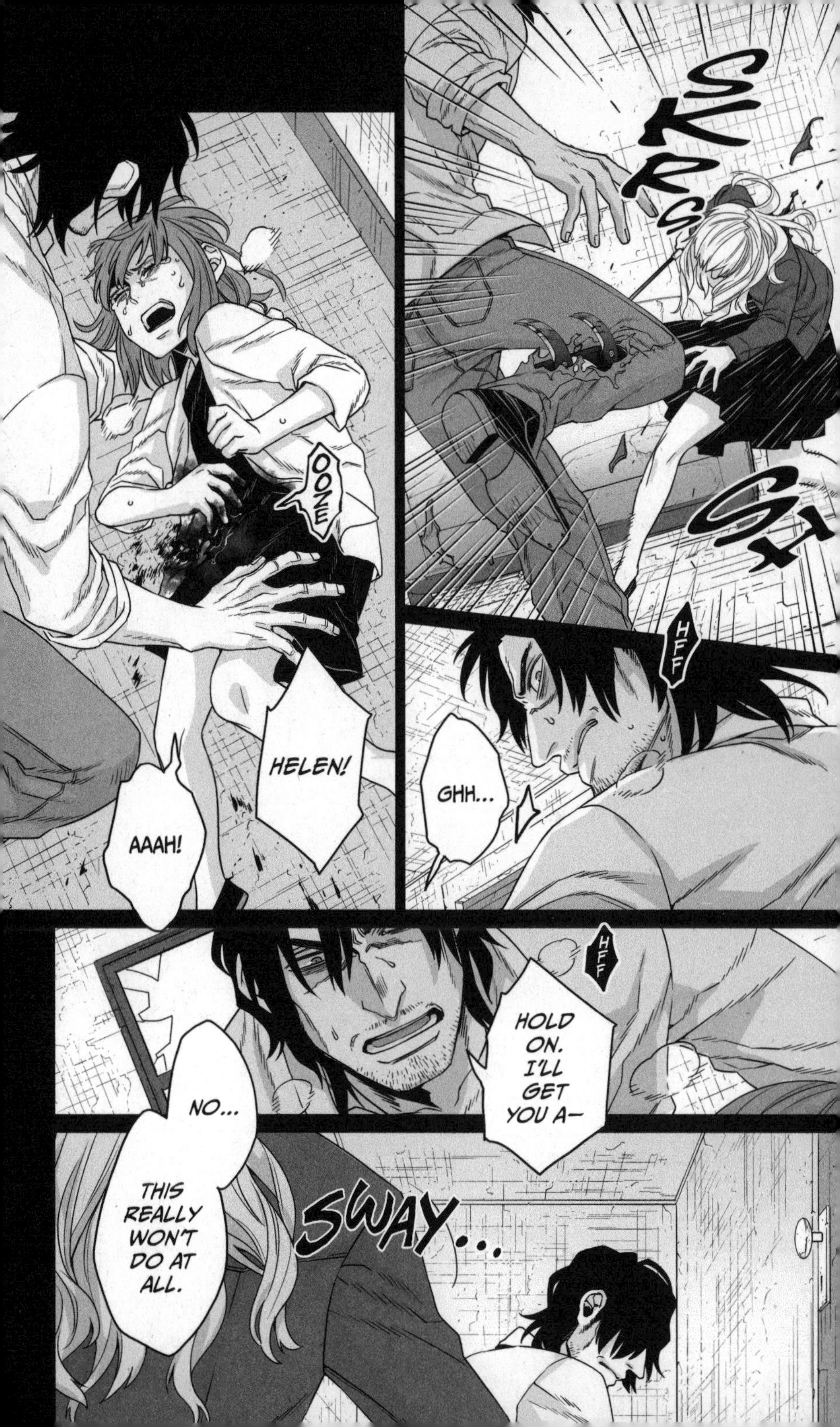
SKRS
SH
HFF
GHH...
OOZE
HELEN!
AAAH!
HFF
HOLD ON. I'LL GET YOU A—
NO...
SWAY...
THIS REALLY WON'T DO AT ALL.

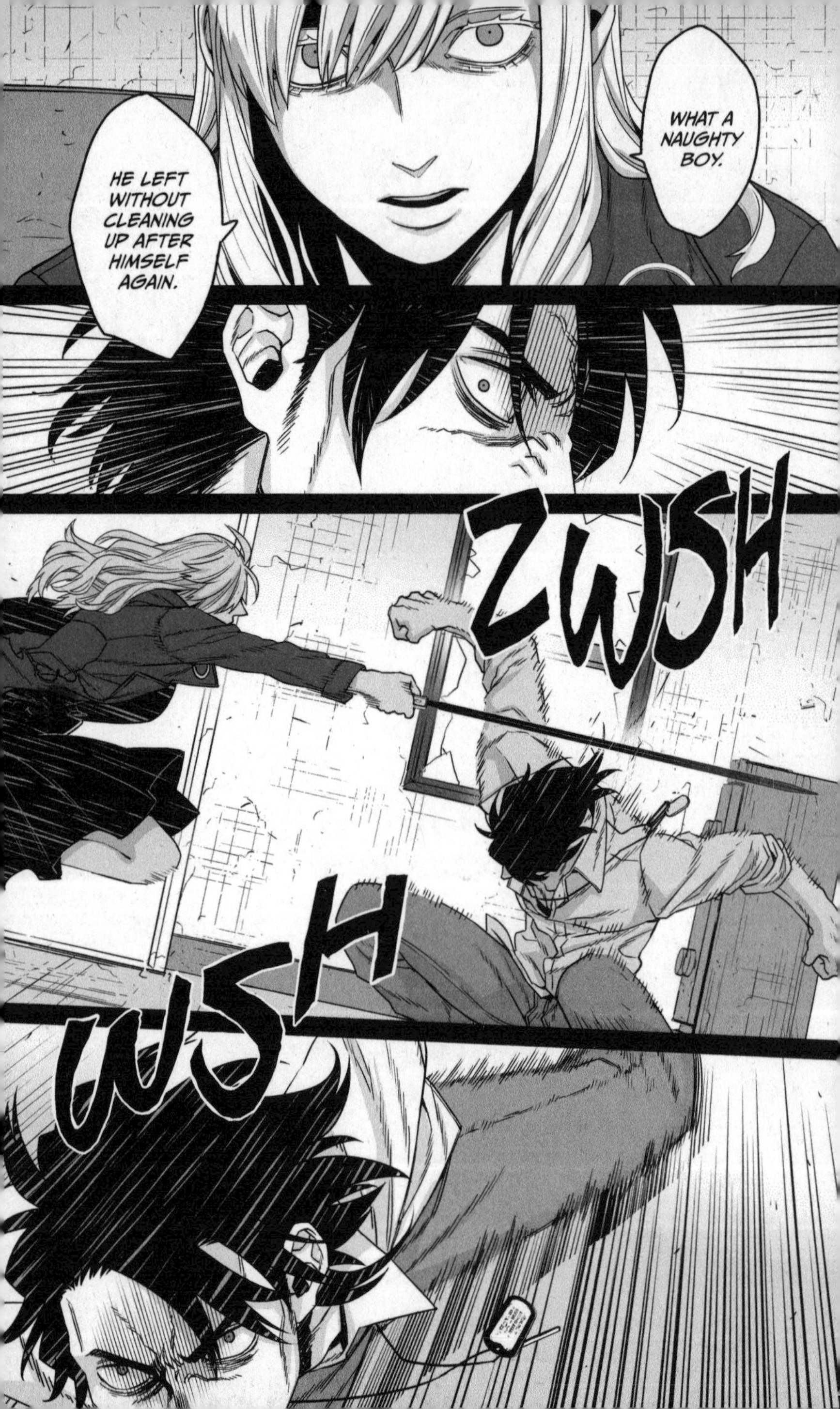
WHAT A NAUGHTY BOY.
HE LEFT WITHOUT CLEANING UP AFTER HIMSELF AGAIN.
ZWSH
WSH

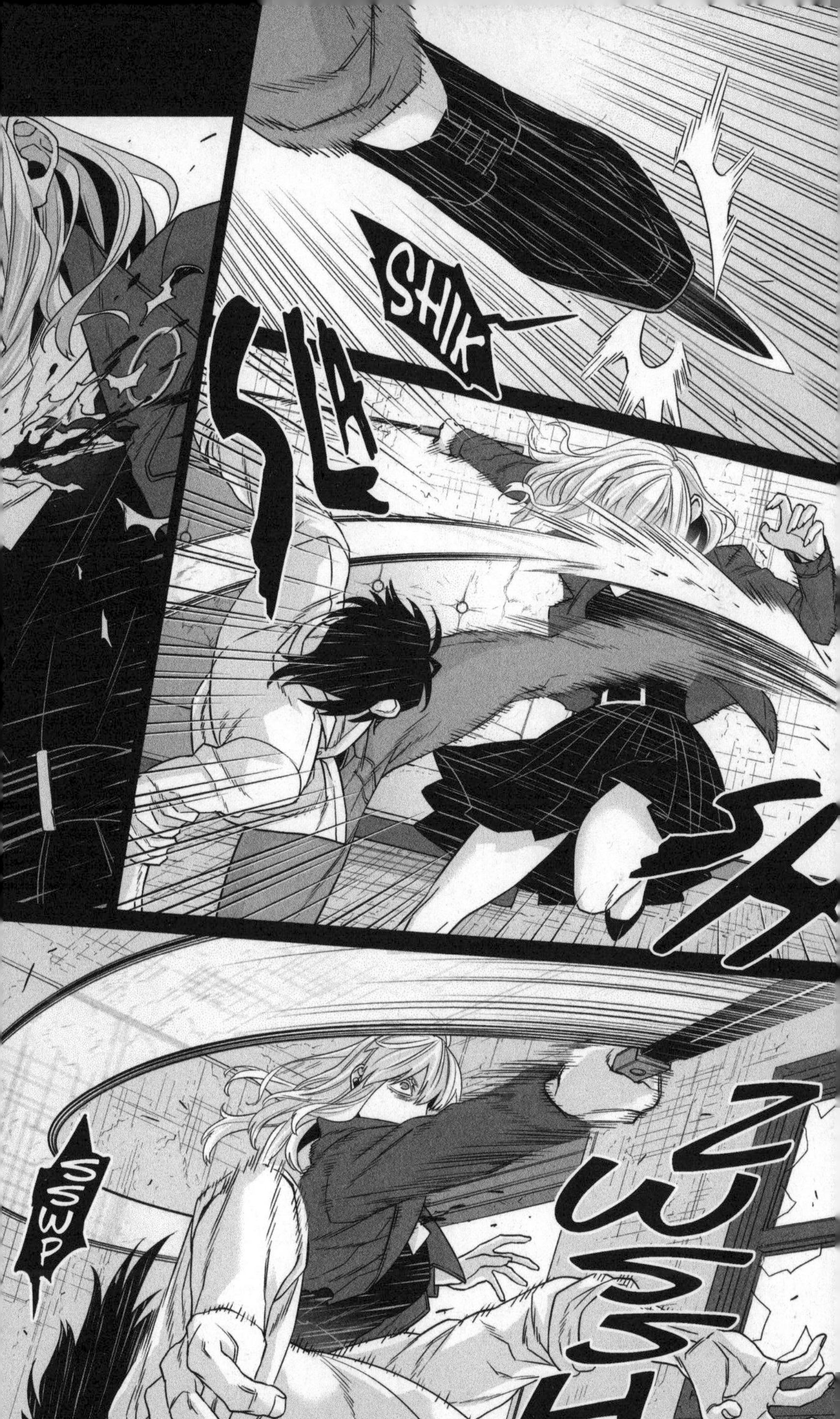
SHIK
SSWP

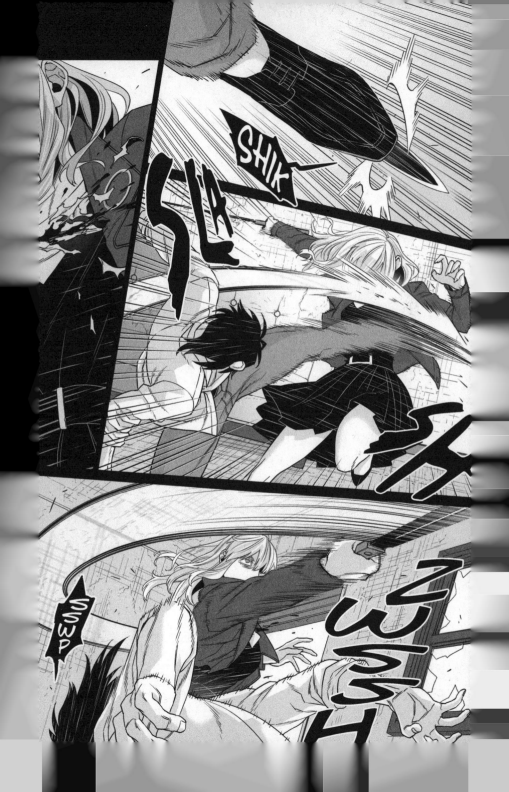

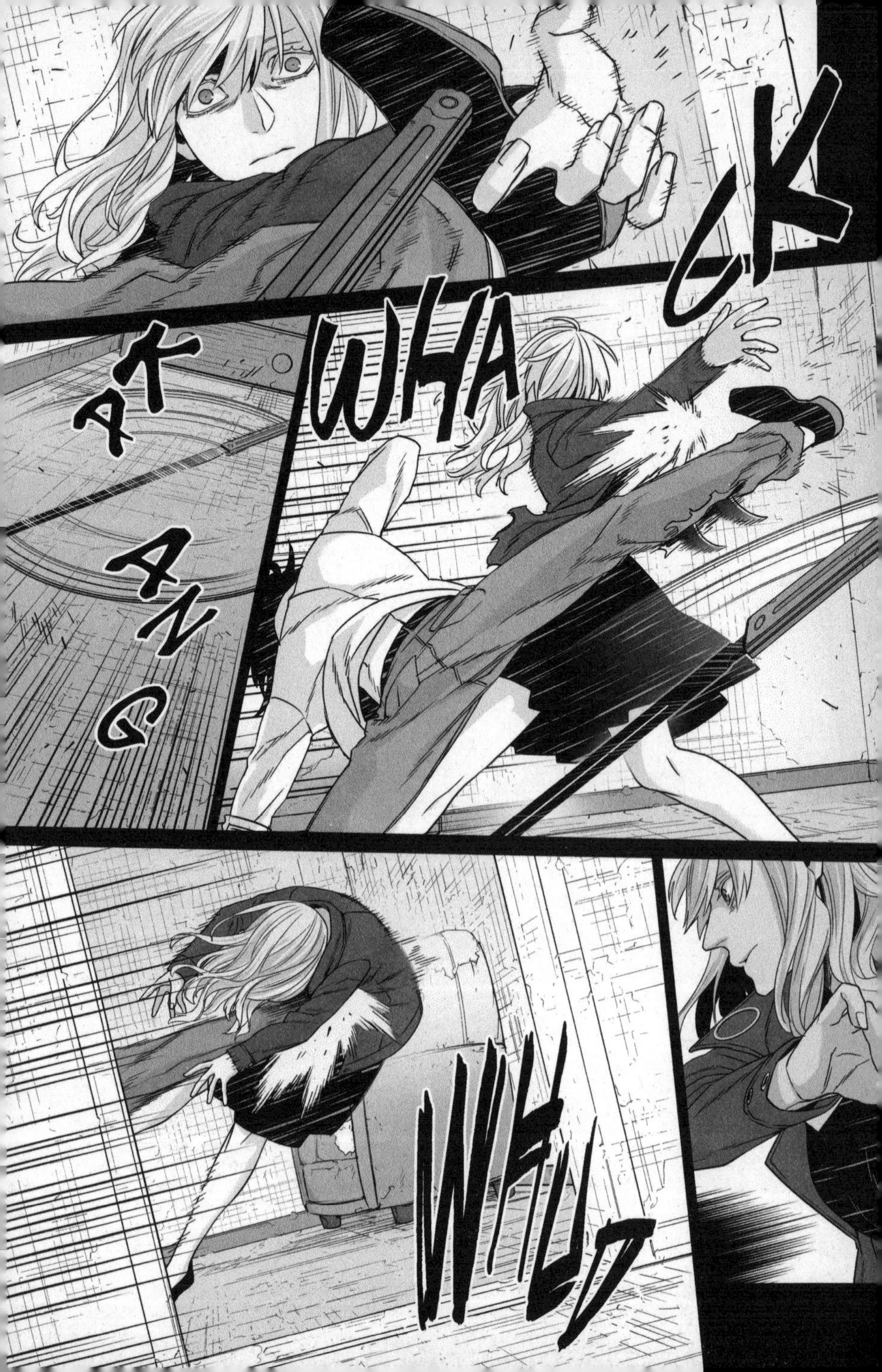

WHACK
ANG
WHUD

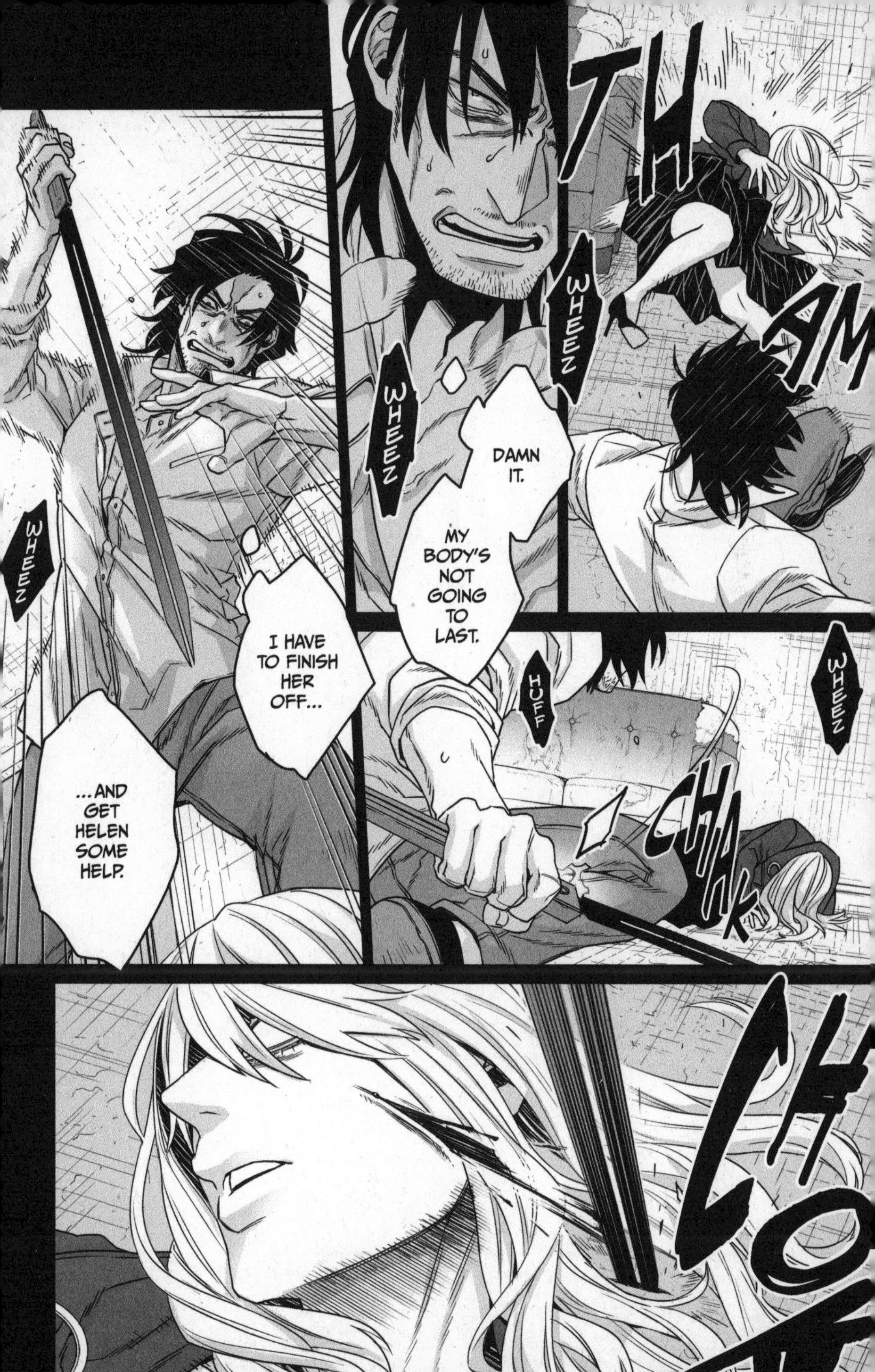
TH
AM
WHEEZ
WHEEZ
DAMN IT.
MY BODY'S NOT GOING TO LAST.
WHEEZ
I HAVE TO FINISH HER OFF...
...AND GET HELEN SOME HELP.
WHEEZ
HUFF
CHAK

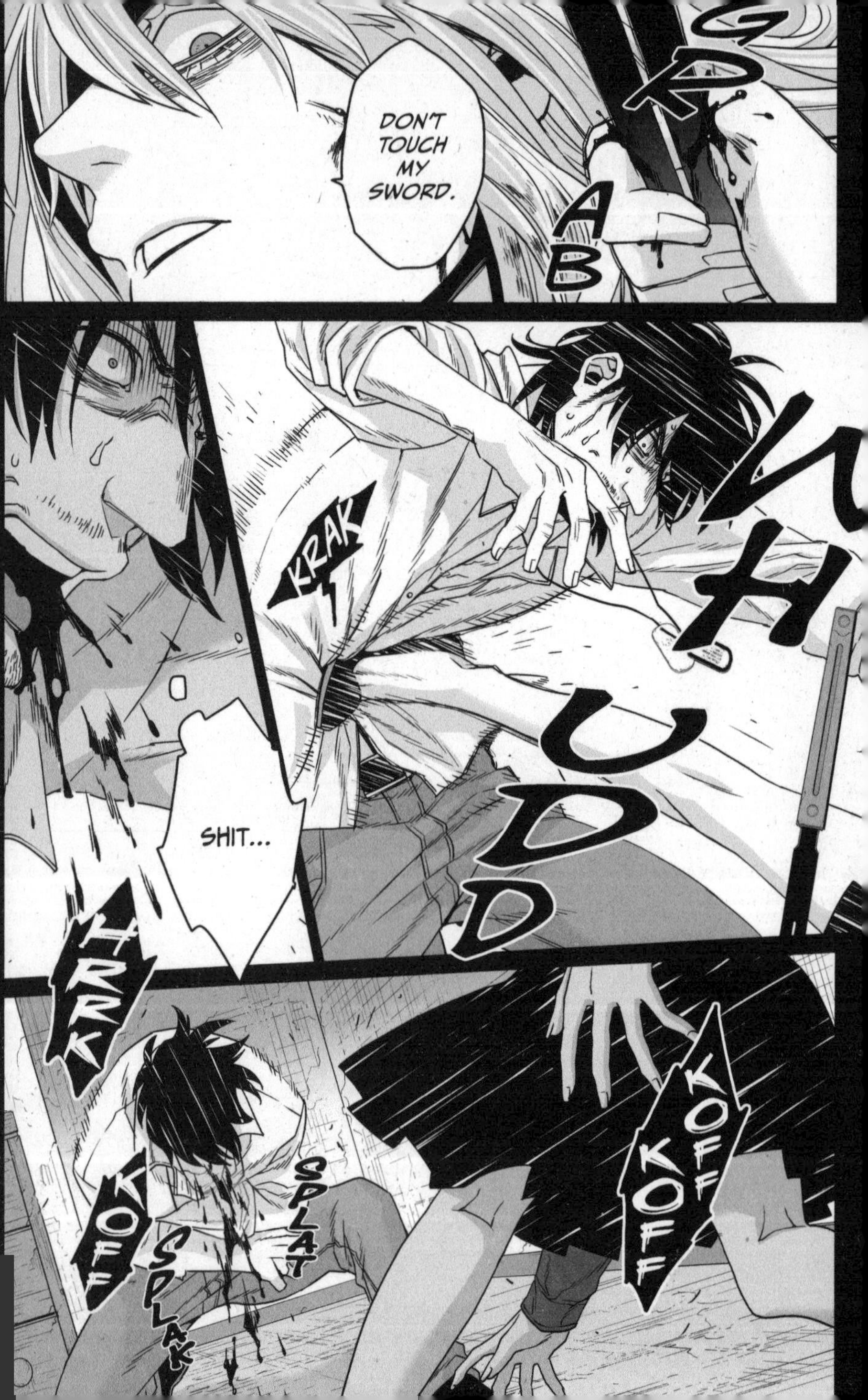
GRAB
DON'T TOUCH MY SWORD.
WHUDD
KRAK
SHIT...
HRRK
KOFF KOFF
KOFF KOFF
SPLAT
SPLAK
KOFF

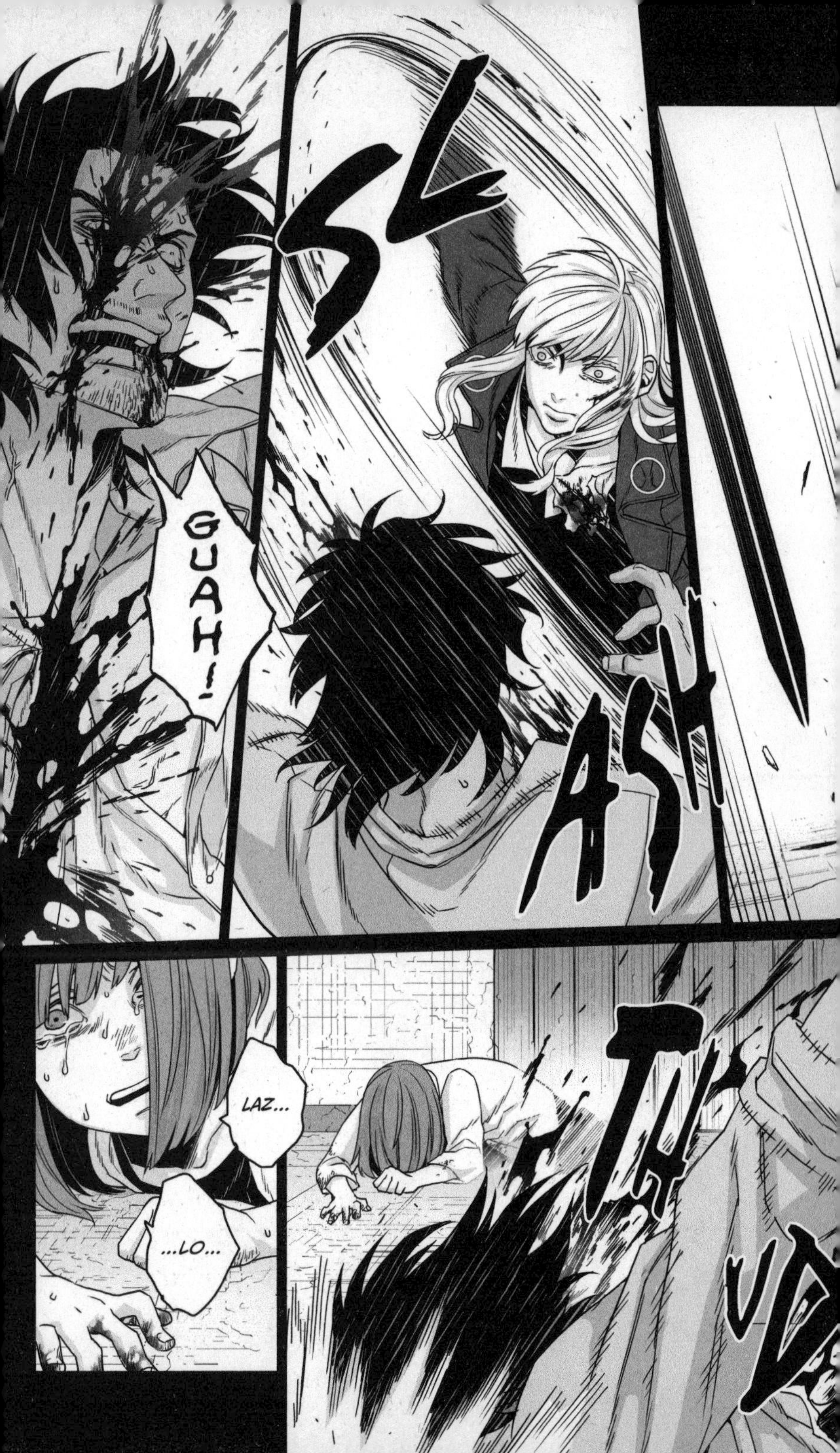
SL
ASH
GUAH!
TH
UD
LAZ...
...LO...

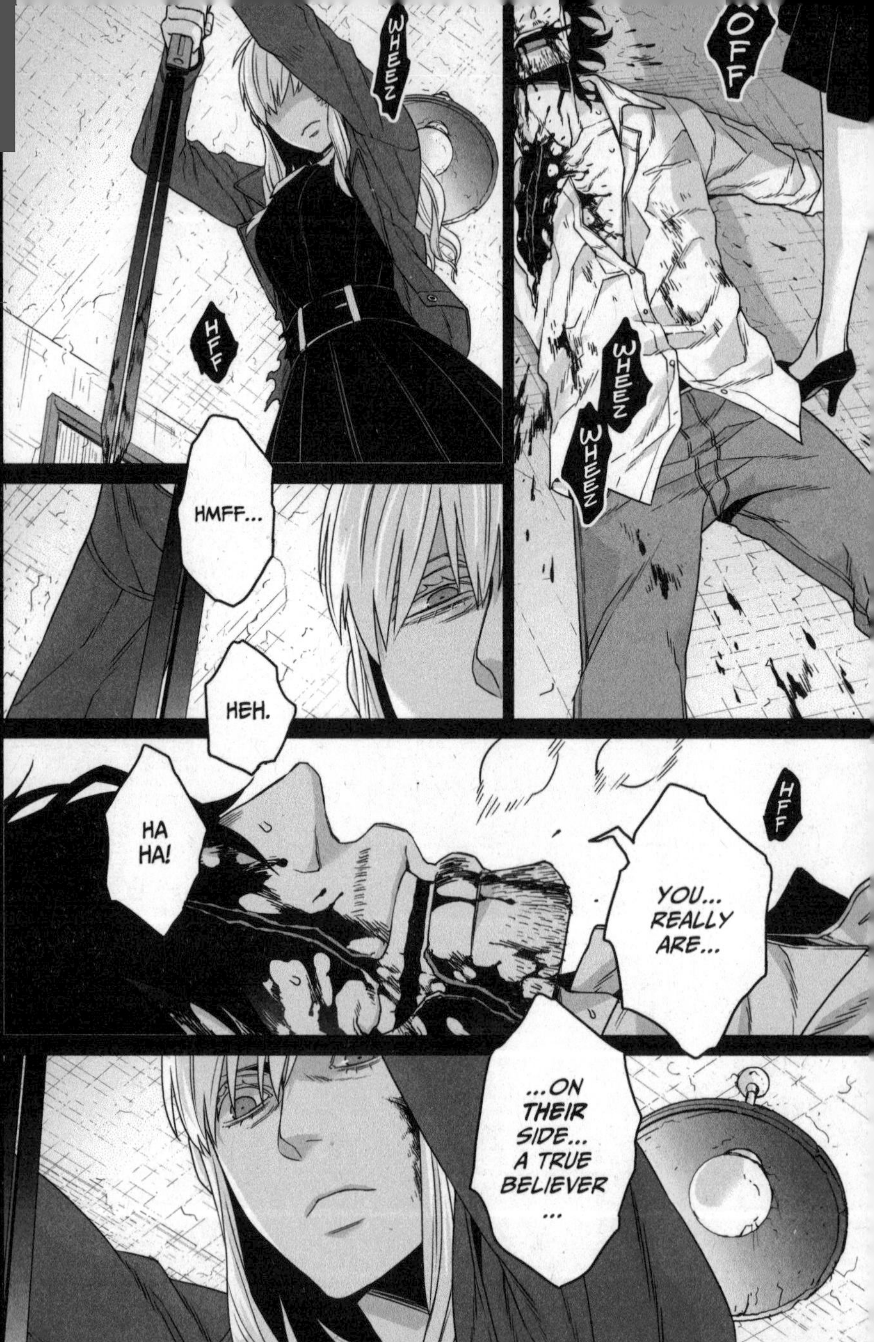
OFF
WHEEZ
WHEEZ
WHEEZ
HFF
HMFF...
HEH.
HFF
YOU... REALLY ARE...
HA HA!
...ON THEIR SIDE... A TRUE BELIEVER ...

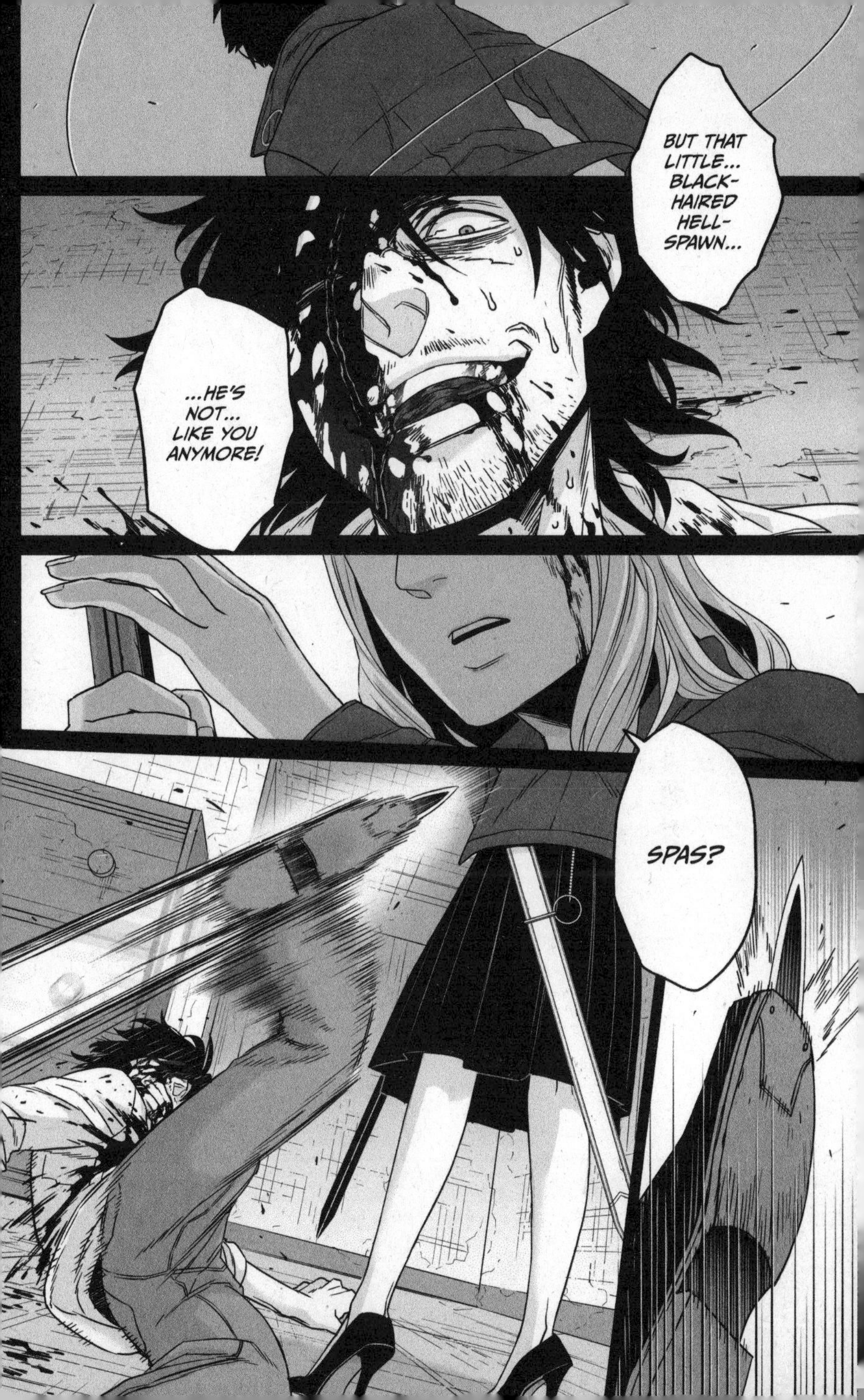

BUT THAT LITTLE... BLACK-HAIRED HELL-SPAWN...
...HE'S NOT... LIKE YOU ANYMORE!
SPAS?

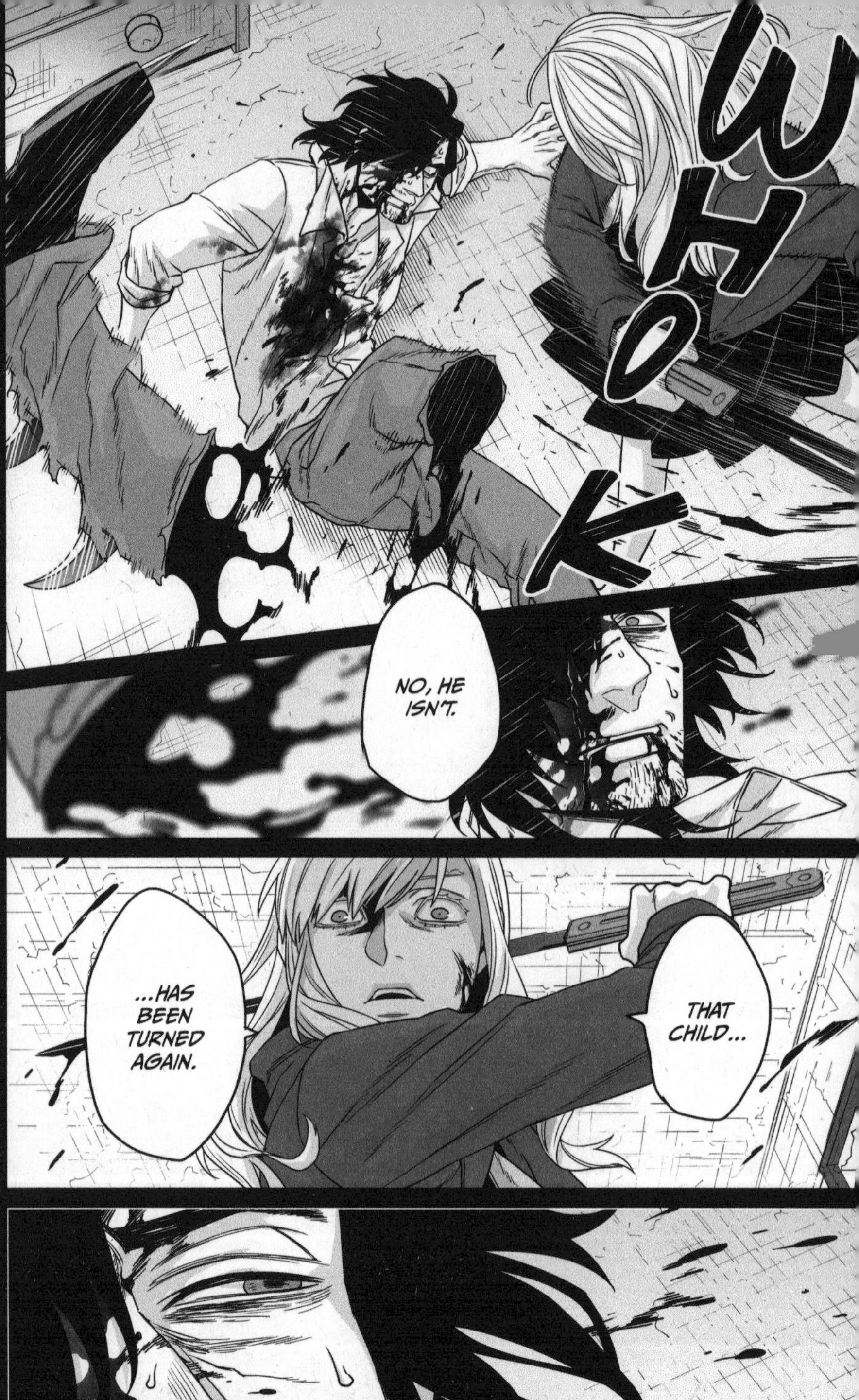
WHOK
NO, HE ISN'T.
THAT CHILD...
...HAS BEEN TURNED AGAIN.

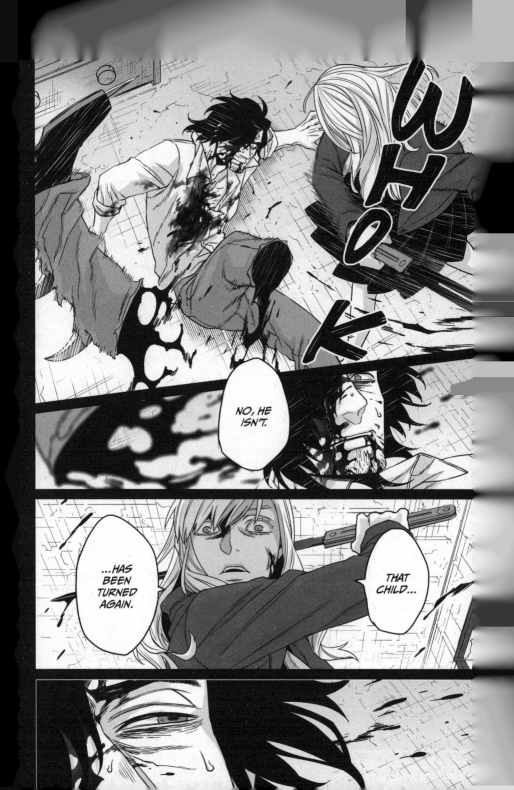

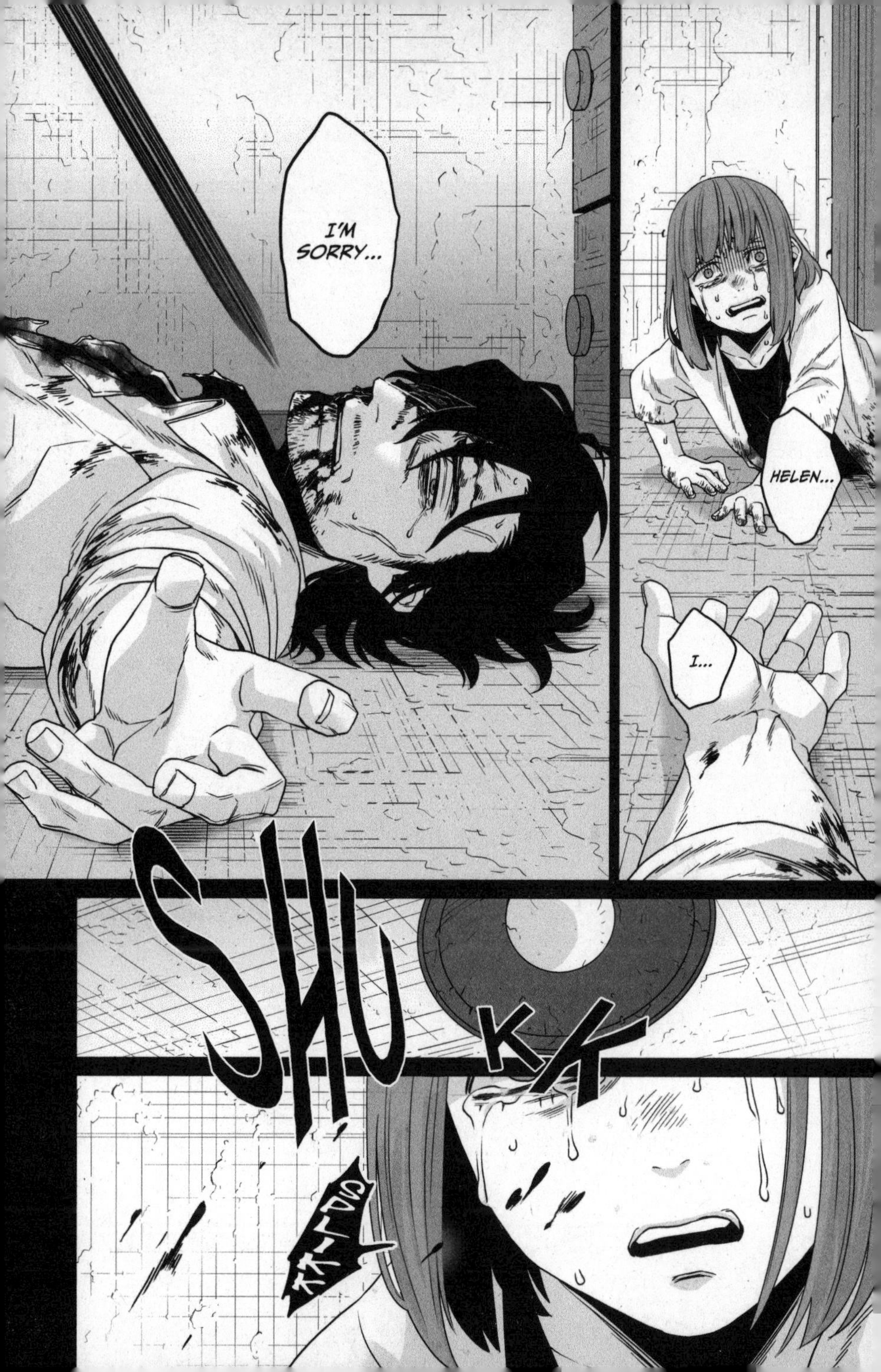
I'M SORRY...
HELEN...
I...
SHUKK
SPLITT

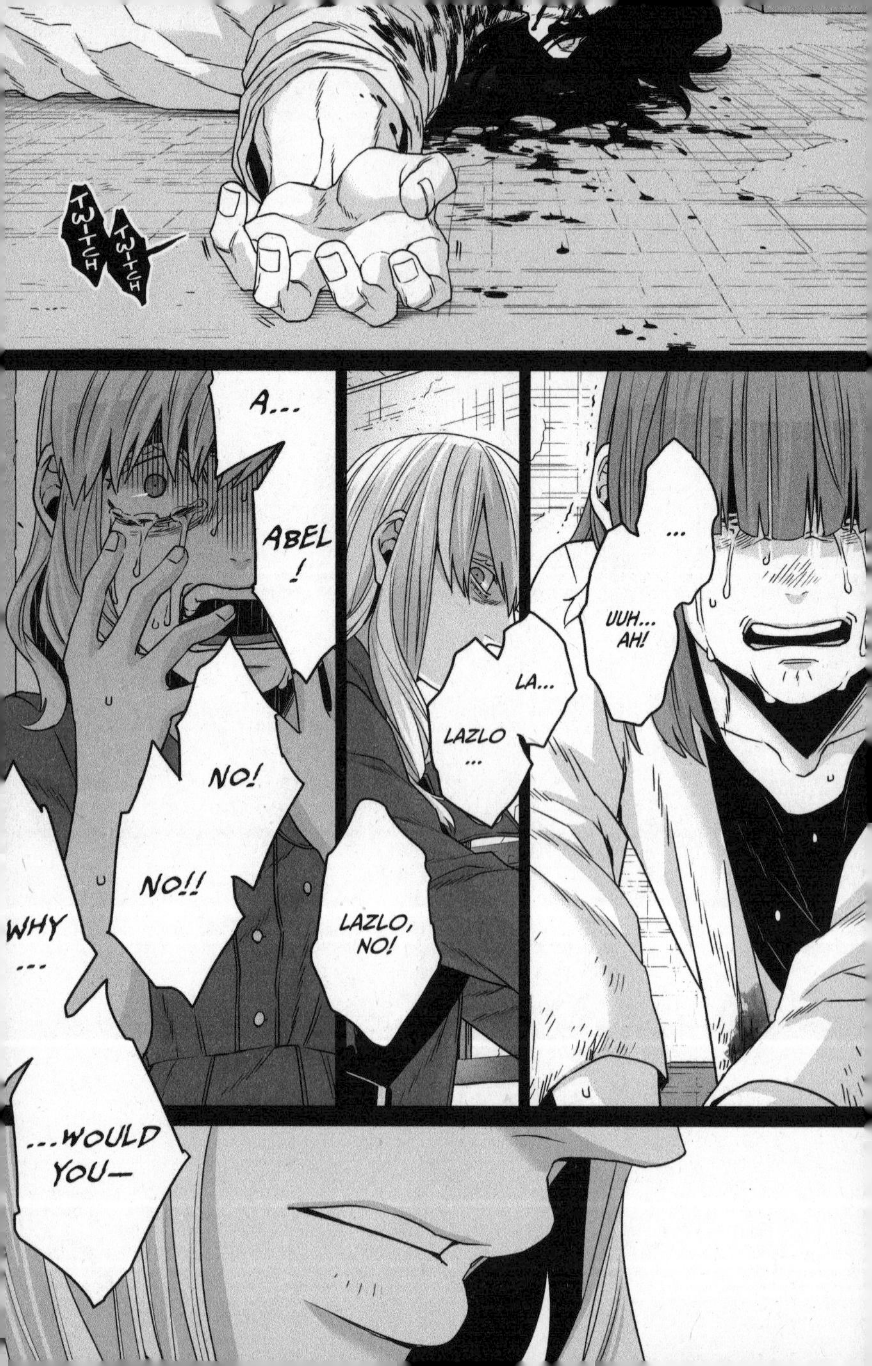

TWITCH TWITCH
...
UUH... AH!
LA...
LAZLO ...
A...
ABEL!
NO!
NO!!
LAZLO, NO!
WHY ...
...WOULD YOU—

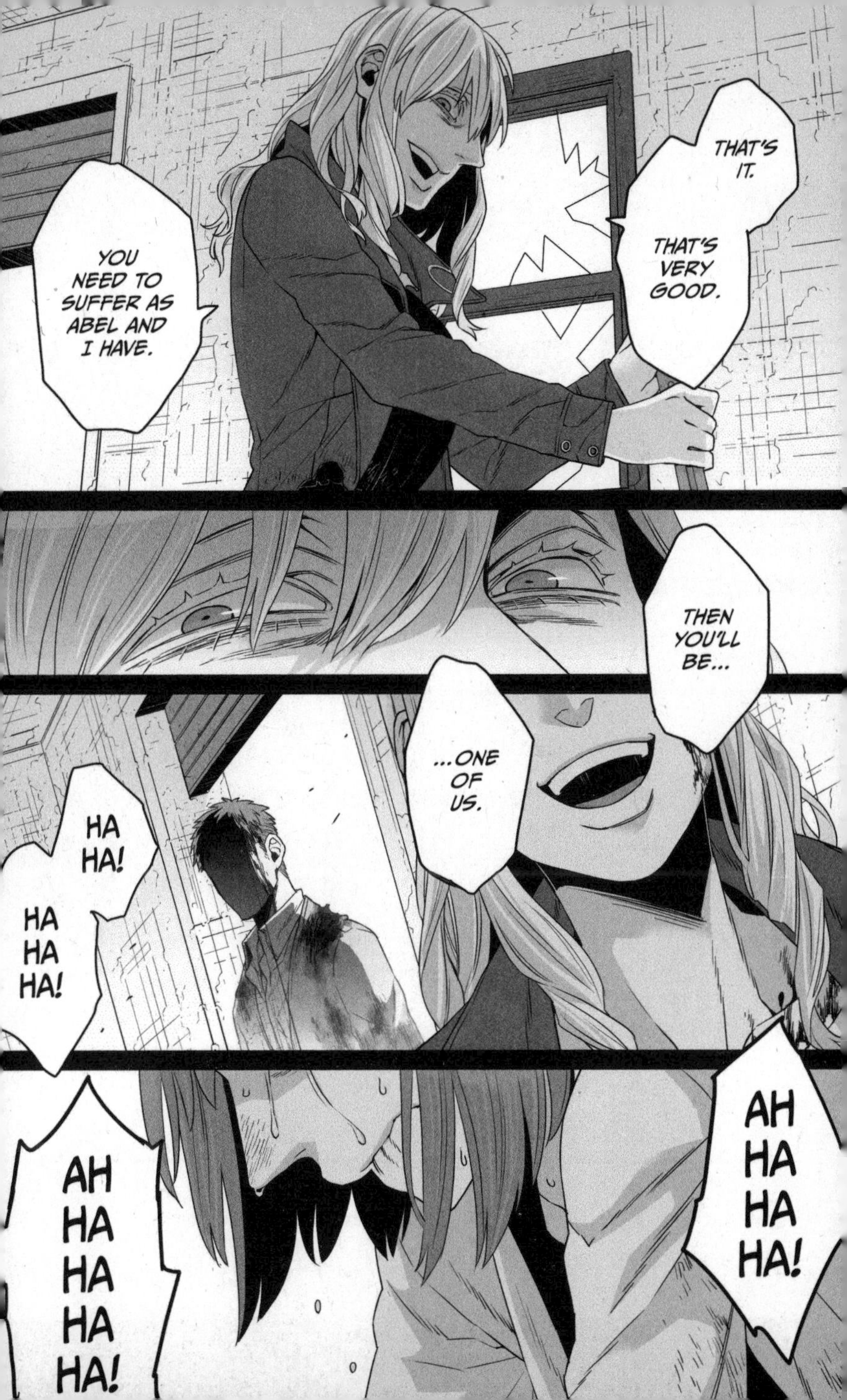
THAT'S IT.
THAT'S VERY GOOD.
YOU NEED TO SUFFER AS ABEL AND I HAVE.
THEN YOU'LL BE...
...ONE OF US.
HA HA!
HA HA HA!
AH HA HA HA!
AH HA HA HA HA HA!

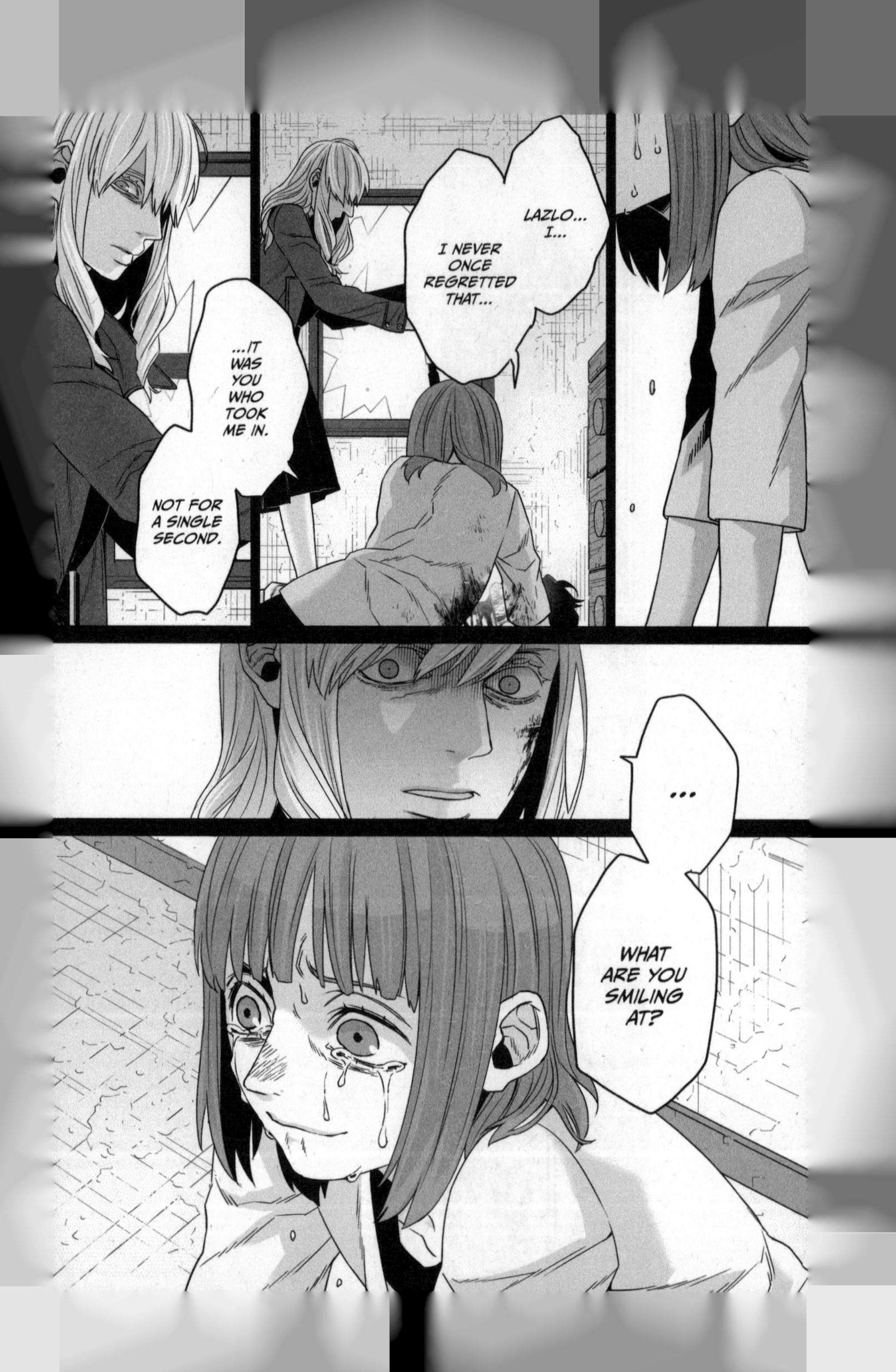
LAZLO... I...
I NEVER ONCE REGRETTED THAT...
...IT WAS YOU WHO TOOK ME IN.
NOT FOR A SINGLE SECOND.
...
WHAT ARE YOU SMILING AT?

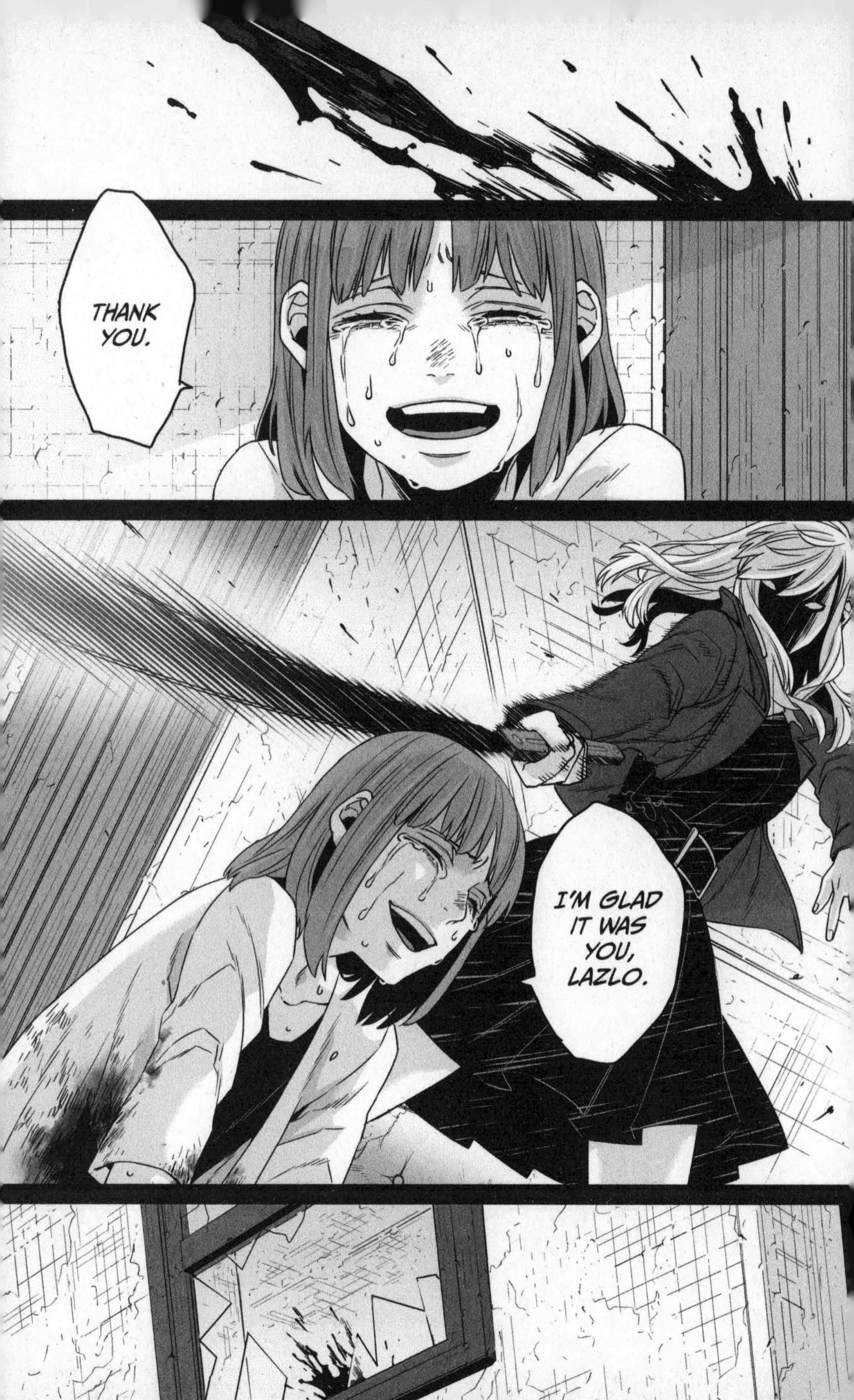
THANK YOU.
I'M GLAD IT WAS YOU, LAZLO.

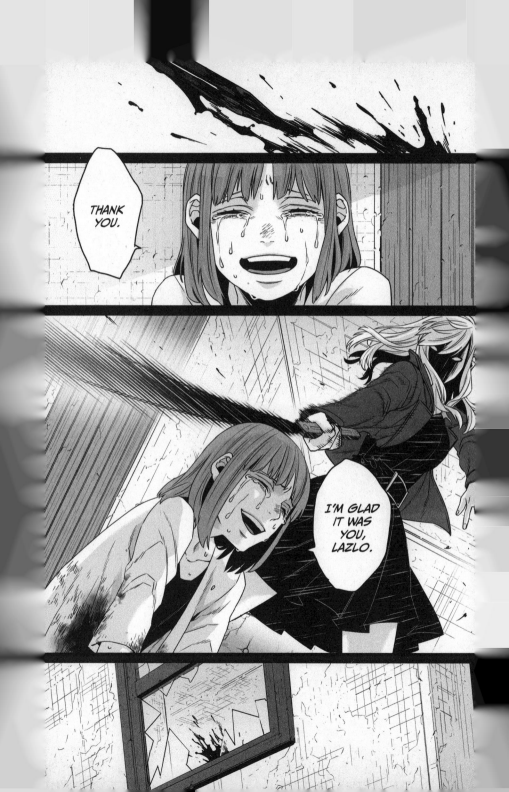

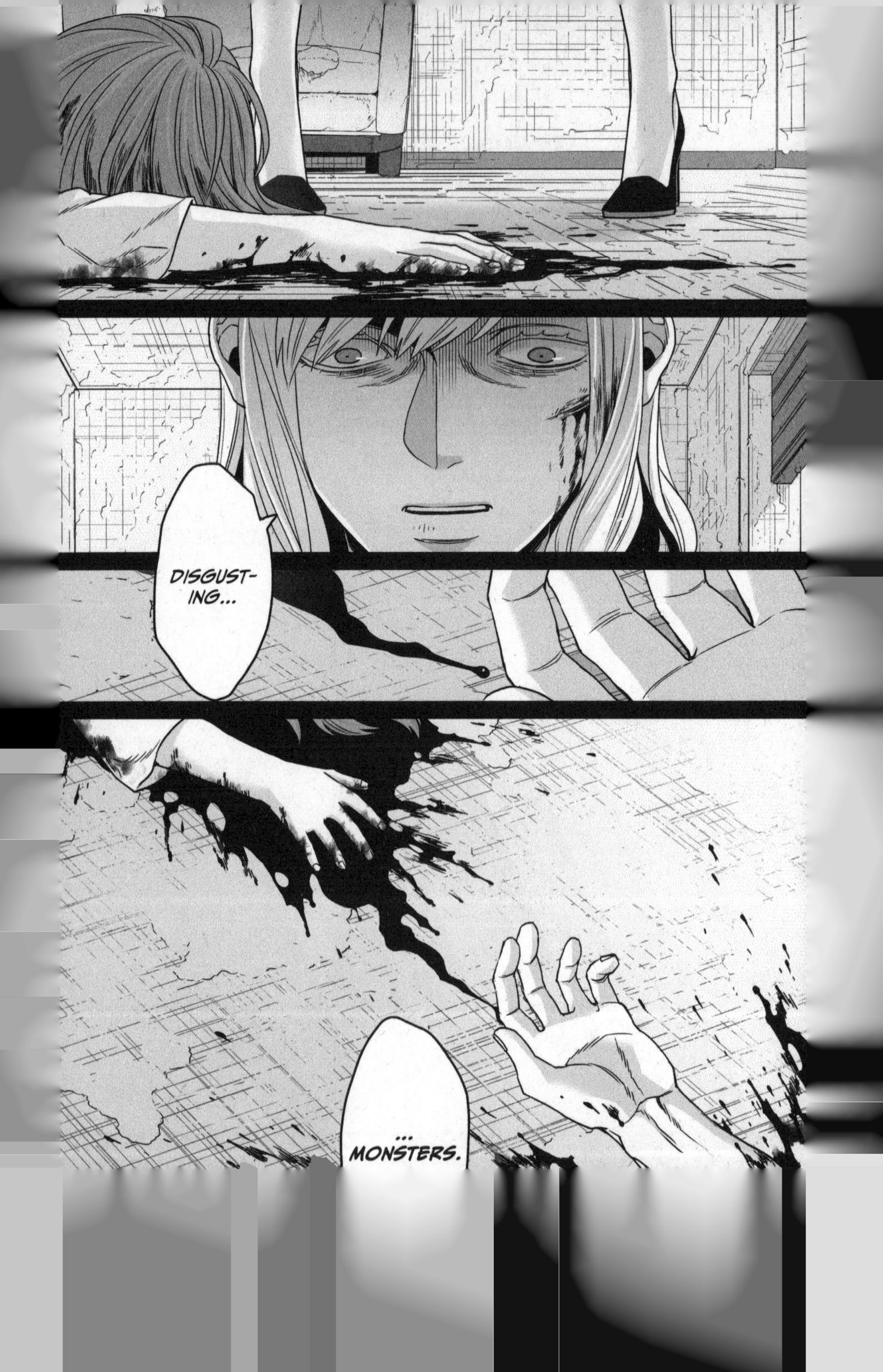
DISGUSTING...
...MONSTERS.

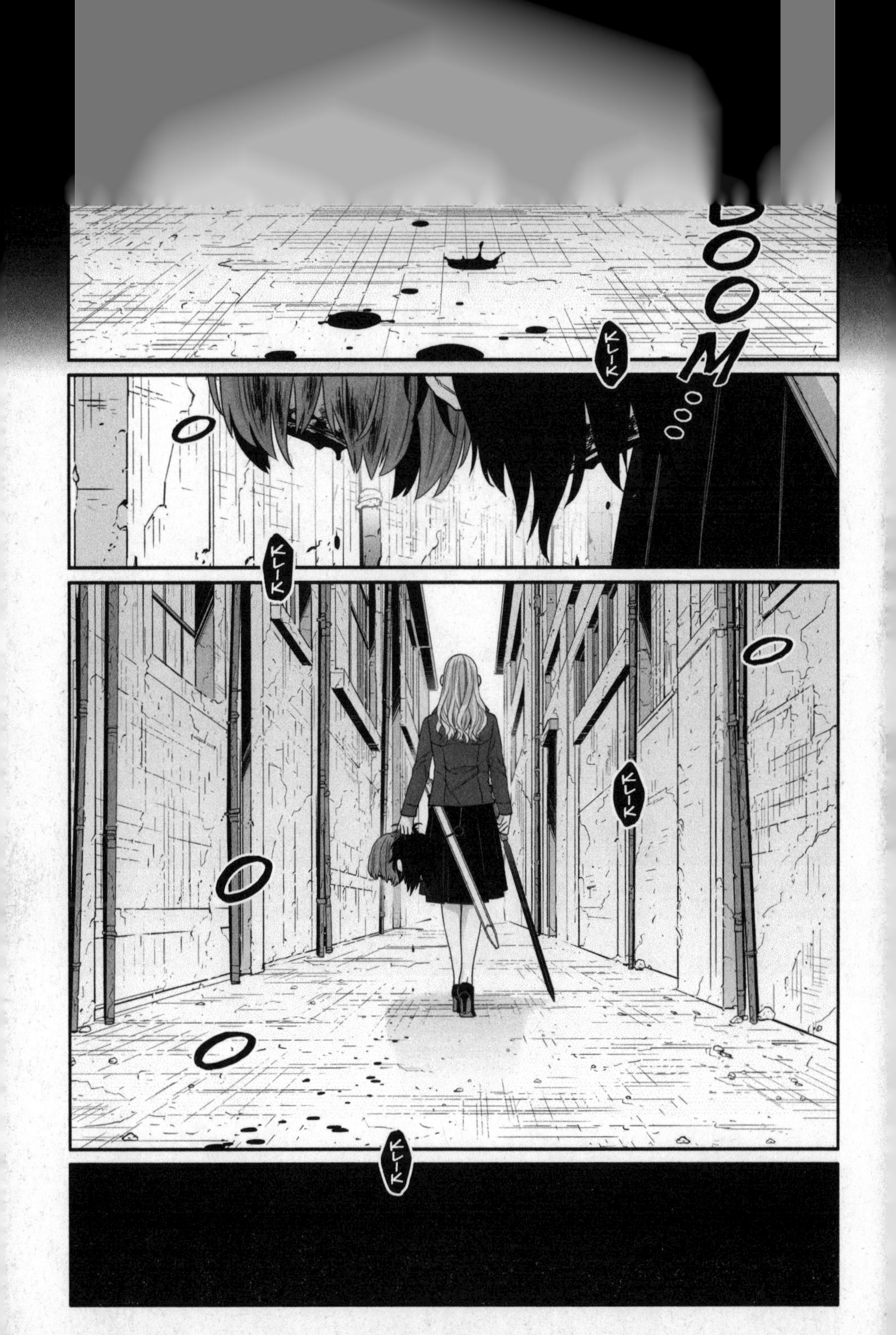
DOOM
KLIK
KLIK
KLIK
KLIK

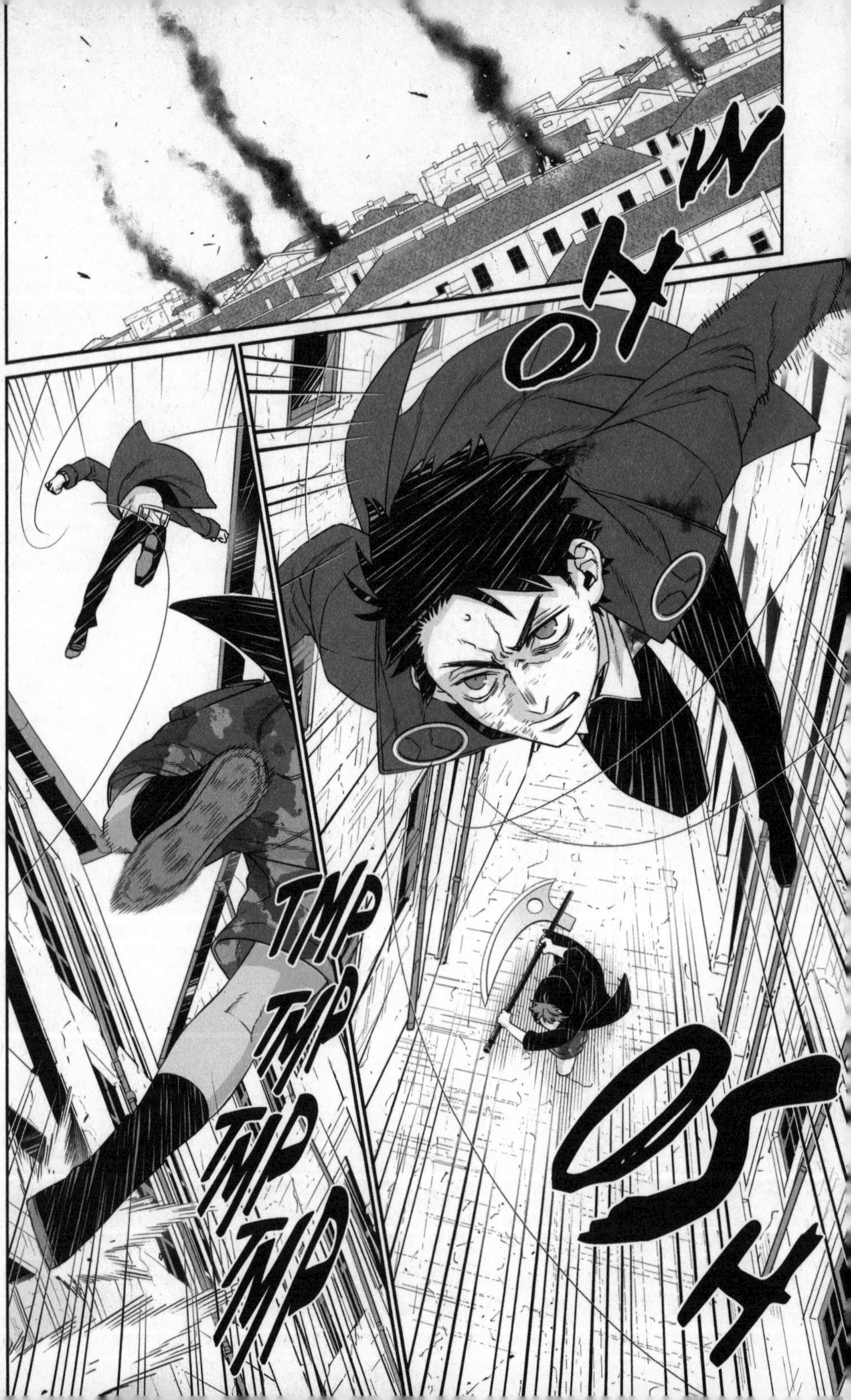
WHOOSH
TMP TMP TMP TMP

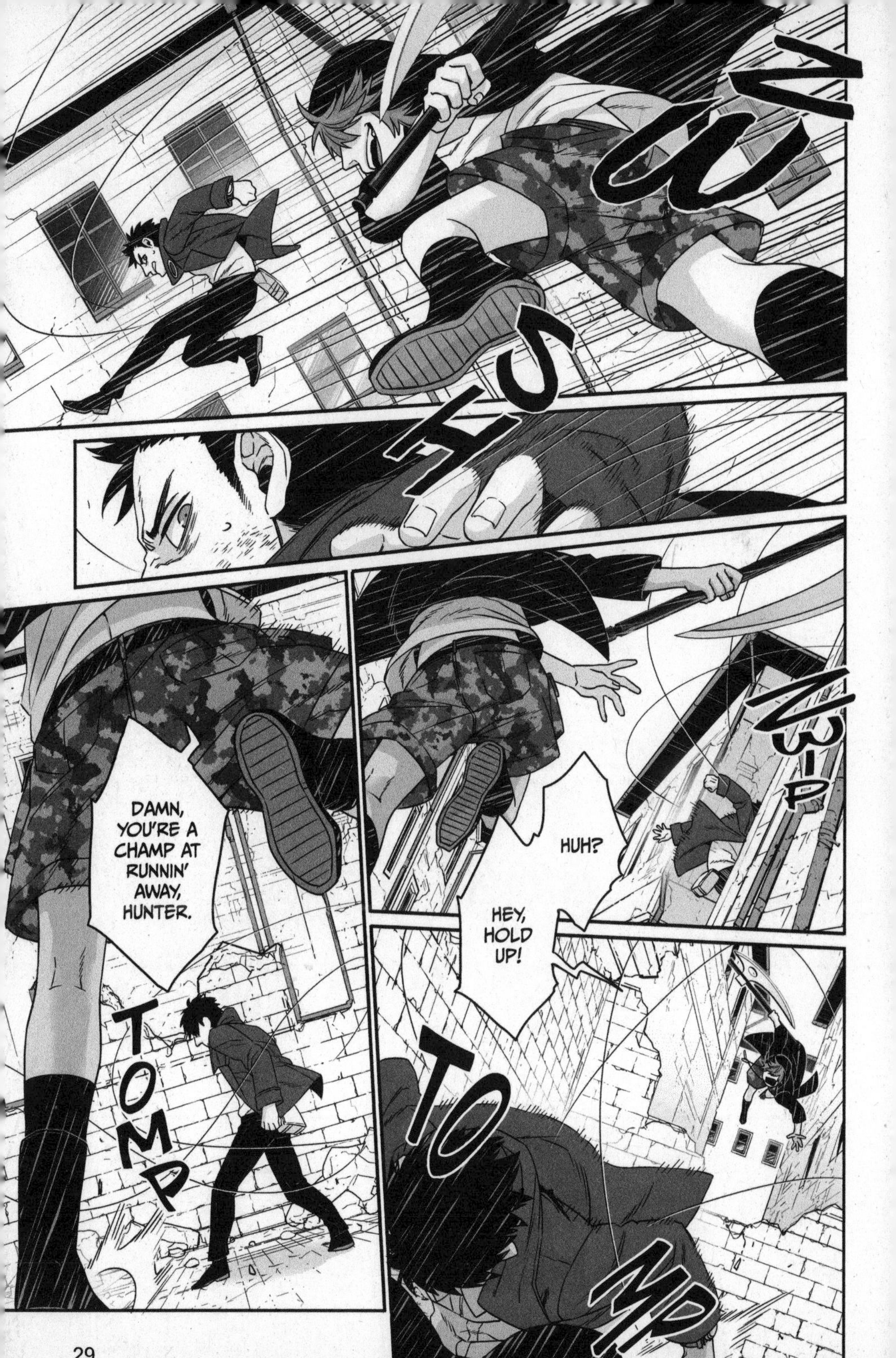

ZWUSH
DAMN, YOU'RE A CHAMP AT RUNNIN' AWAY, HUNTER.
ZWIP
HUH?
HEY, HOLD UP!
TOMP
TOMP

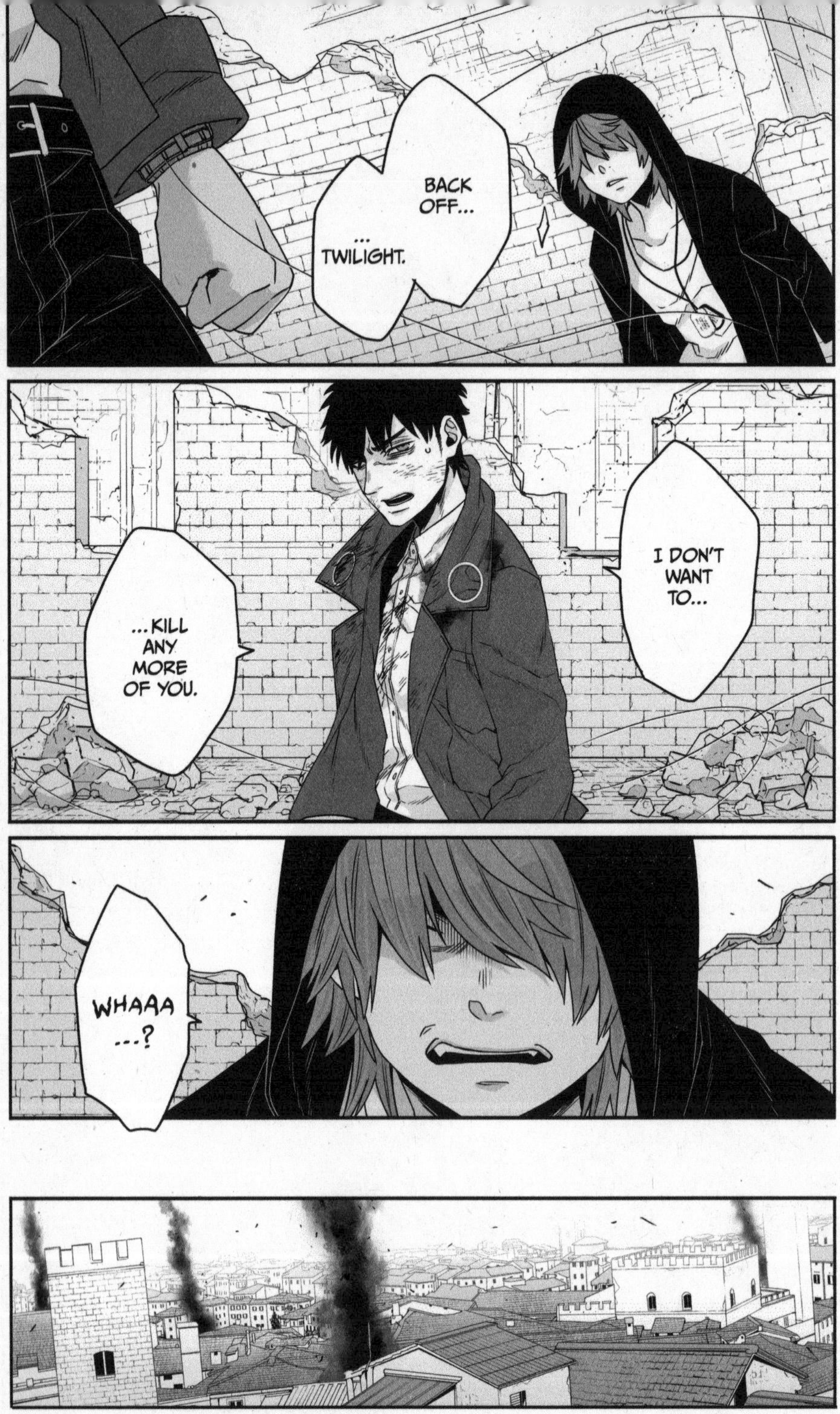
BACK OFF... ...TWILIGHT.
I DON'T WANT TO...
...KILL ANY MORE OF YOU.
WHAAA ...?

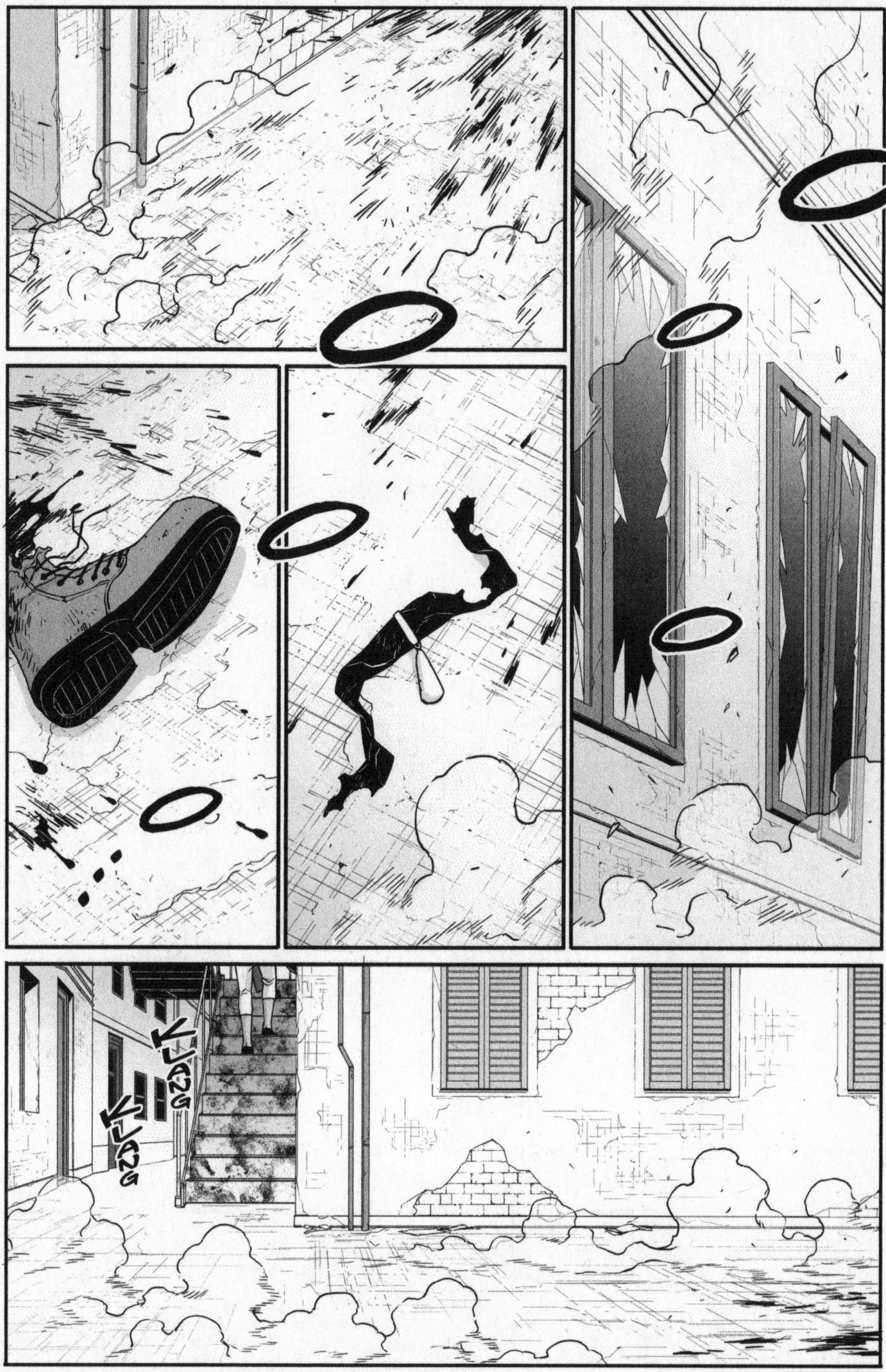
KLANG
KLANG

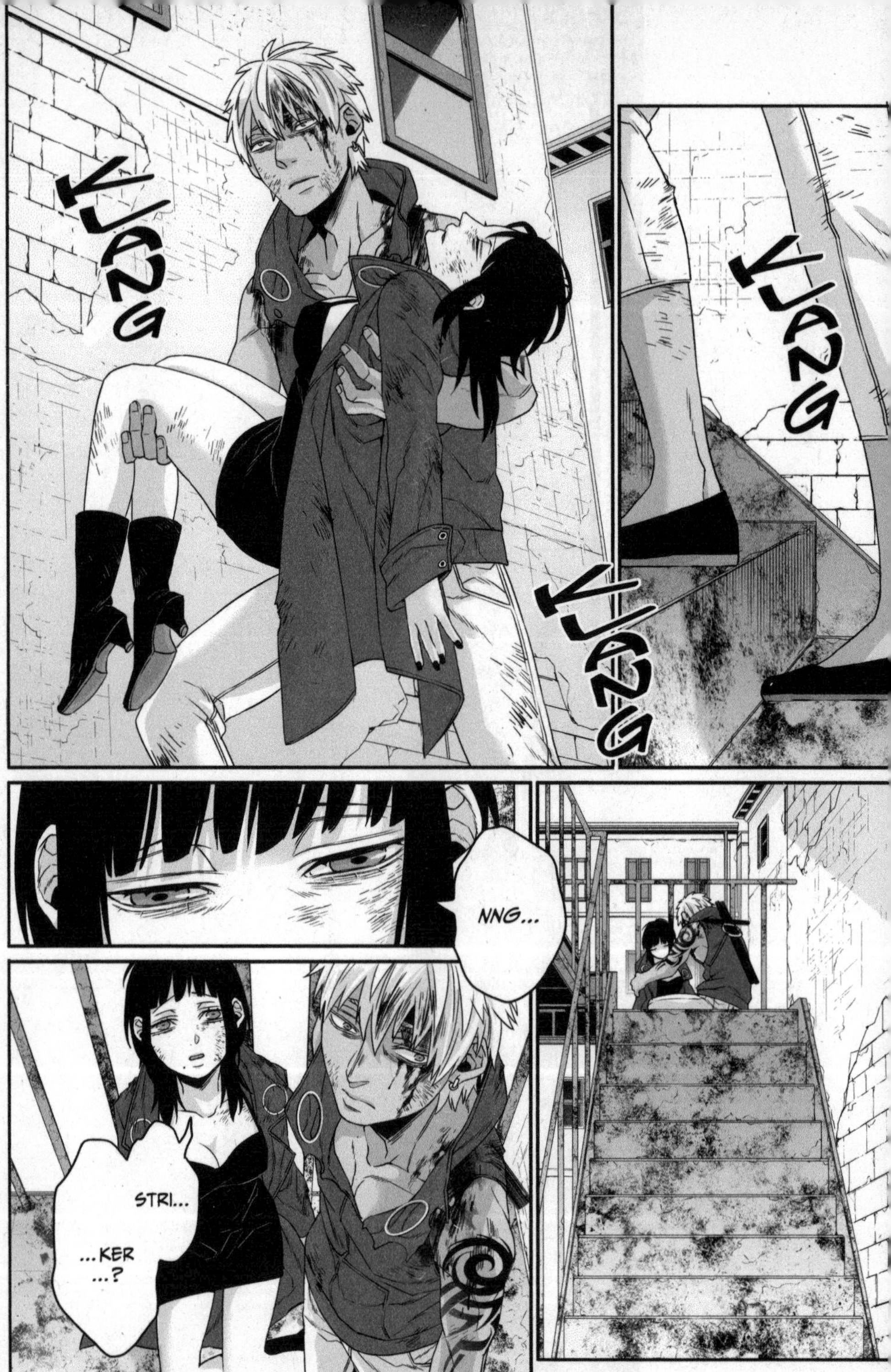
KLANG
KLANG
KLANG
NNG...
STRI...
...KER
...?

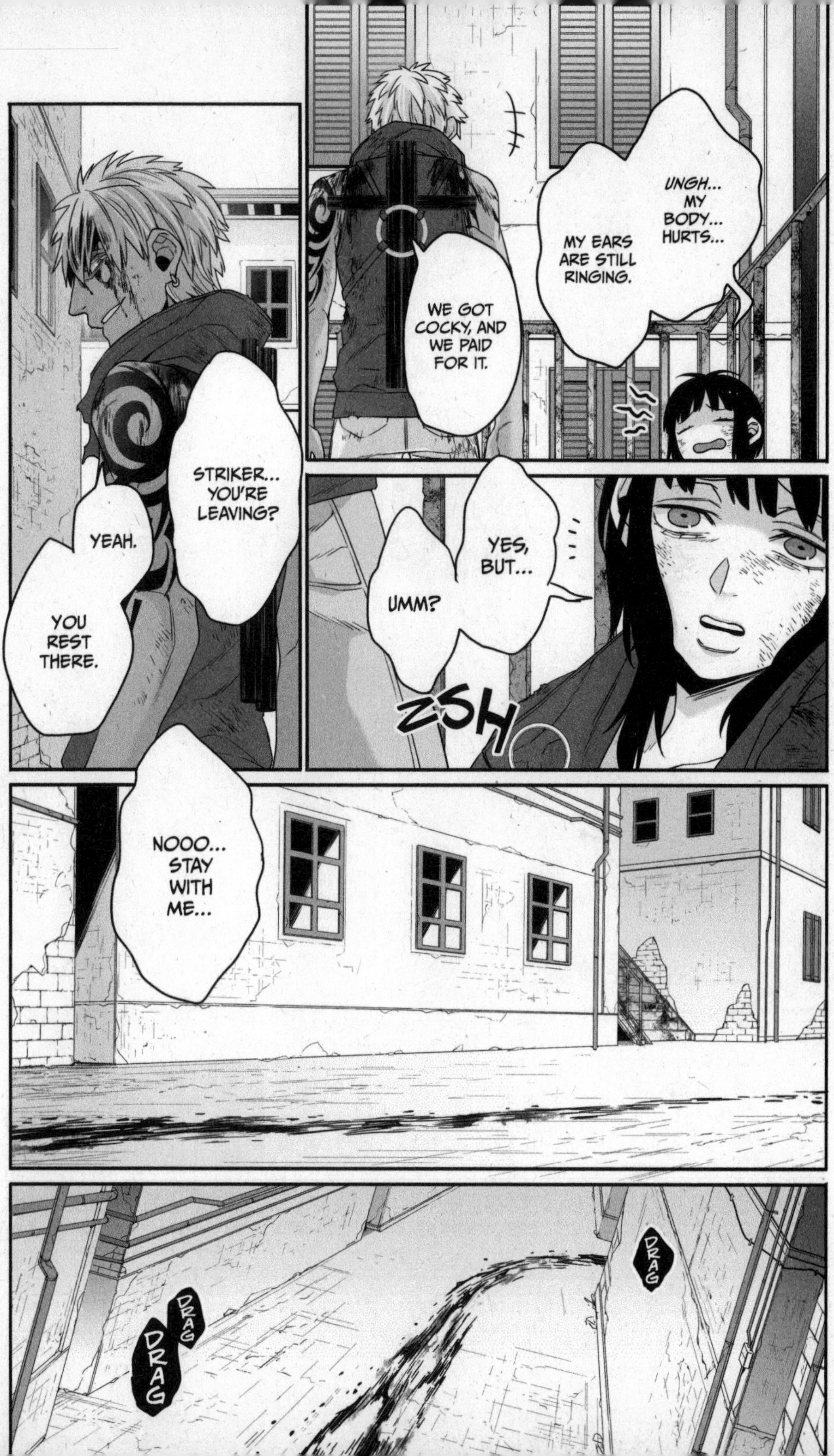
UNGH... MY BODY... HURTS...
MY EARS ARE STILL RINGING.
WE GOT COCKY, AND WE PAID FOR IT.
STRIKER... YOU'RE LEAVING?
YEAH.
YOU REST THERE.
YES, BUT...
UMM?
ZSH
NOOO... STAY WITH ME...
DRAG
DRAG
DRAG

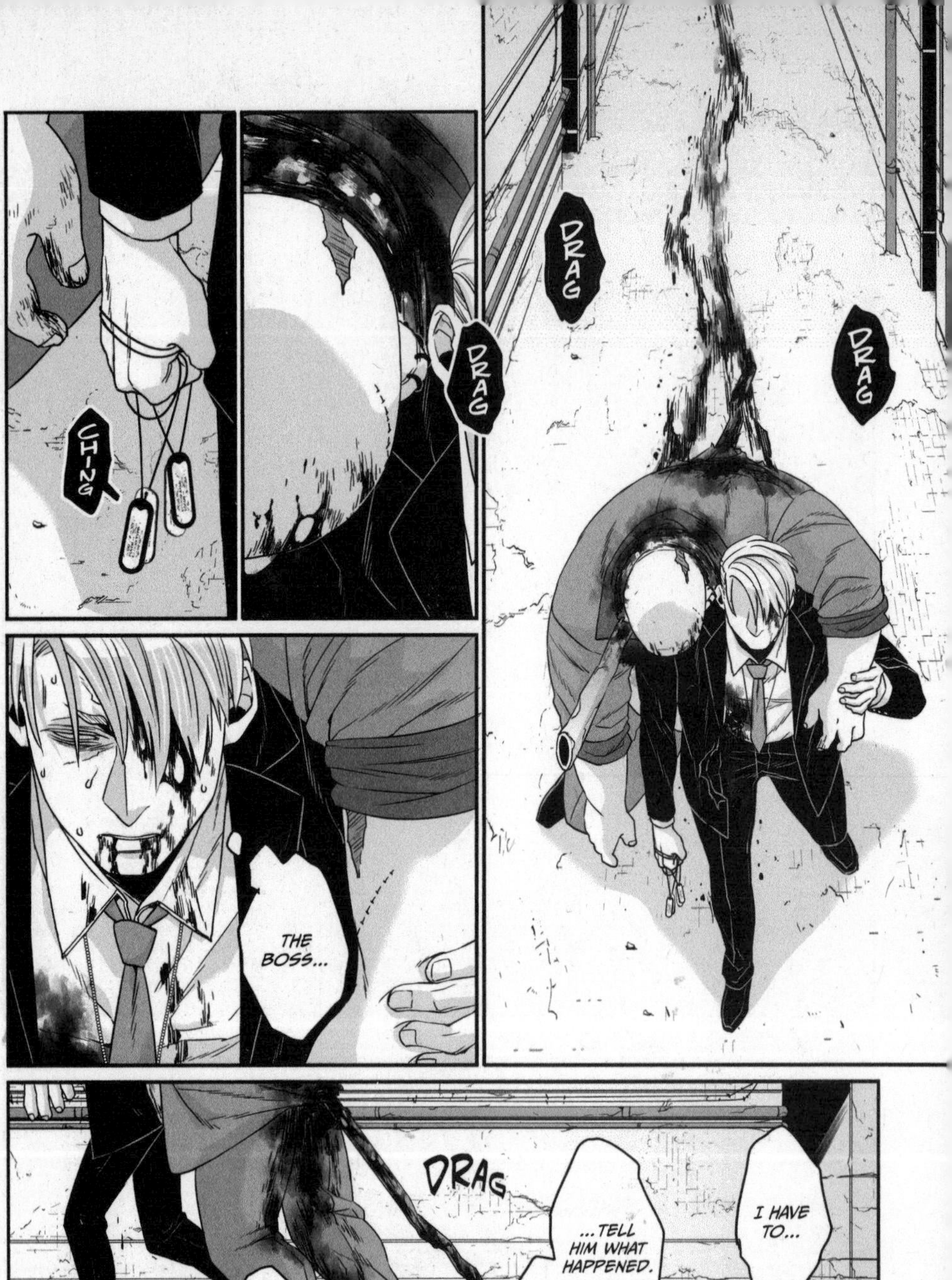
DRAG
DRAG
DRAG
CHING
THE BOSS...
I HAVE TO...
...TELL HIM WHAT HAPPENED.
HAVE TO...
DRAG
...TELL HIM...
DRAG

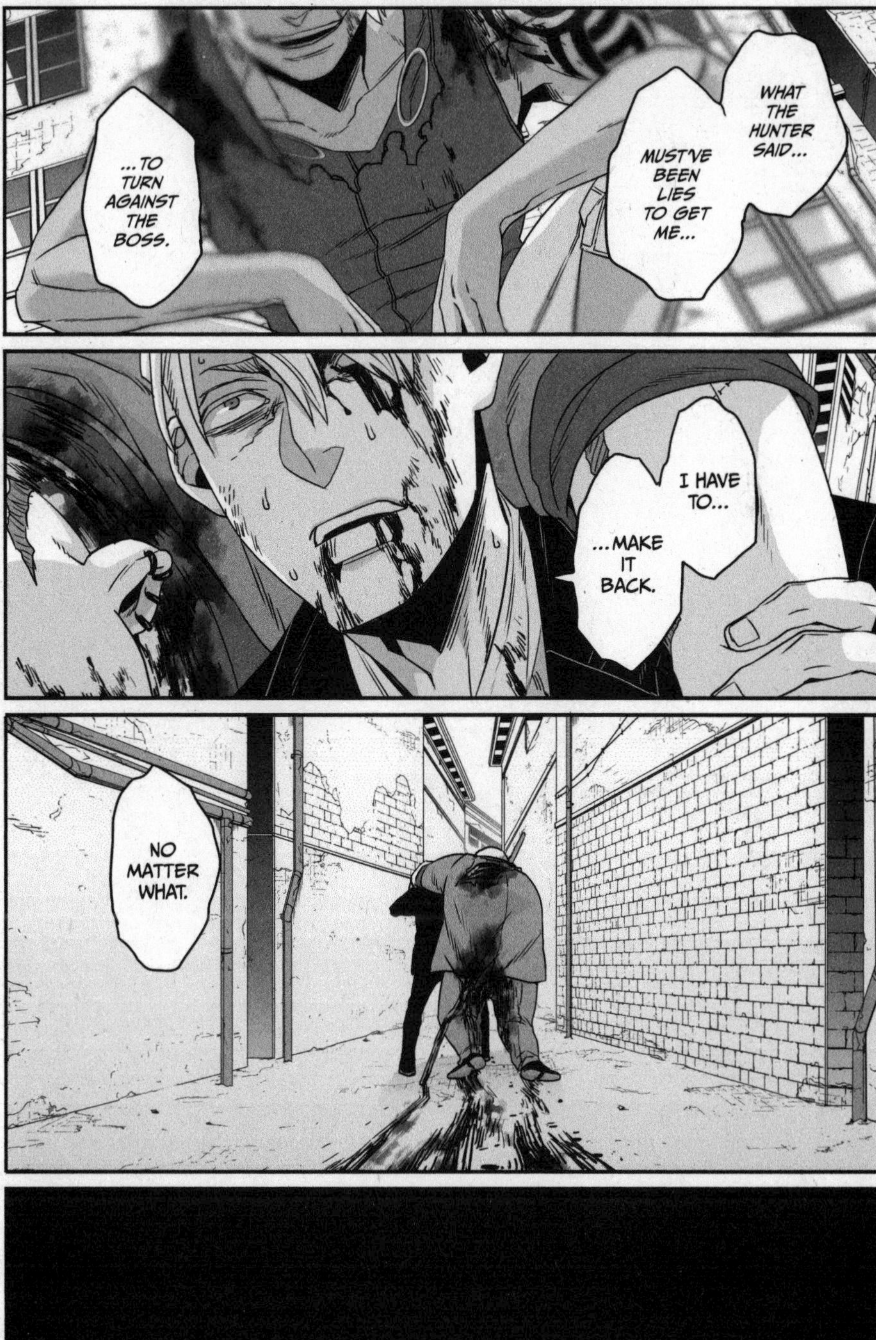
WHAT THE HUNTER SAID...
MUST'VE BEEN LIES TO GET ME...
...TO TURN AGAINST THE BOSS.
I HAVE TO...
...MAKE IT BACK.
NO MATTER WHAT.

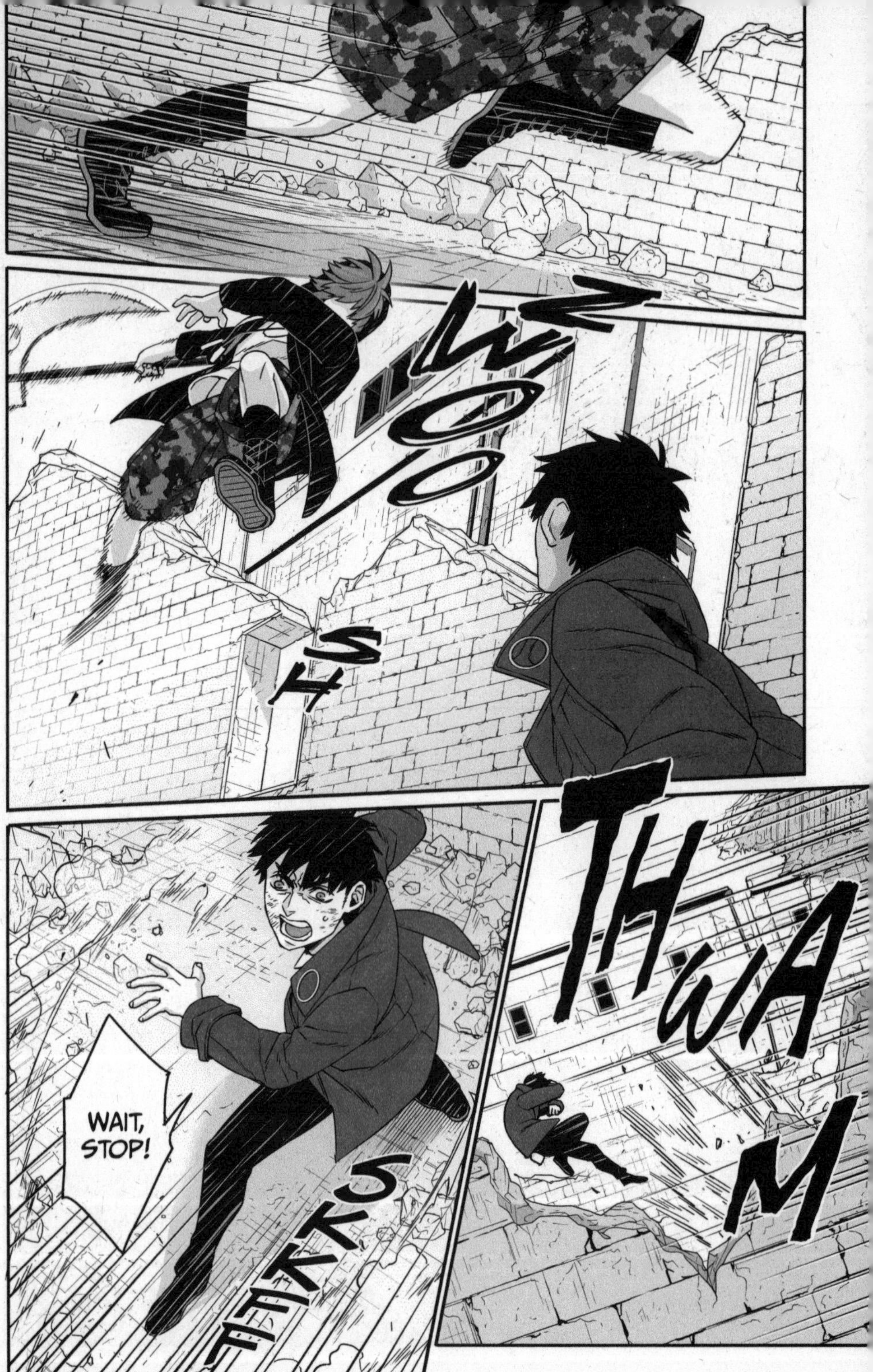
ZWOOO
SH
THWAM
WAIT, STOP!
SKKFFF

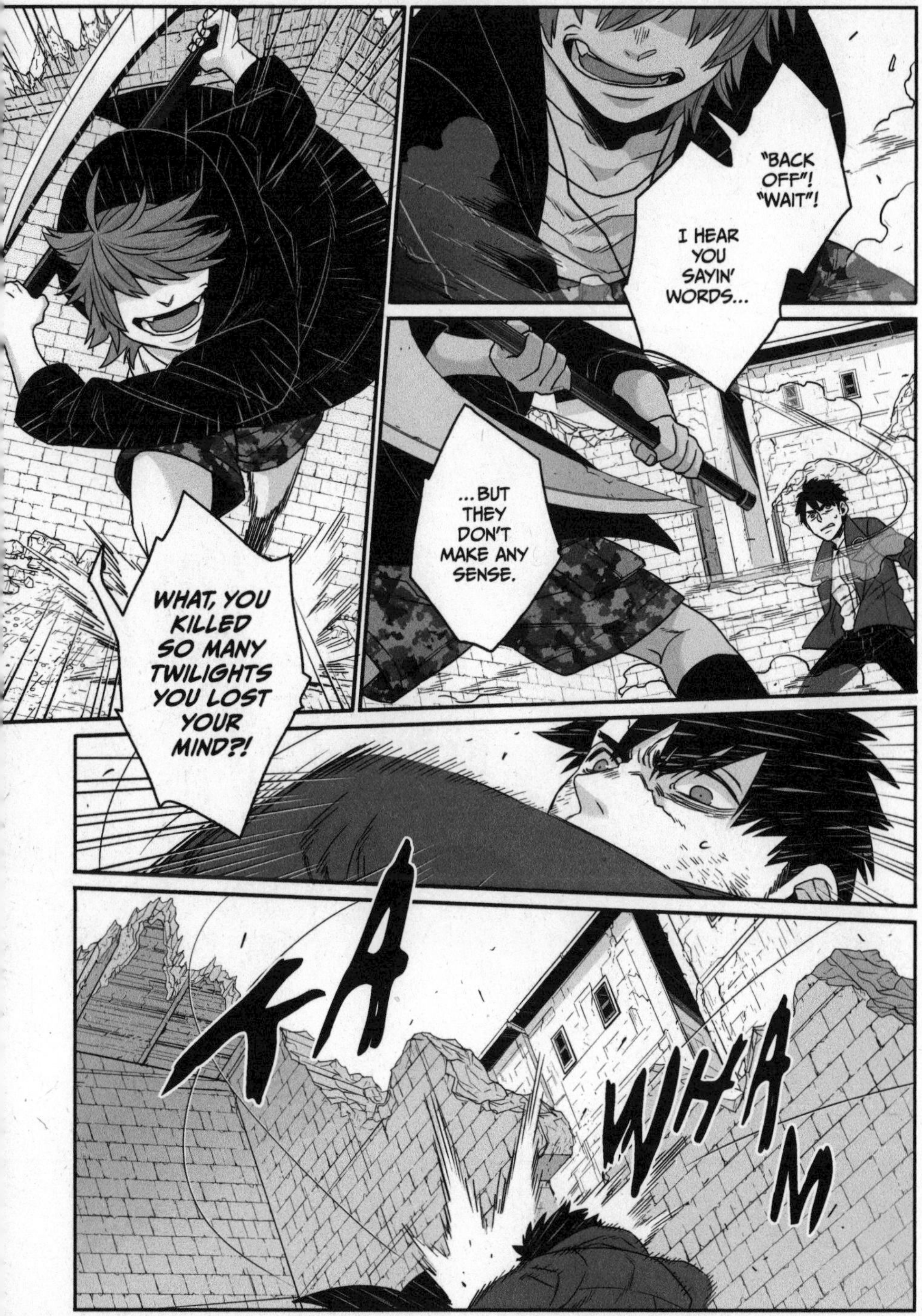
"BACK OFF"! "WAIT"!
I HEAR YOU SAYIN' WORDS...
...BUT THEY DON'T MAKE ANY SENSE.
WHAT, YOU KILLED SO MANY TWILIGHTS YOU LOST YOUR MIND?!
KA
WHAM

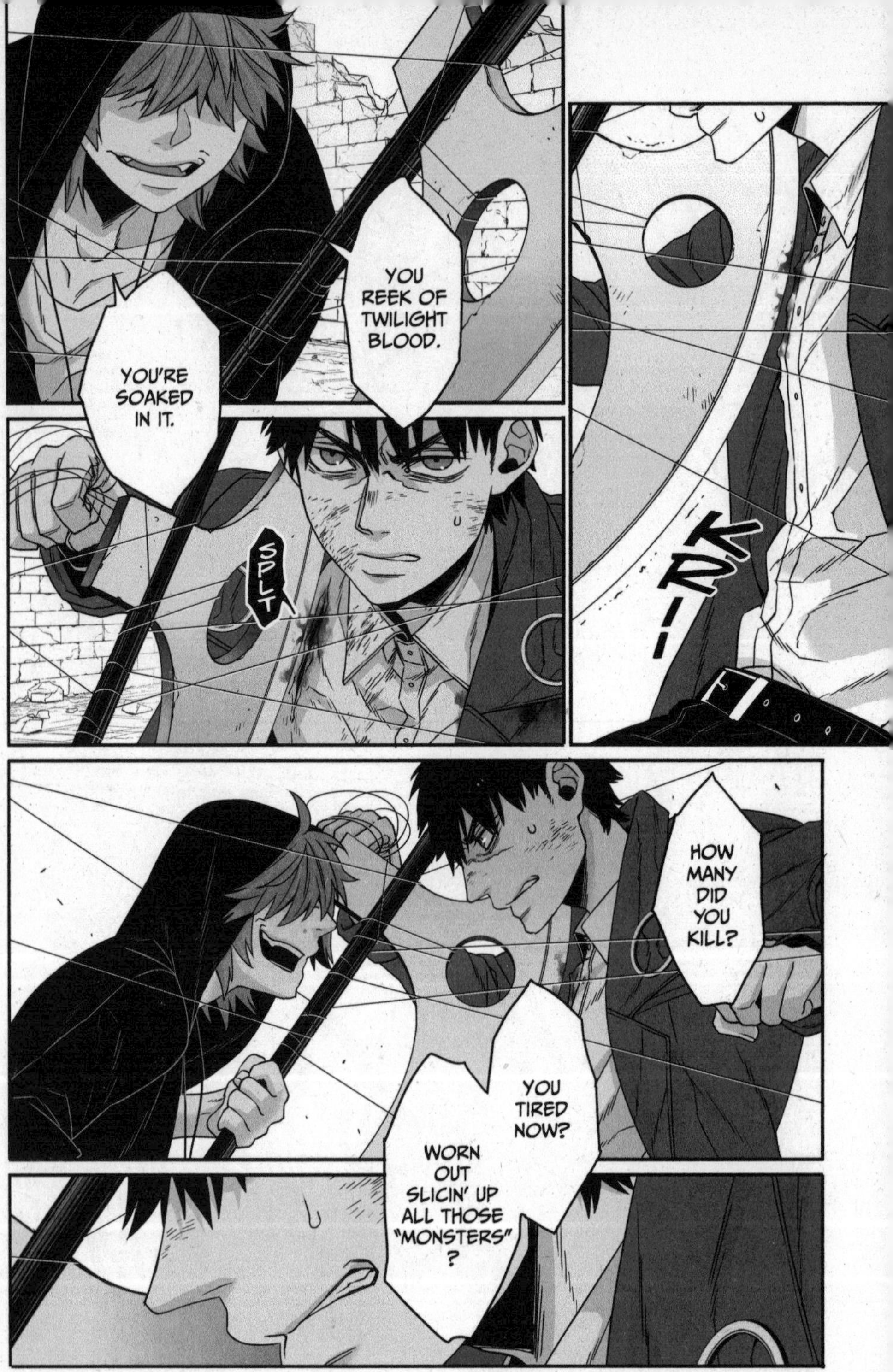
KRI
YOU REEK OF TWILIGHT BLOOD.
YOU'RE SOAKED IN IT.
SPLT
HOW MANY DID YOU KILL?
YOU TIRED NOW?
WORN OUT SLICIN' UP ALL THOSE "MONSTERS"?

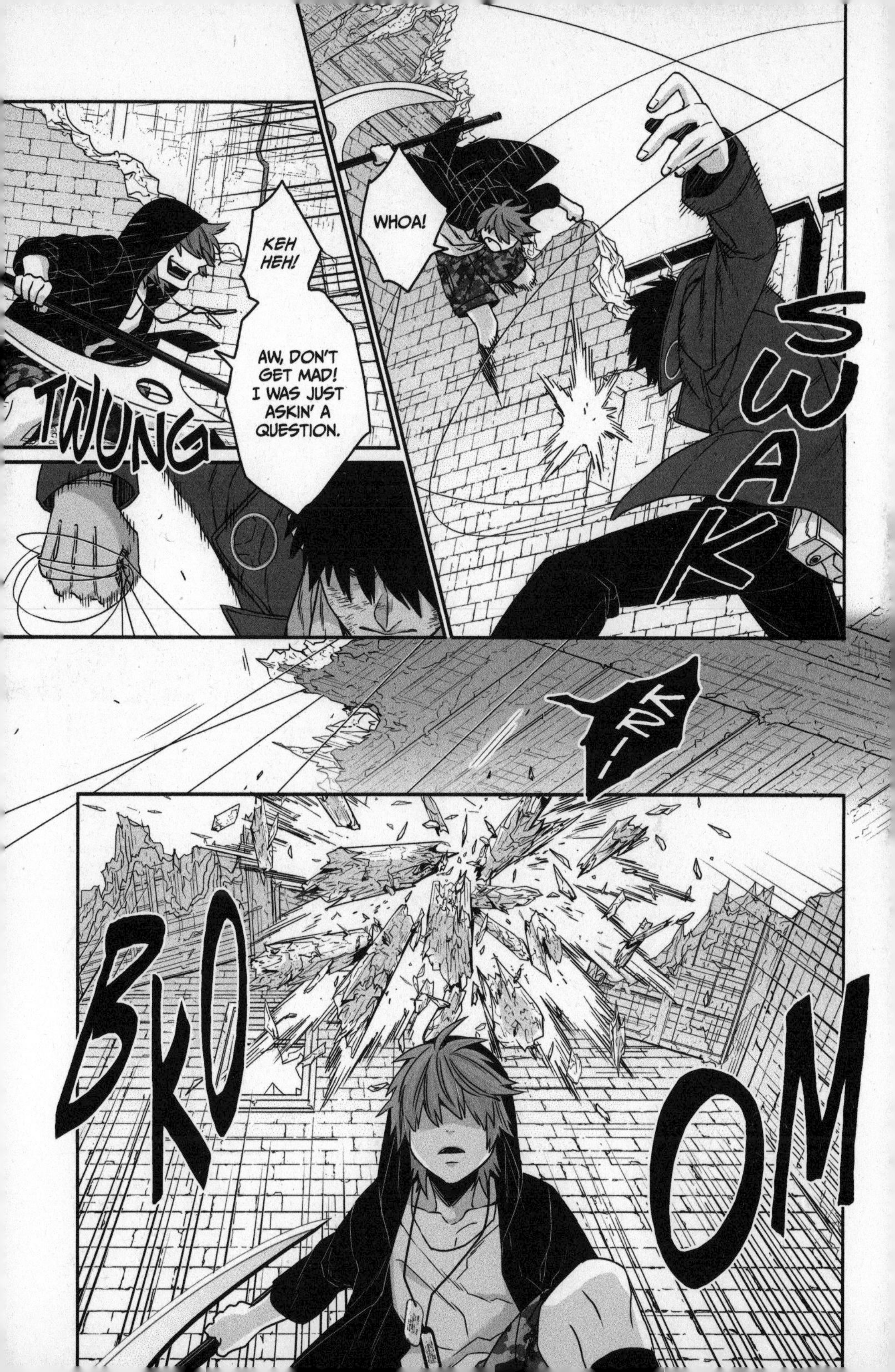
WHOA!
SWAK
KEH HEH!
AW, DON'T GET MAD! I WAS JUST ASKIN' A QUESTION.
TWUNG
KRI--
BROOM

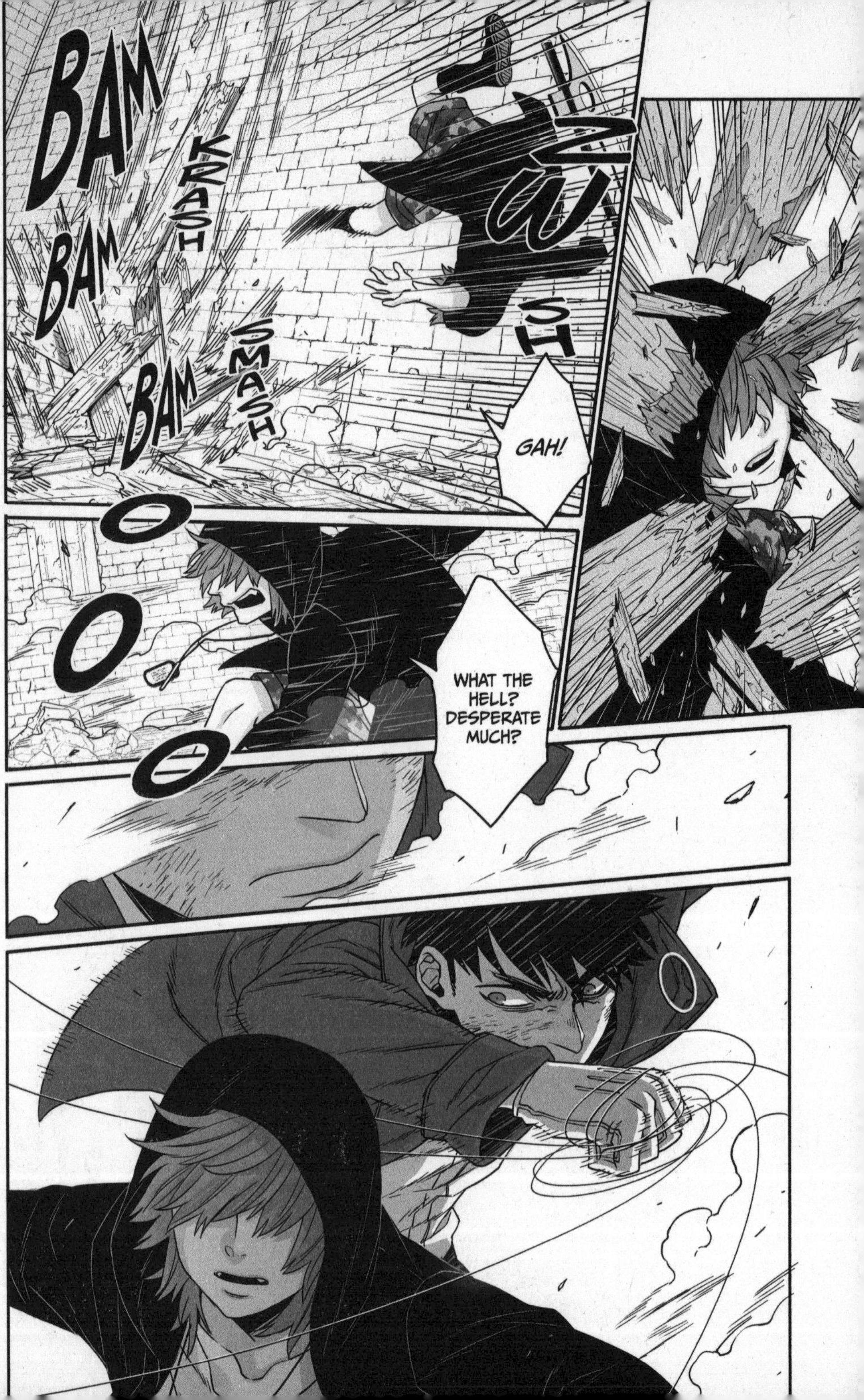
BAM
BAM
BAM
KRASH
SMASH
GAH!
WHAT THE HELL? DESPERATE MUCH?

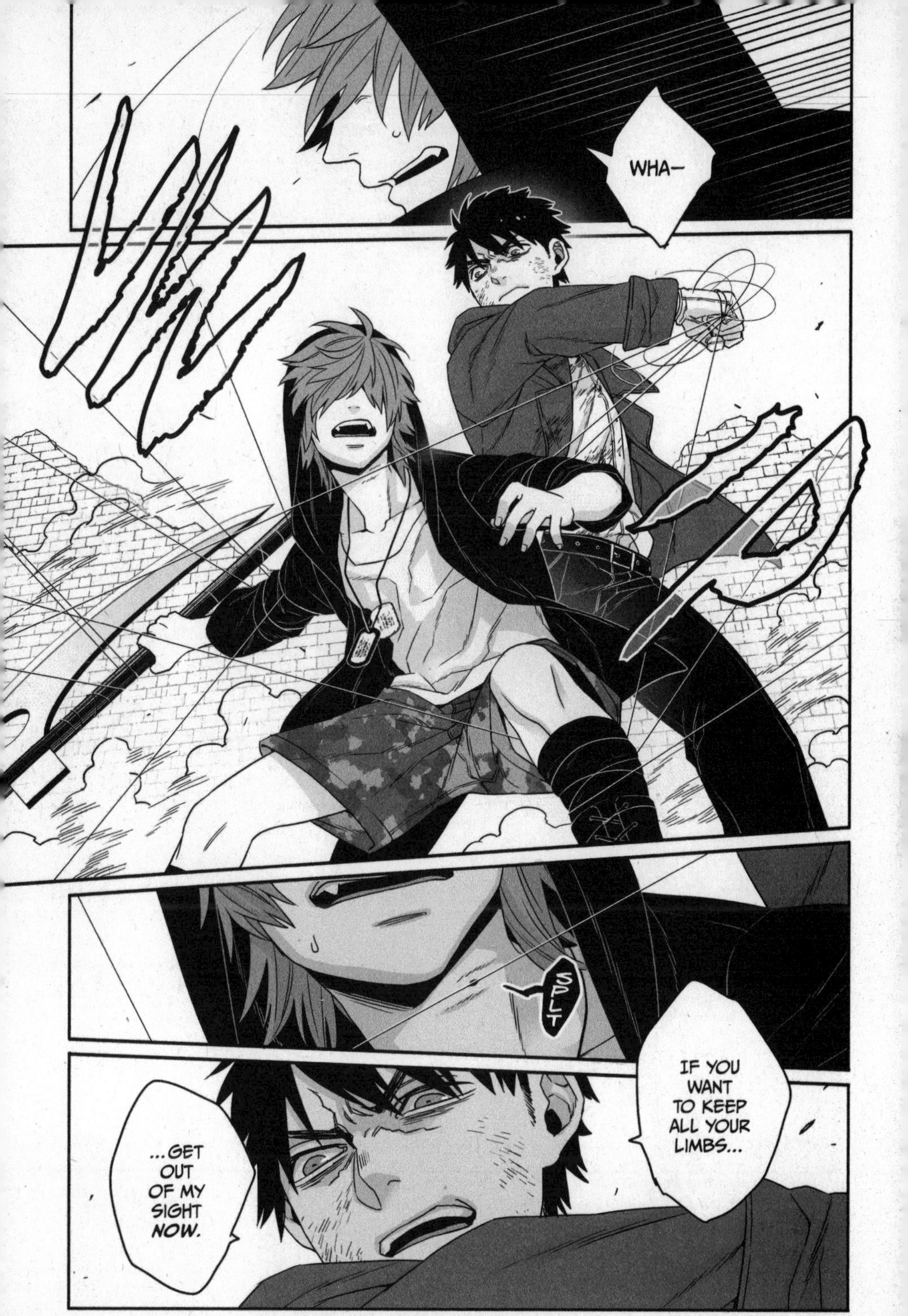
WHA–
SPLT
IF YOU WANT TO KEEP ALL YOUR LIMBS...
...GET OUT OF MY SIGHT NOW.

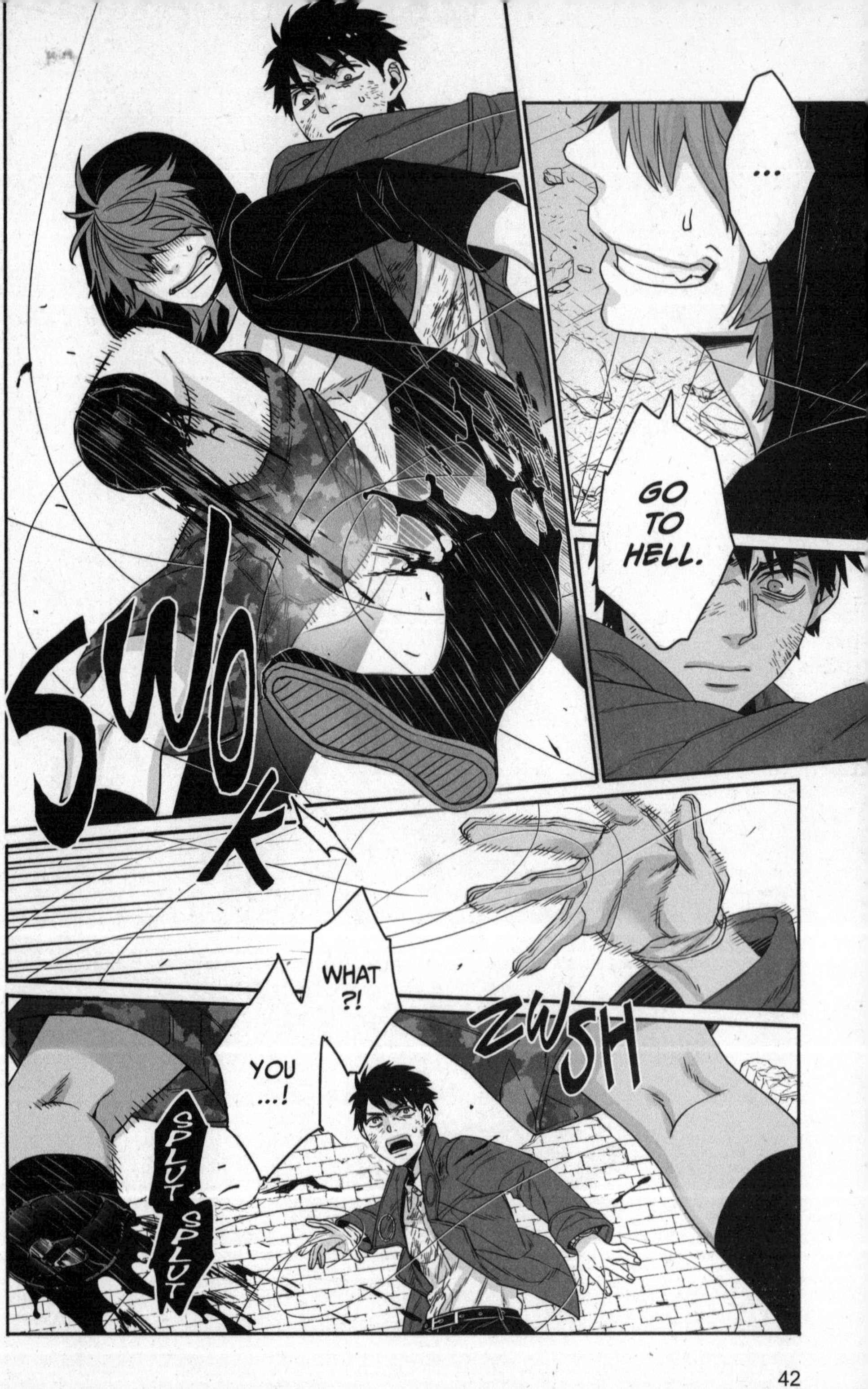
...
GO TO HELL.
SWOK
WHAT?!
YOU ...!
ZWSH
SPLUT SPLUT SPLUT

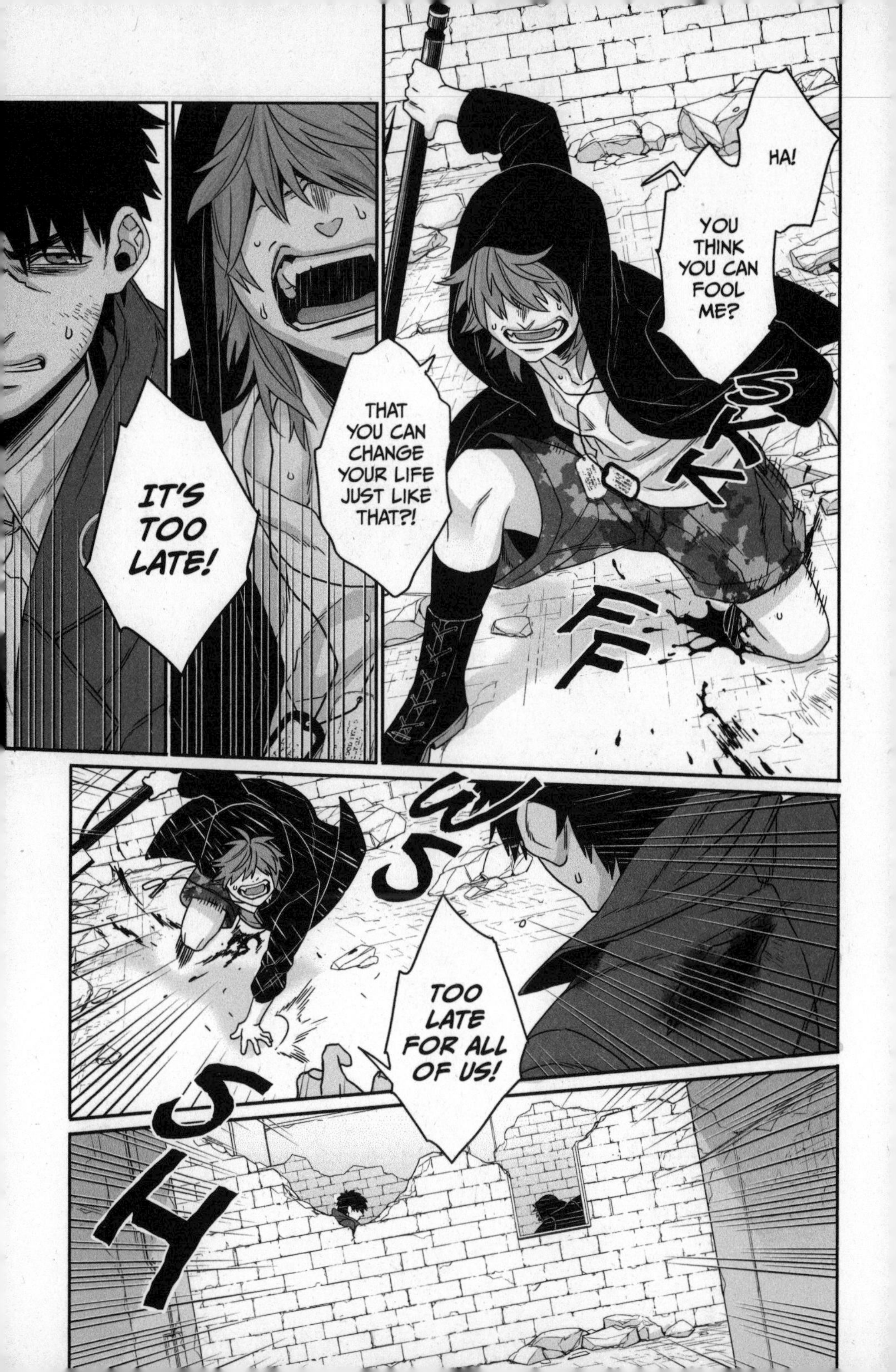
HA!
YOU THINK YOU CAN FOOL ME?
THAT YOU CAN CHANGE YOUR LIFE JUST LIKE THAT?!
SKK
FF
IT'S TOO LATE!
WS
TOO LATE FOR ALL OF US!
SH

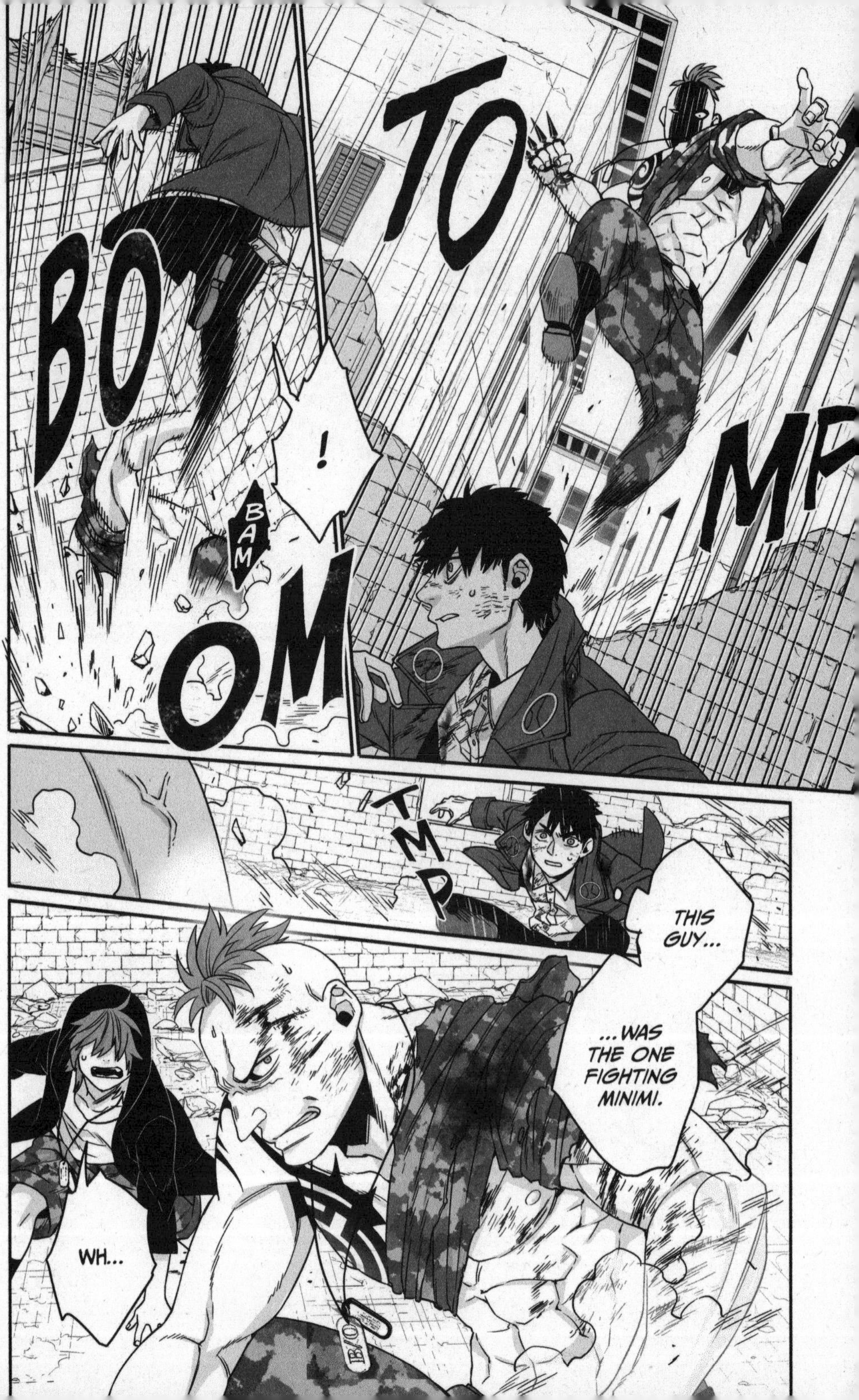
TO
MP
BO
OM
!
BAM
TMP
THIS GUY...
...WAS THE ONE FIGHTING MINIMI.
WH...

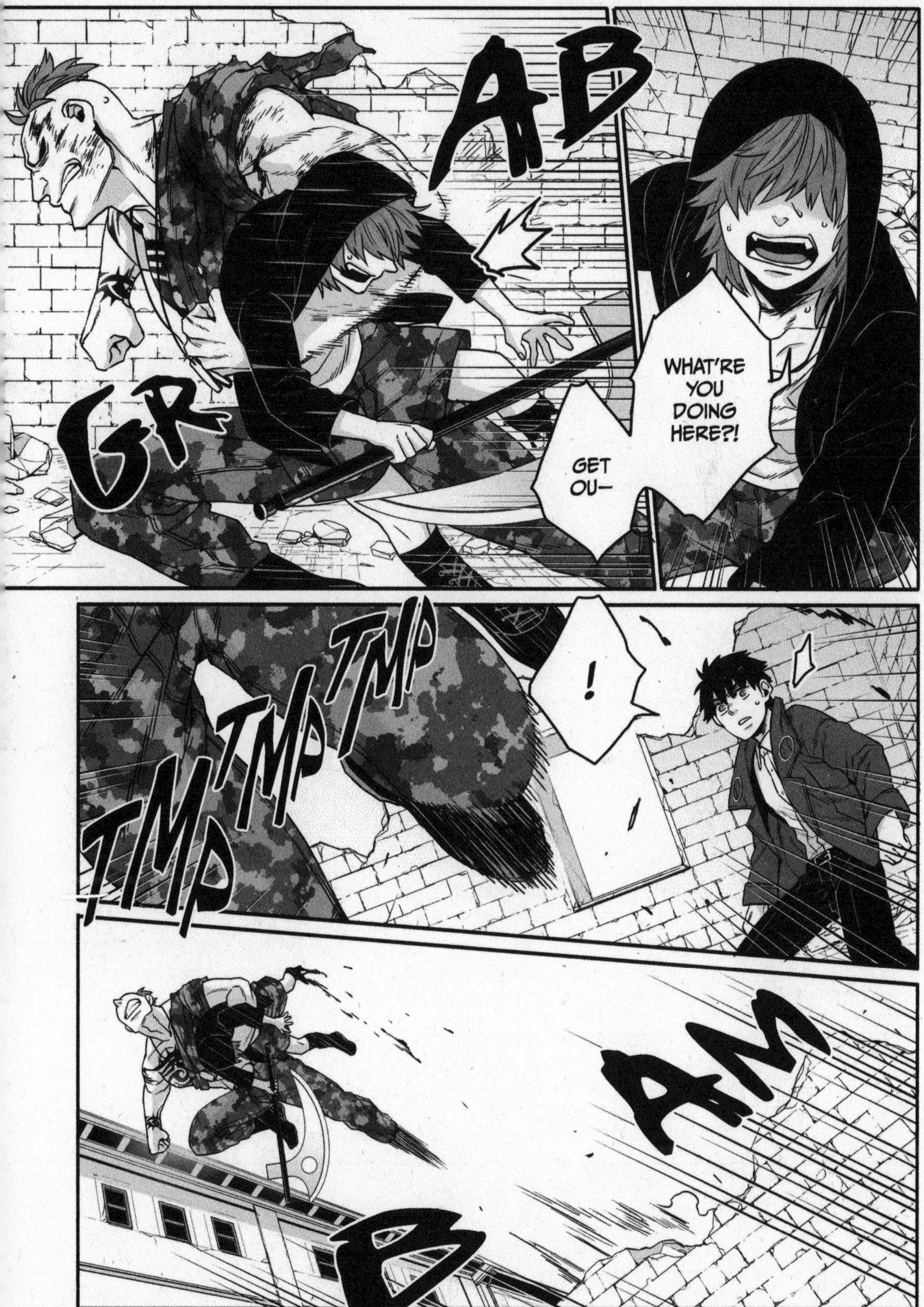
AB
GR
WHAT'RE YOU DOING HERE?!
GET OU–
!
TMP TMP TMP TMP
BAM

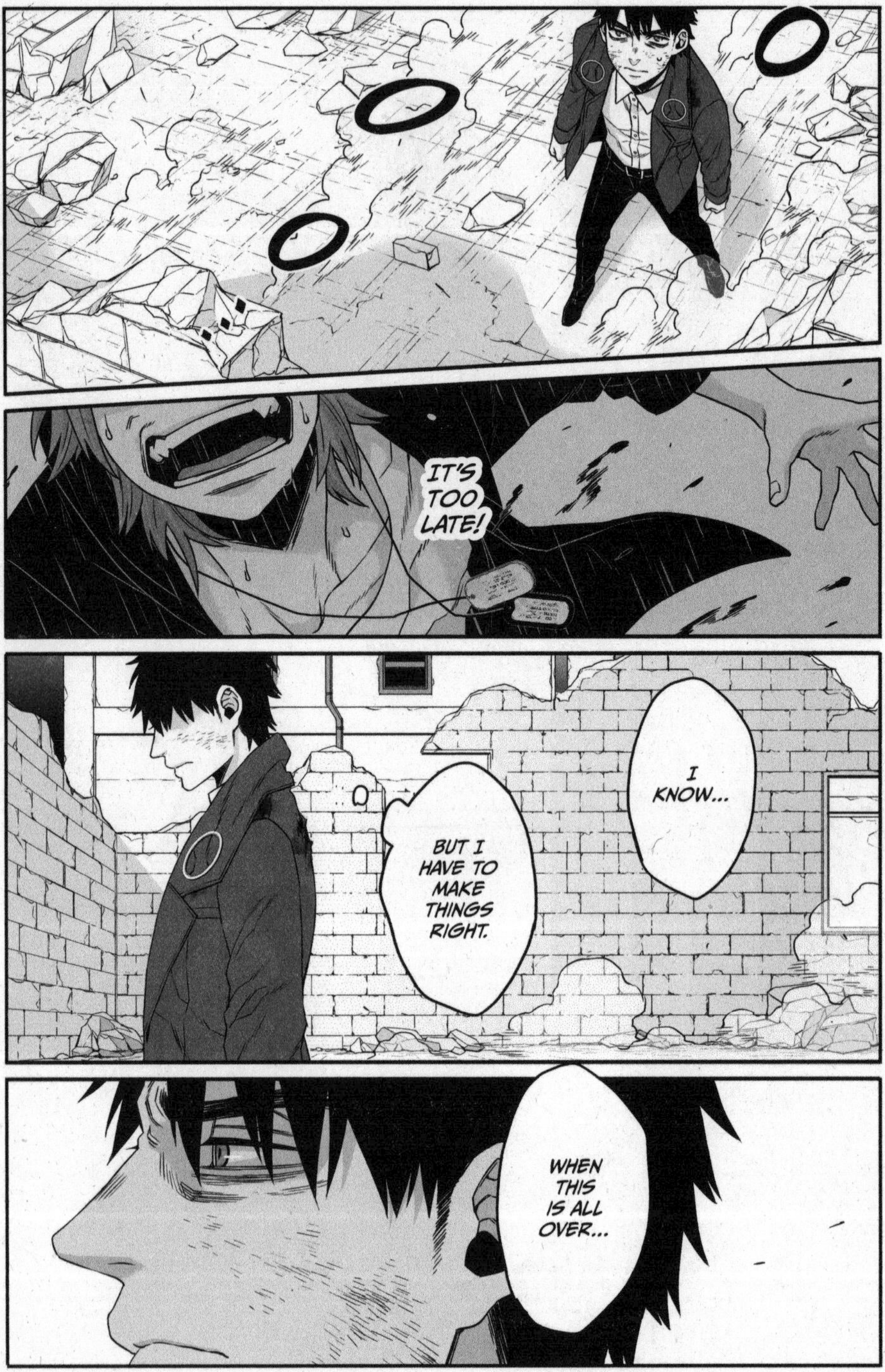
IT'S TOO LATE!
I KNOW...
BUT I HAVE TO MAKE THINGS RIGHT.
WHEN THIS IS ALL OVER...

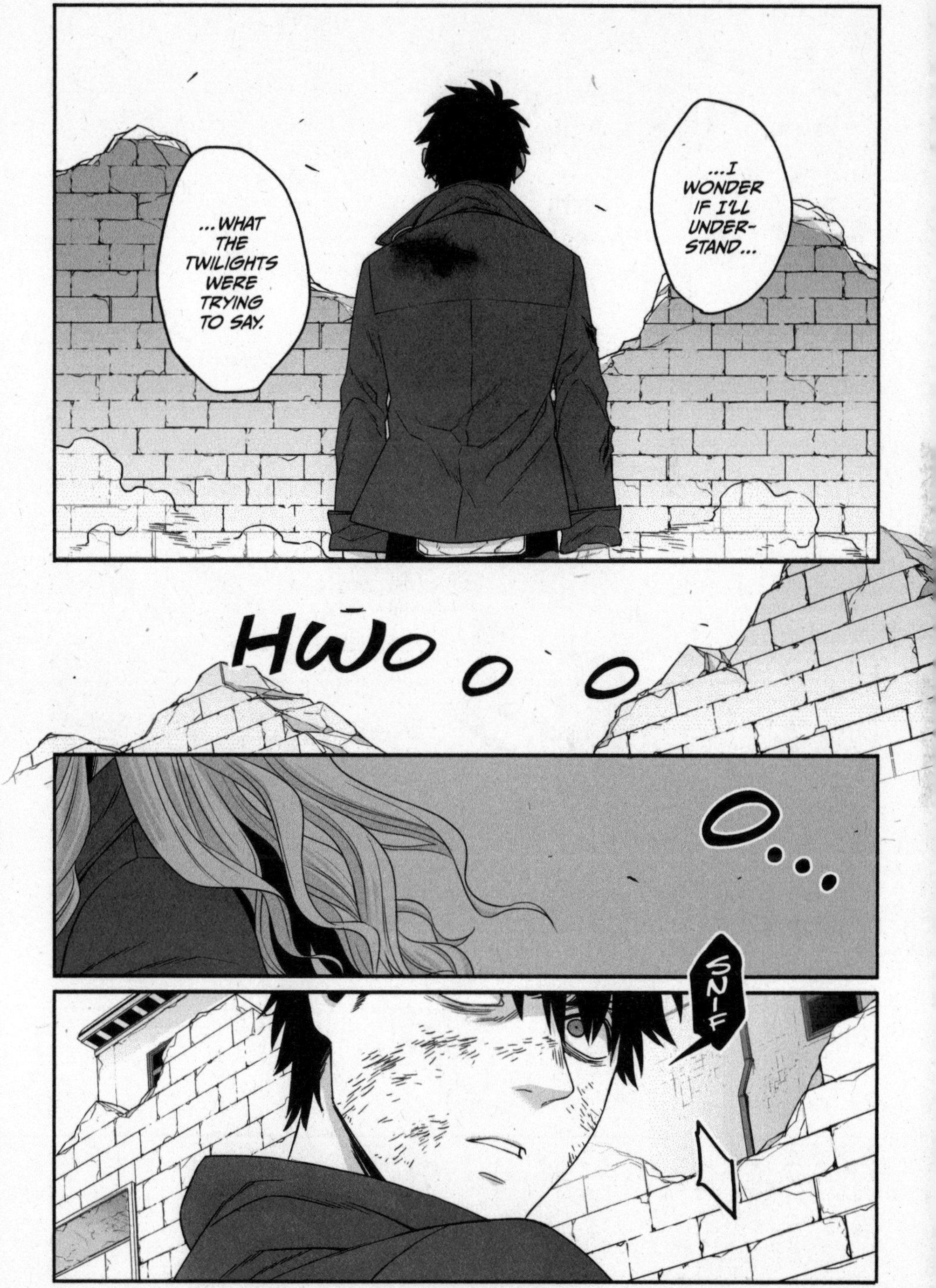
...I WONDER IF I'LL UNDER-STAND...
...WHAT THE TWILIGHTS WERE TRYING TO SAY.
HWO O O
O...
SNIF

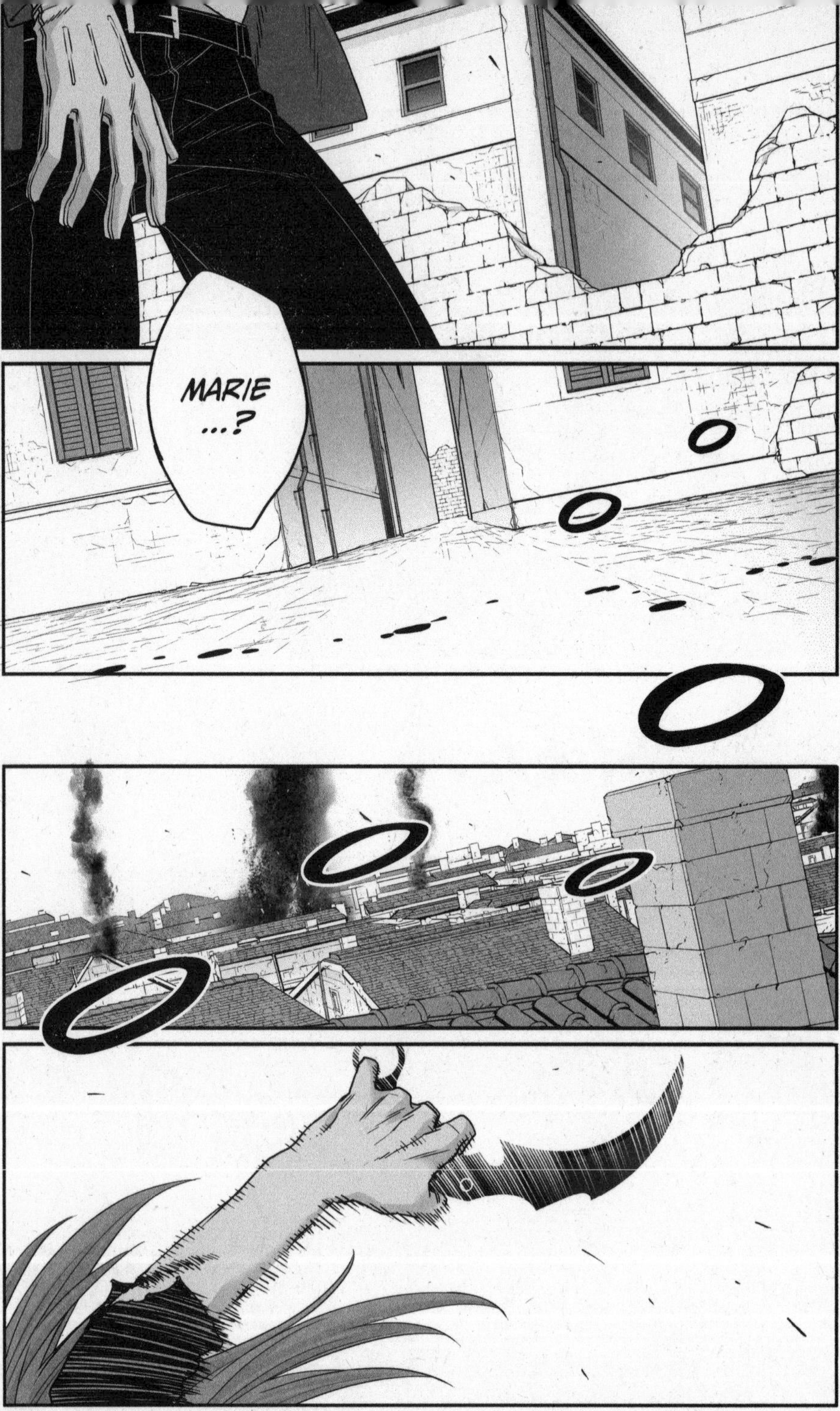
MARIE ...?

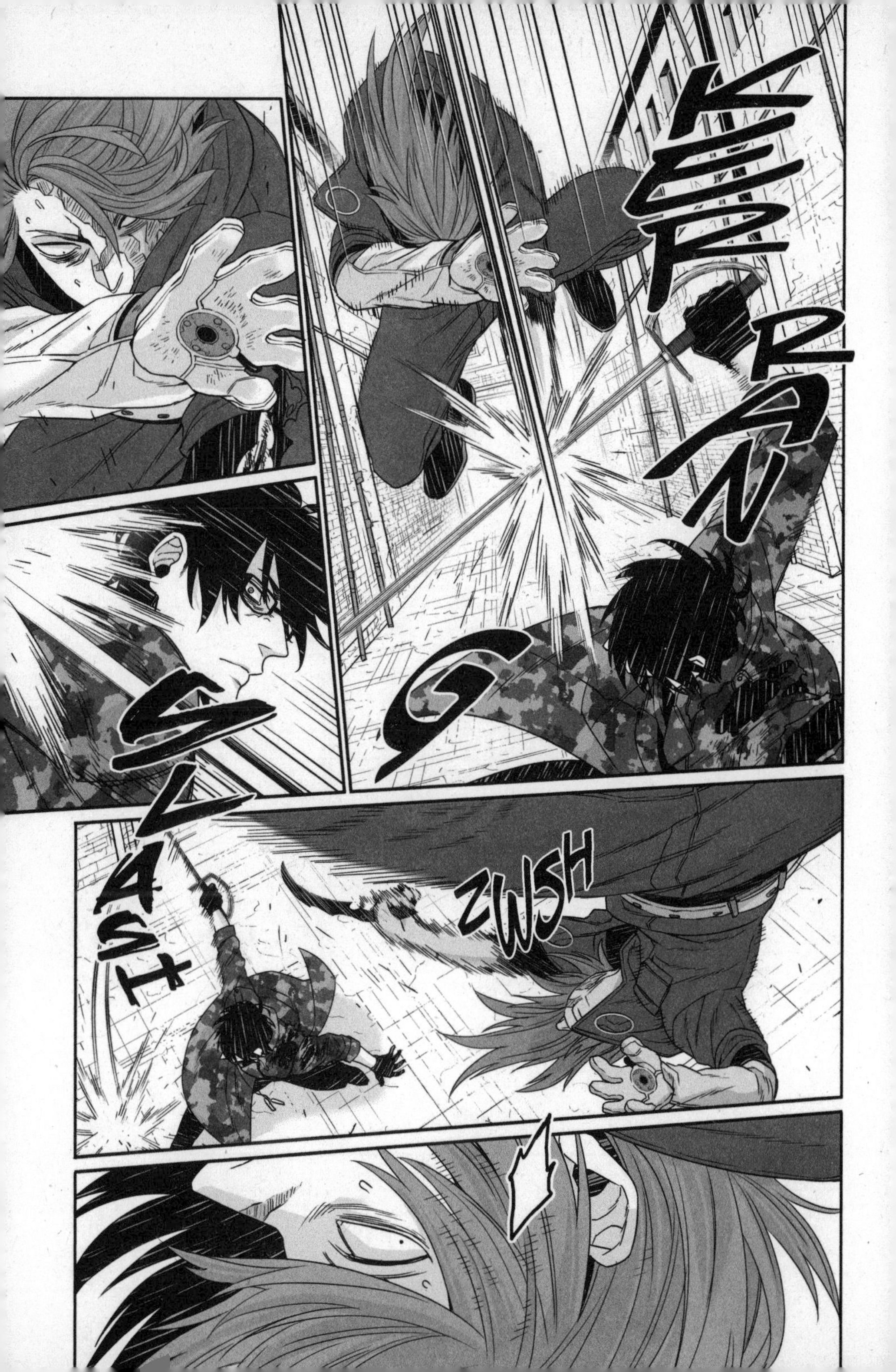
KERRANG
SLAST
ZWSH

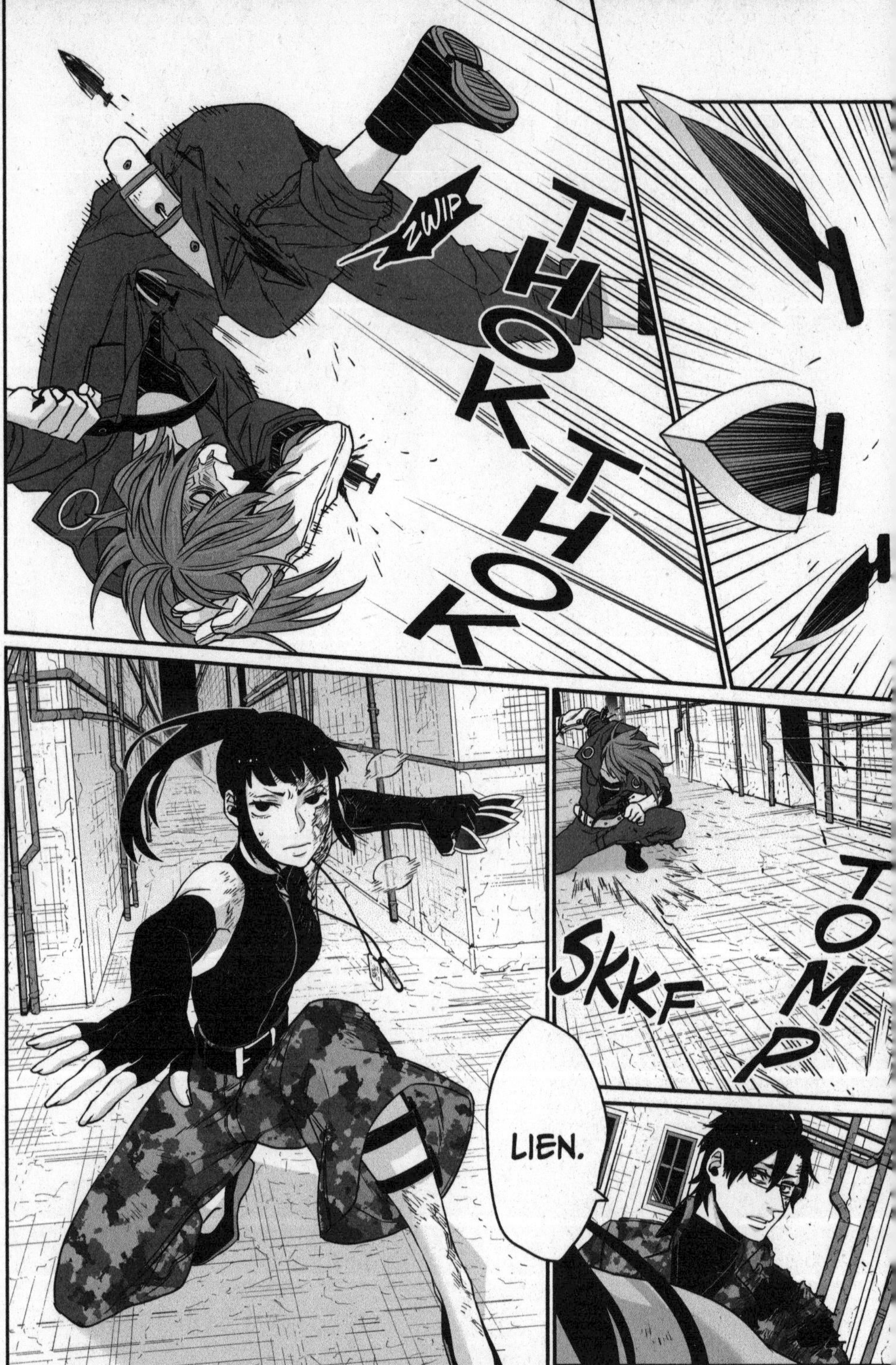
THOKTHOK
ZWIP
TOMP
SKKF
LIEN.

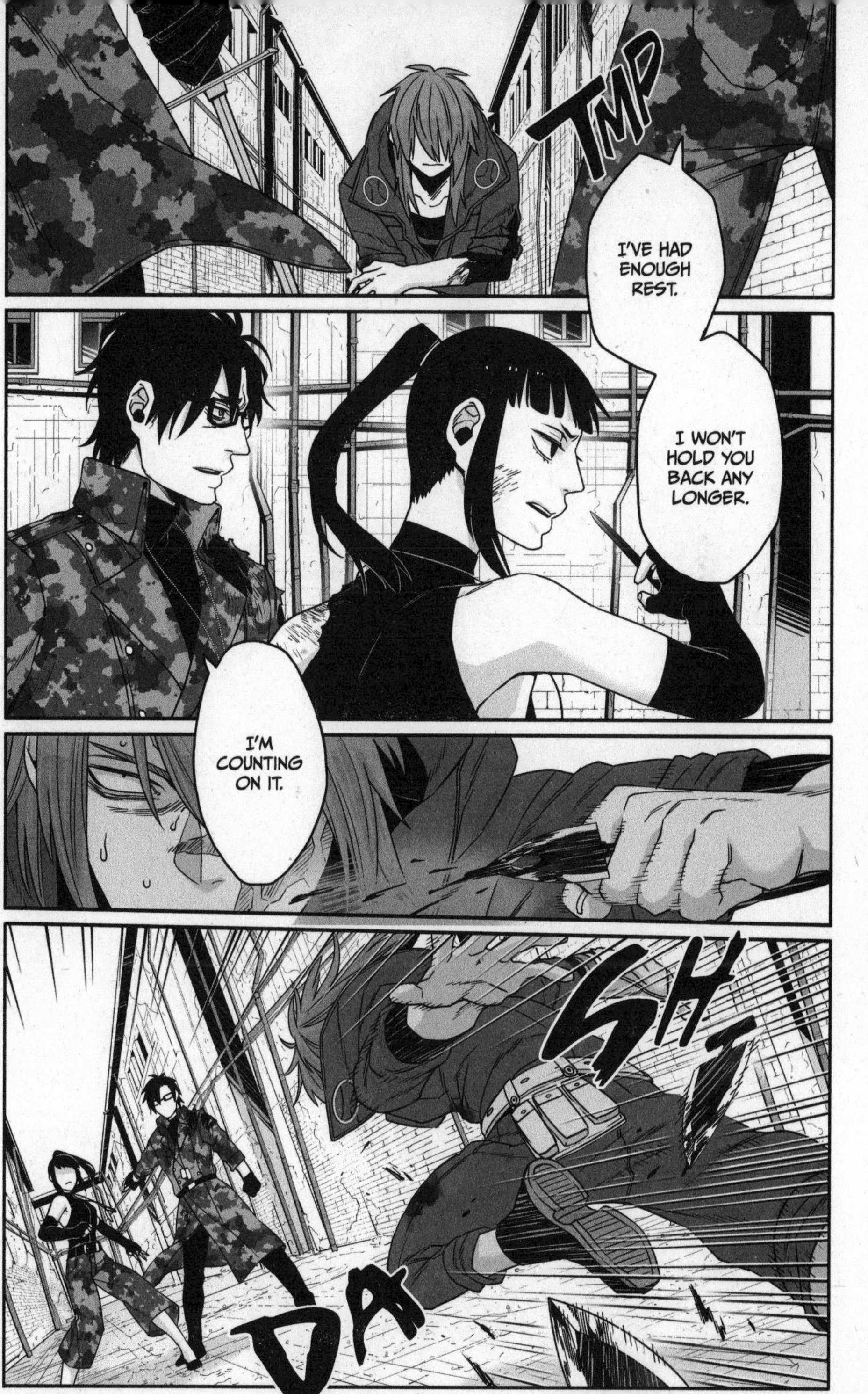
TMP
I'VE HAD ENOUGH REST.
I WON'T HOLD YOU BACK ANY LONGER.
I'M COUNTING ON IT.
SH
DA

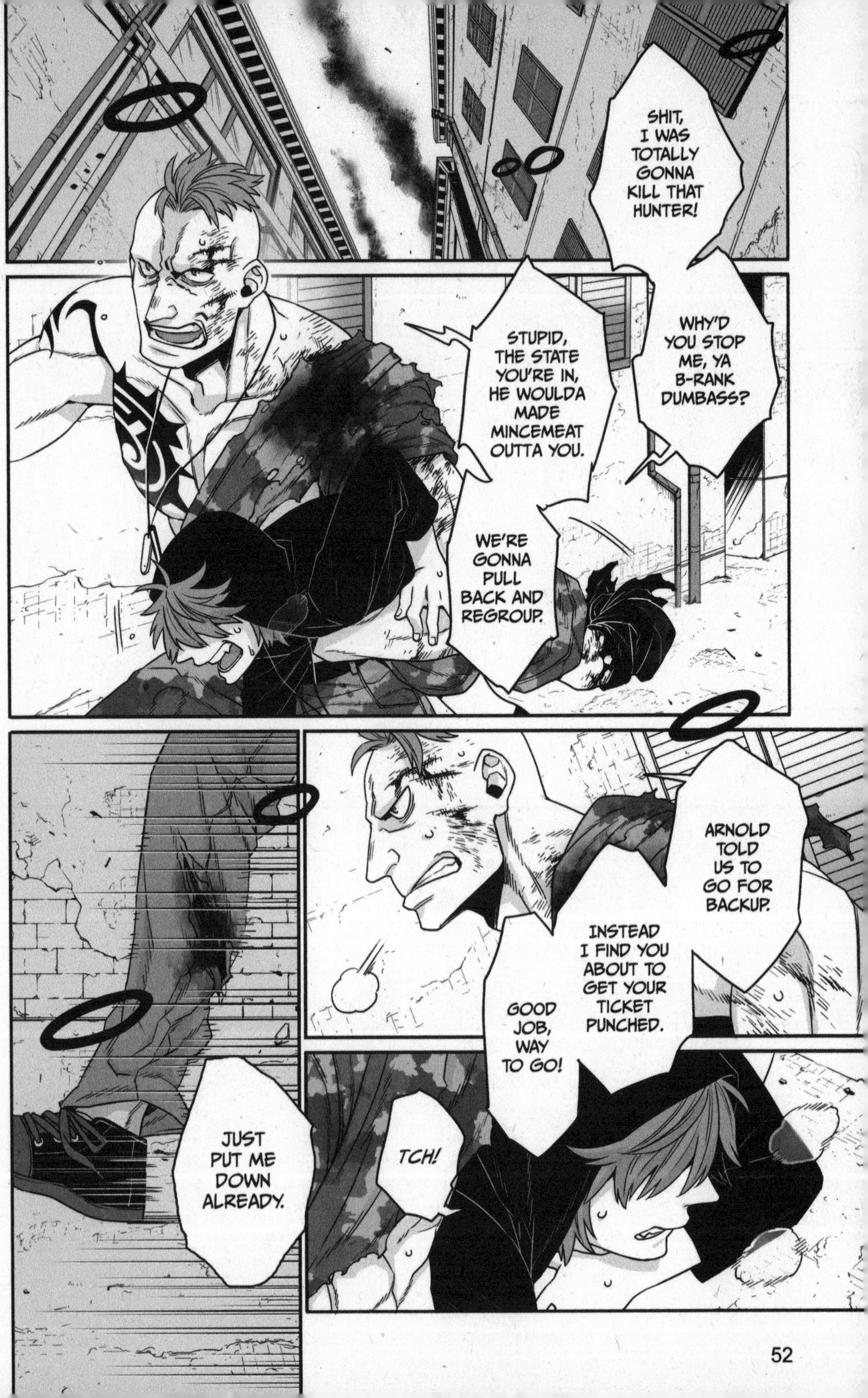
SHIT, I WAS TOTALLY GONNA KILL THAT HUNTER!
WHY'D YOU STOP ME, YA B-RANK DUMBASS?
STUPID, THE STATE YOU'RE IN, HE WOULDA MADE MINCEMEAT OUTTA YOU.
WE'RE GONNA PULL BACK AND REGROUP.
ARNOLD TOLD US TO GO FOR BACKUP.
INSTEAD I FIND YOU ABOUT TO GET YOUR TICKET PUNCHED.
GOOD JOB, WAY TO GO!
TCH!
JUST PUT ME DOWN ALREADY.

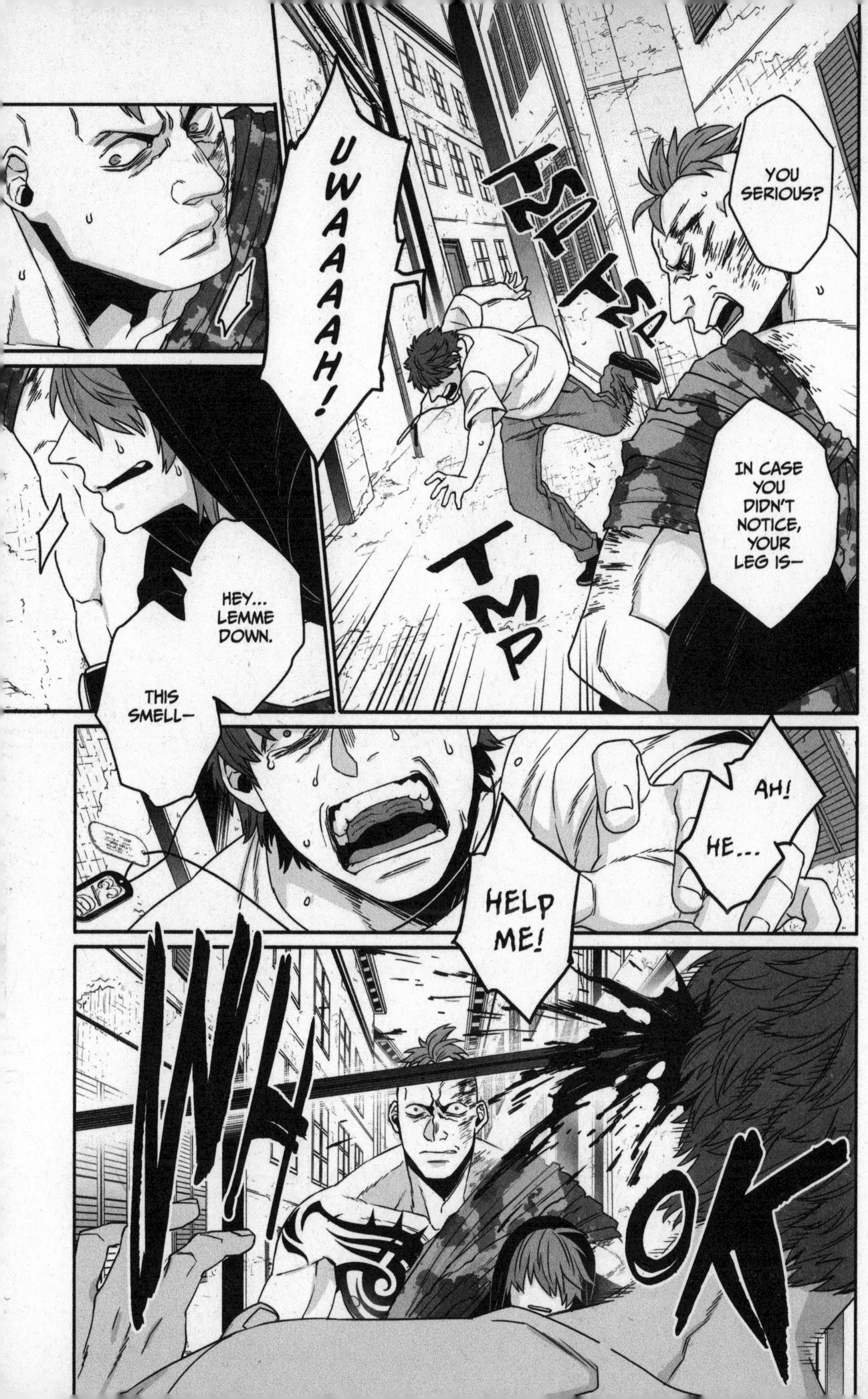
YOU SERIOUS?
TMP TMP TMP
IN CASE YOU DIDN'T NOTICE, YOUR LEG IS—
UWAAAAAH!
TMP
HEY... LEMME DOWN.
THIS SMELL—
AH!
HE...
HELP ME!
WHOK

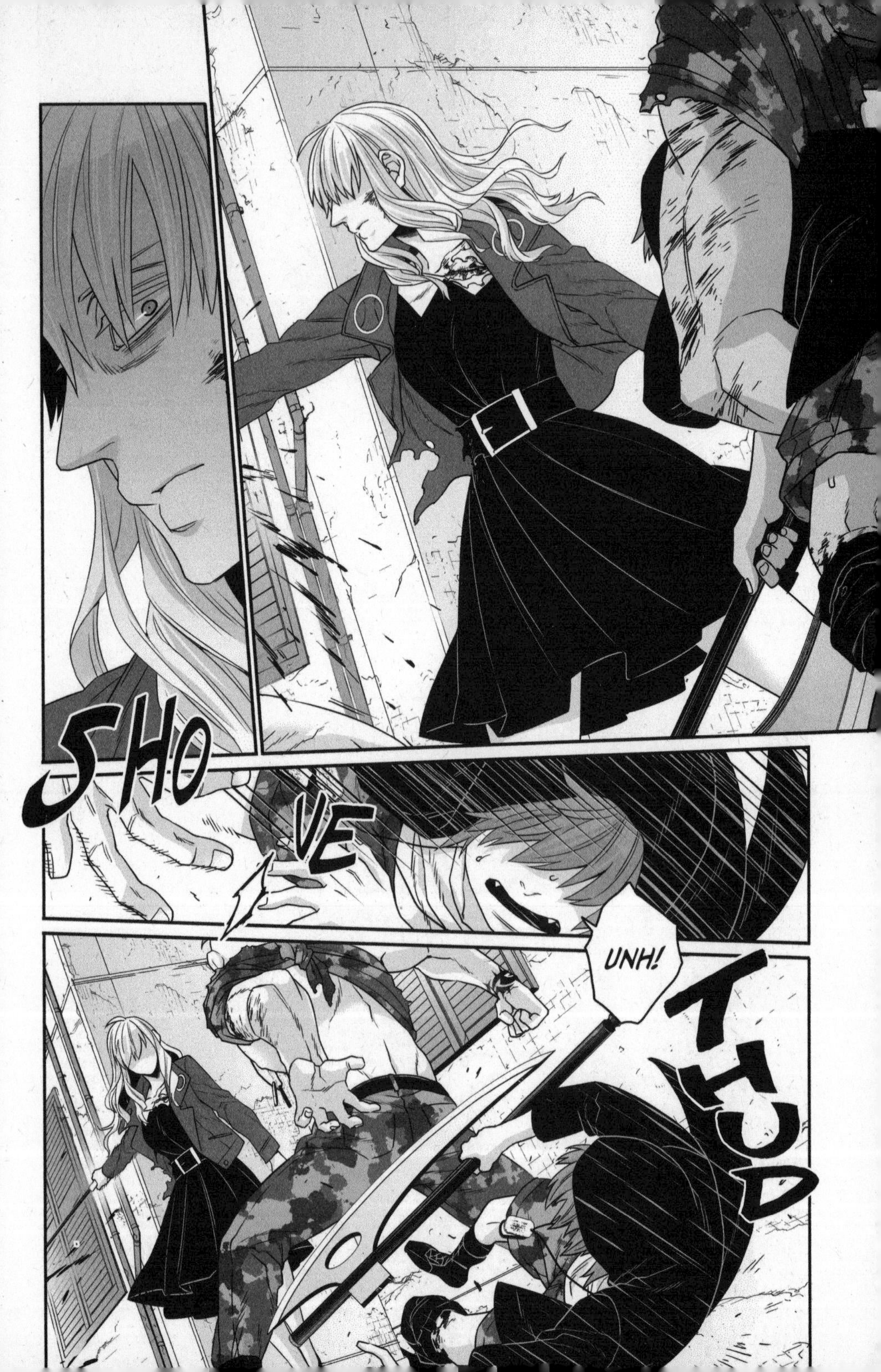
SHOVE
UNH!
THUD

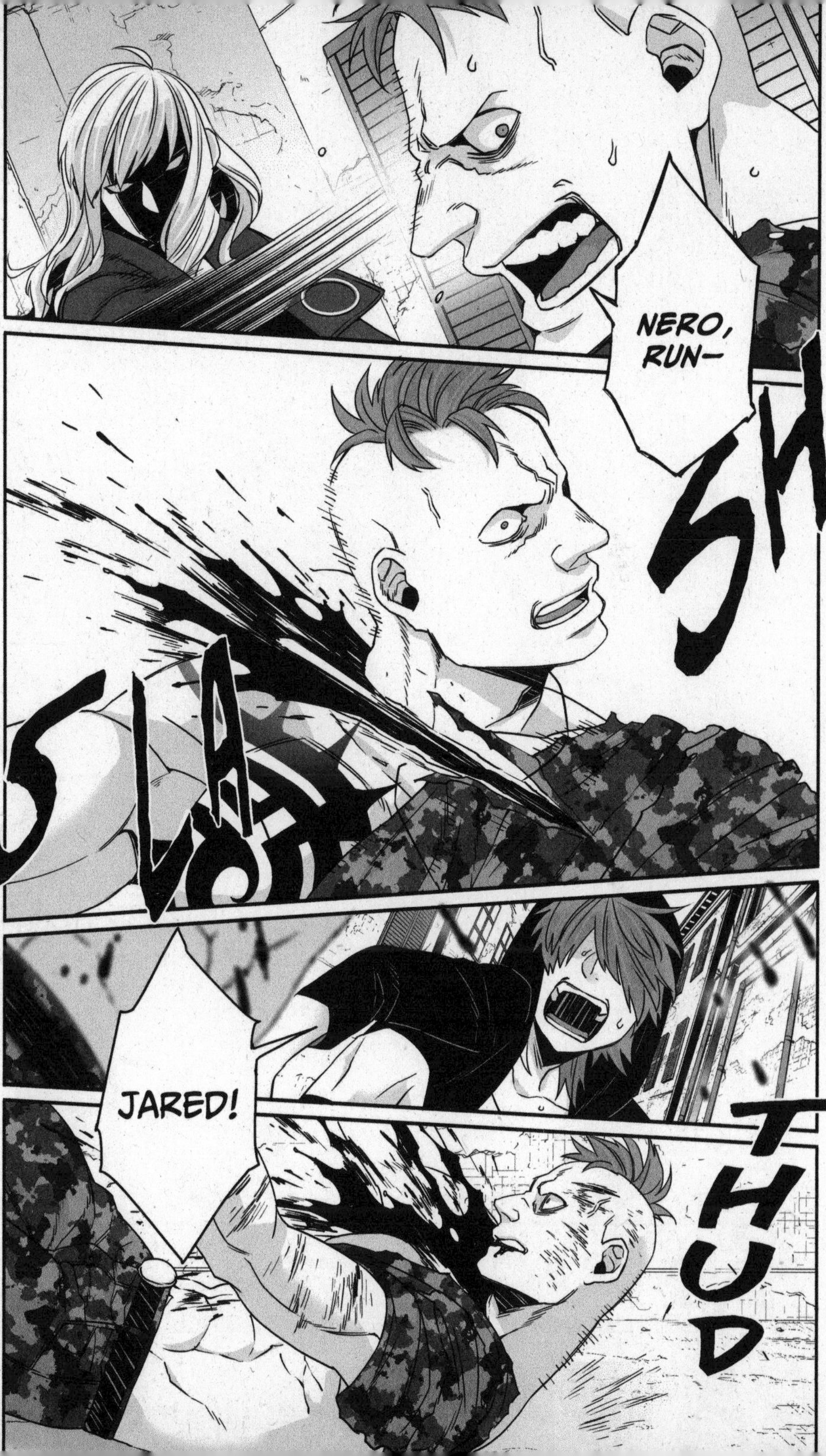
NERO, RUN—
SLA
SH
JARED!
THUD

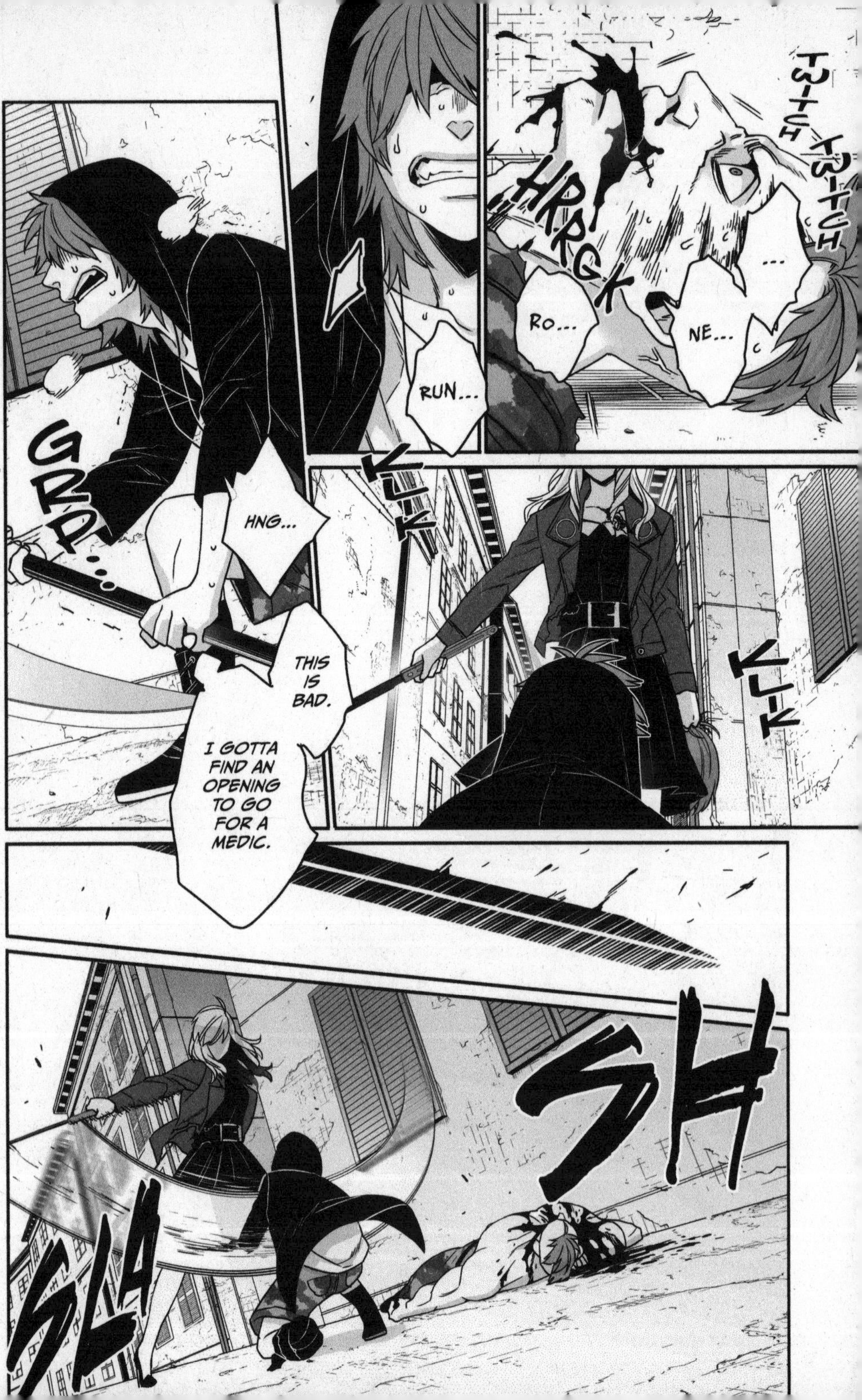
TWITCH TWITCH
HRRGK
...
NE...
RO...
RUN...
GRP...
HNG...
KLIK
KLIK
THIS IS BAD.
I GOTTA FIND AN OPENING TO GO FOR A MEDIC.
SHH
SLA

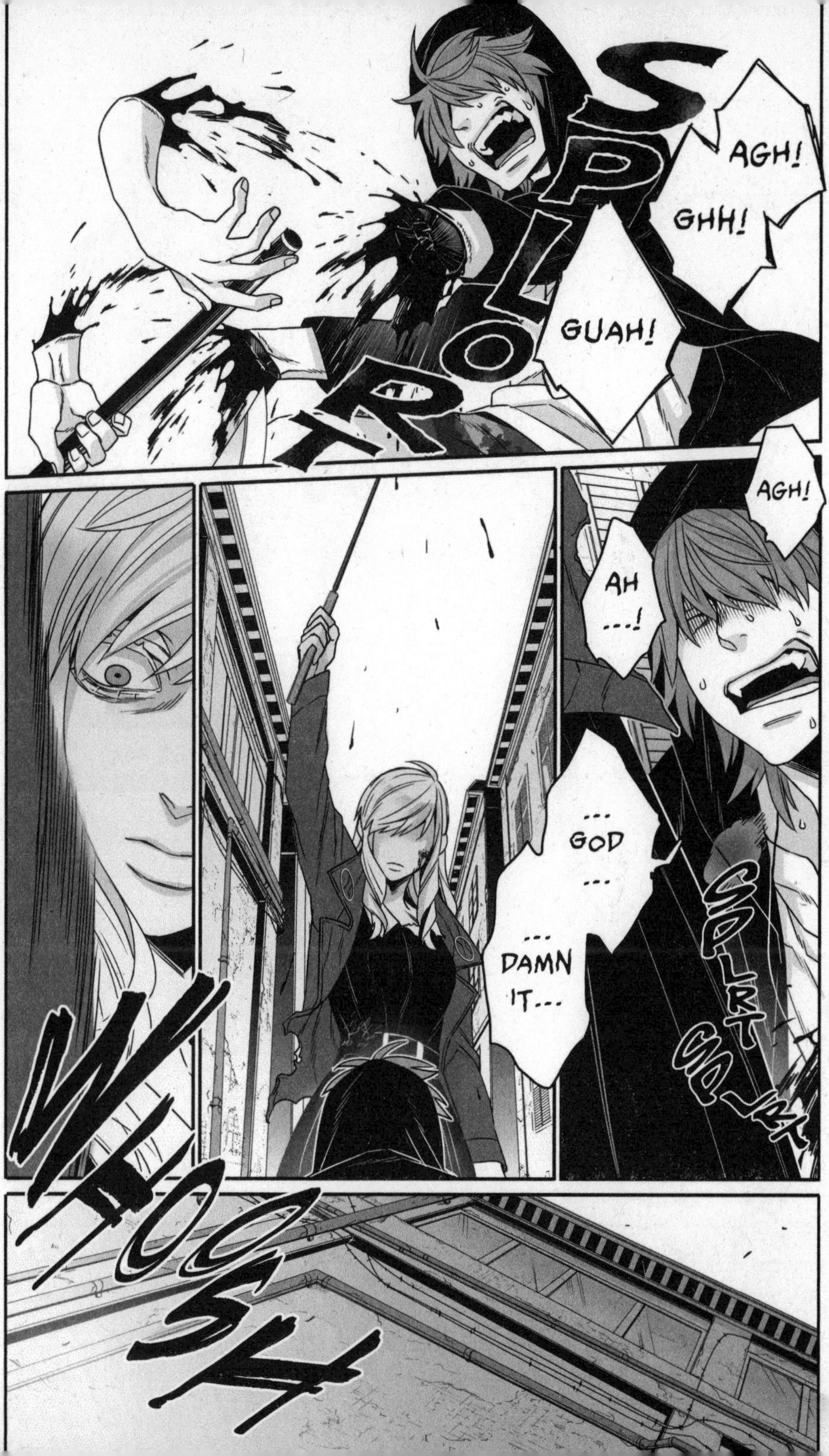
AGH!
GHH!
GUAH!
SPLORT
AGH!
AH ...!
... GOD ...
... DAMN IT...
SPLRT
WHOOSH

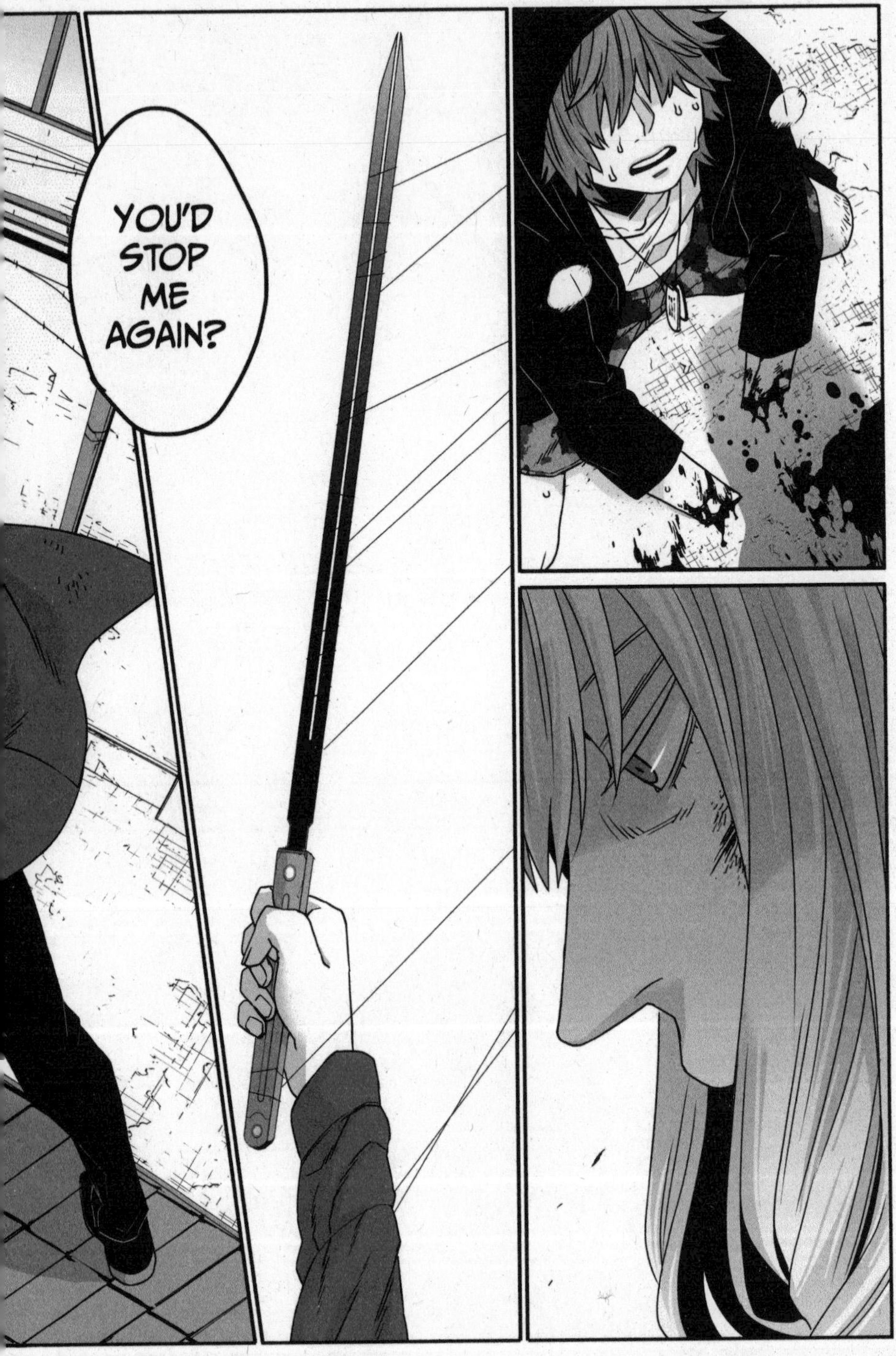
YOU'D STOP ME AGAIN?

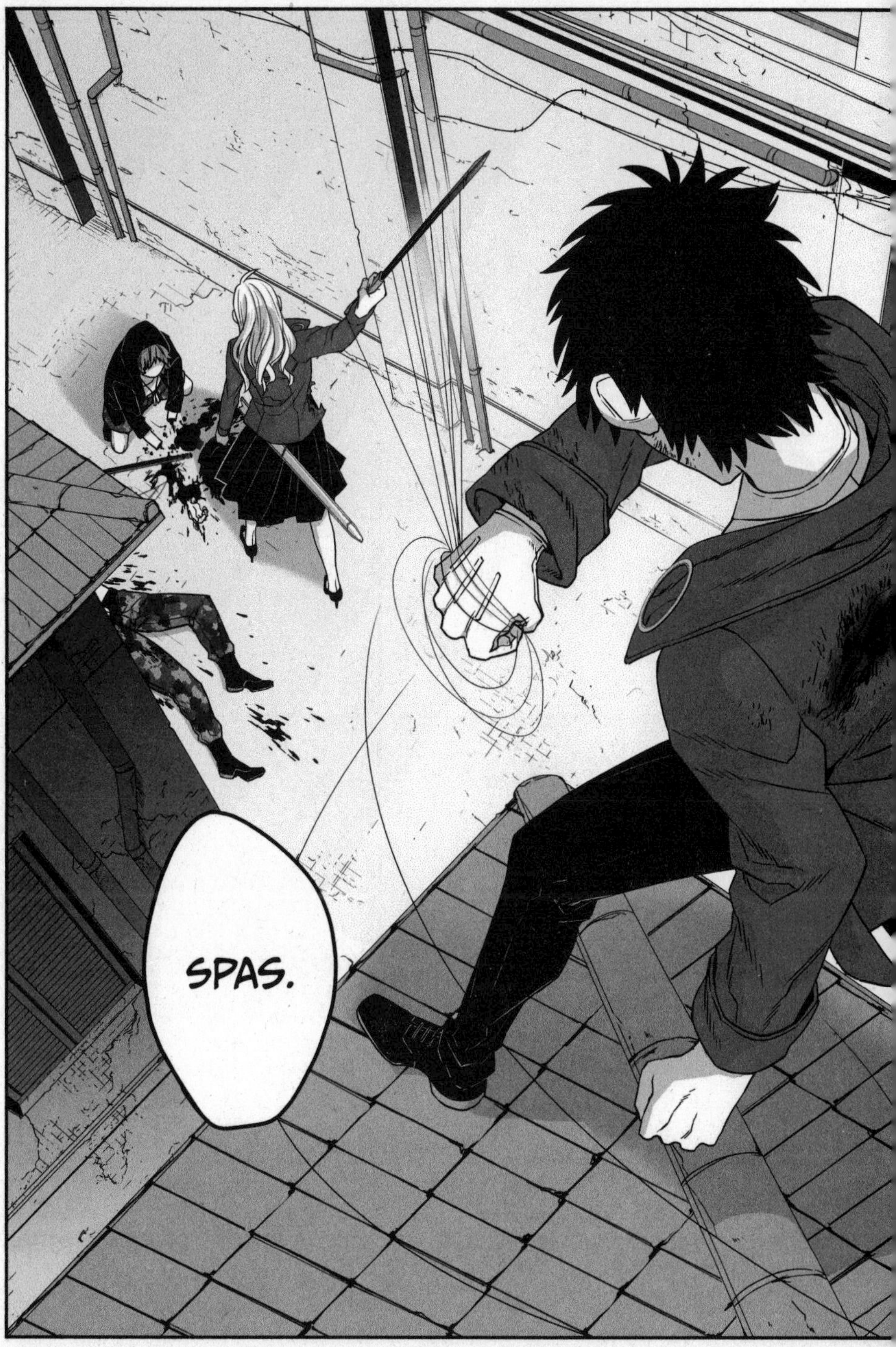
SPAS.

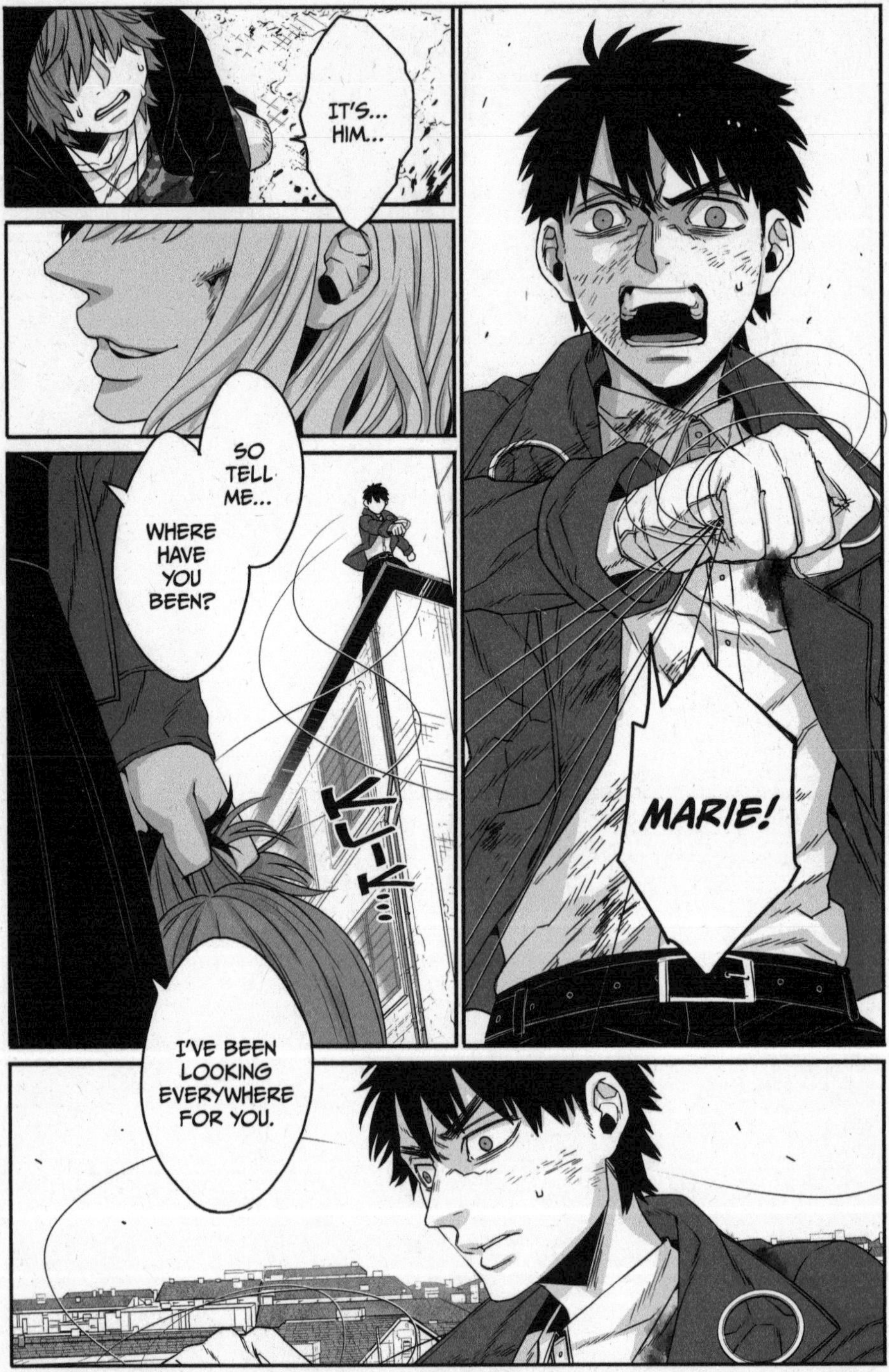
MARIE!
IT'S... HIM...
SO TELL ME...
WHERE HAVE YOU BEEN?
I'VE BEEN LOOKING EVERYWHERE FOR YOU.

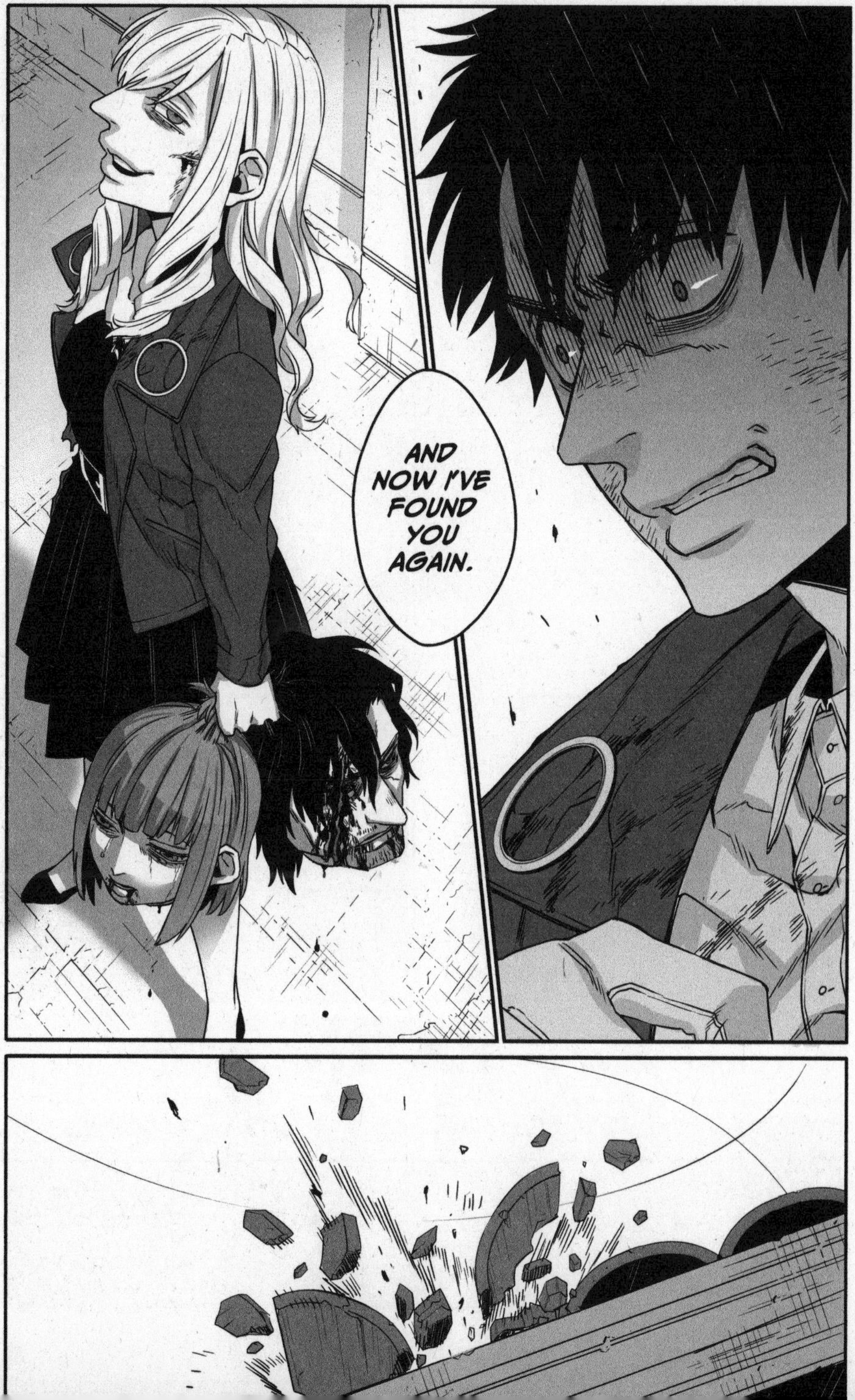
AND NOW I'VE FOUND YOU AGAIN.

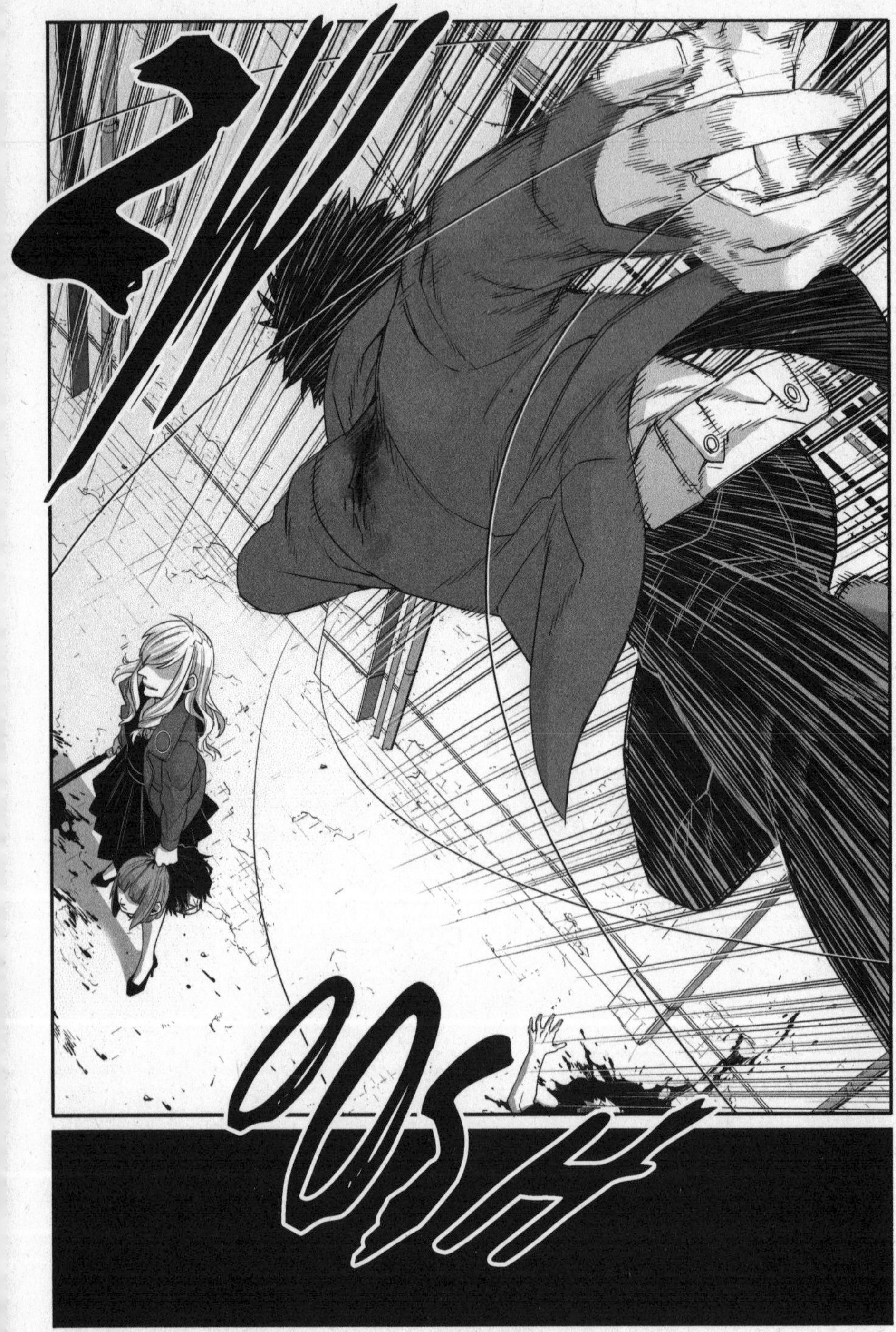
SWI
WOOSH

#10 END

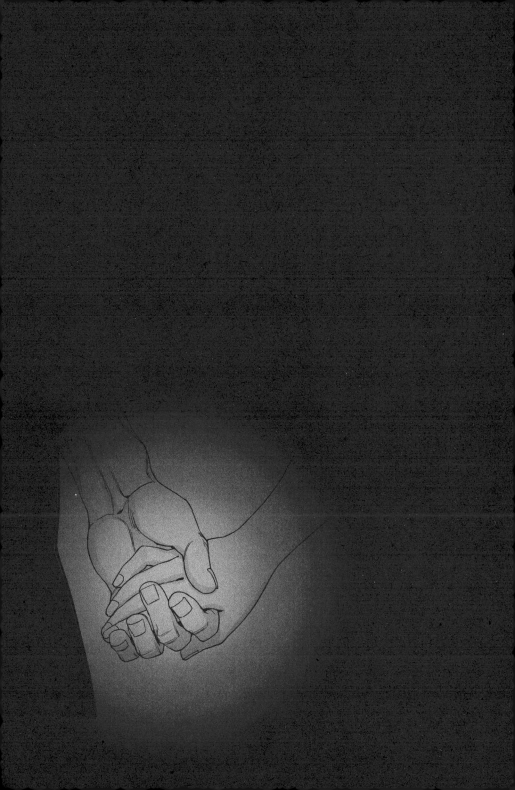

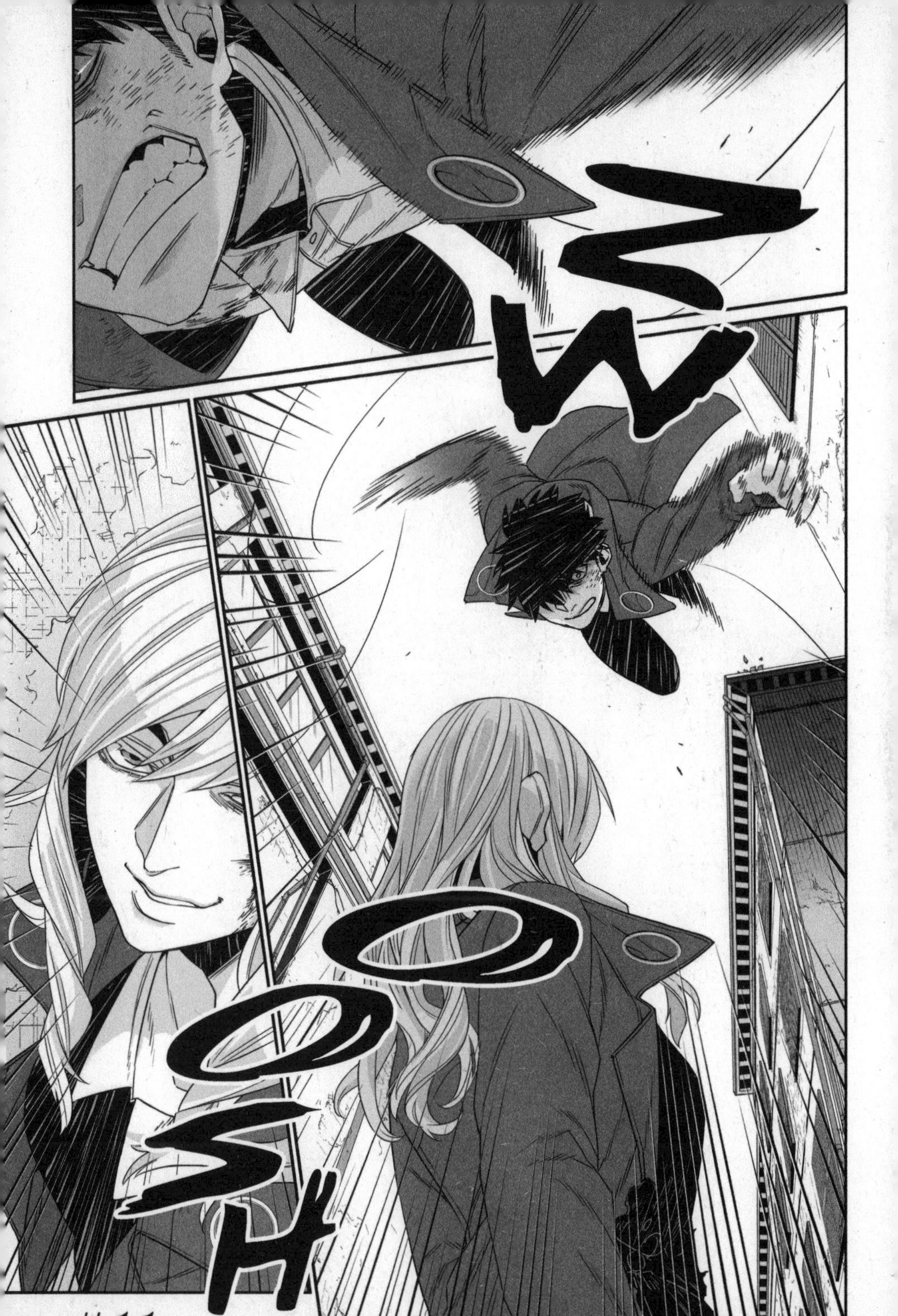
SWOOSH

#11

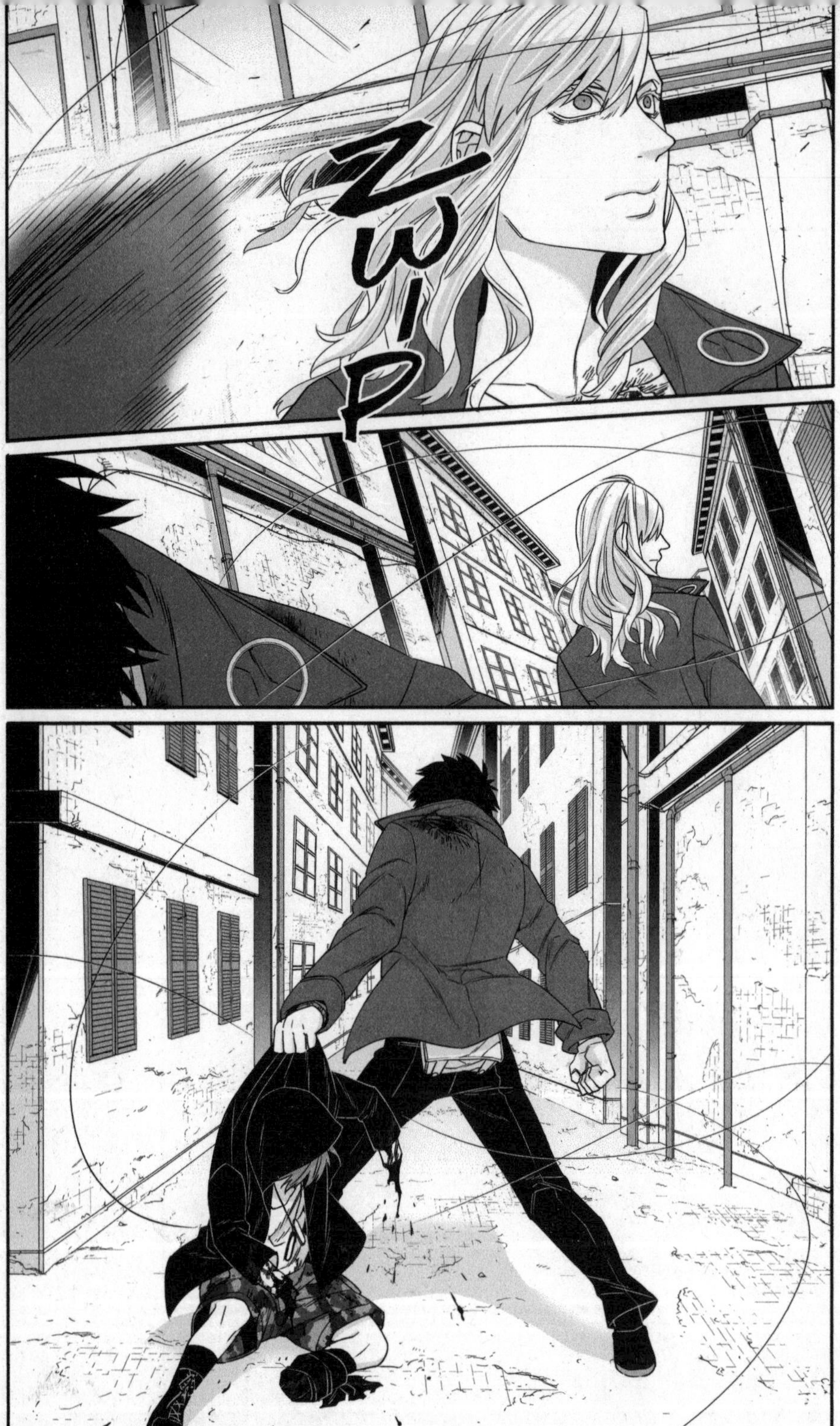
ZWIP

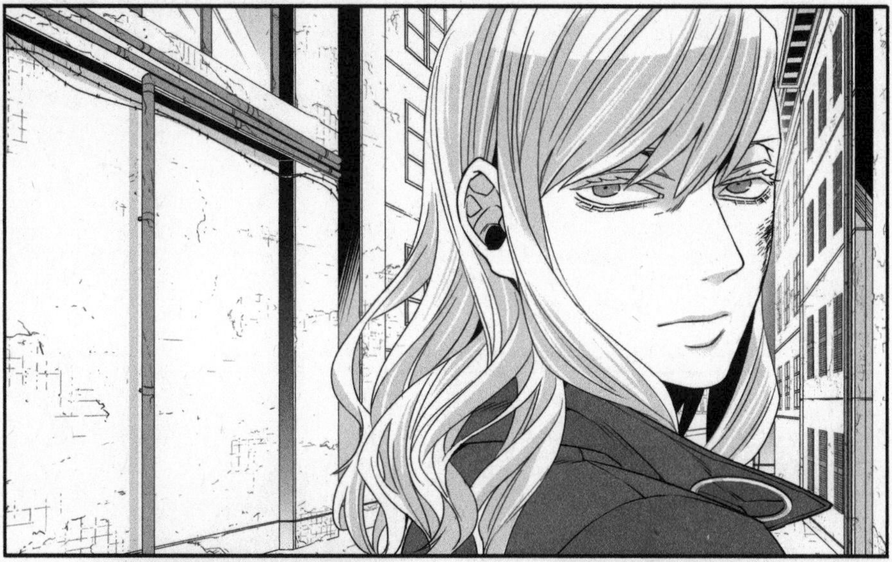

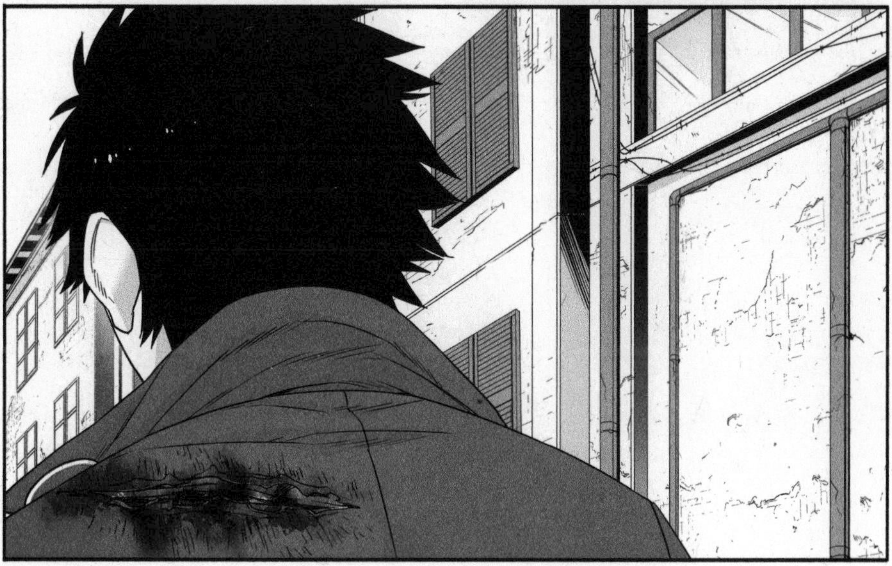

#11

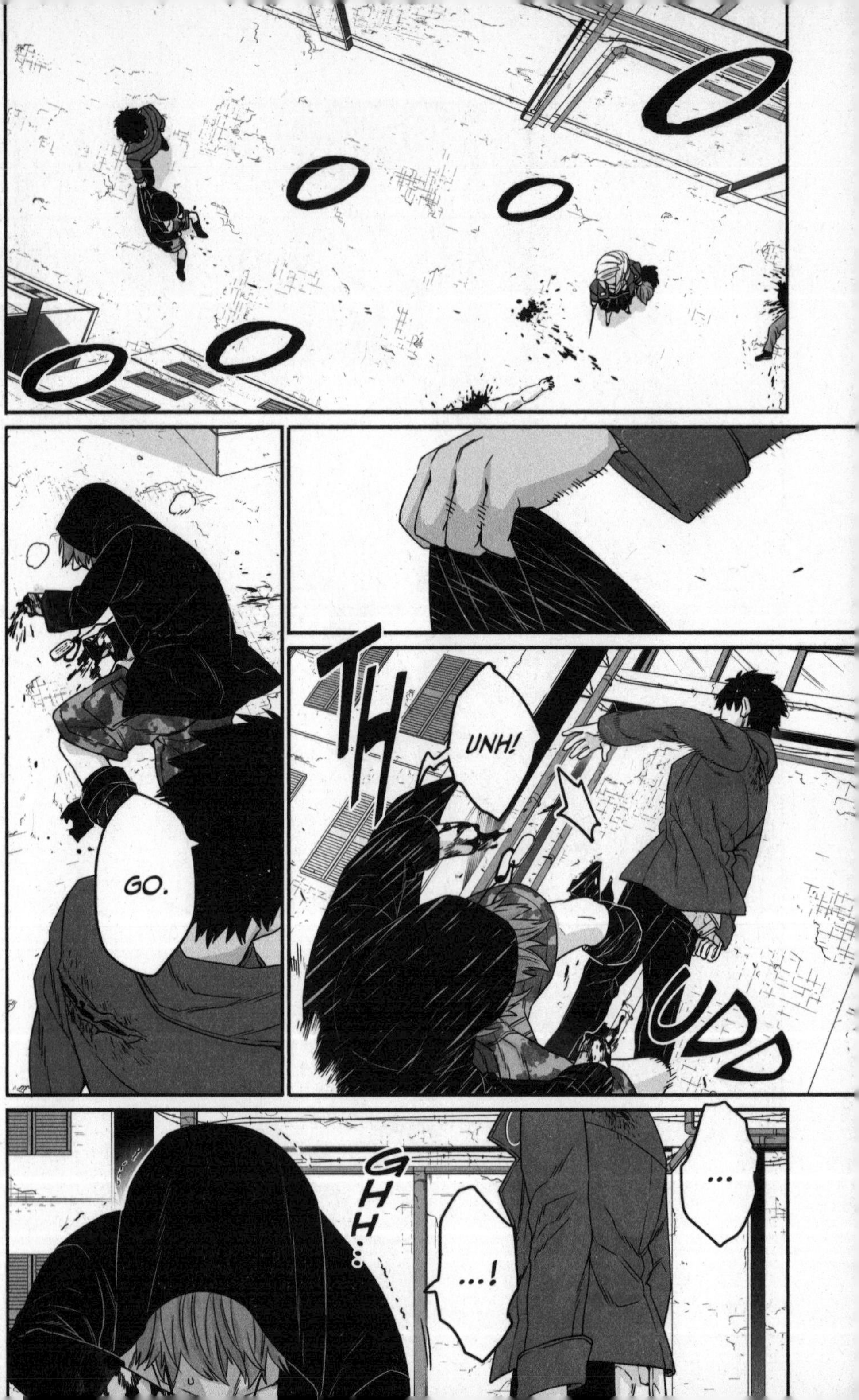
UNH!
THUDD
GO.
...
...!
GHH..

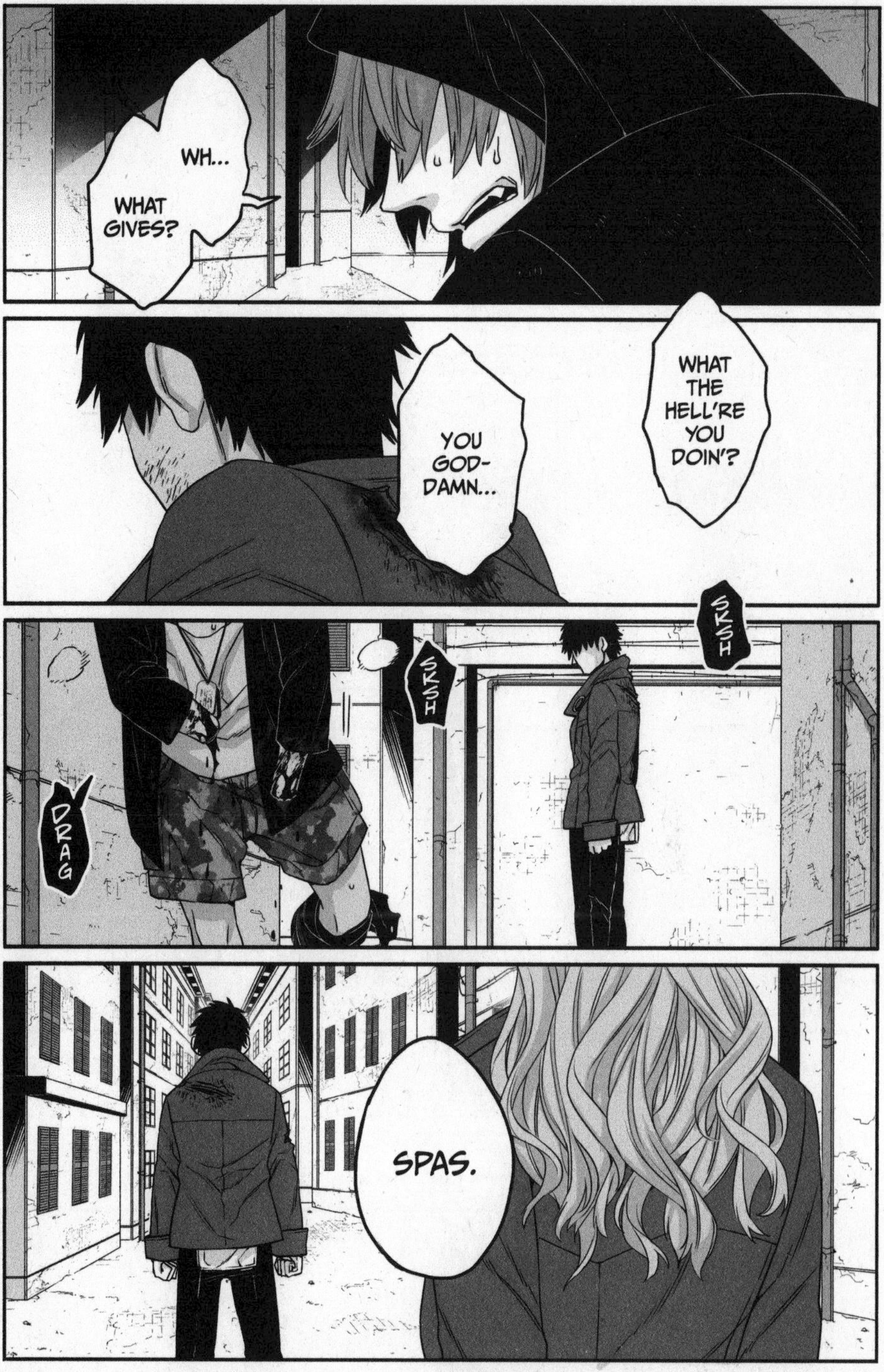
WH...
WHAT GIVES?
WHAT THE HELL'RE YOU DOIN'?
YOU GOD-DAMN...
SKSH
SKSH
DRAG
SPAS.

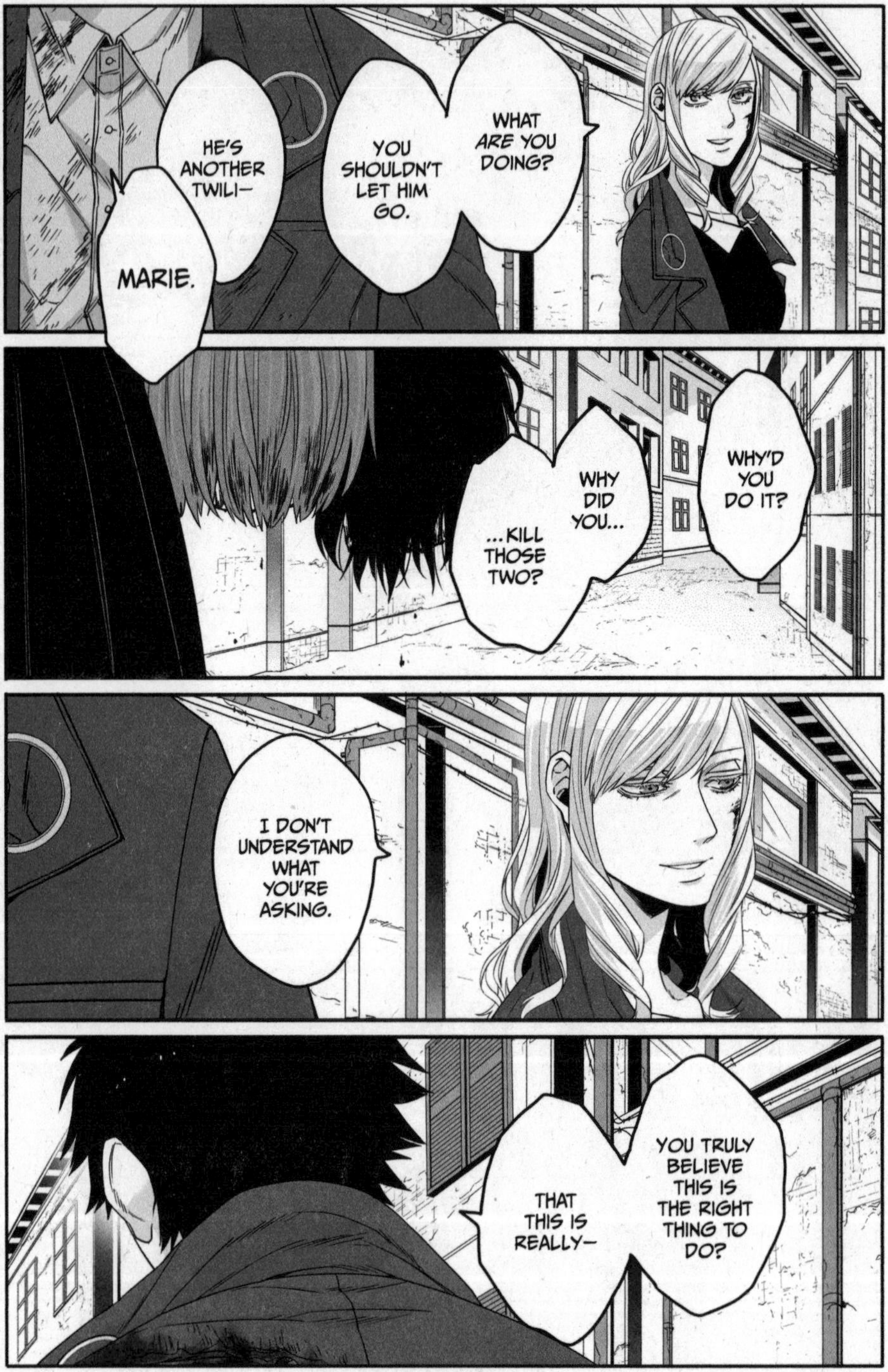
WHAT ARE YOU DOING?
YOU SHOULDN'T LET HIM GO.
HE'S ANOTHER TWILI—
MARIE.
WHY'D YOU DO IT?
WHY DID YOU...
...KILL THOSE TWO?
I DON'T UNDERSTAND WHAT YOU'RE ASKING.
YOU TRULY BELIEVE THIS IS THE RIGHT THING TO DO?
THAT THIS IS REALLY—

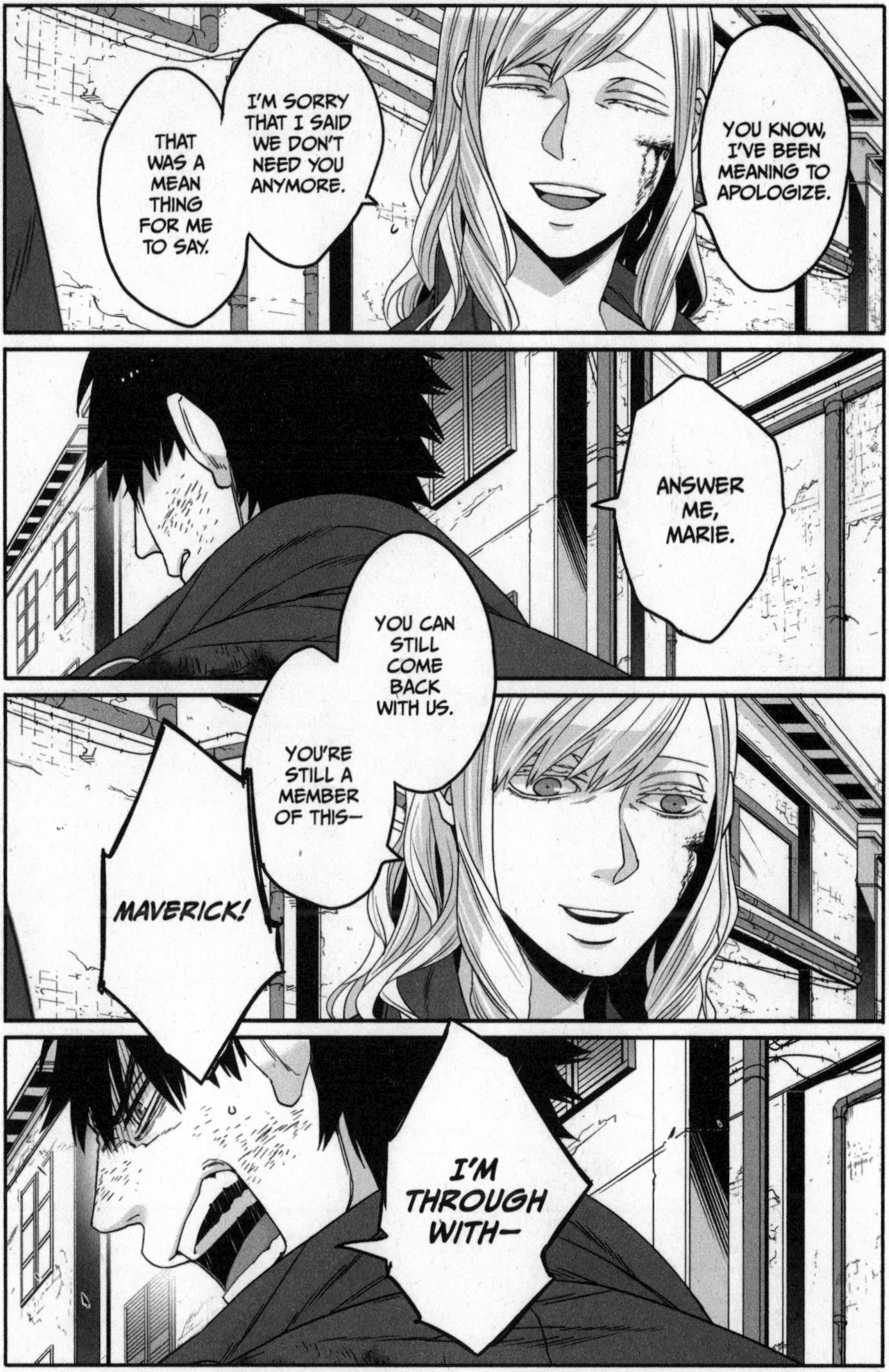
YOU KNOW, I'VE BEEN MEANING TO APOLOGIZE.
I'M SORRY THAT I SAID WE DON'T NEED YOU ANYMORE.
THAT WAS A MEAN THING FOR ME TO SAY.
ANSWER ME, MARIE.
YOU CAN STILL COME BACK WITH US.
YOU'RE STILL A MEMBER OF THIS—
MAVERICK!
I'M THROUGH WITH—

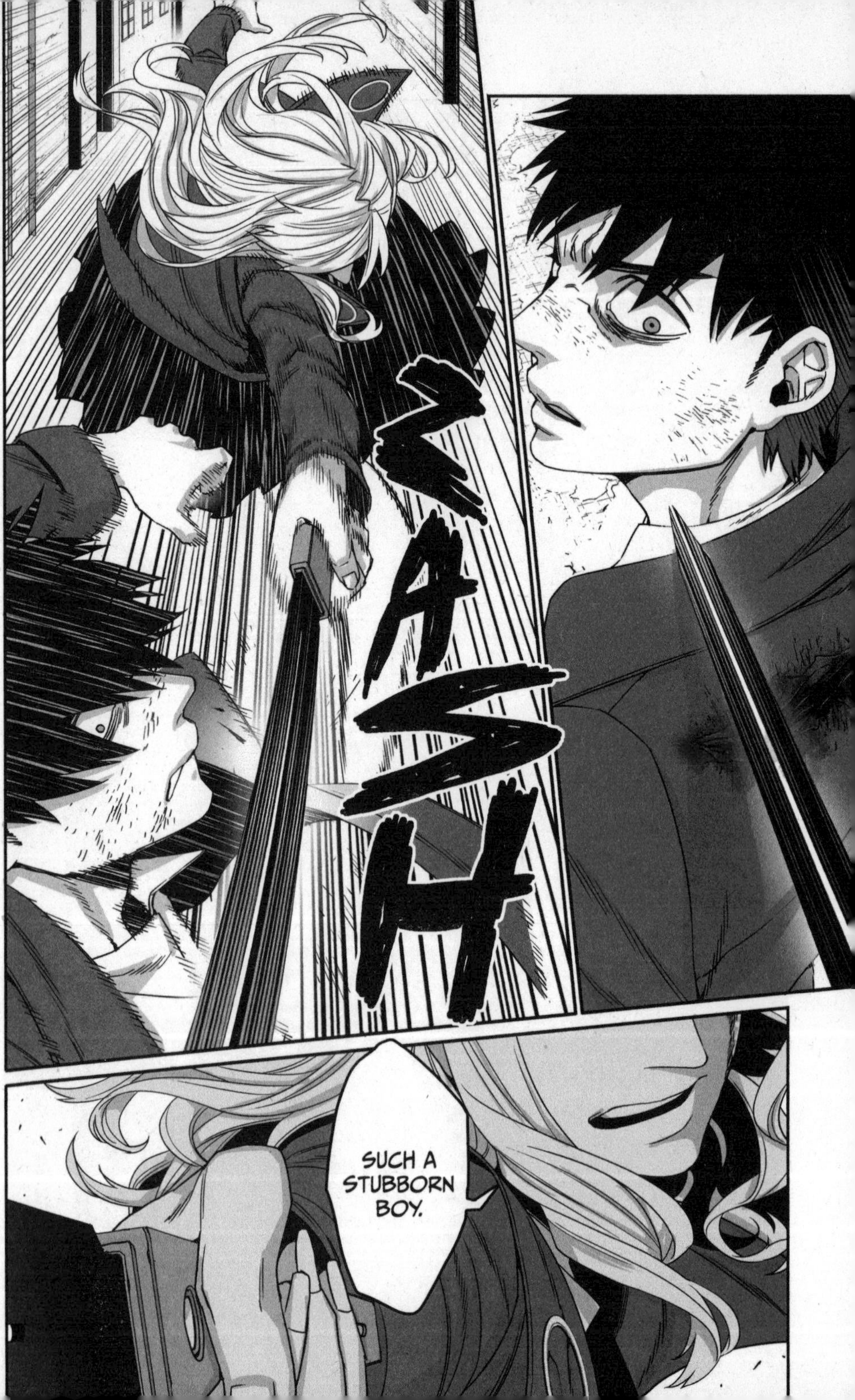
ZASH
SUCH A STUBBORN BOY.

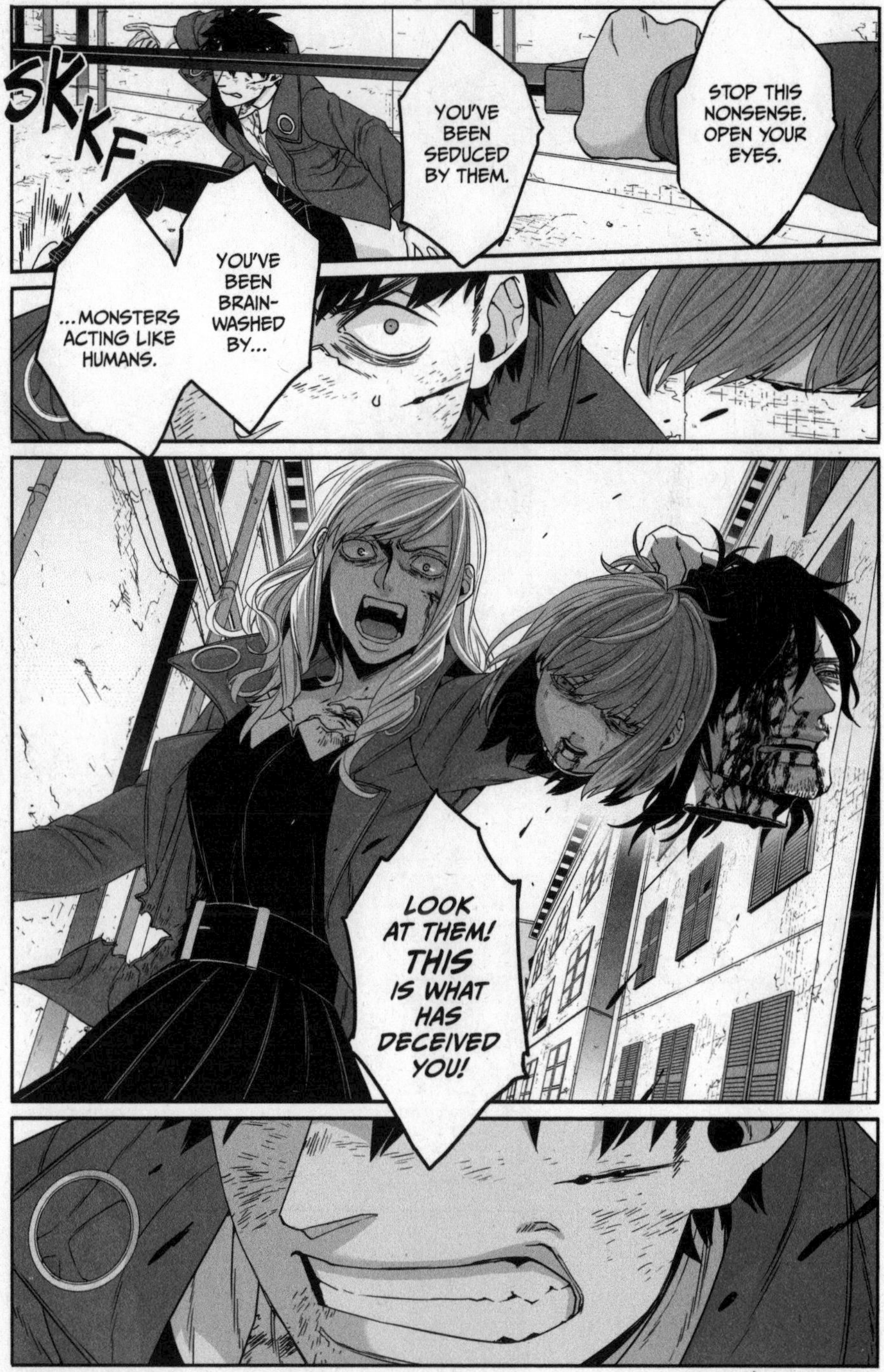
STOP THIS NONSENSE. OPEN YOUR EYES.
YOU'VE BEEN SEDUCED BY THEM.
SKKF
YOU'VE BEEN BRAIN-WASHED BY...
...MONSTERS ACTING LIKE HUMANS.
LOOK AT THEM! THIS IS WHAT HAS DECEIVED YOU!

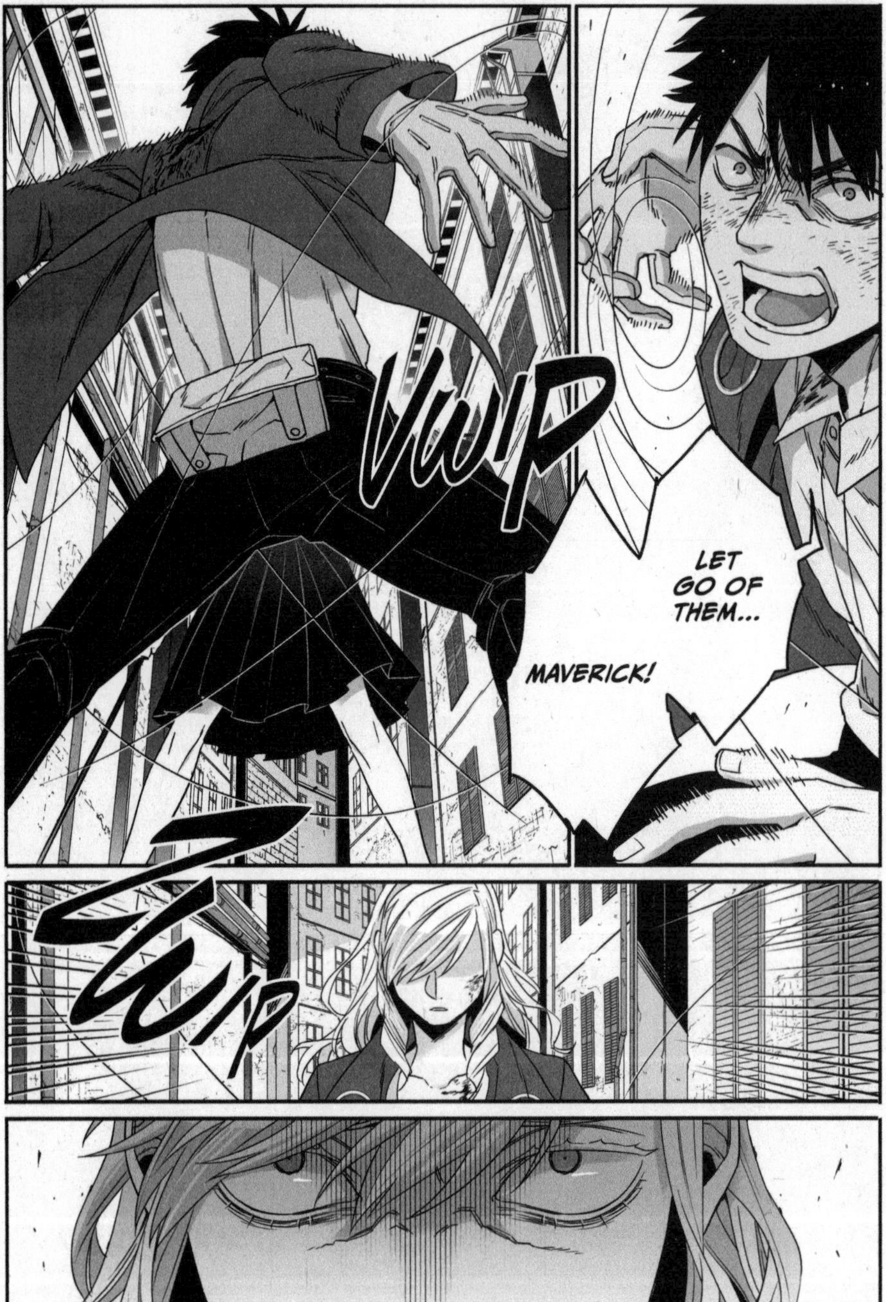
VWIP
LET GO OF THEM...
MAVERICK!
VWIP

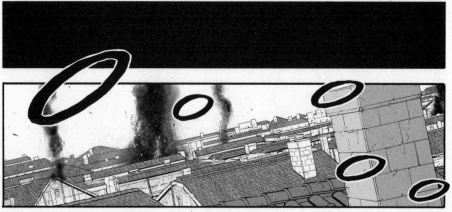

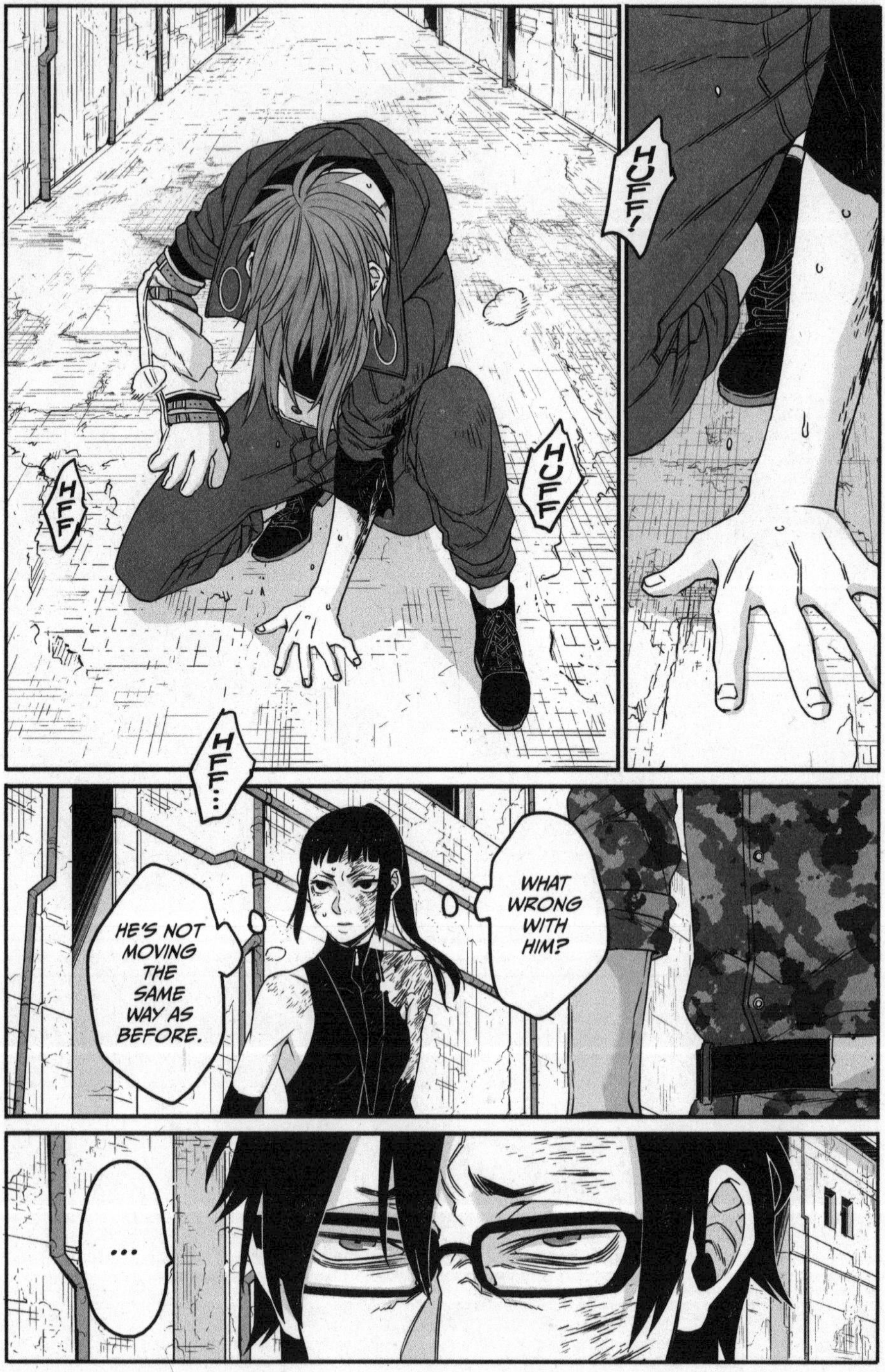
HUFF!
HUFF
HFF
HFF...
WHAT WRONG WITH HIM?
HE'S NOT MOVING THE SAME WAY AS BEFORE.
...

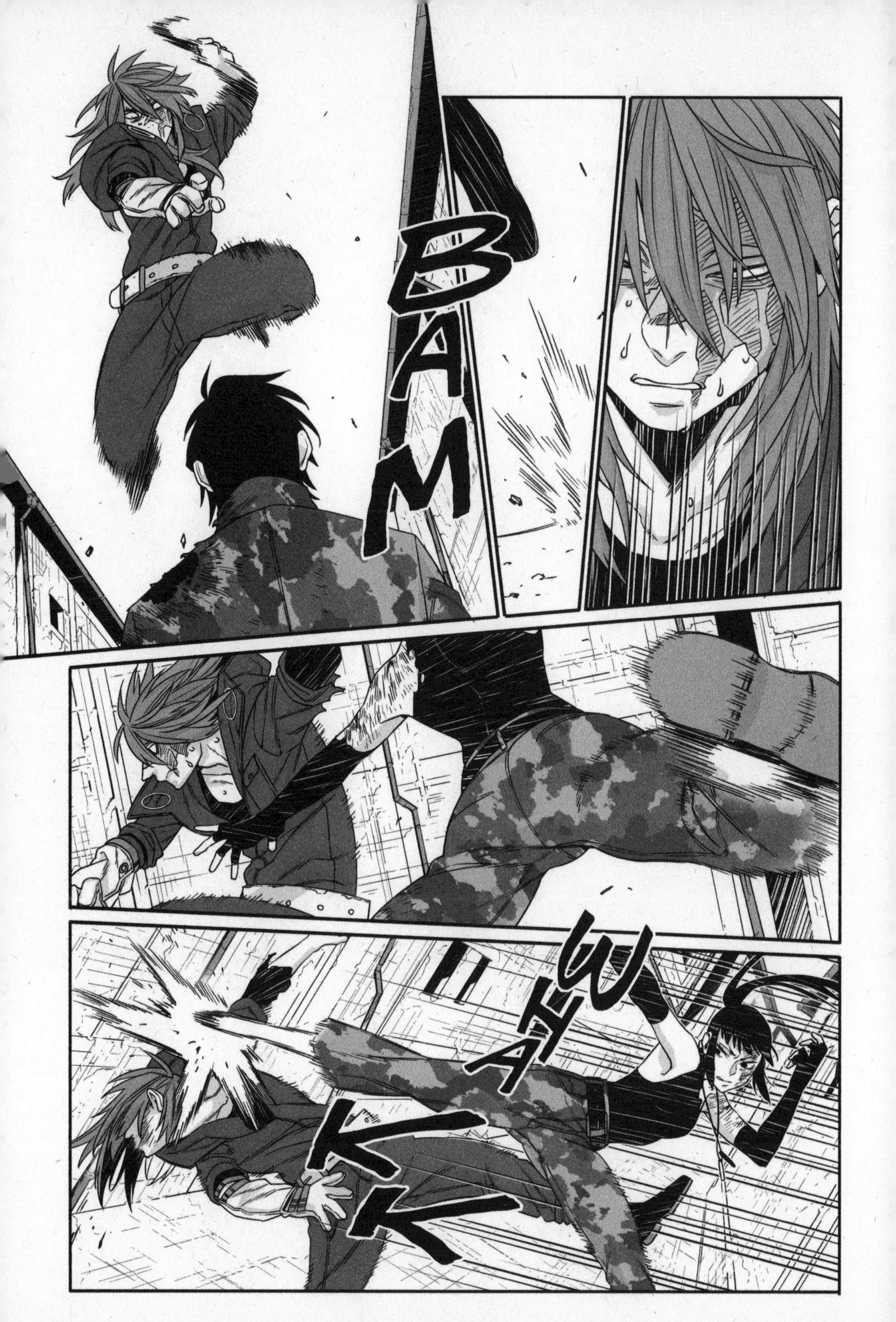
BAM
WHAKK

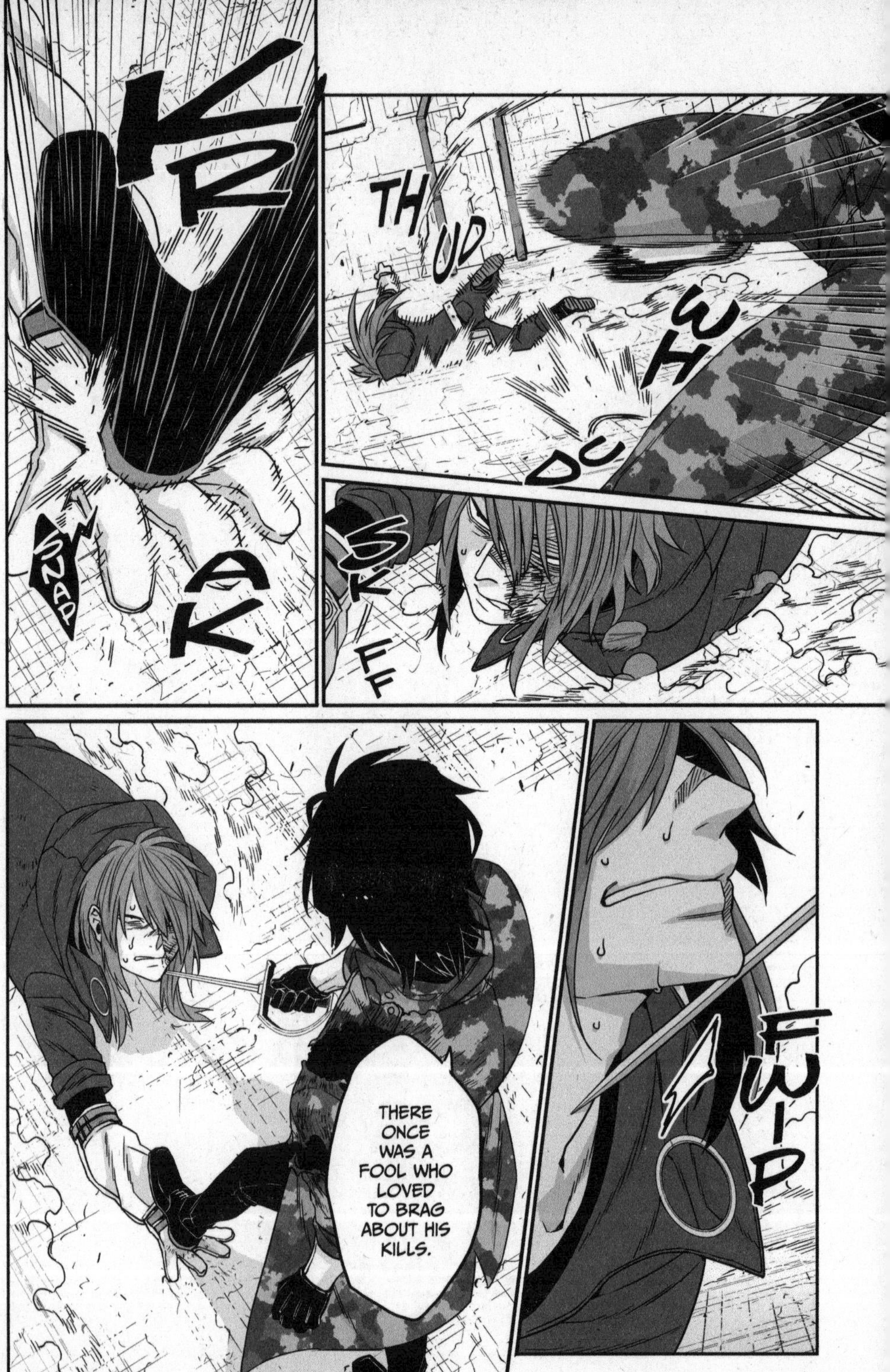
THUD
WHUD
SKFF
KRAK
SNAP
FWIP
THERE ONCE WAS A FOOL WHO LOVED TO BRAG ABOUT HIS KILLS.

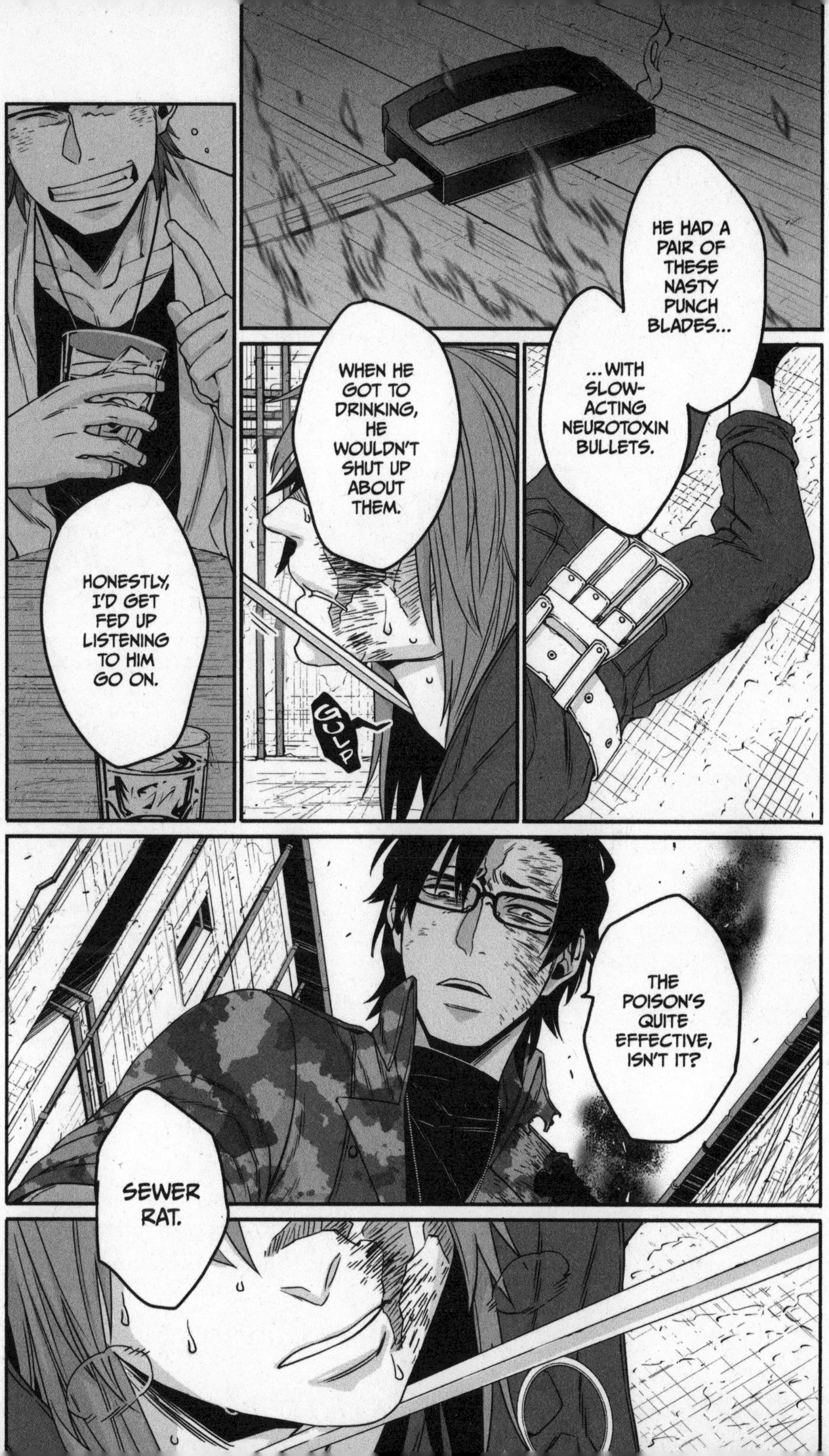

HE HAD A PAIR OF THESE NASTY PUNCH BLADES...
...WITH SLOW-ACTING NEUROTOXIN BULLETS.
WHEN HE GOT TO DRINKING, HE WOULDN'T SHUT UP ABOUT THEM.
HONESTLY, I'D GET FED UP LISTENING TO HIM GO ON.
GULP
THE POISON'S QUITE EFFECTIVE, ISN'T IT?
SEWER RAT.

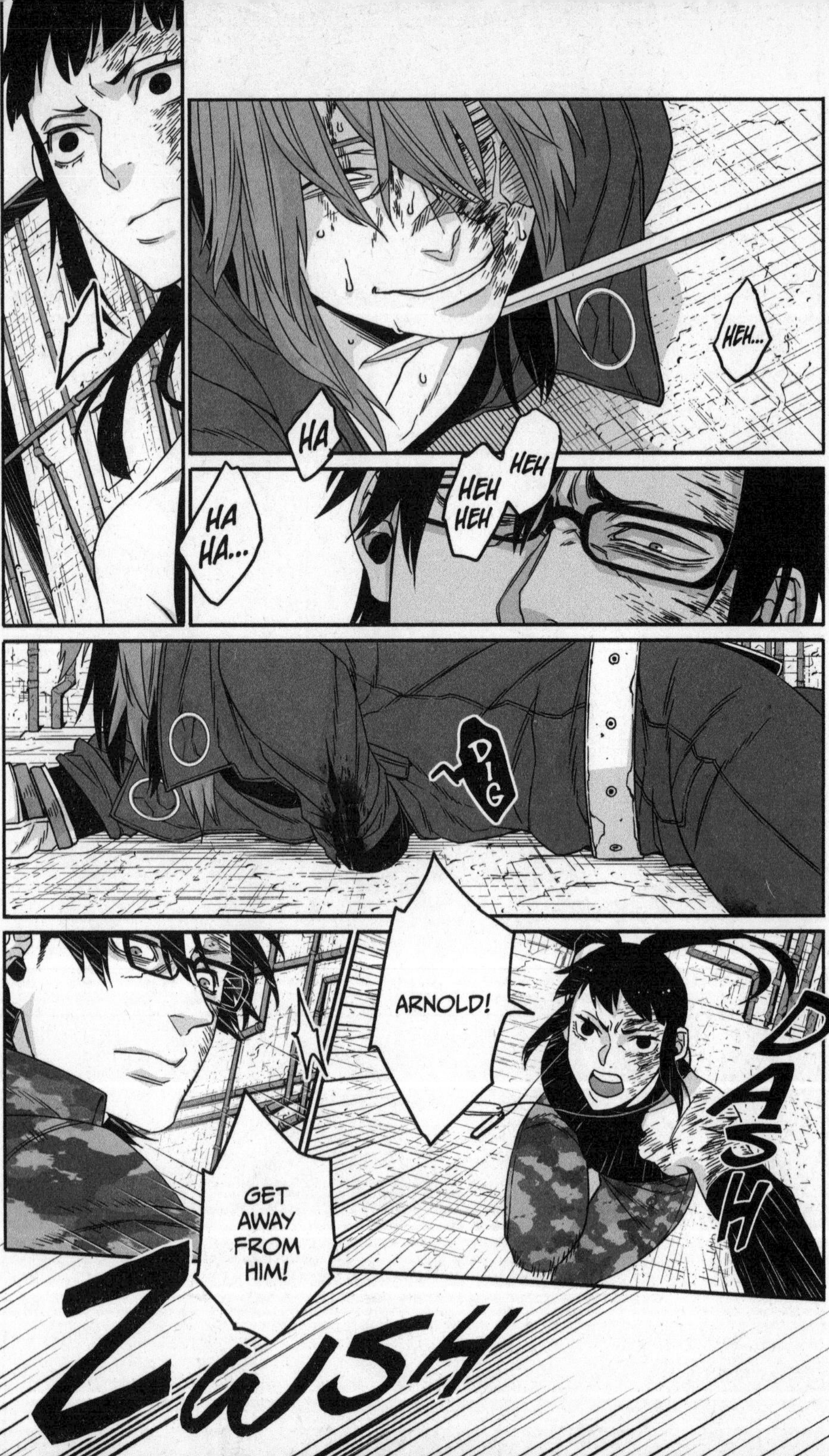
HEH...
HA
HEH HEH HEH
HA HA...
DIG
ARNOLD!
DASH
GET AWAY FROM HIM!
ZWSH

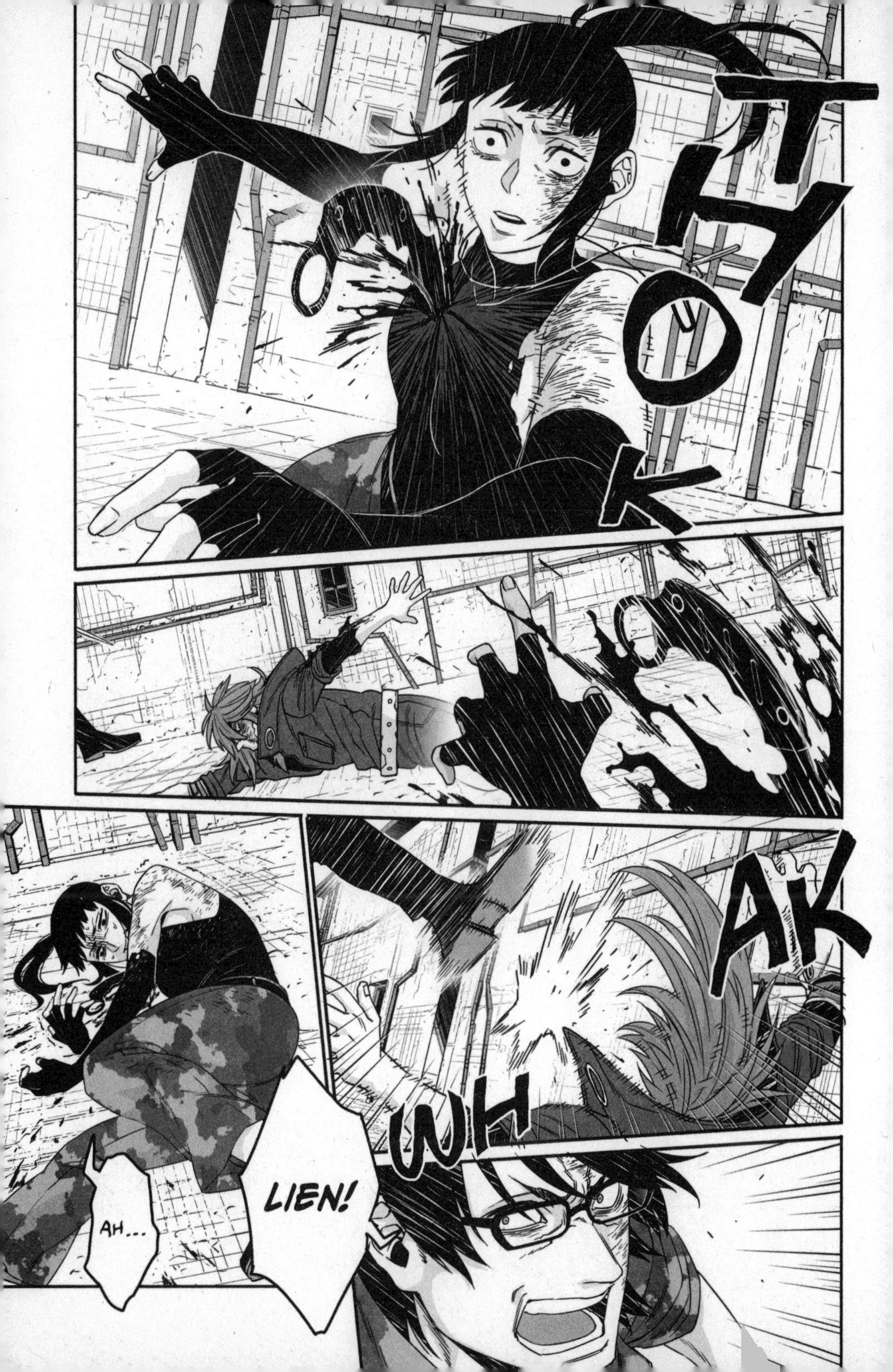
THOK
WHAK
LIEN!
AH...

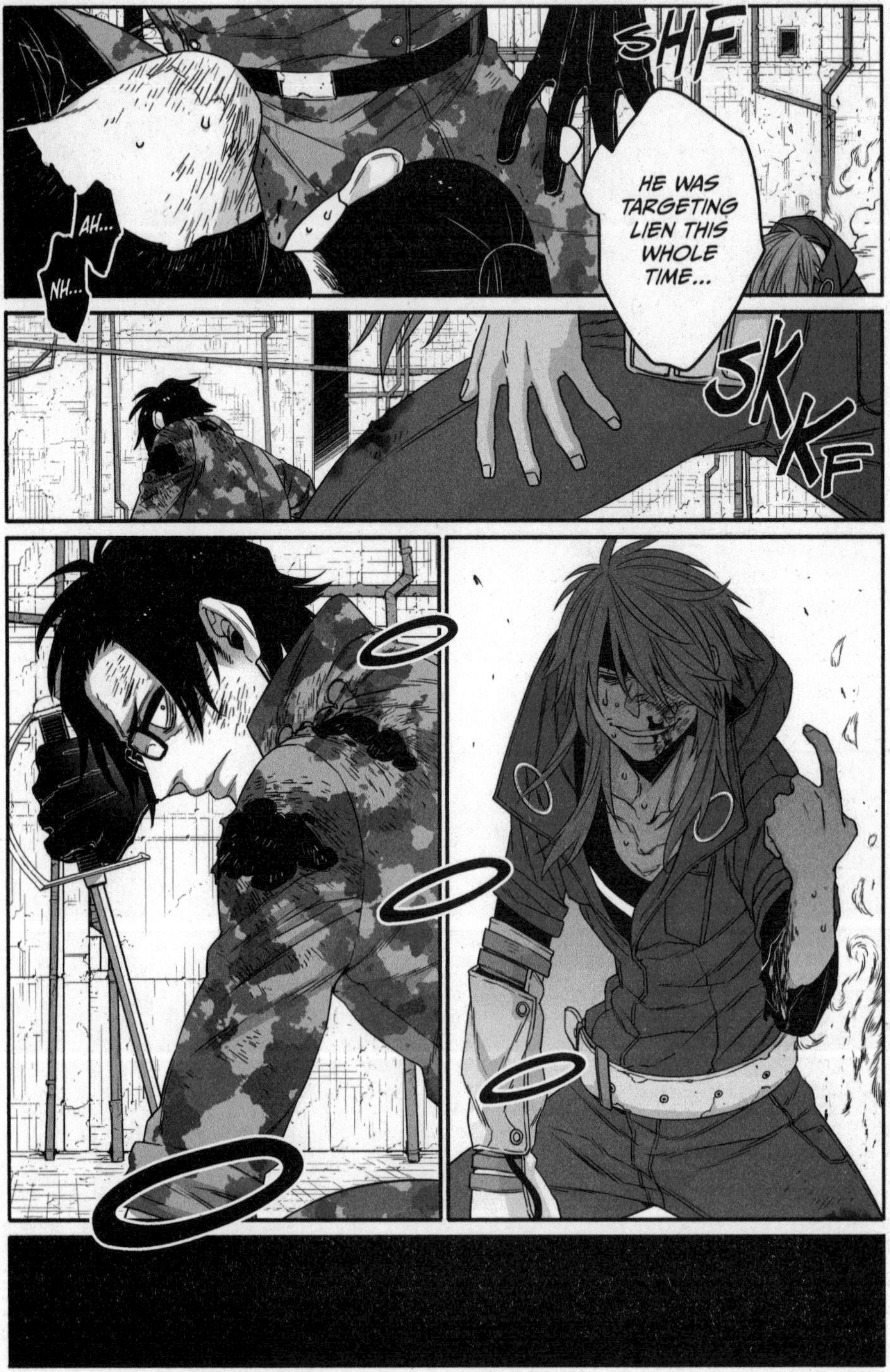
SHF
AH...
NH...
HE WAS TARGETING LIEN THIS WHOLE TIME...
SKKF

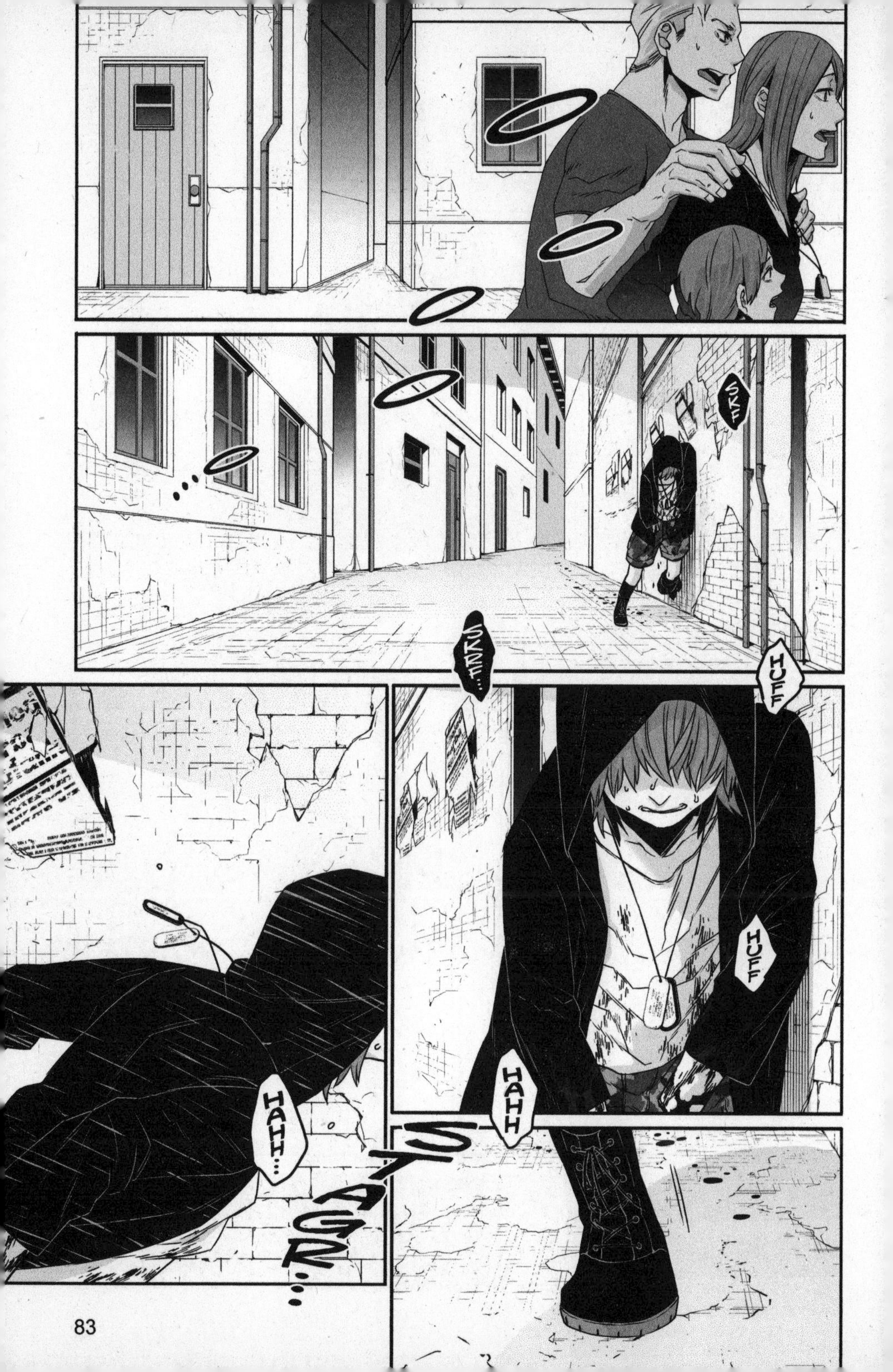
SKF
...
SKRF...
HUFF
HUFF
HAHH
HAHH...
STAGR...

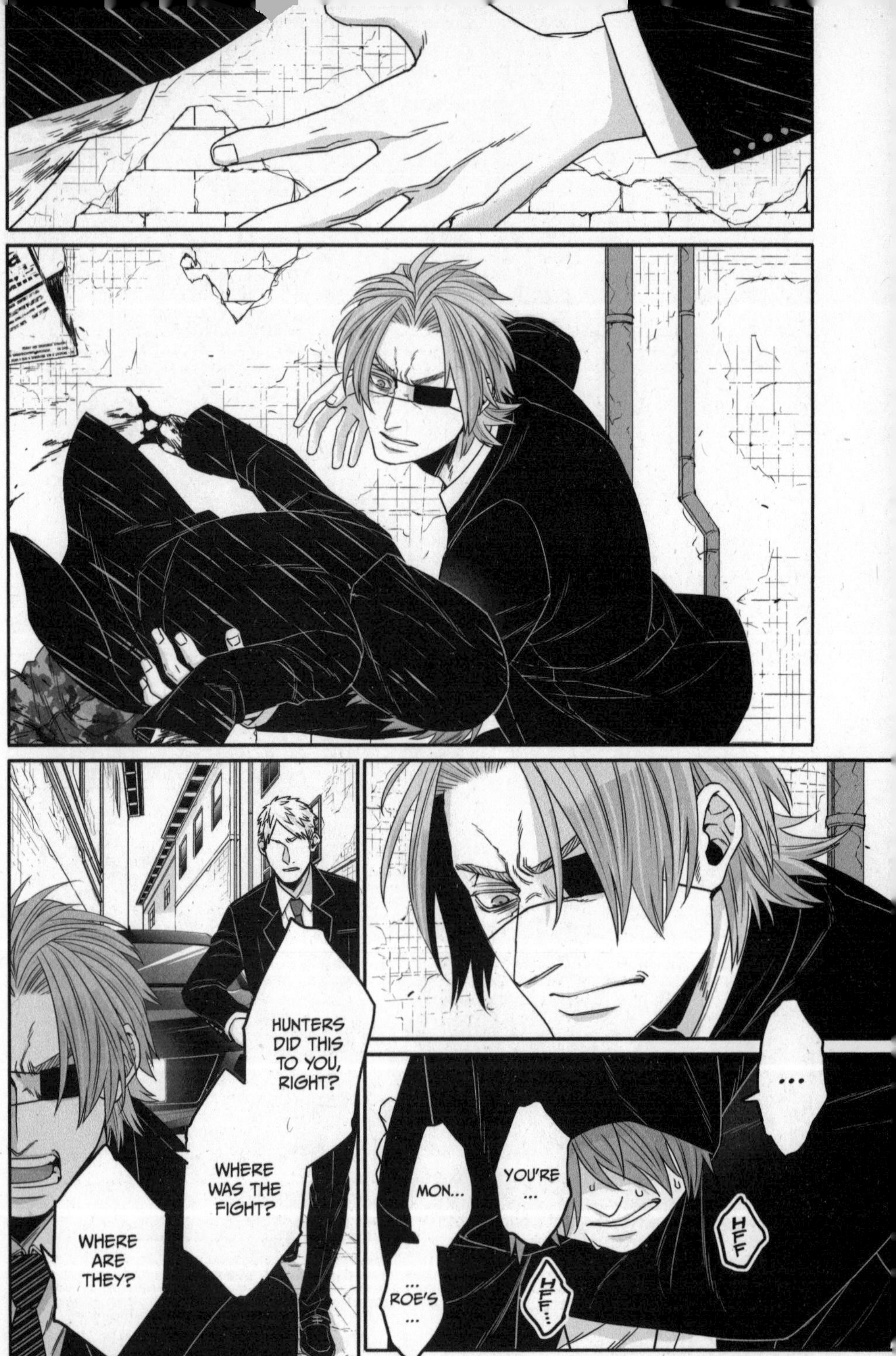
...
YOU'RE ...
MON...
... ROE'S ...
HFF
HFF...
HUNTERS DID THIS TO YOU, RIGHT?
WHERE WAS THE FIGHT?
WHERE ARE THEY?

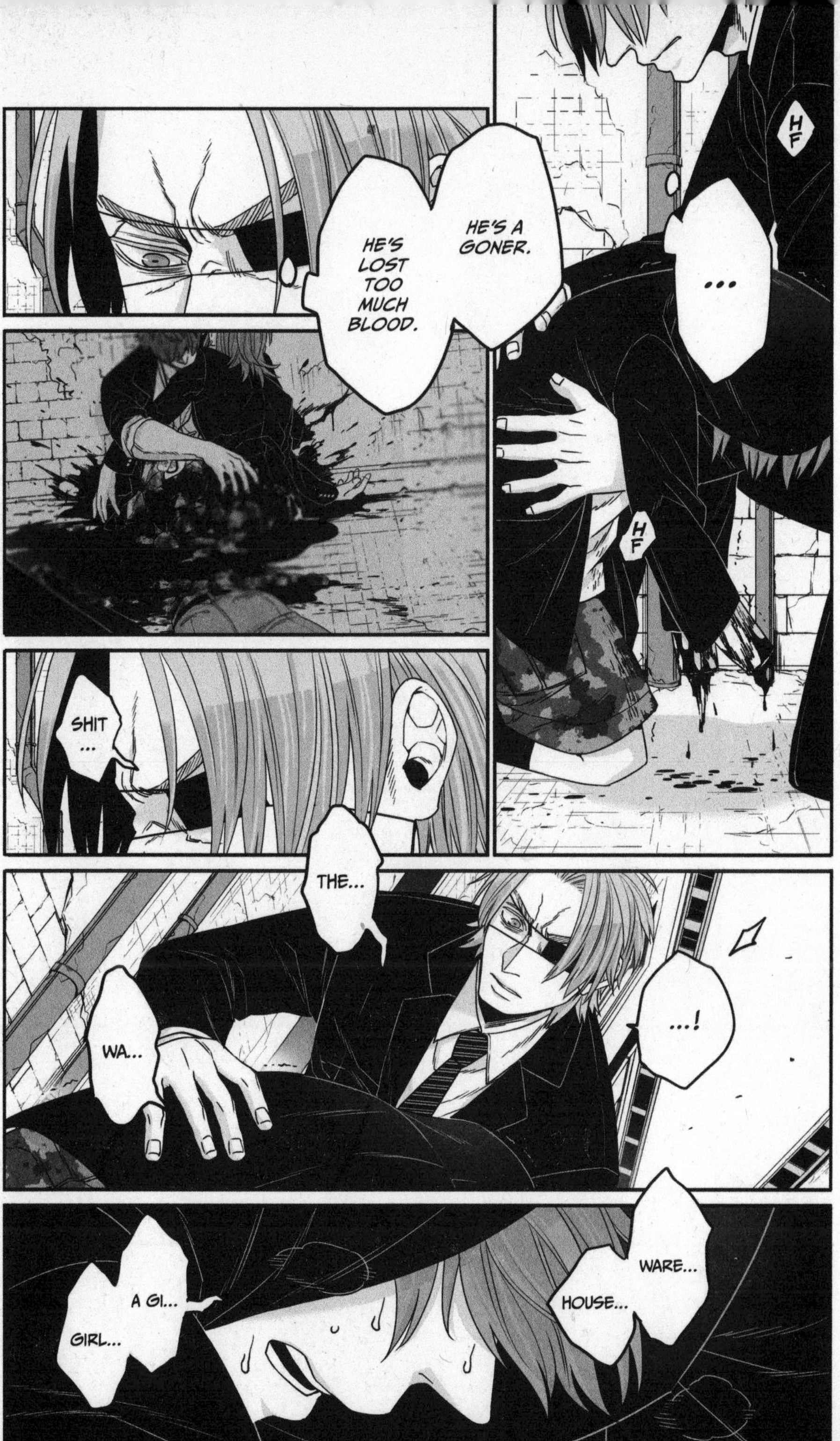
HF
...
HE'S A GONER.
HE'S LOST TOO MUCH BLOOD.
HF
SHIT ...
...!
THE...
WA...
WARE...
HOUSE...
A GI...
GIRL...

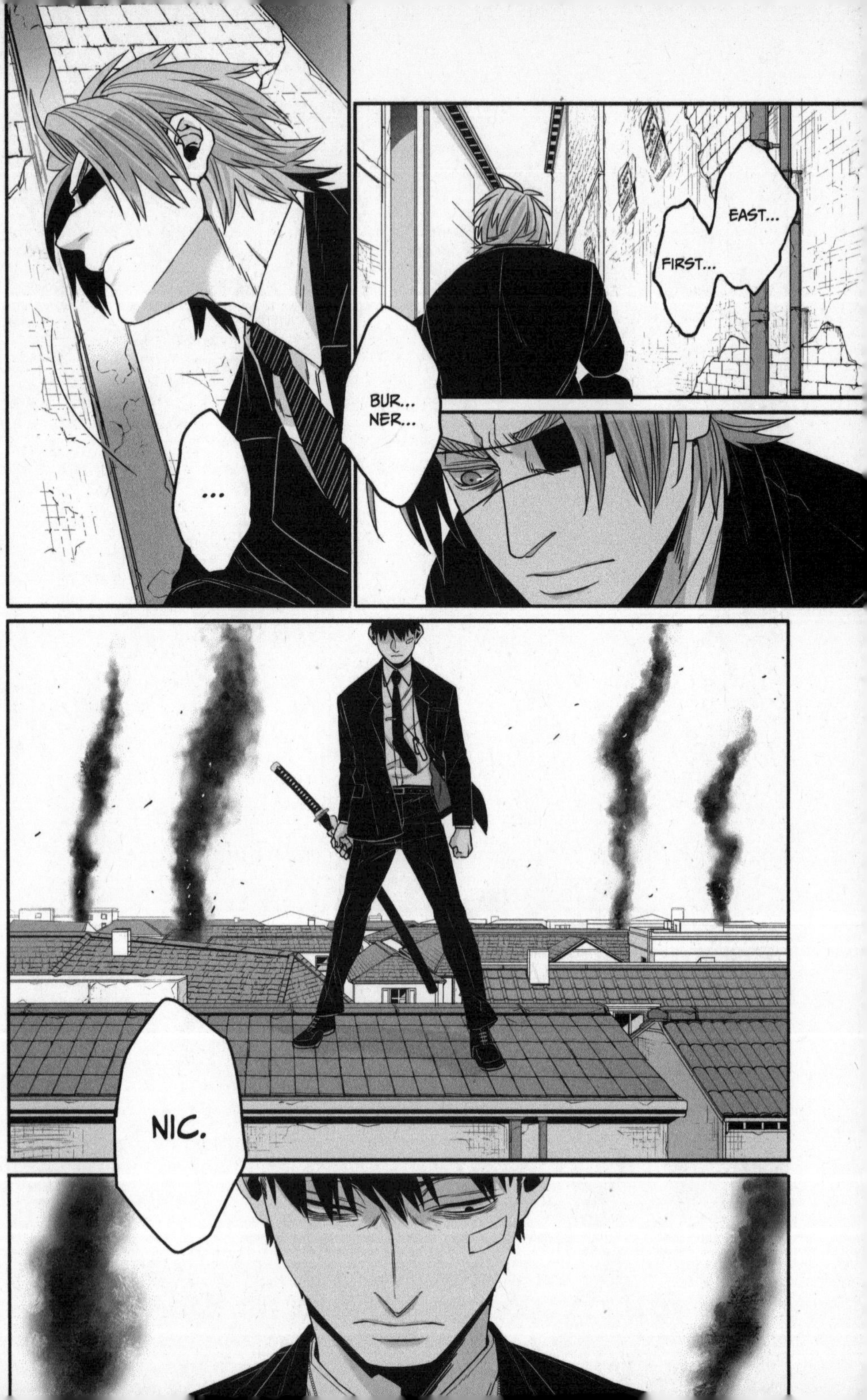
EAST...
FIRST...
BUR...
NER...
...
NIC.

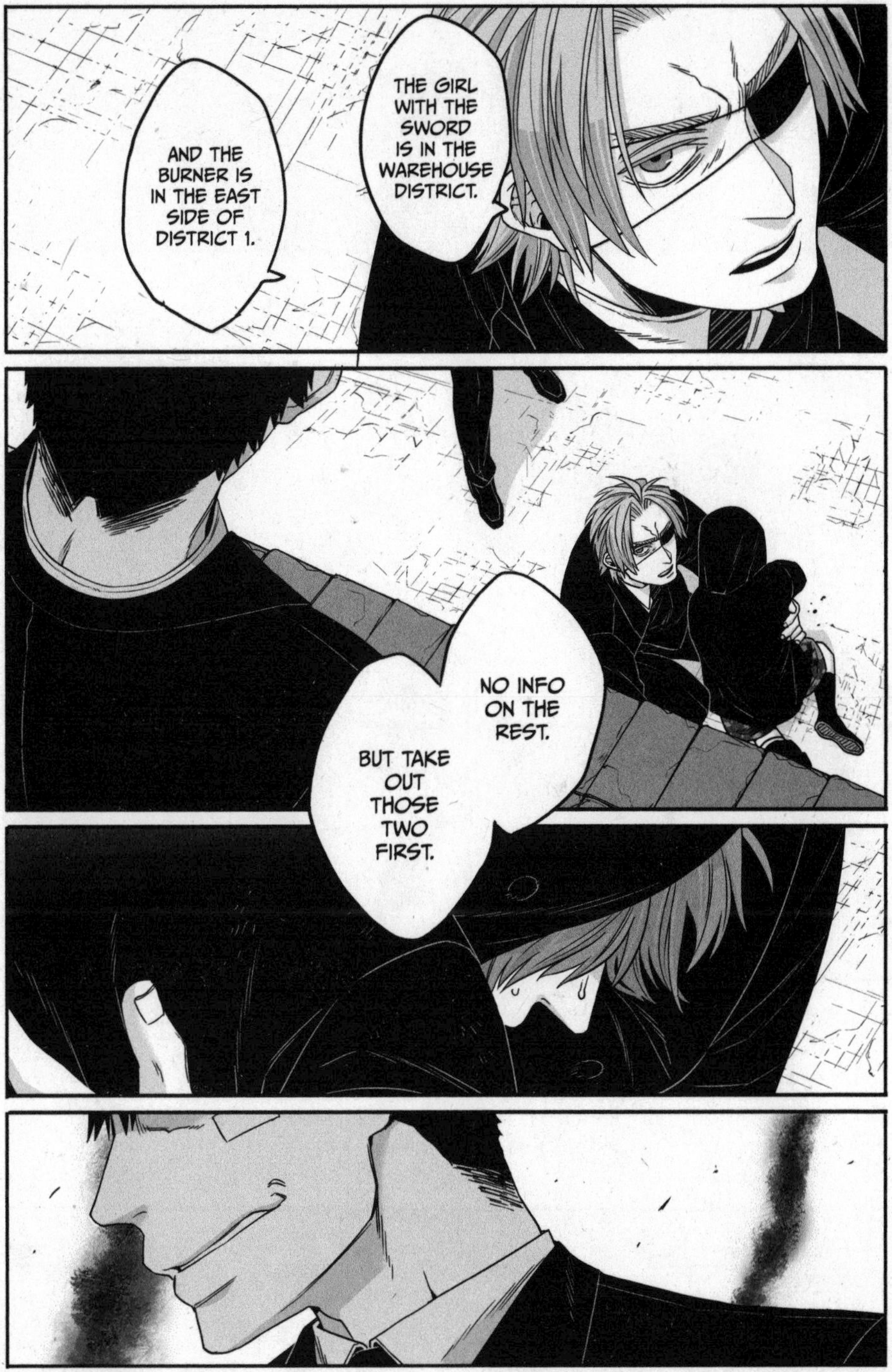
THE GIRL WITH THE SWORD IS IN THE WAREHOUSE DISTRICT.
AND THE BURNER IS IN THE EAST SIDE OF DISTRICT 1.
NO INFO ON THE REST.
BUT TAKE OUT THOSE TWO FIRST.

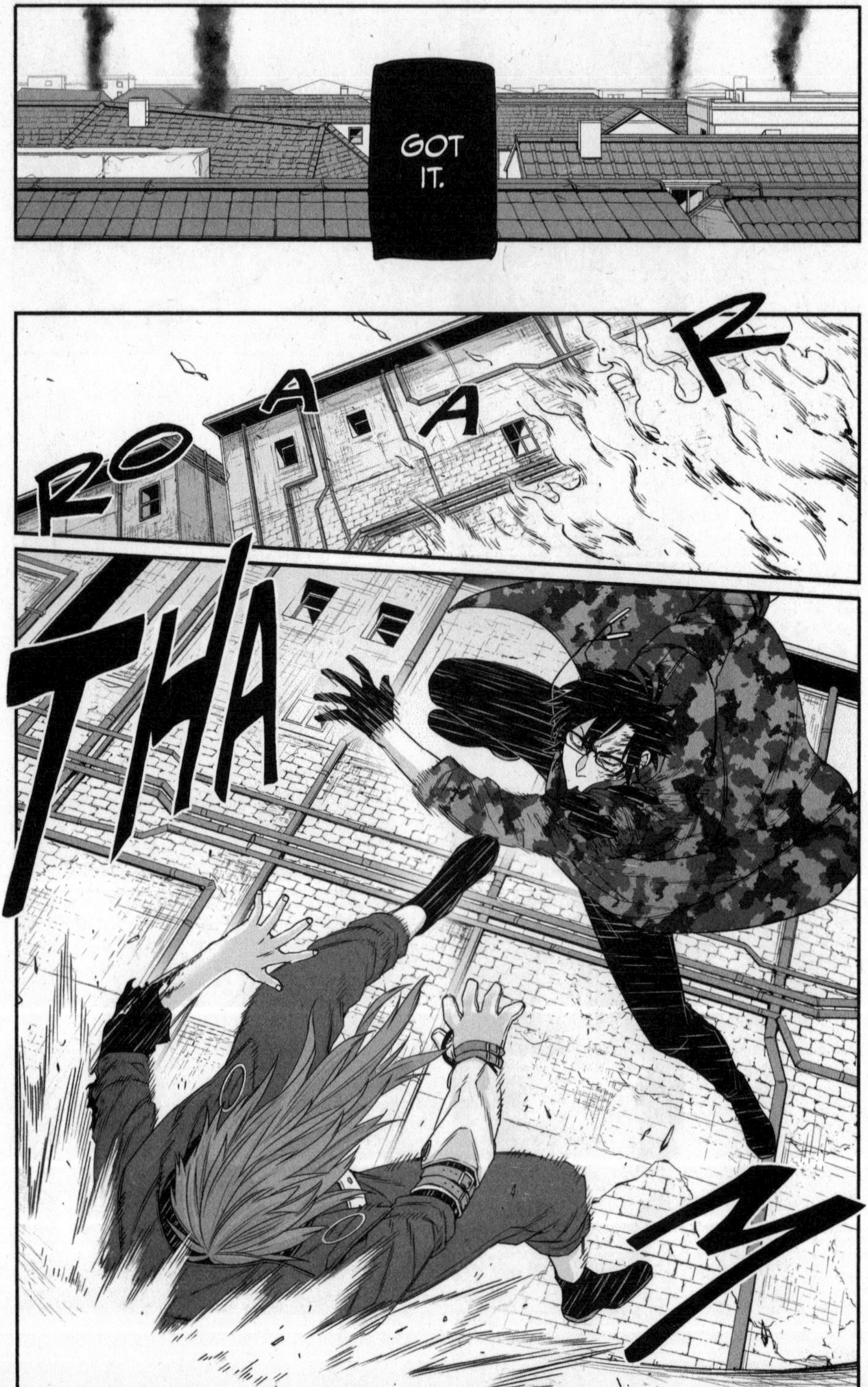
GOT IT.
ROAAR
THAM

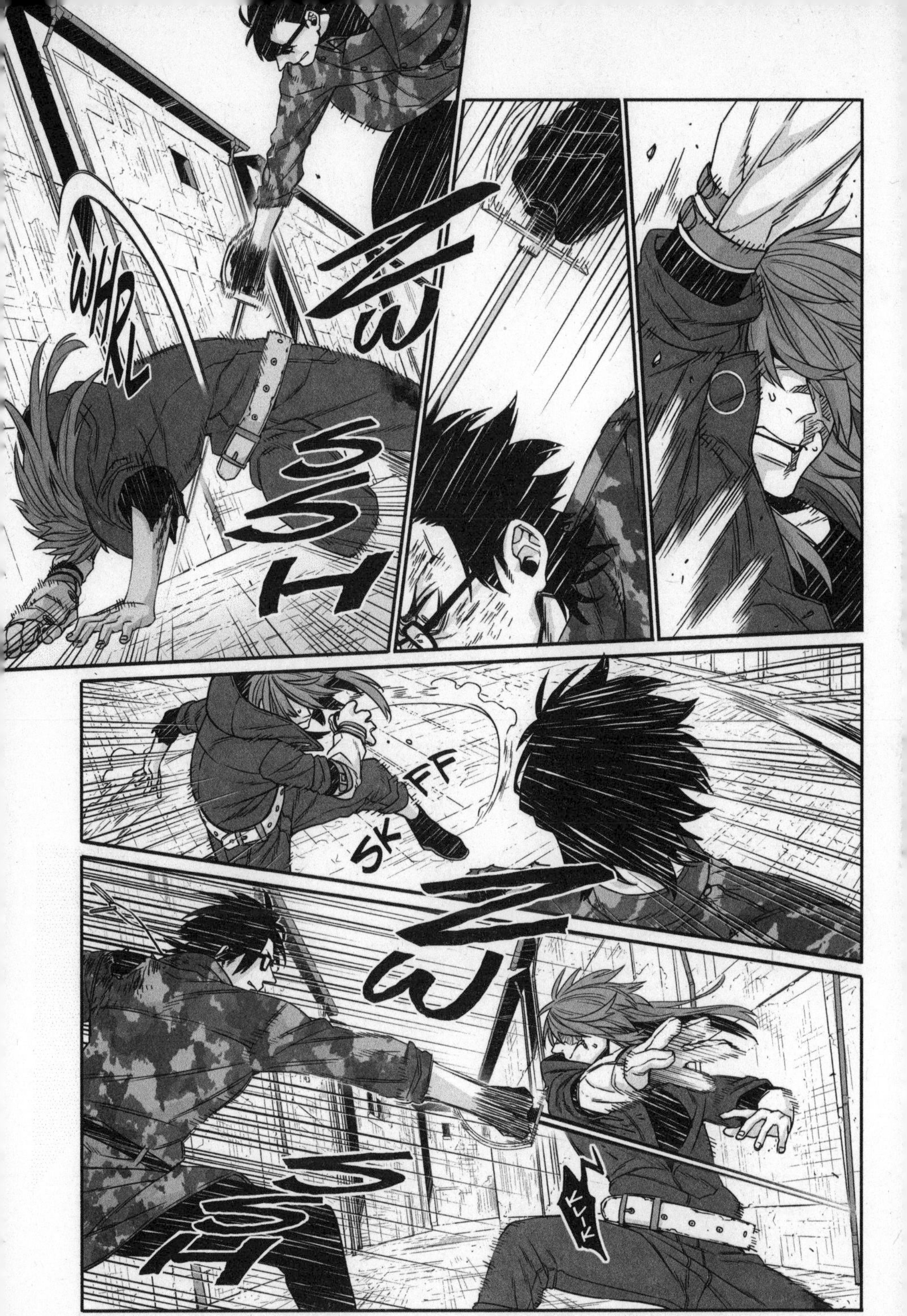
WHRL
SKFF
KLIK

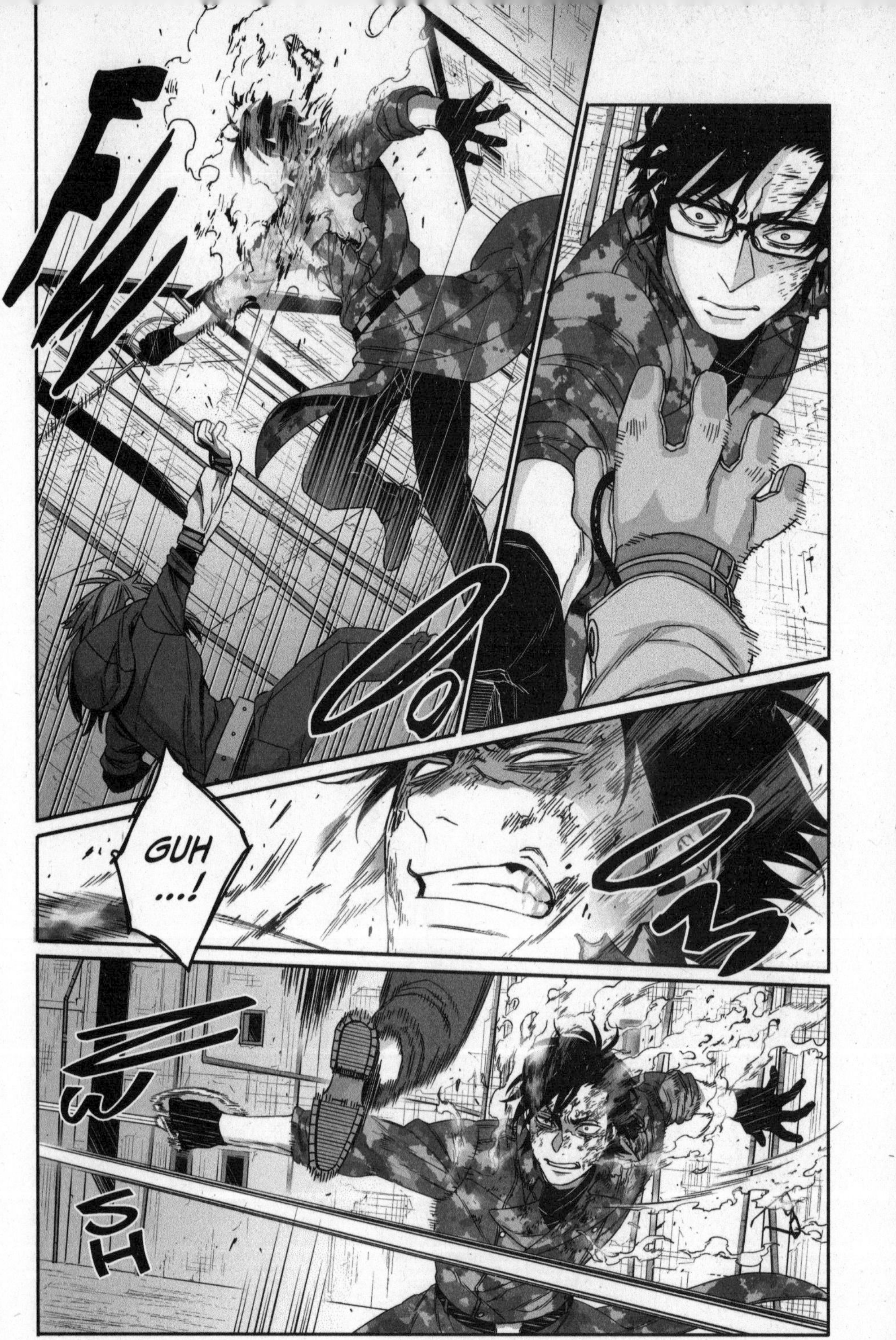
GUH
...!

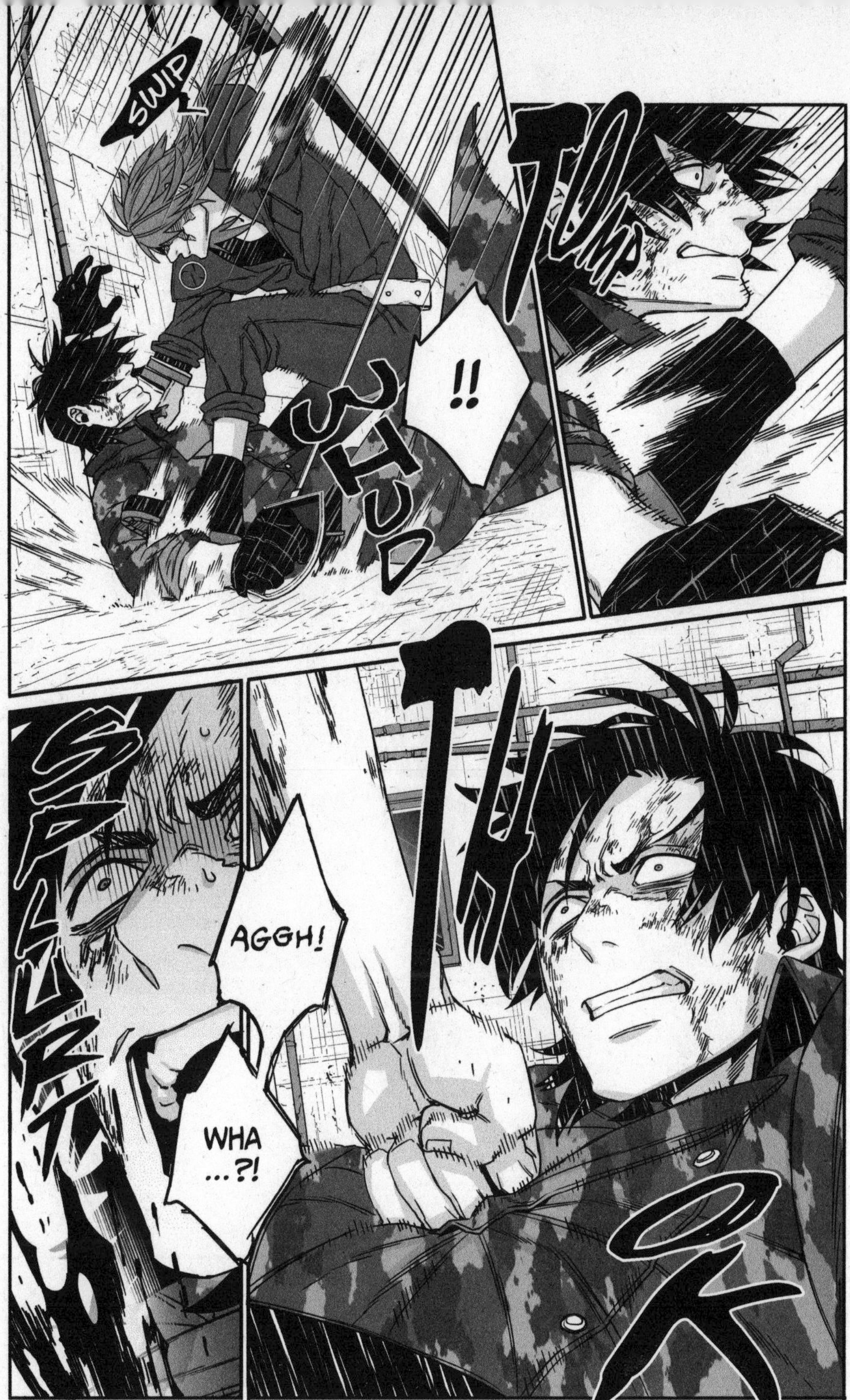
SWIP
TUMP
!!
SHUD
THOK
AGGH!
WHA ...?!
SPLURT

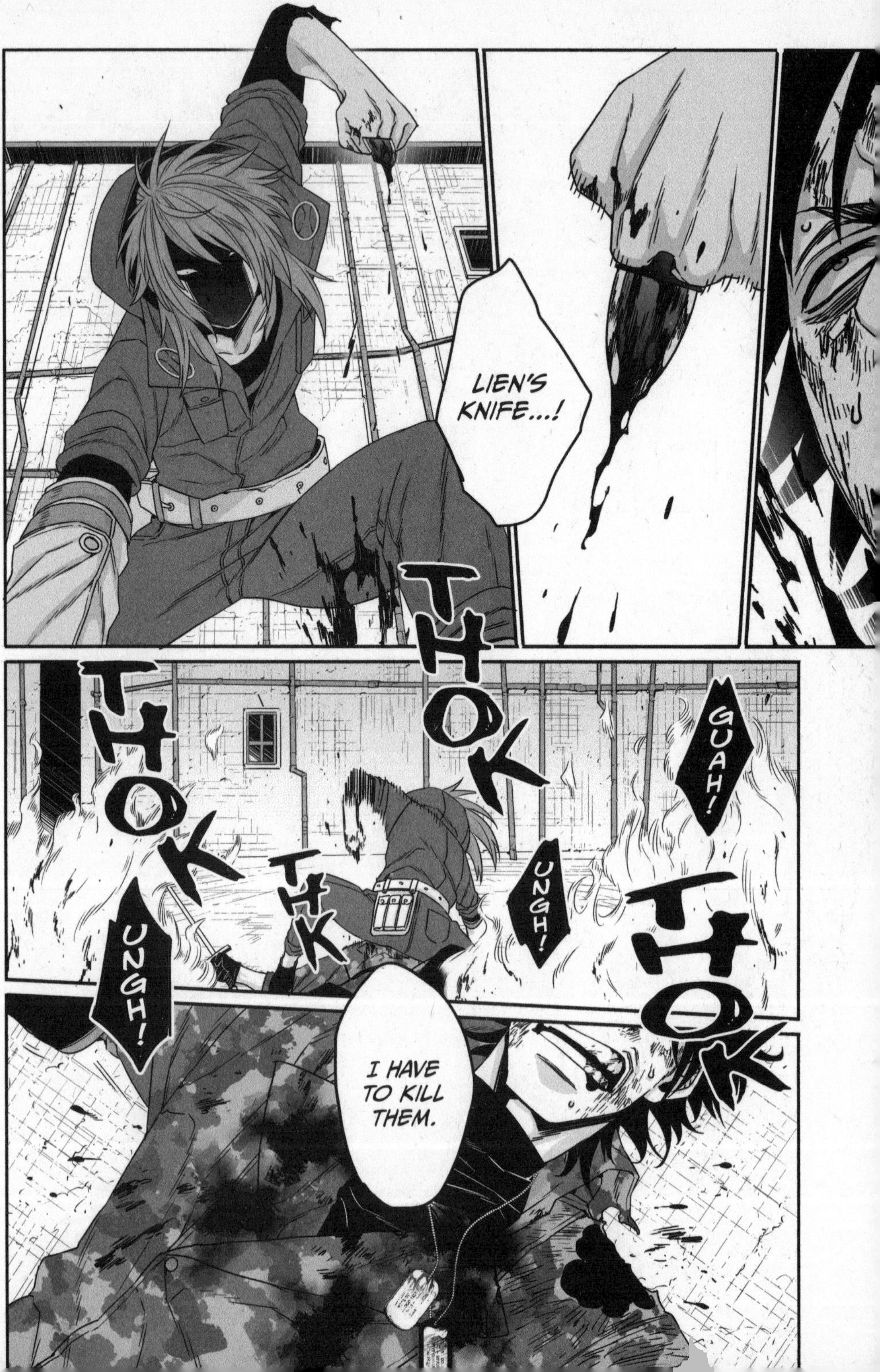
LIEN'S KNIFE...!
THOK
GUAH!
UNGH!
THOK
THK
THOK
UNGH!
I HAVE TO KILL THEM.

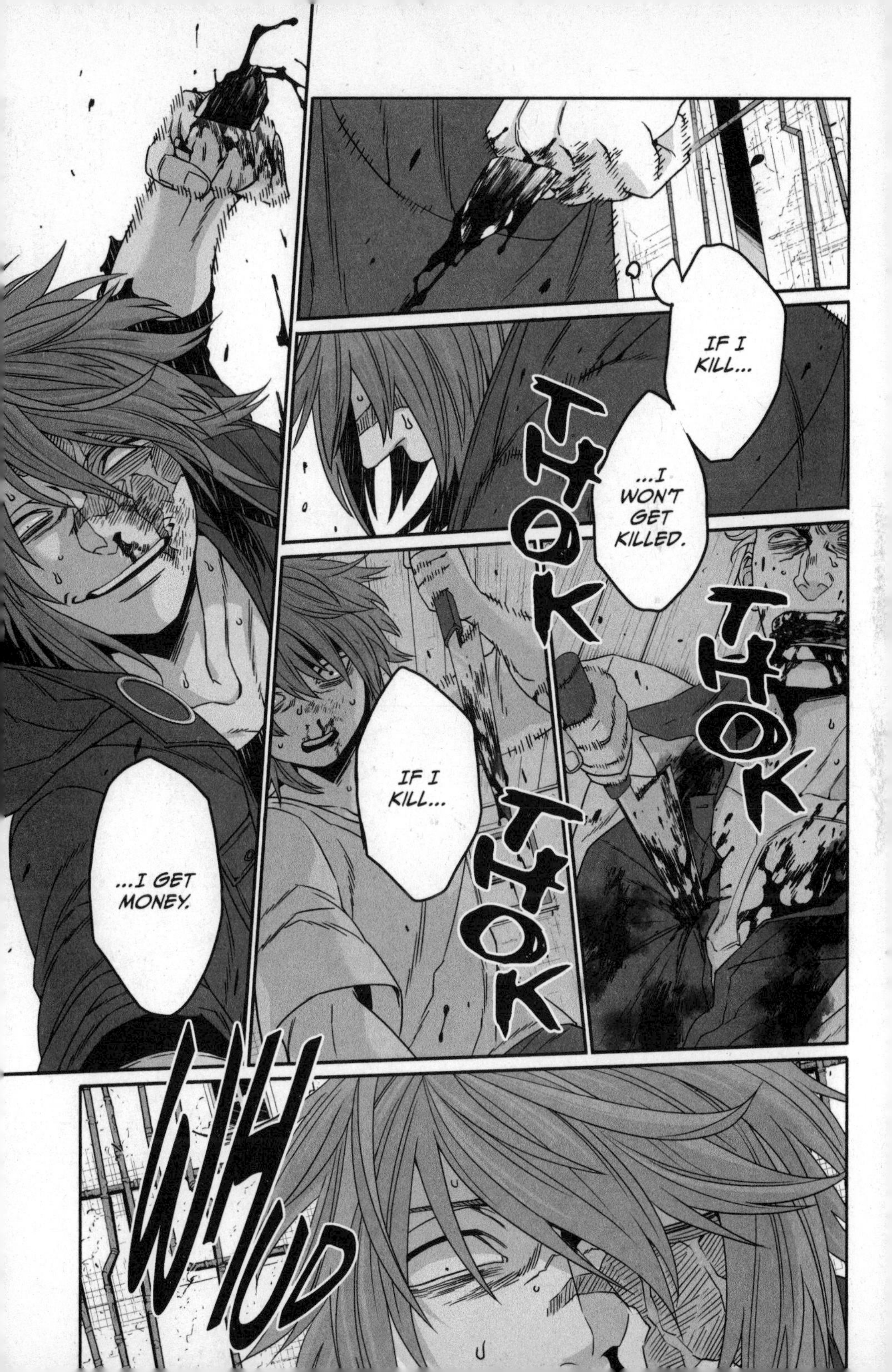
IF I KILL...
...I WON'T GET KILLED.
THOK
THOK
IF I KILL...
...I GET MONEY.
THOK
WHUD

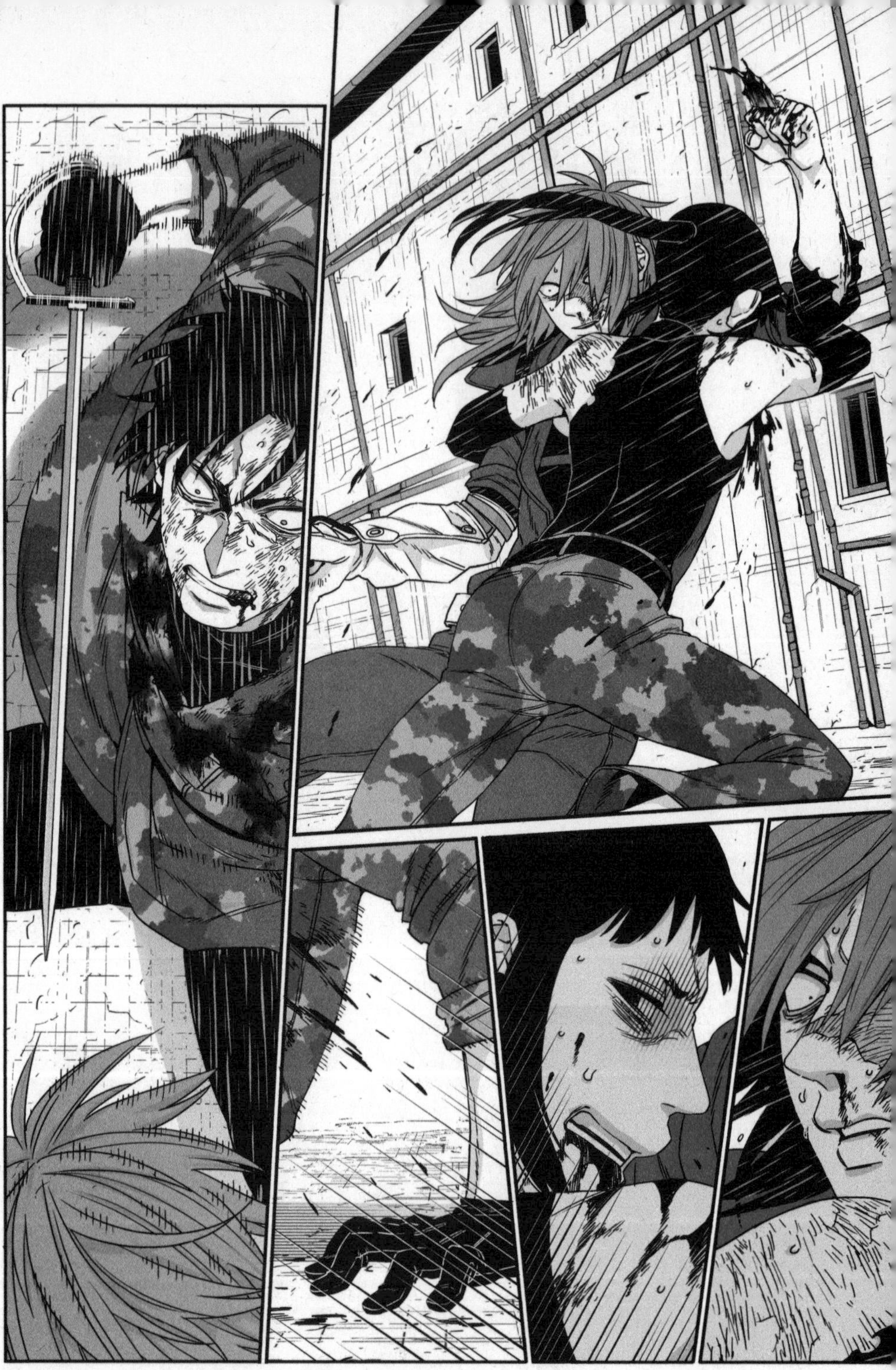

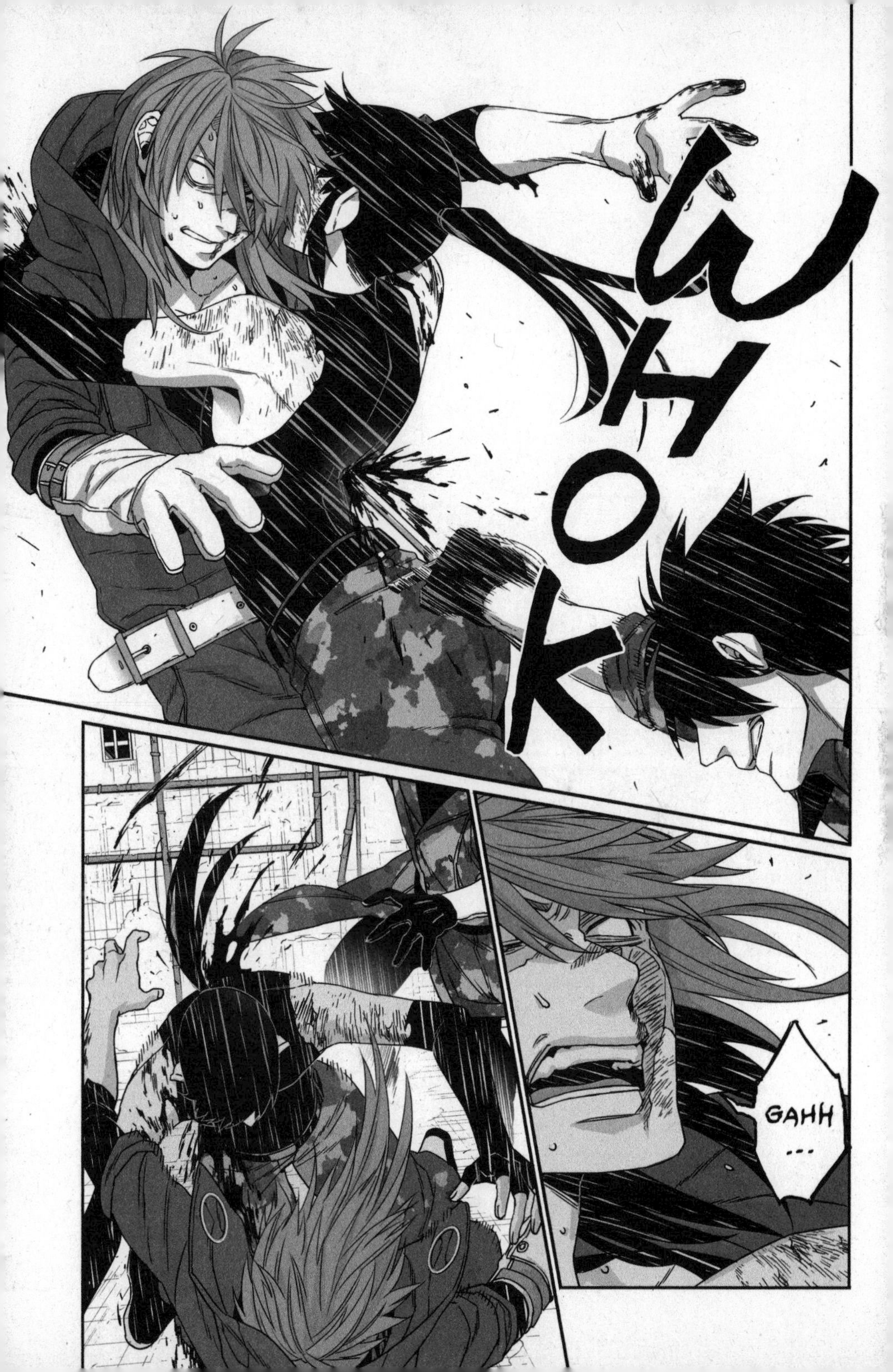
WHOK
GAHH ...

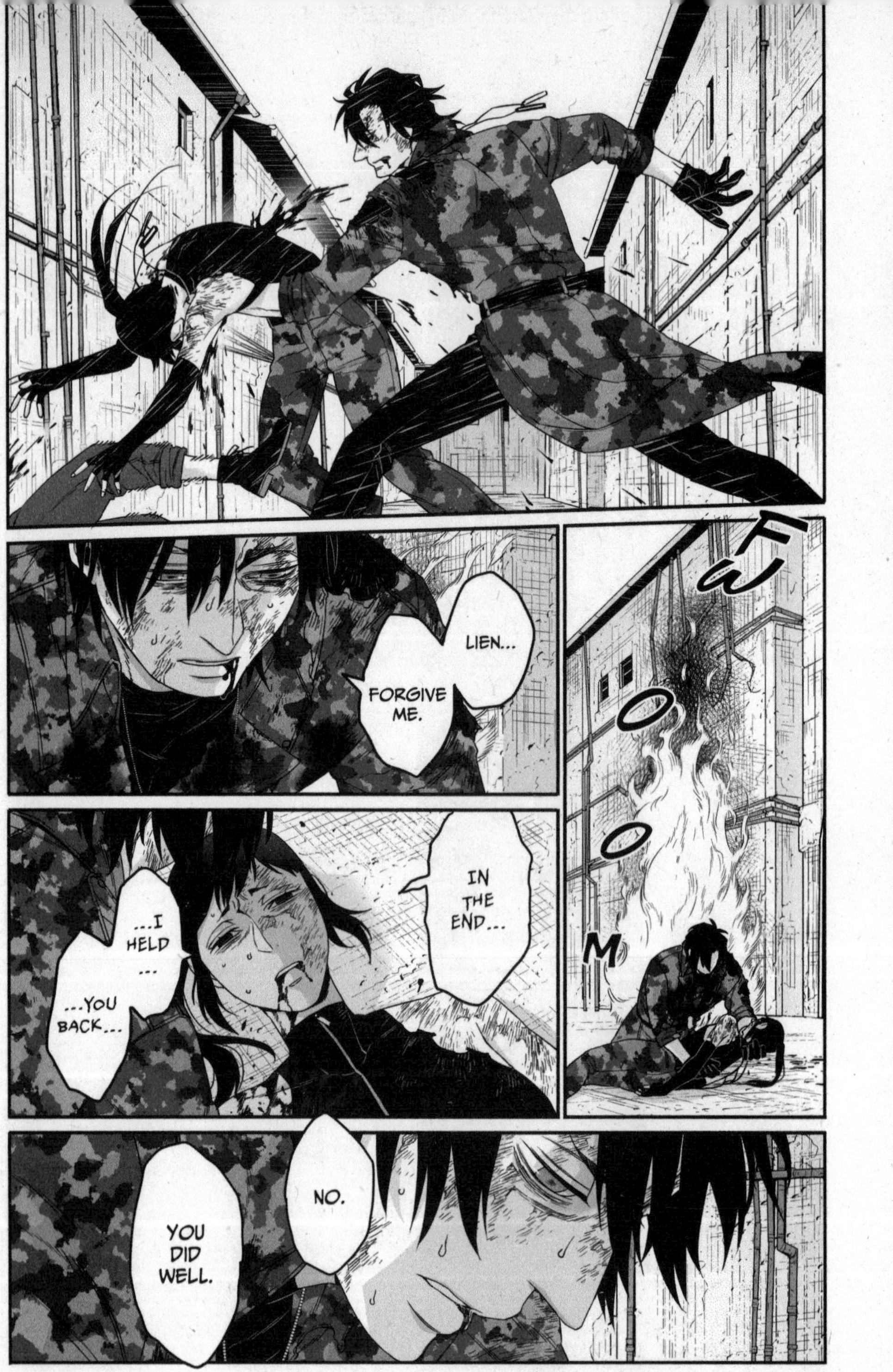
FWOOOM
LIEN...
FORGIVE ME.
IN THE END...
...I HELD ... ...YOU BACK...
NO.
YOU DID WELL.

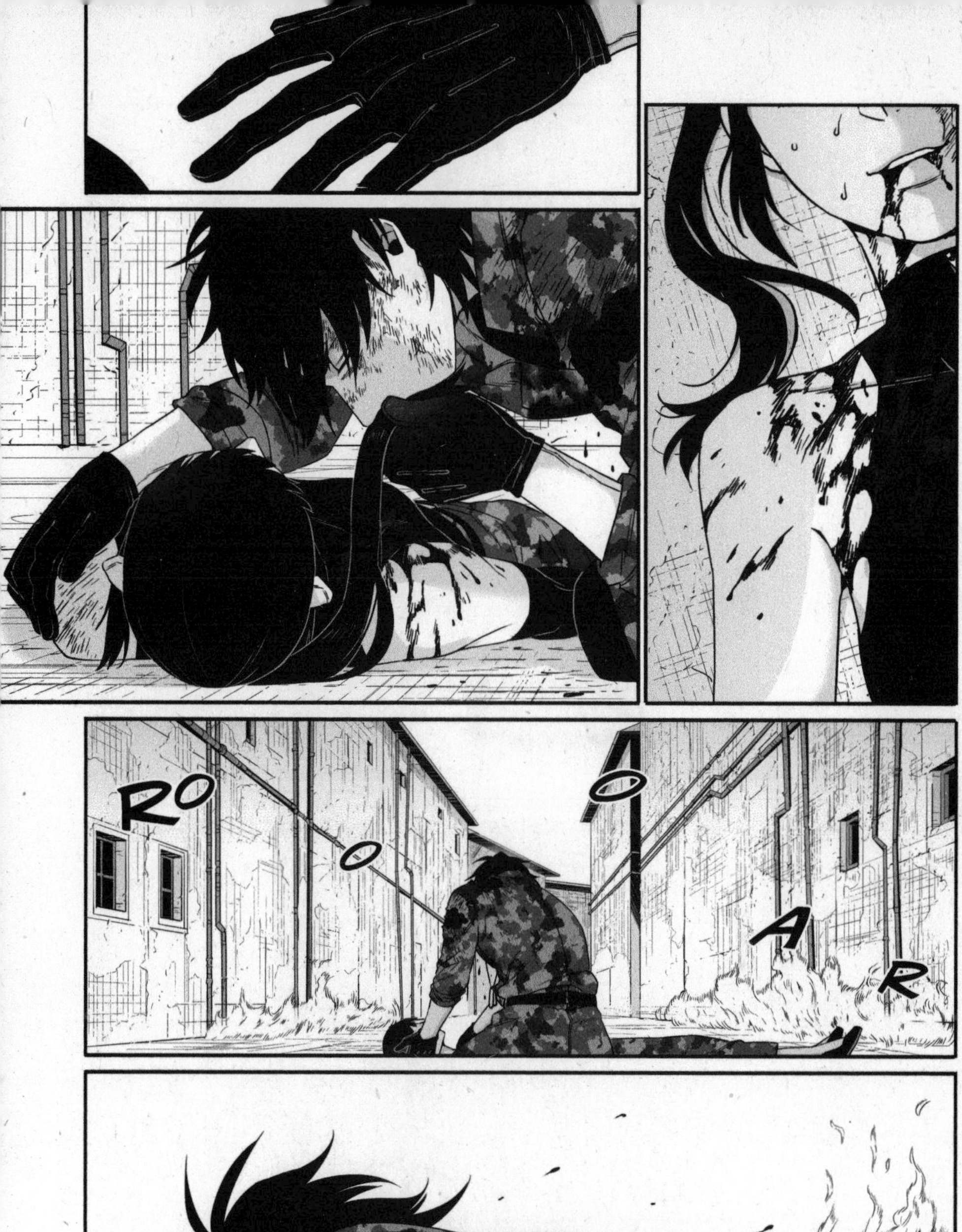
ROOOAR

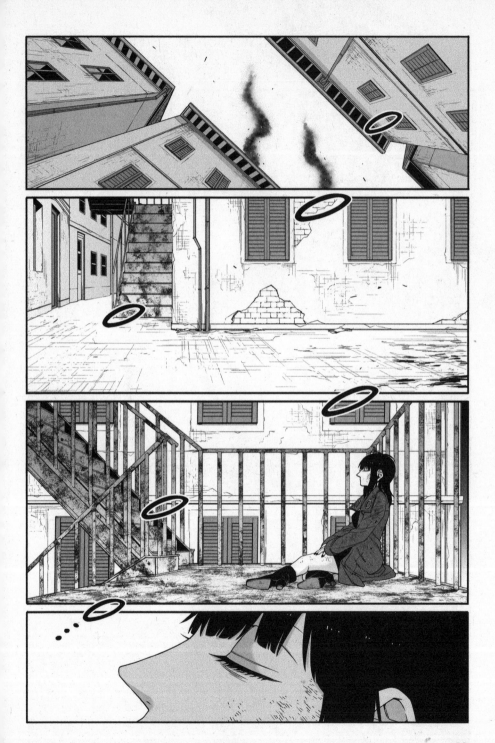

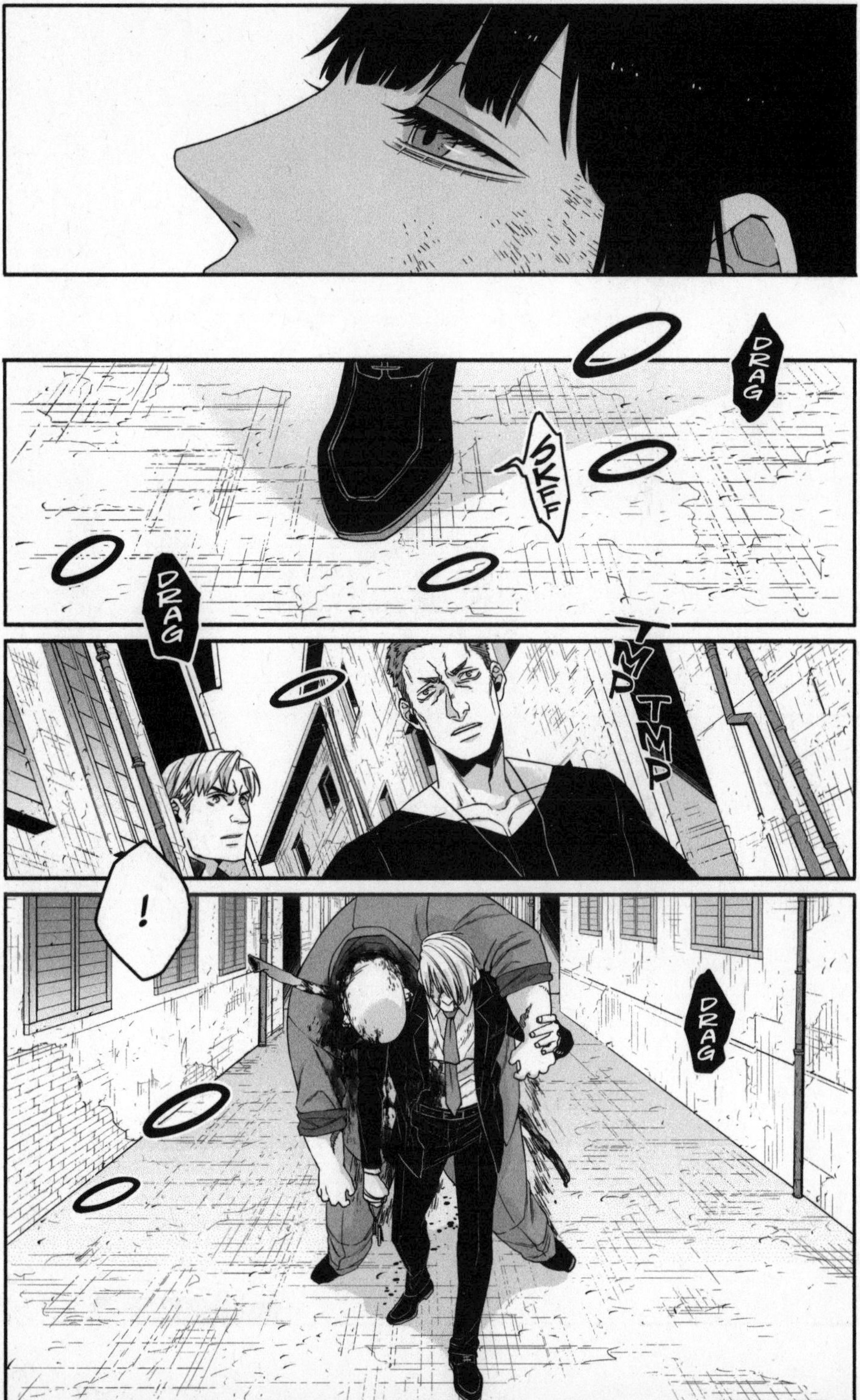
DRAG
SKFF
DRAG
TMP TMP
TMP TMP
!
DRAG

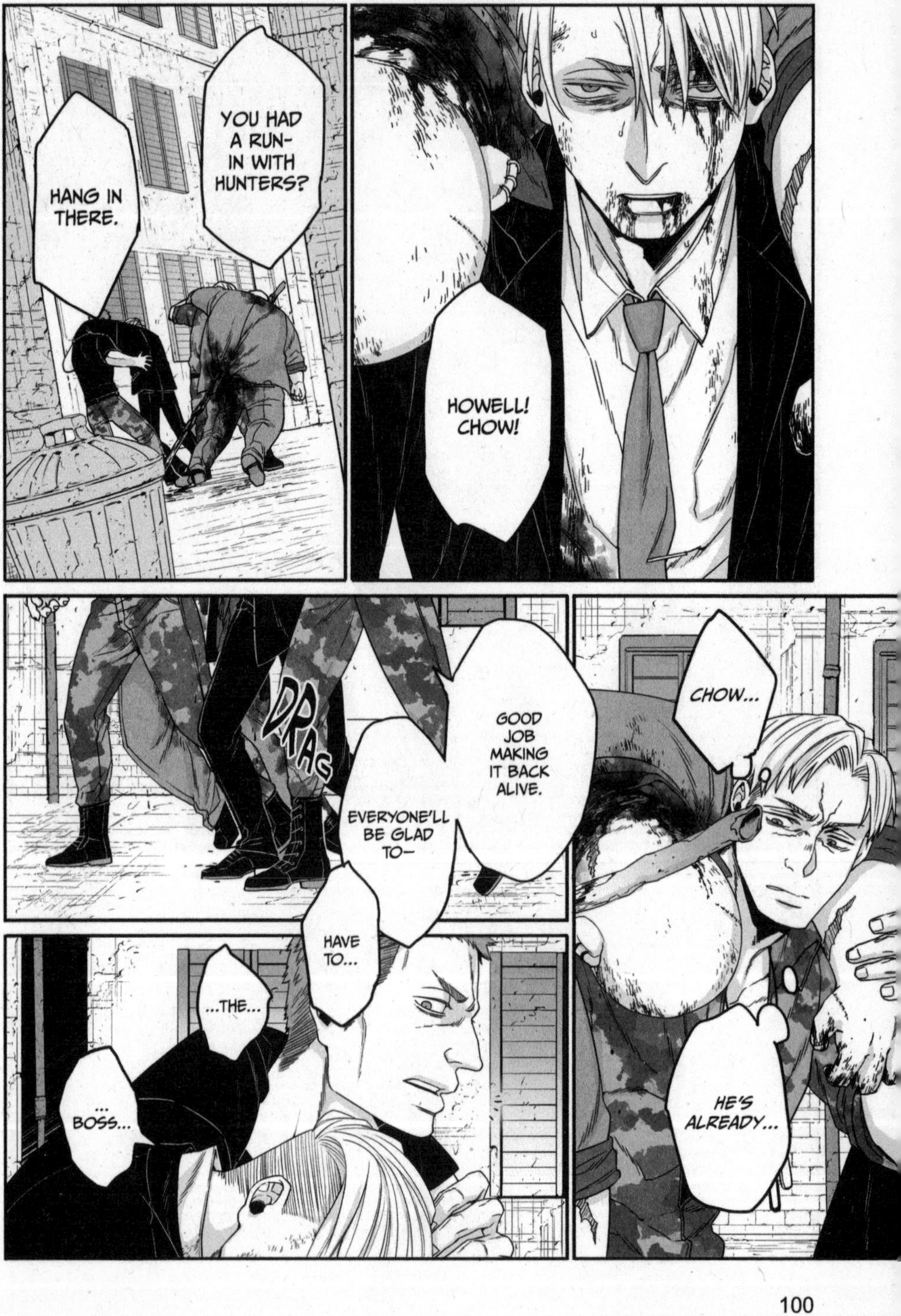
HOWELL! CHOW!
YOU HAD A RUN-IN WITH HUNTERS?
HANG IN THERE.
DRAG
GOOD JOB MAKING IT BACK ALIVE.
EVERYONE'LL BE GLAD TO—
CHOW...
HE'S ALREADY...
HAVE TO...
...THE...
... BOSS...

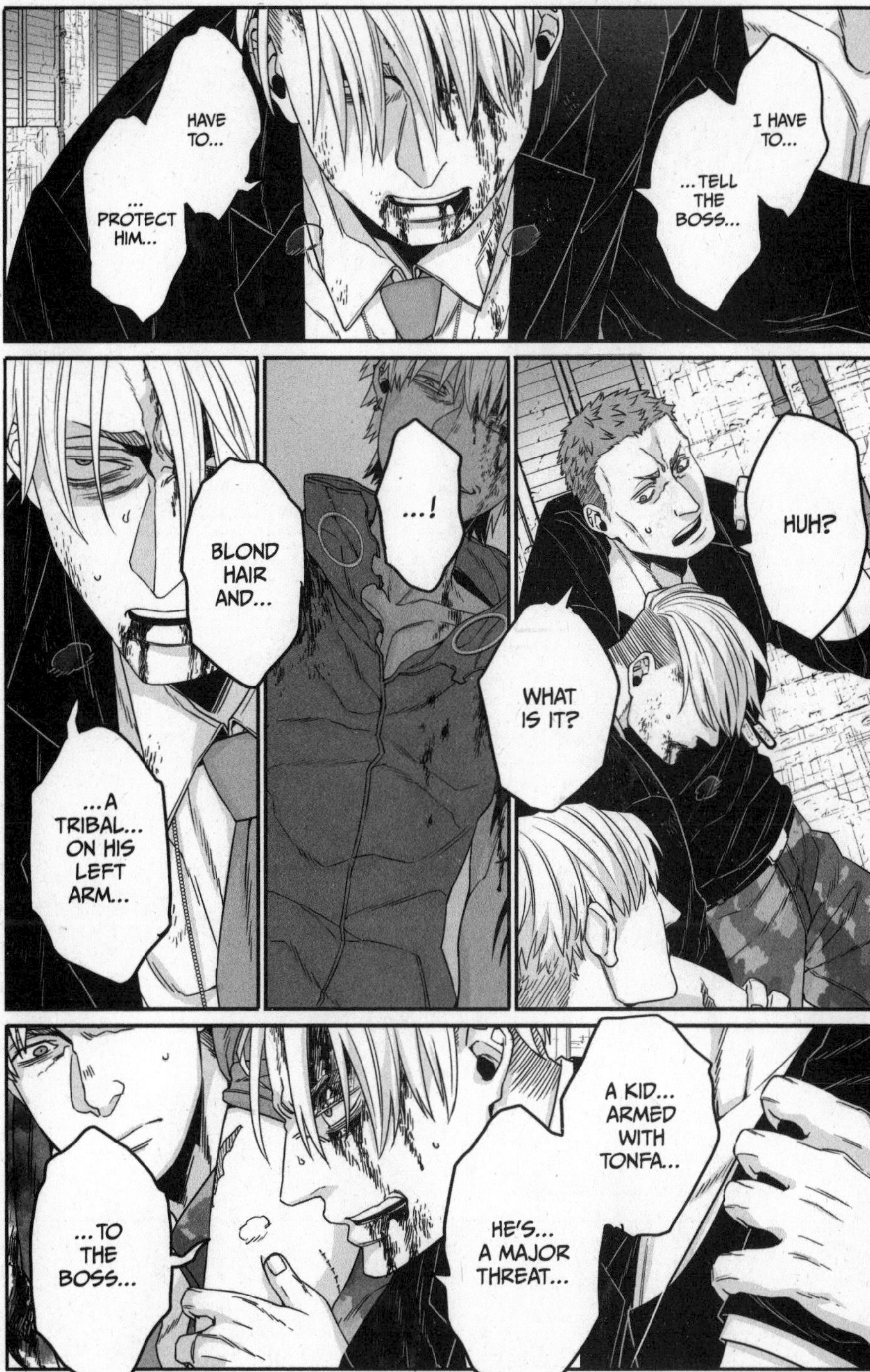
I HAVE TO...
...TELL THE BOSS...
HAVE TO...
... PROTECT HIM...
HUH?
WHAT IS IT?
...!
BLOND HAIR AND...
...A TRIBAL... ON HIS LEFT ARM...
A KID... ARMED WITH TONFA...
HE'S... A MAJOR THREAT...
...TO THE BOSS...

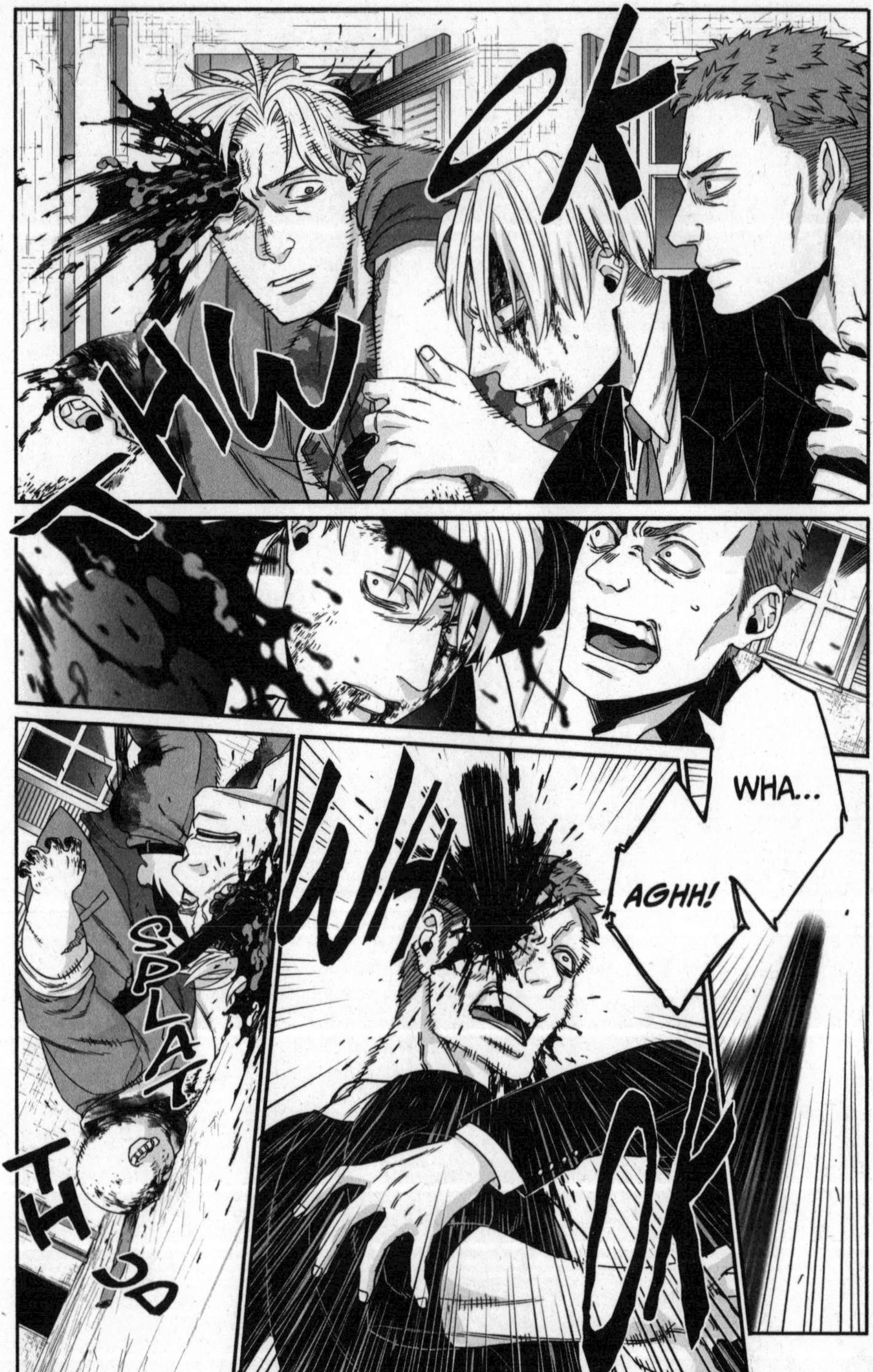
THWOK
WHA...
AGHH!
WHOK
SPLAT
THUD

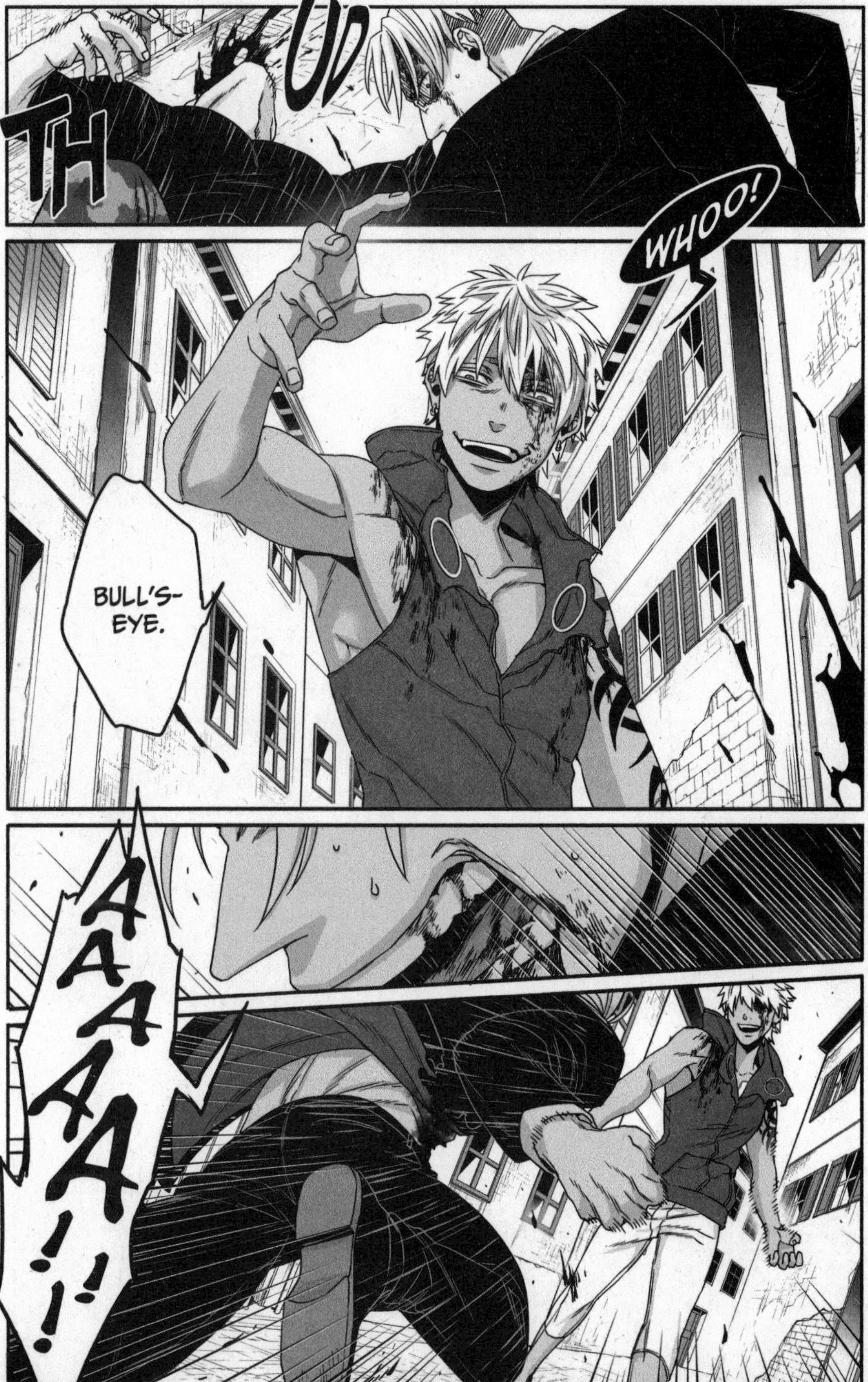
THUD
WHOO!
BULL'S-EYE.
AAAAAA!!!

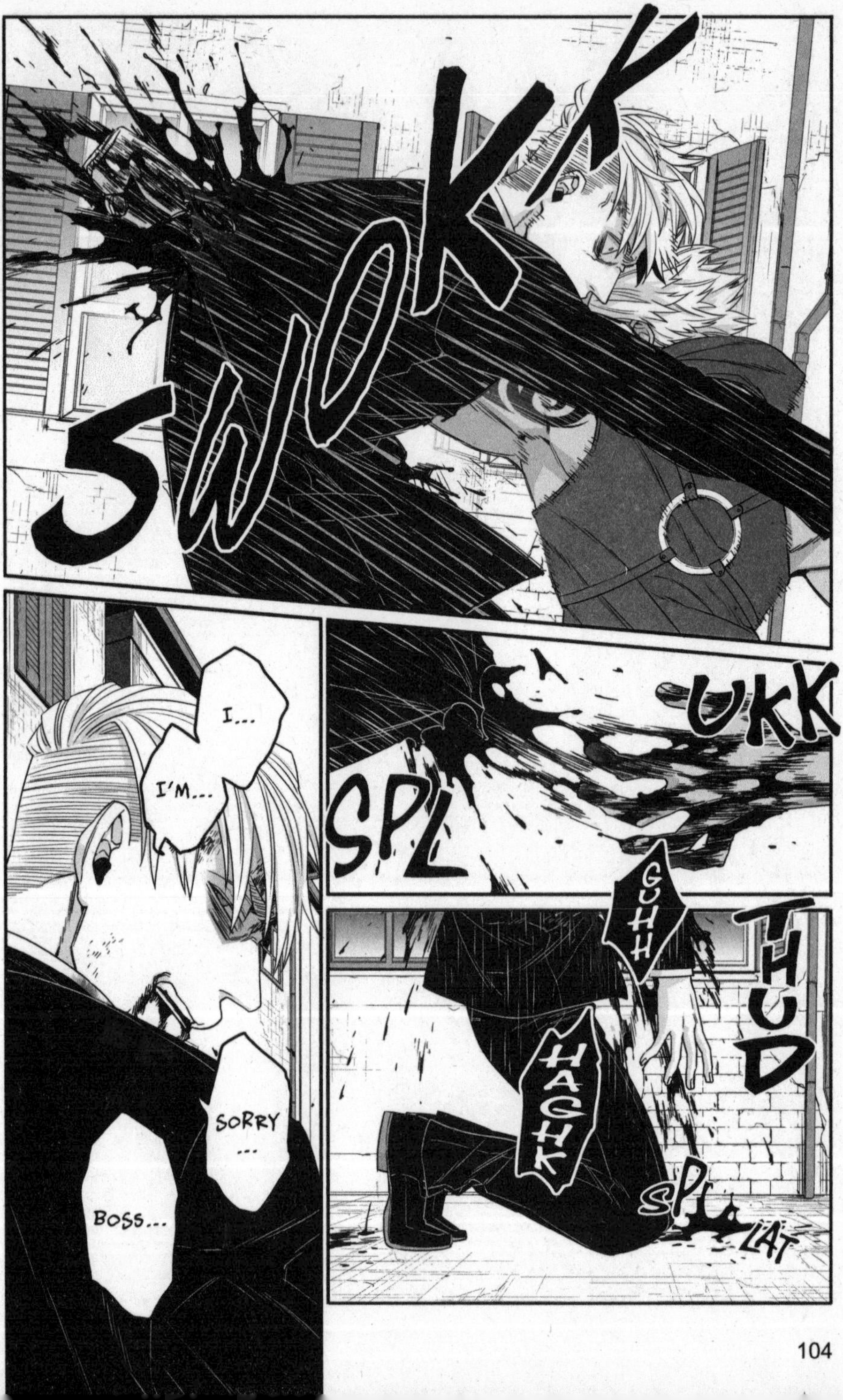
SWOKK
UKK
SPL
GUHH
THUD
HAGHK
SPLAT
I...
I'M...
SORRY...
BOSS...

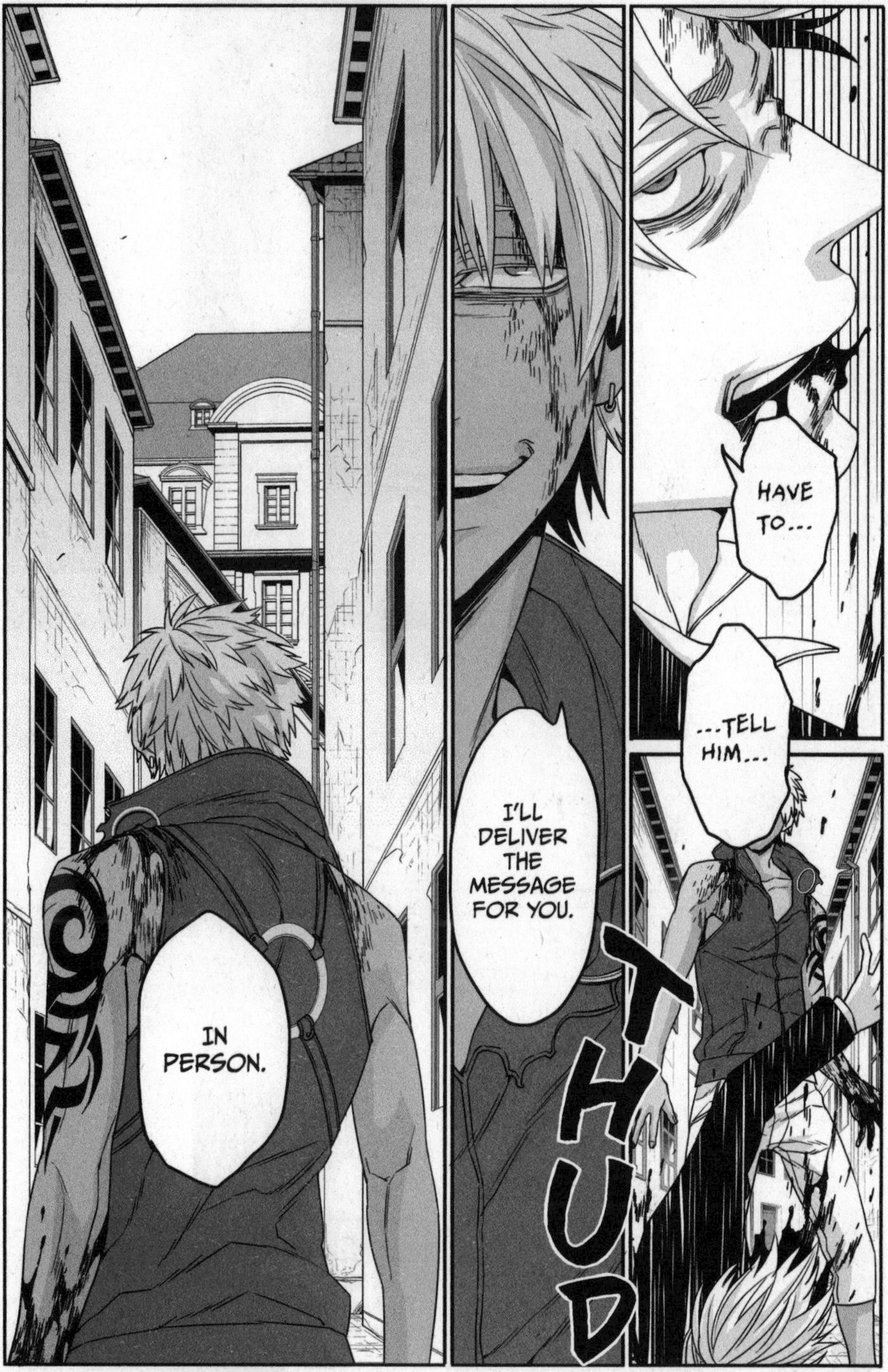
HAVE TO...
...TELL HIM...
THUD
I'LL DELIVER THE MESSAGE FOR YOU.
IN PERSON.

THANKS FOR...

...LEADING ME TO HIM.

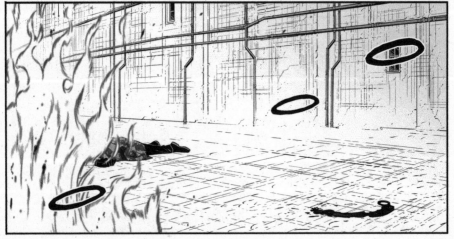

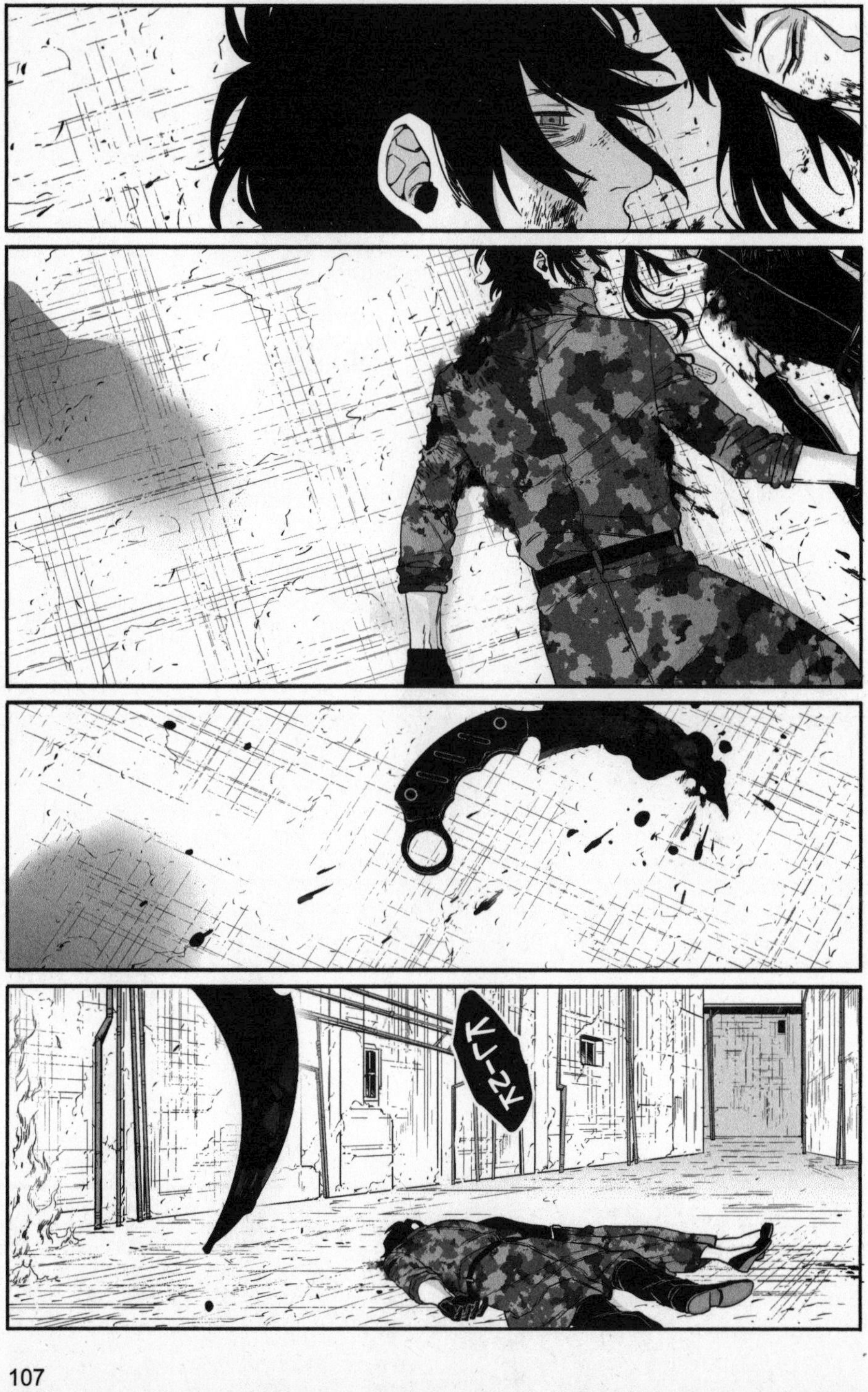
KLINK

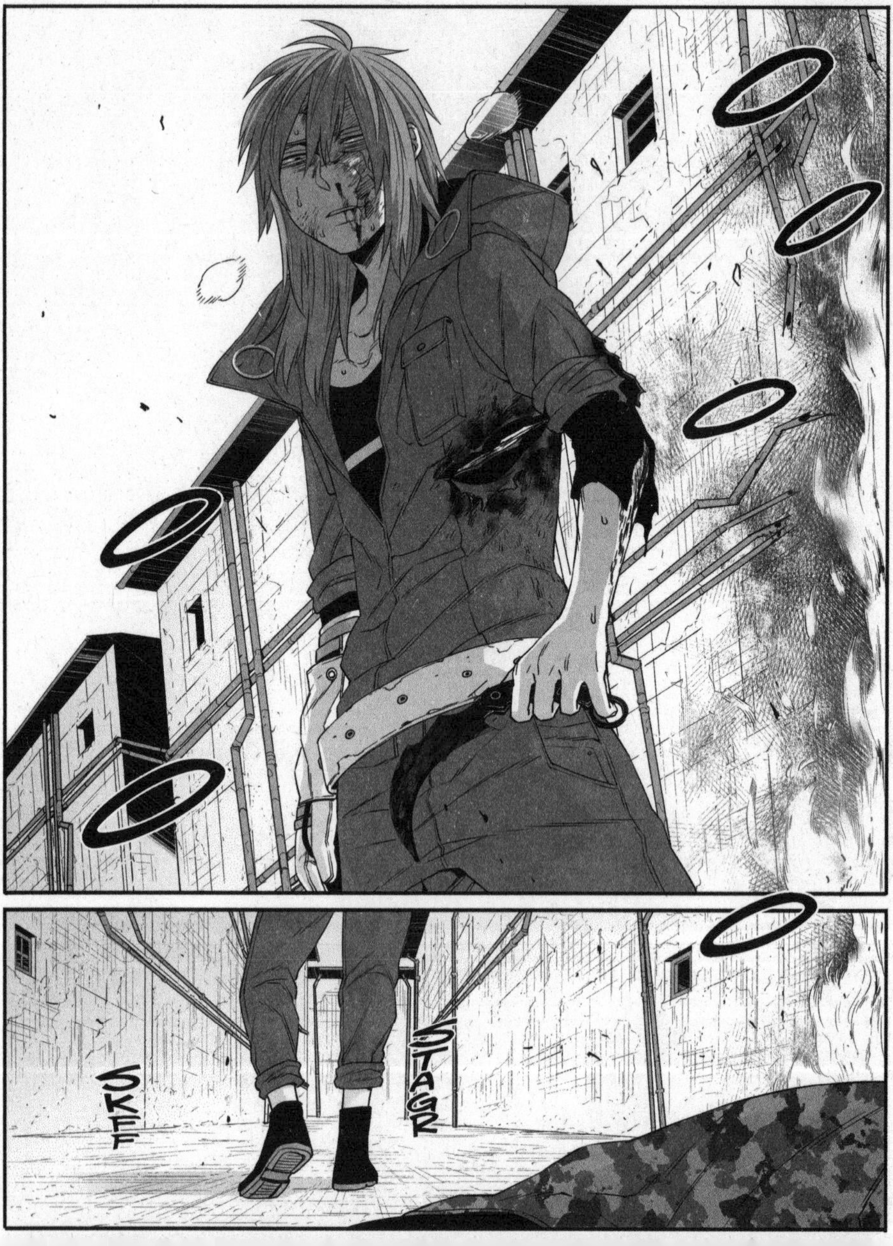
STAGR
SKFF

#12

KWHAAM
EEK!
TING
THIS WAY. COME ON!
TMP TMP TMP
LET'S HEAD TO BASTARD.
THEY'LL PROTECT US.
RIGHT.
WE NEED TO HURRY...

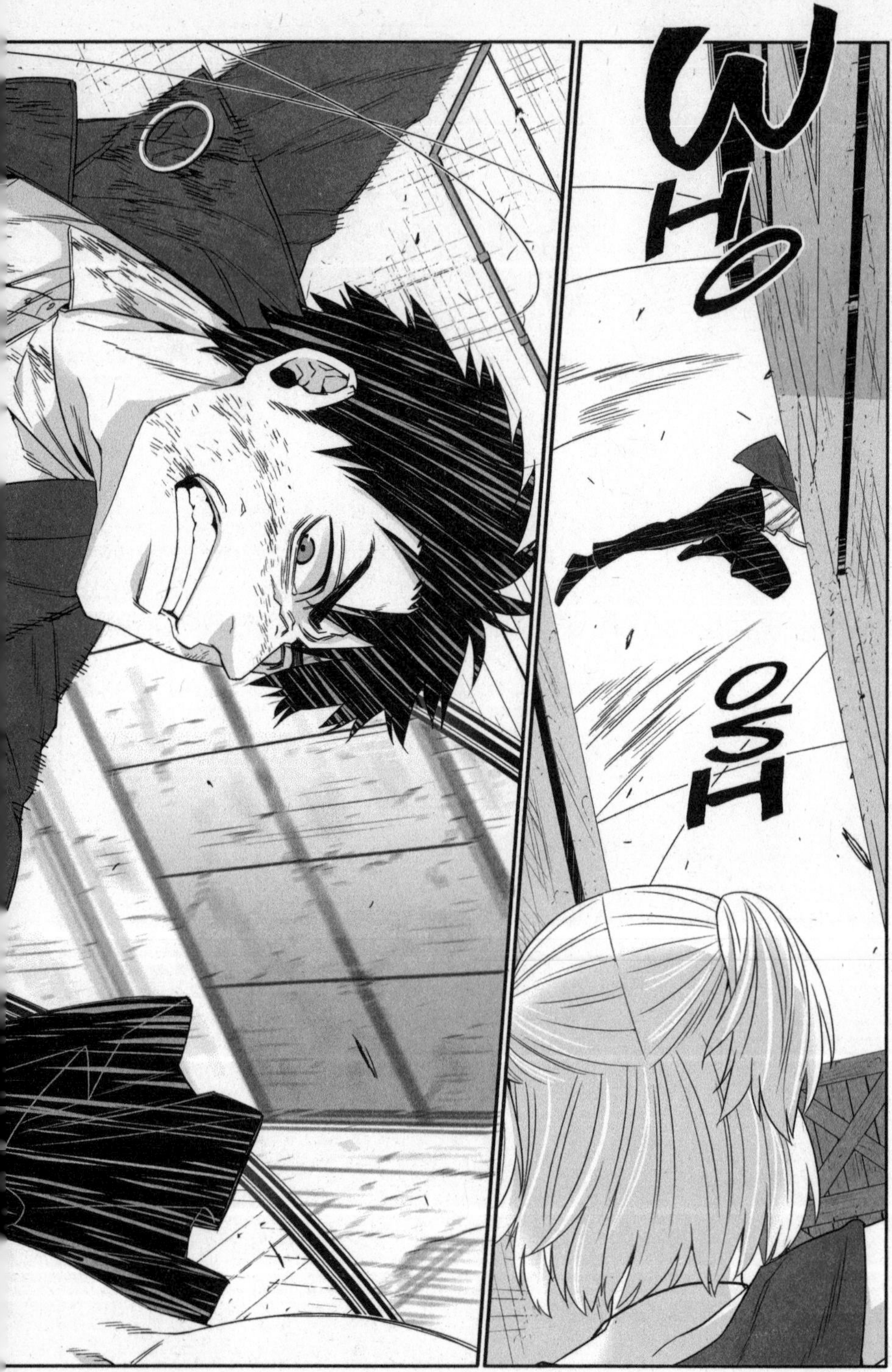
WHOOSH

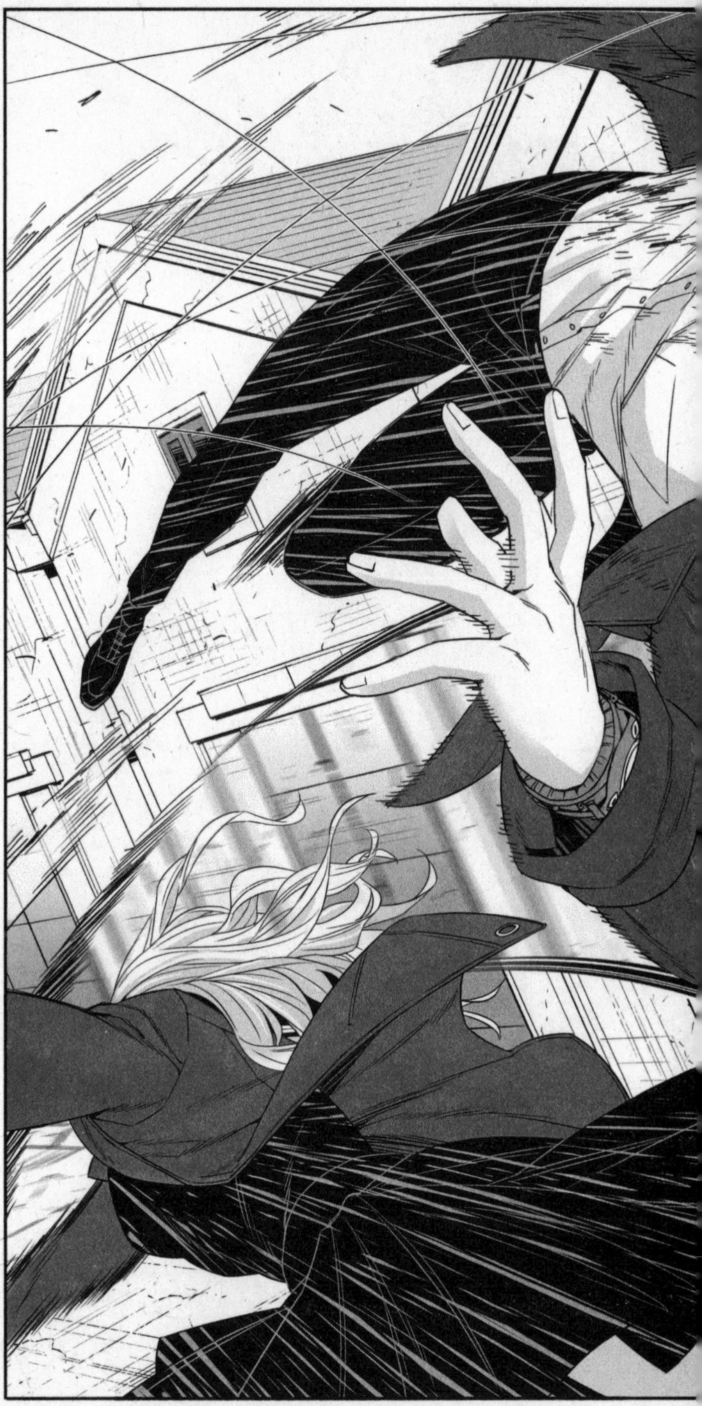

#12

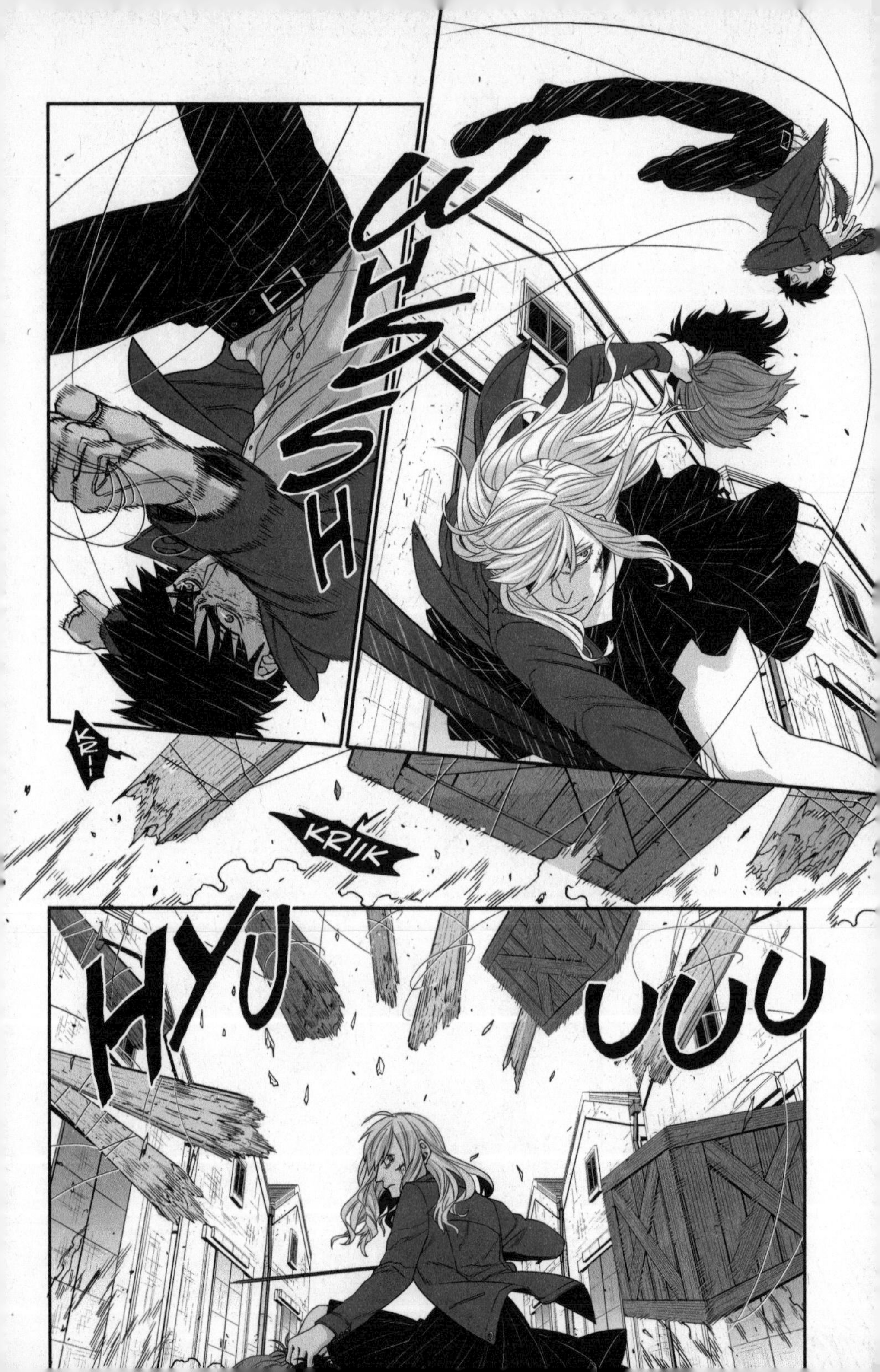
WHSSSH
KRI-I
KRIIK
HYU UUU

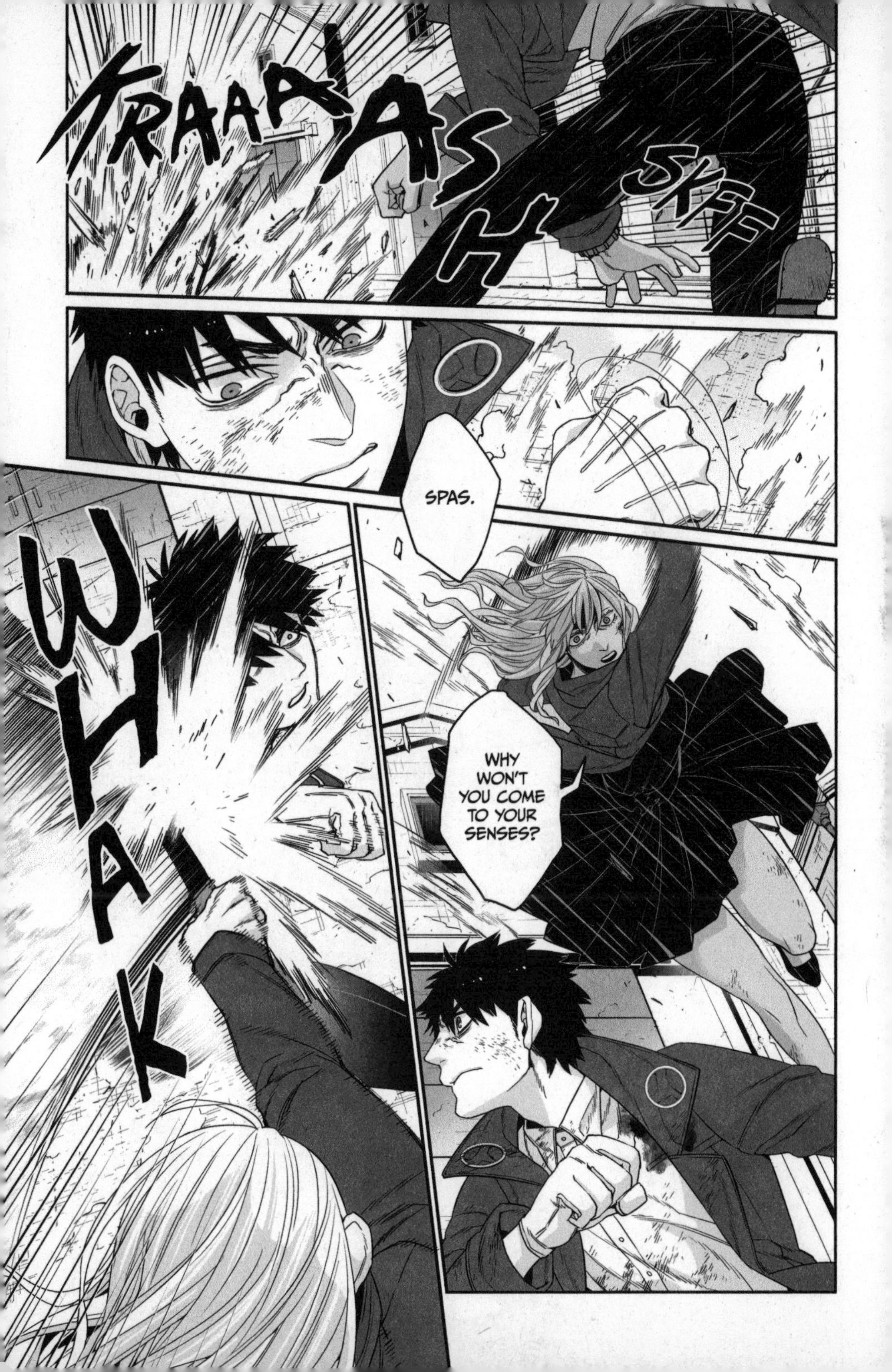

SKFF
TRAAAASH
SPAS.
WHY WON'T YOU COME TO YOUR SENSES?
WHAK

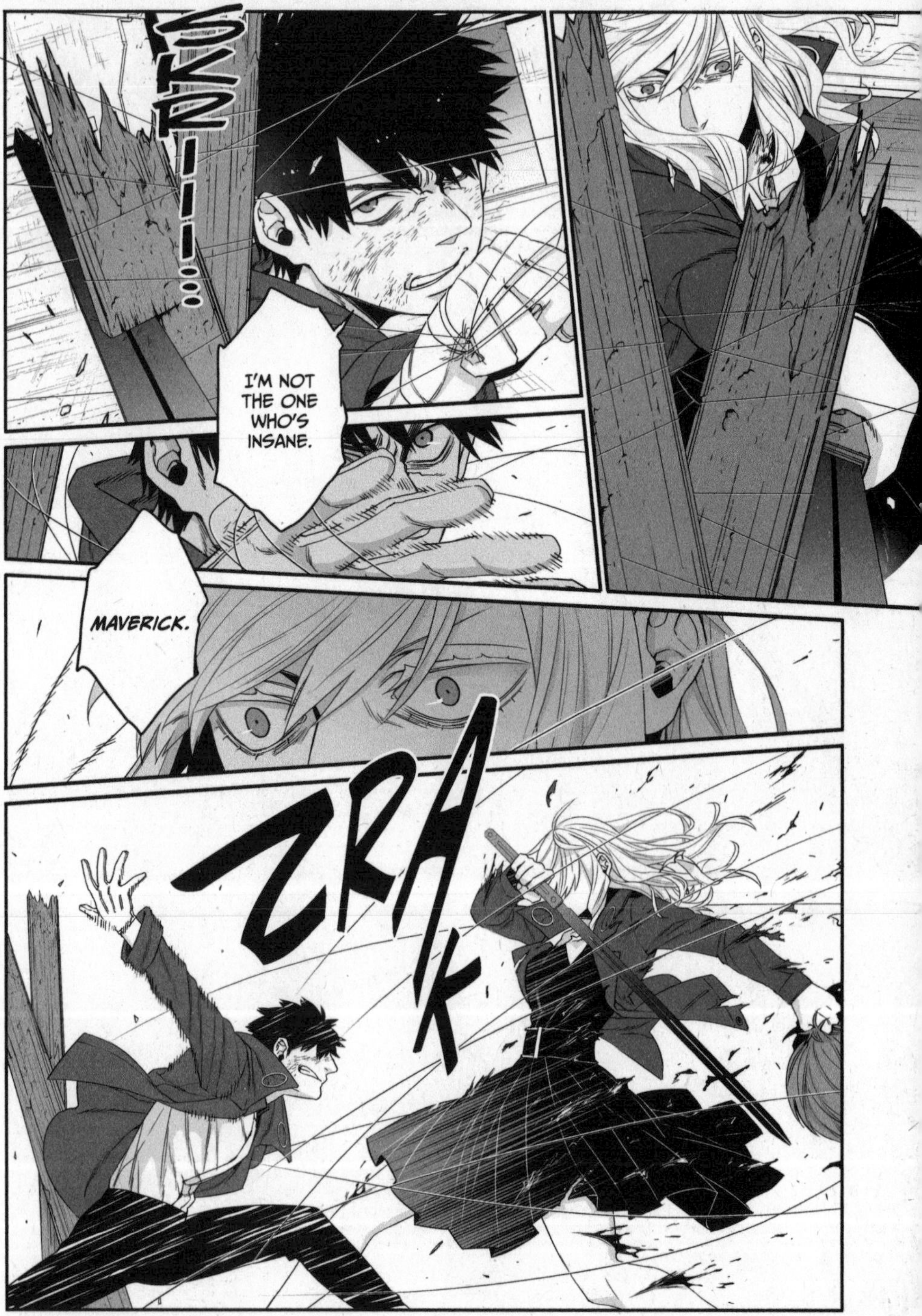

SKRIIII...
I'M NOT THE ONE WHO'S INSANE.
MAVERICK.
ZRAK

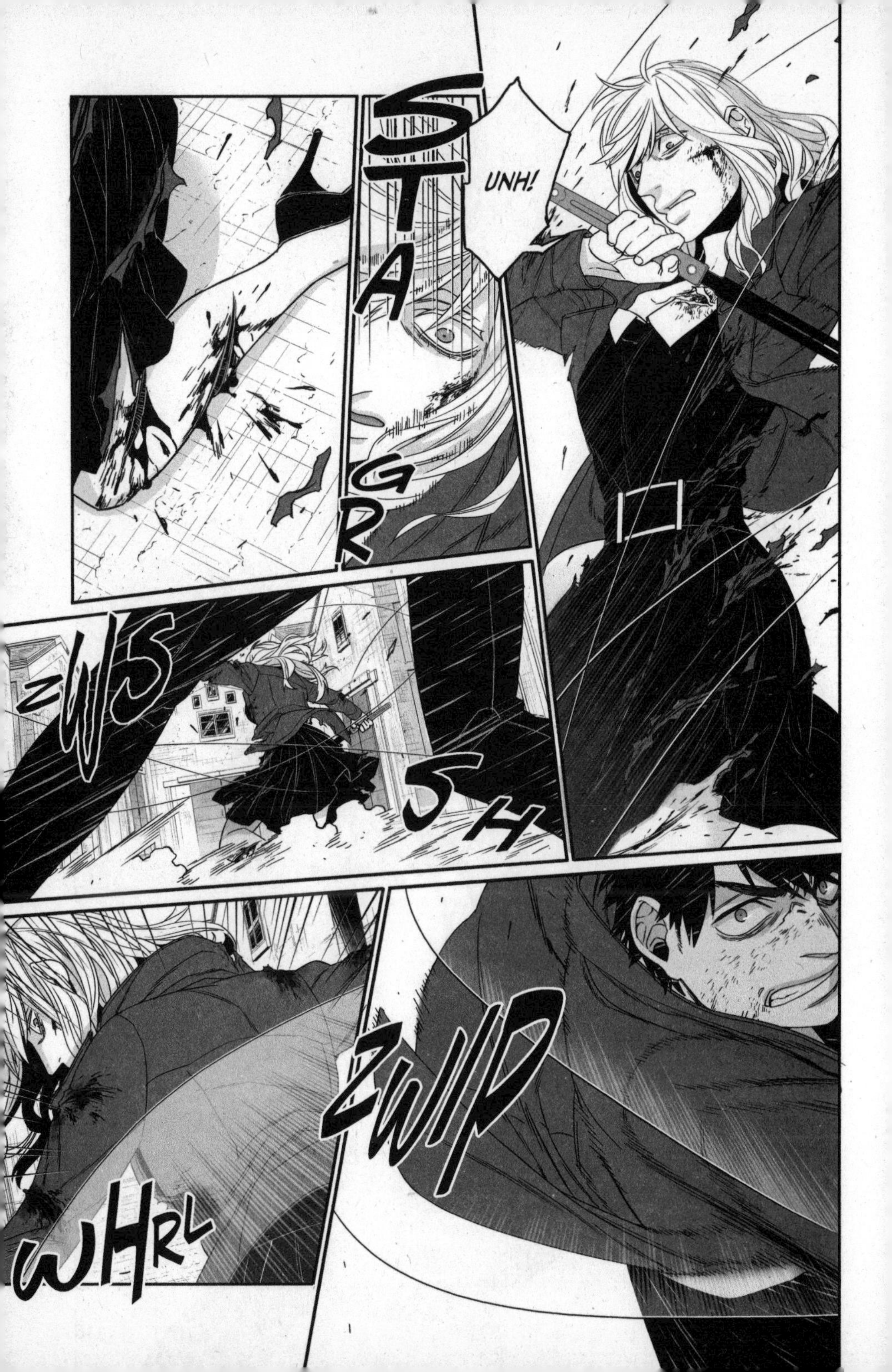
UNH!
STAGGR
ZWS
SH
ZWIP
WHRL

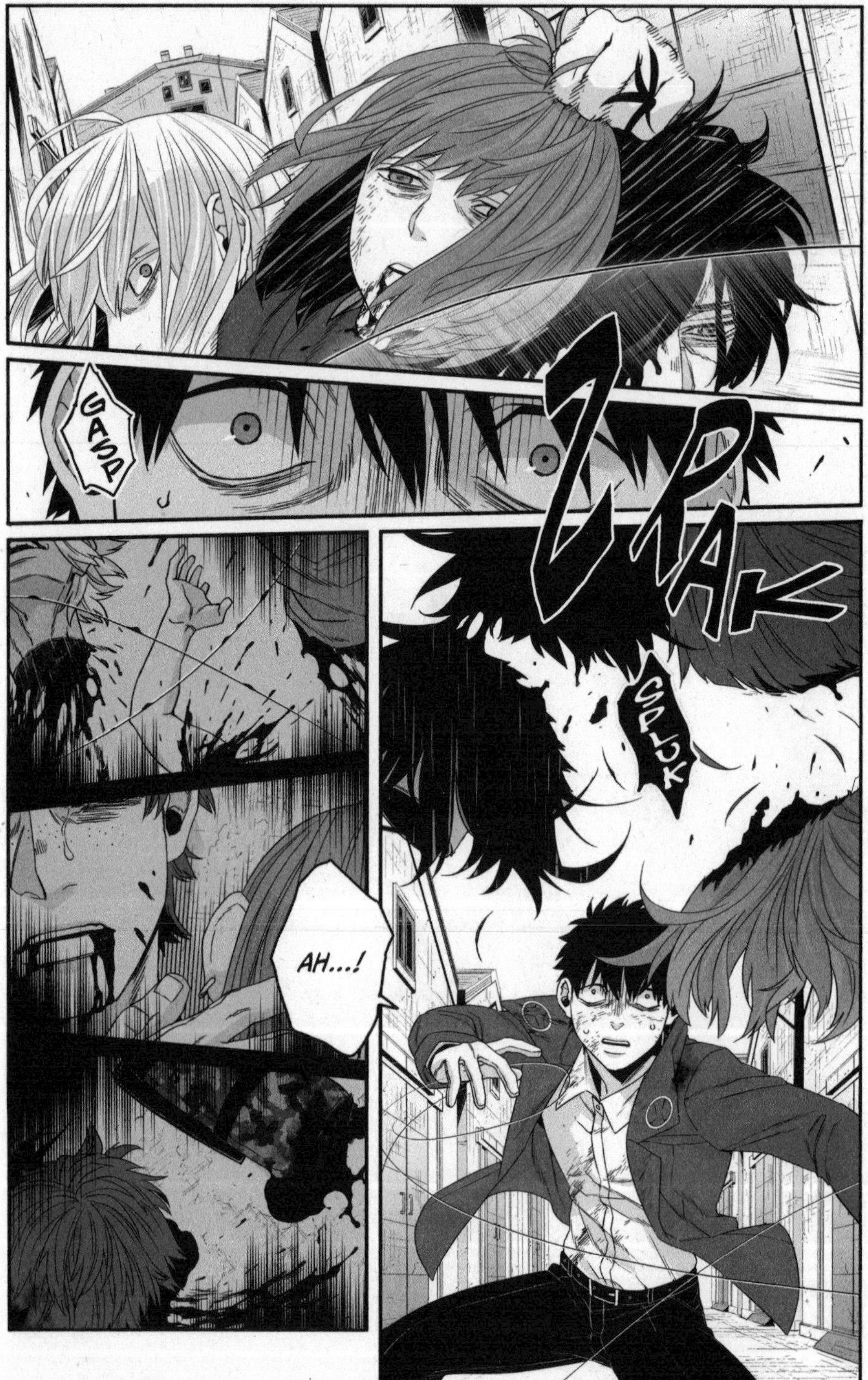
GASP
ZPAK
SPLUK
AH...!

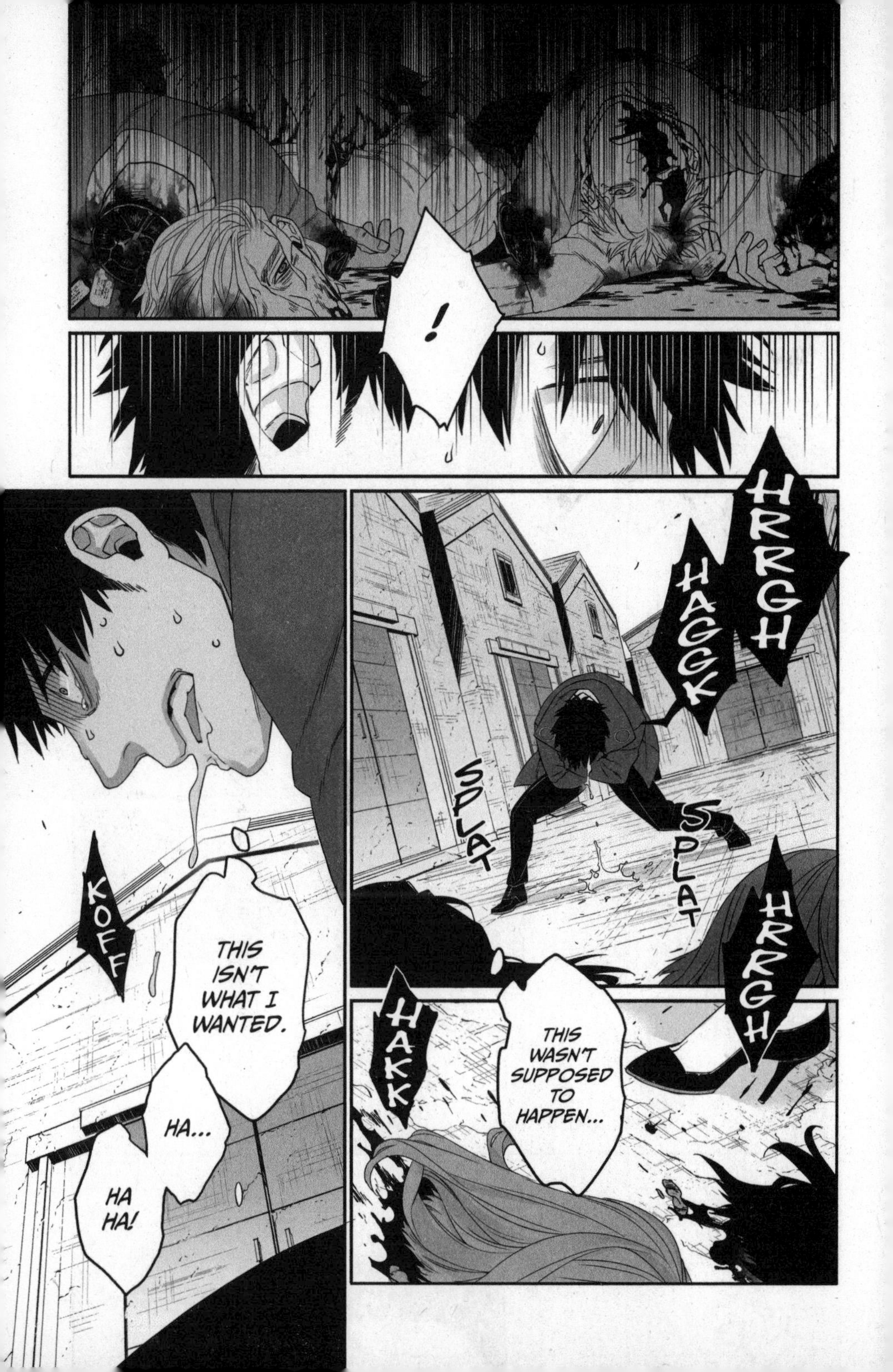
!
HRRGH
HAGGK
SPLAT
SPLAT
HRRGH
HAKK
THIS WASN'T SUPPOSED TO HAPPEN...
KOFF
THIS ISN'T WHAT I WANTED.
HA...
HA HA!

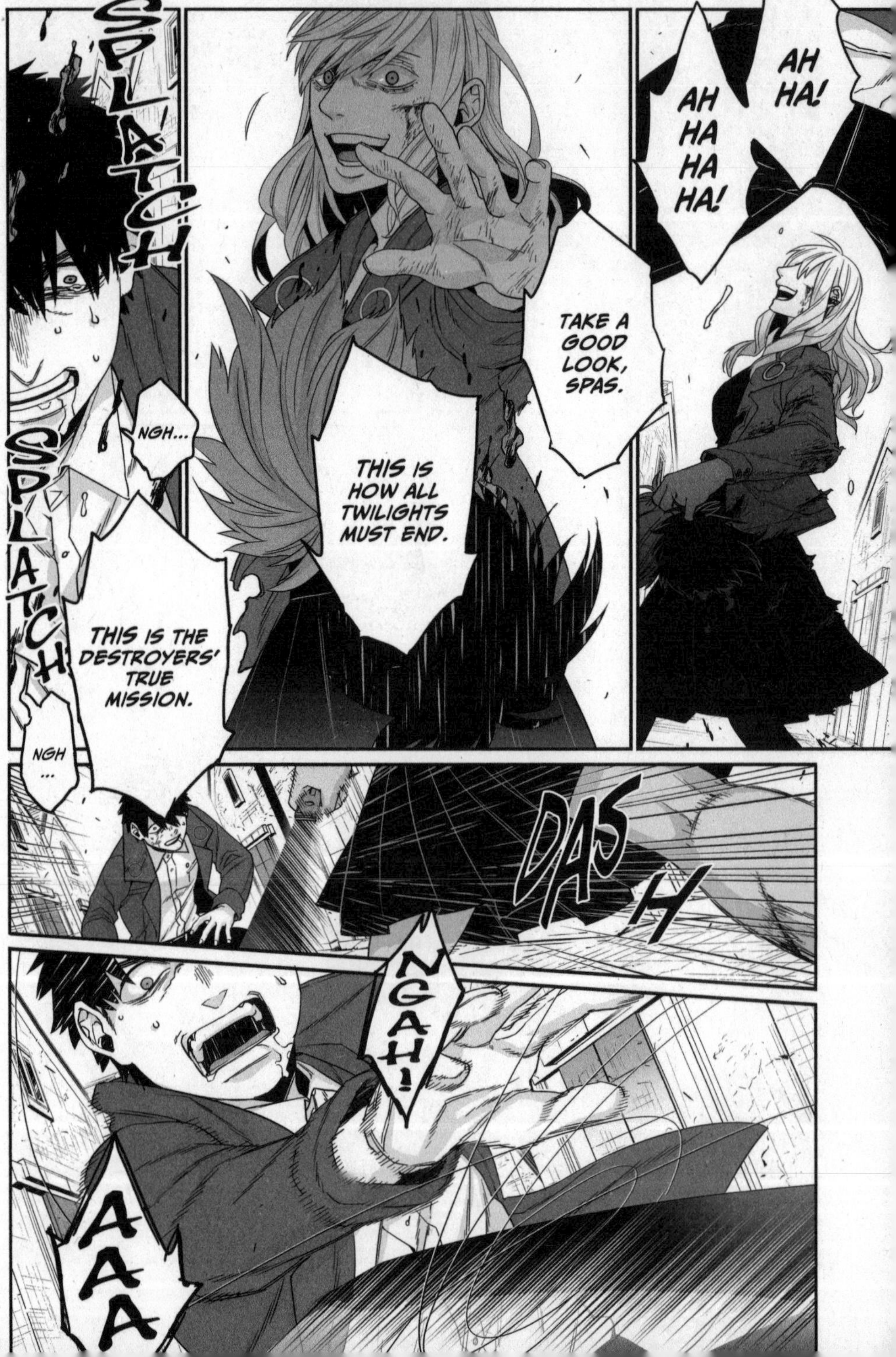
AH HA!
AH HA HA HA!
TAKE A GOOD LOOK, SPAS.
THIS IS HOW ALL TWILIGHTS MUST END.
SPLATCH
NGH...
SPLATCH
THIS IS THE DESTROYERS' TRUE MISSION.
NGH ...
DASH
NGAH!
AAA

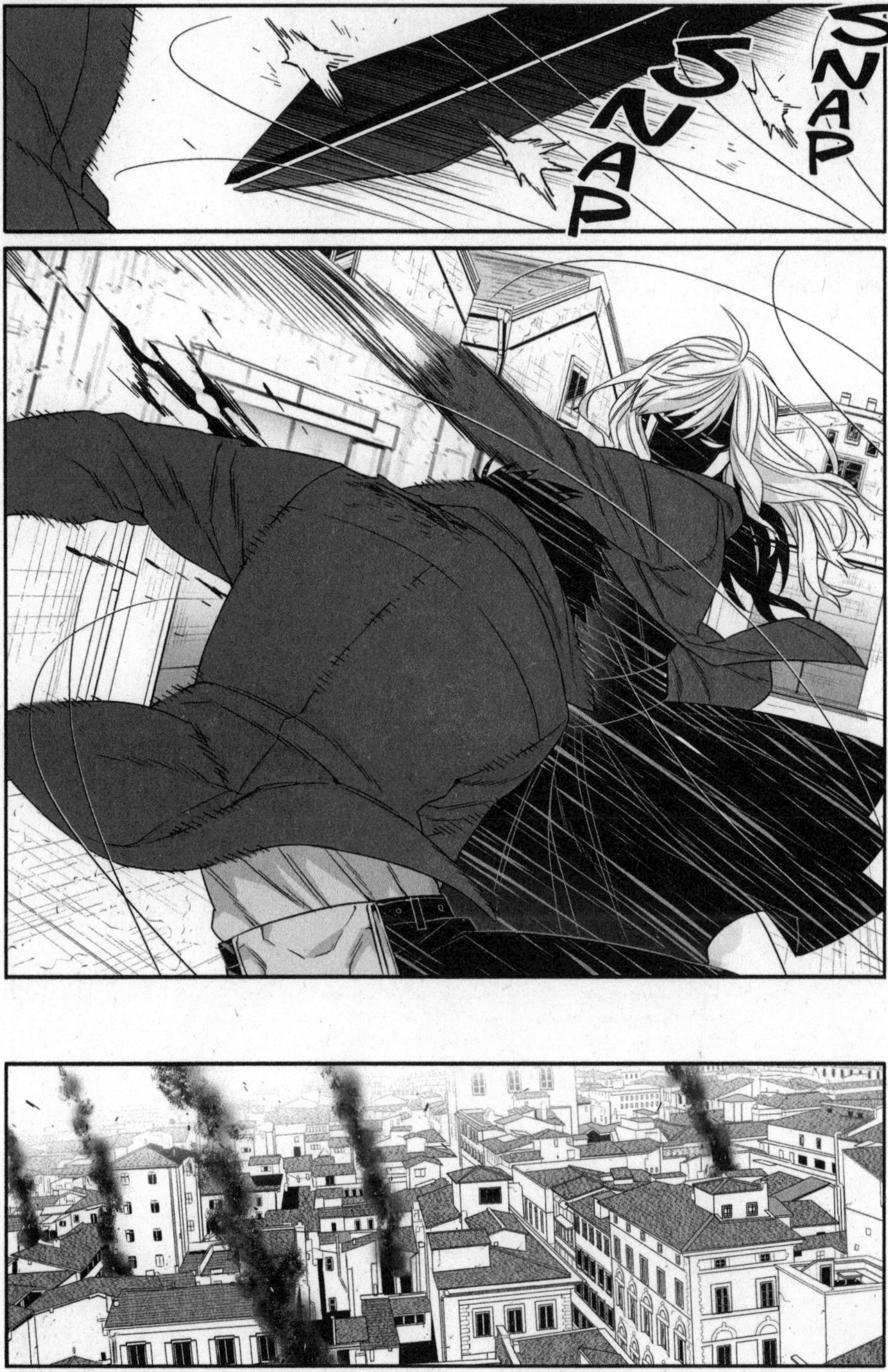
SNAP
SNAP

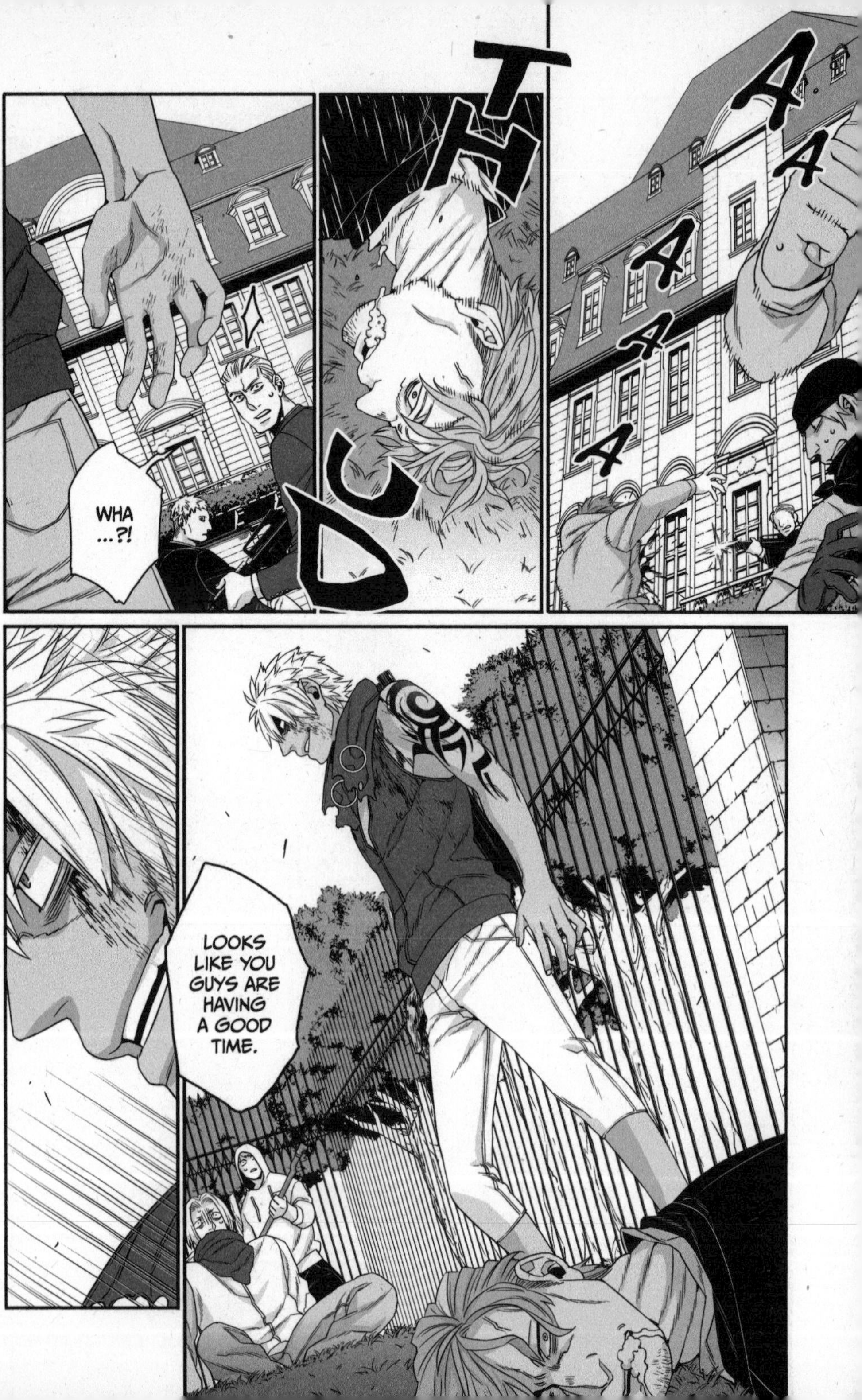
AAAAAA
THUD
WHA ...?!
LOOKS LIKE YOU GUYS ARE HAVING A GOOD TIME.

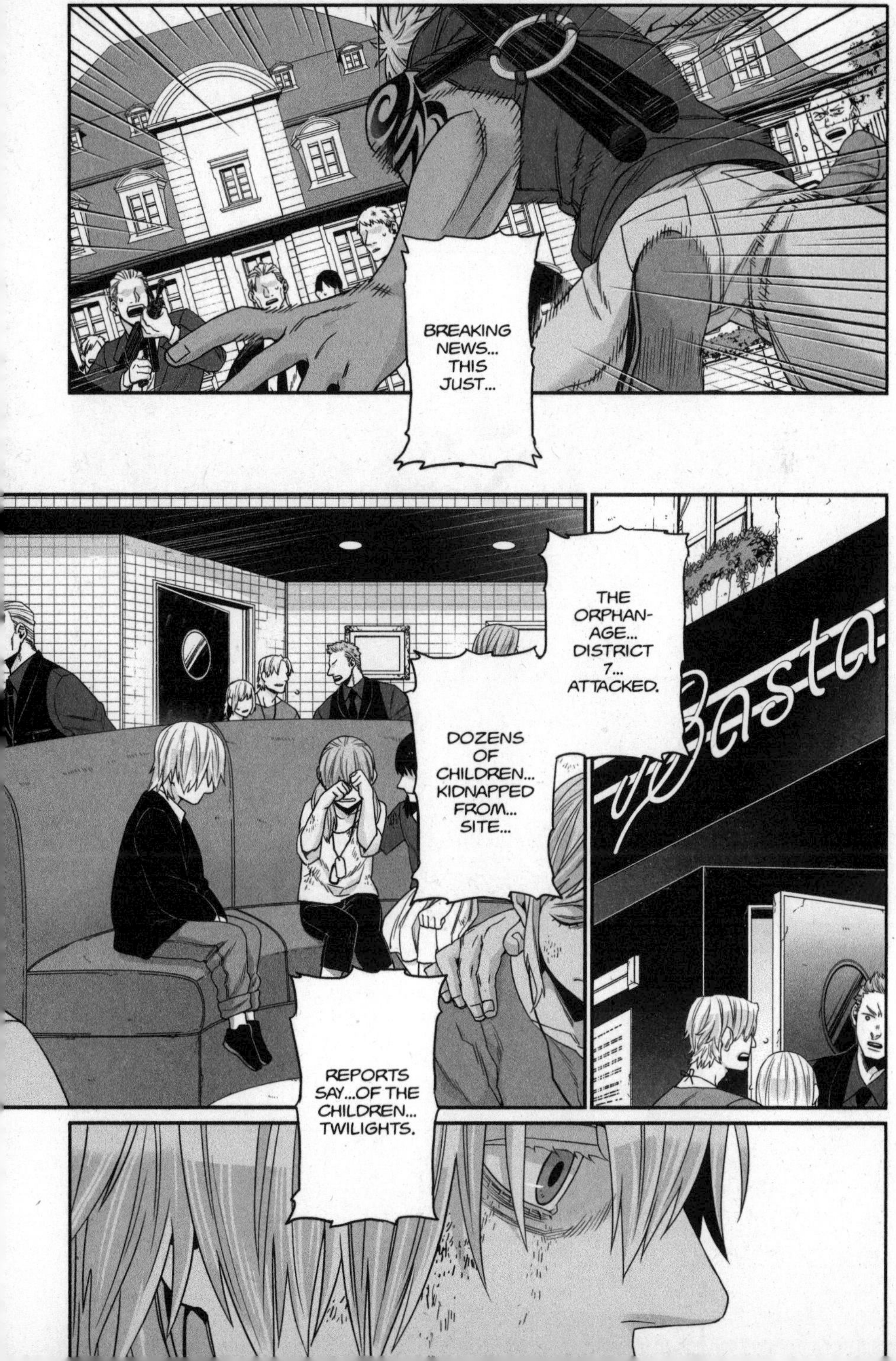
BREAKING NEWS... THIS JUST...
THE ORPHANAGE... DISTRICT 7... ATTACKED.
DOZENS OF CHILDREN... KIDNAPPED FROM... SITE...
REPORTS SAY...OF THE CHILDREN... TWILIGHTS.

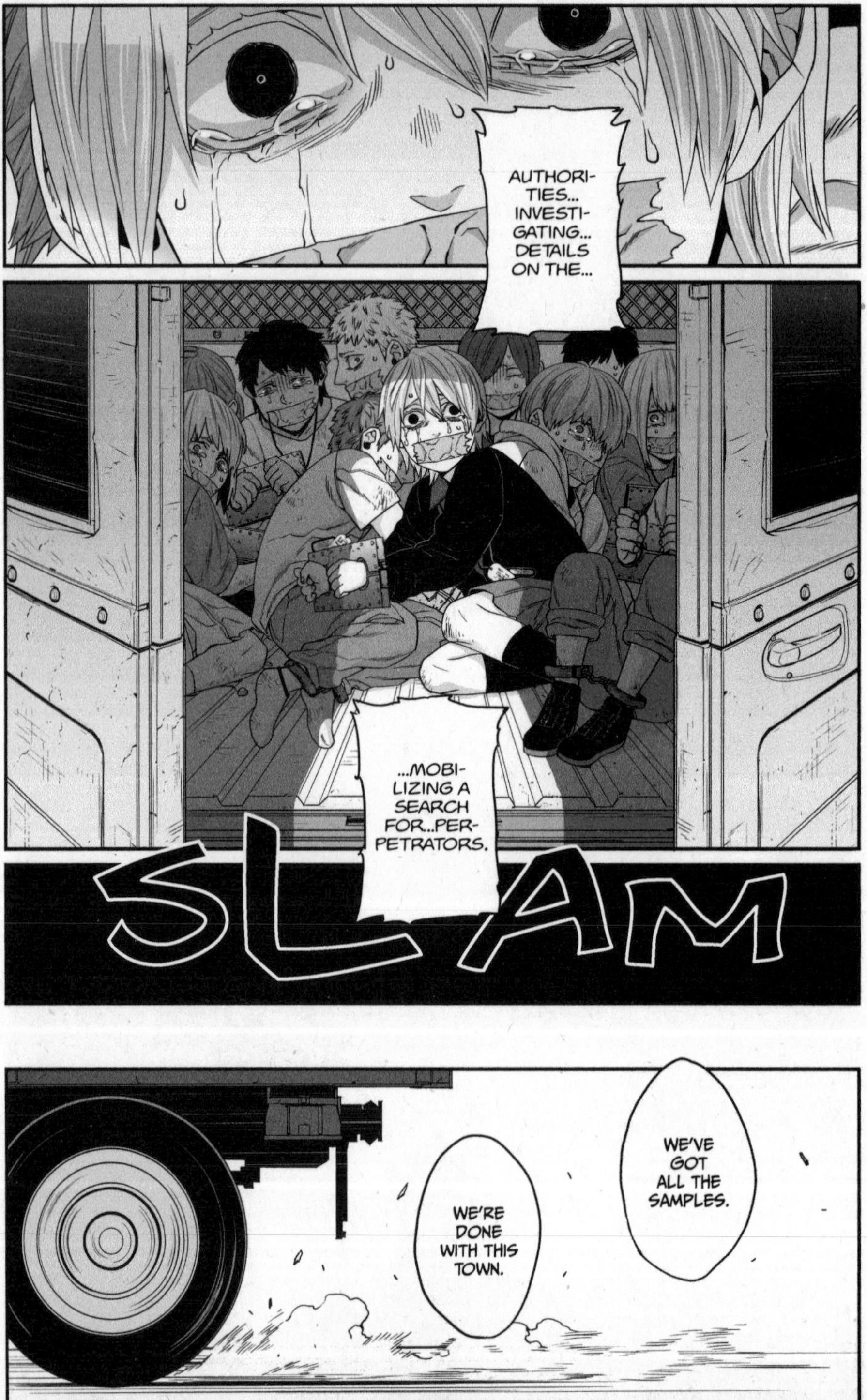
AUTHORI-TIES... INVESTI-GATING... DETAILS ON THE...
...MOBI-LIZING A SEARCH FOR...PER-PETRATORS.
SLAM
WE'VE GOT ALL THE SAMPLES.
WE'RE DONE WITH THIS TOWN.

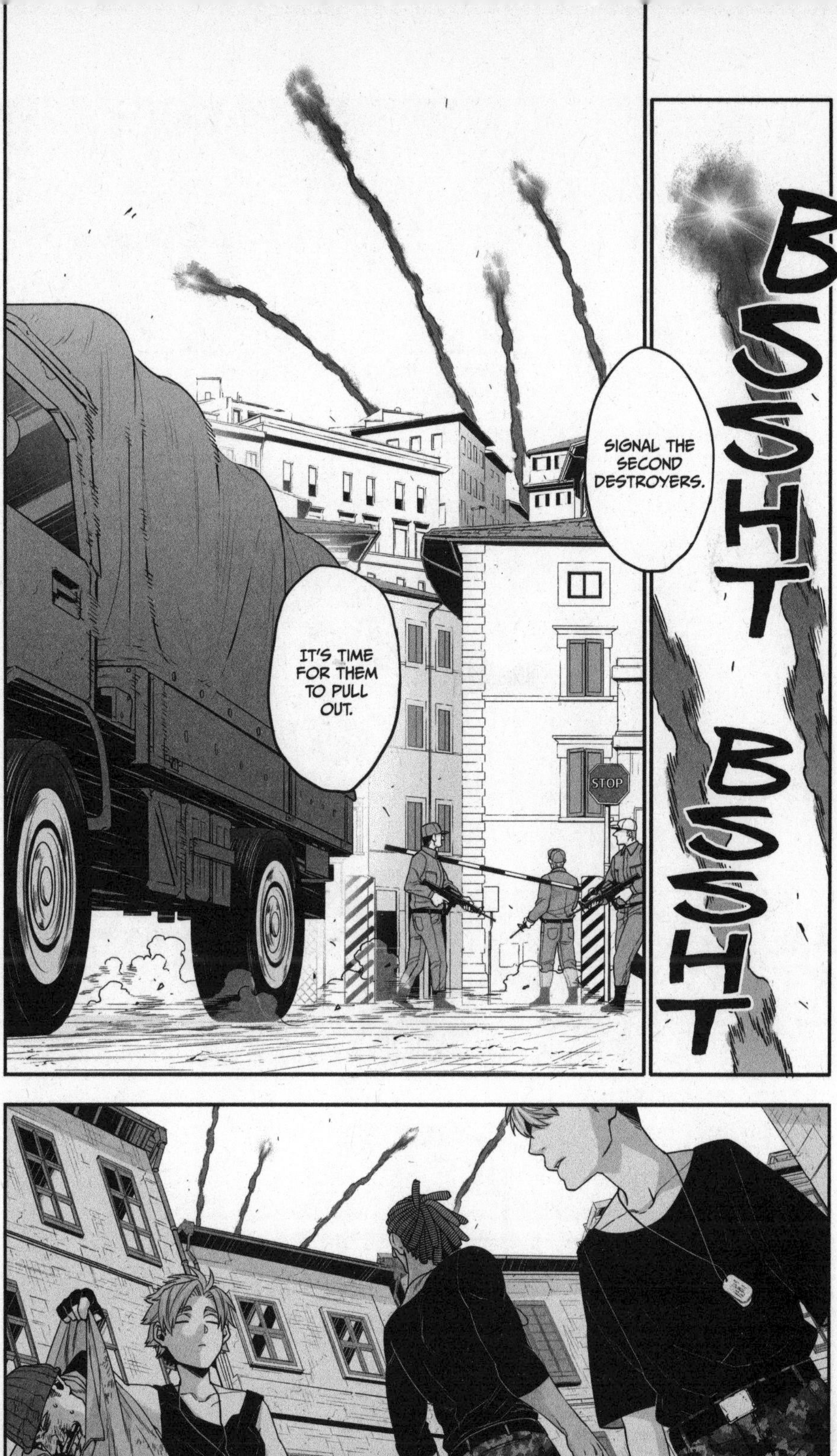
BSSHT BSSHT
SIGNAL THE SECOND DESTROYERS.
IT'S TIME FOR THEM TO PULL OUT.
STOP

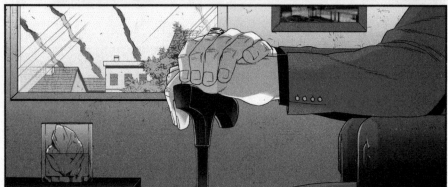

BLAM BLAM BLAM BLAM BLAM

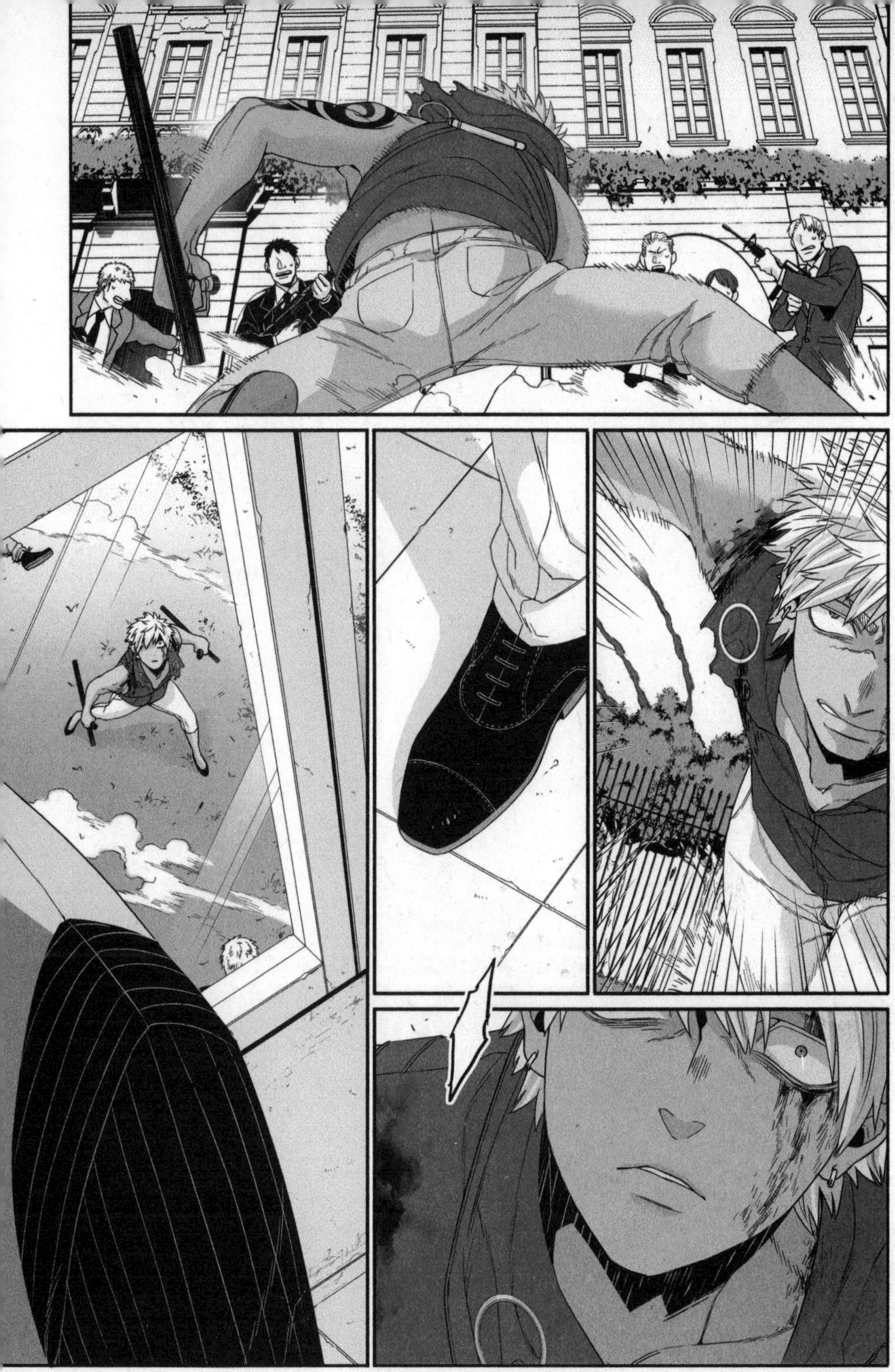

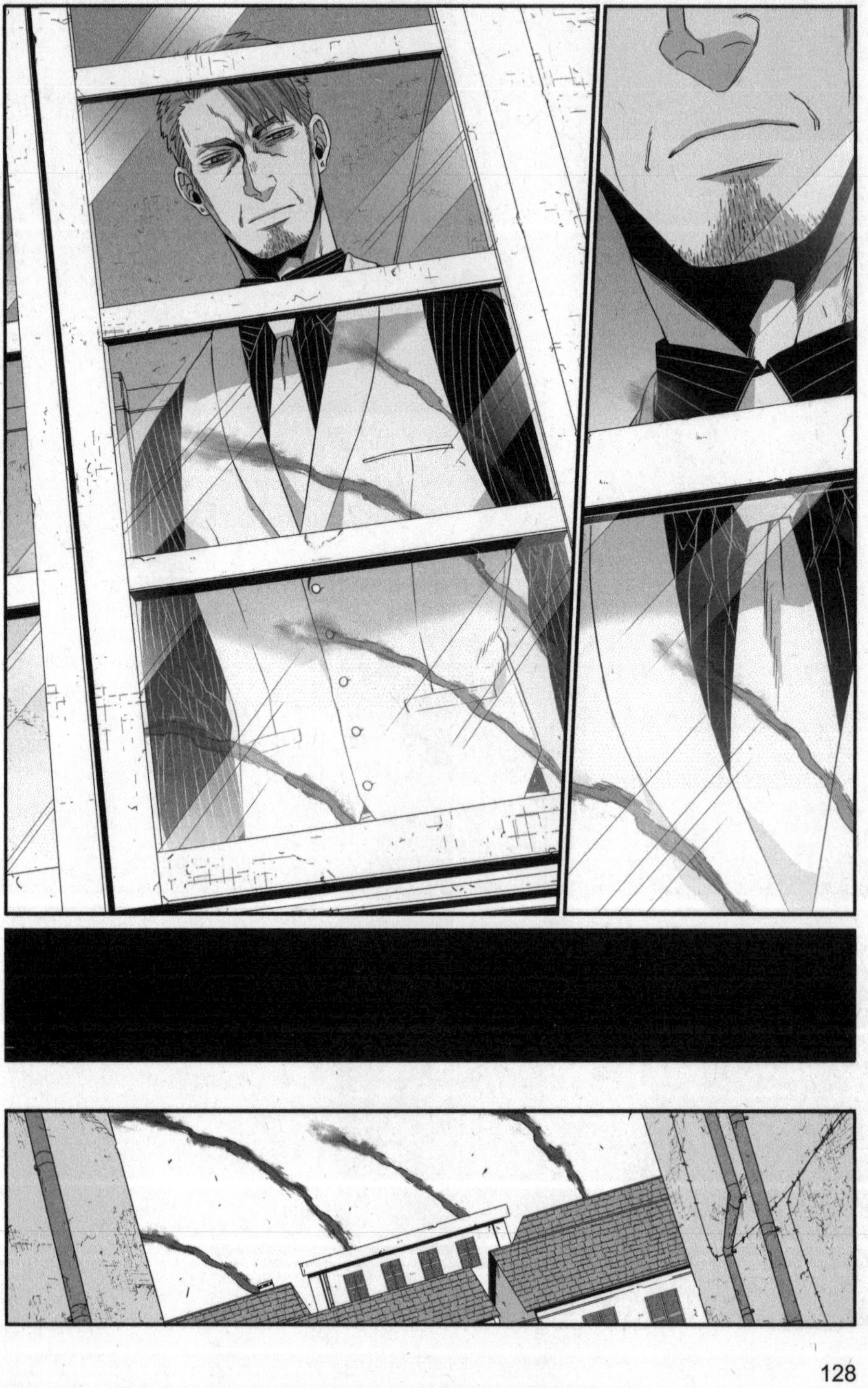

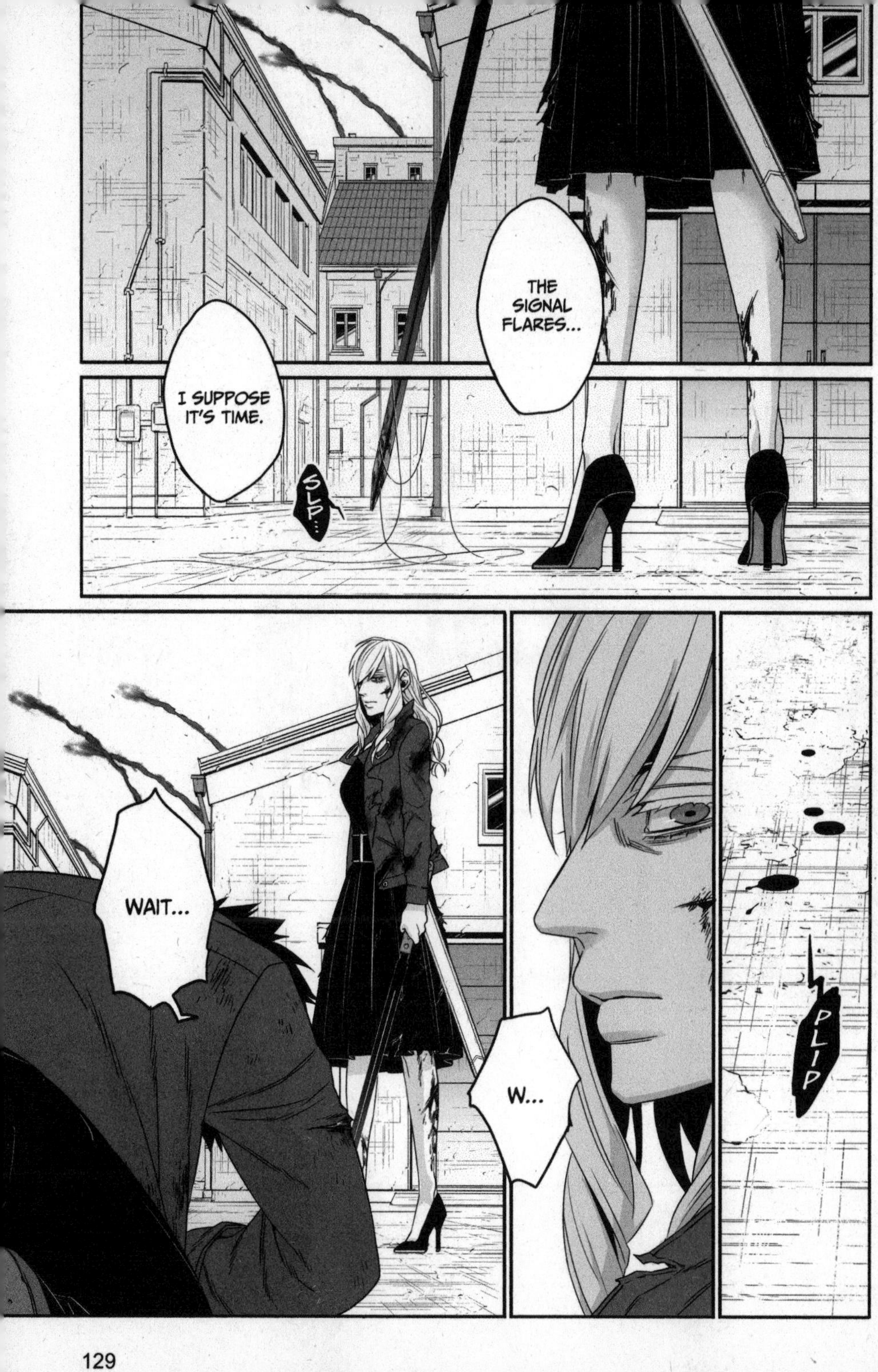
THE SIGNAL FLARES...
I SUPPOSE IT'S TIME.
SLP...
W...
PLIP
WAIT...

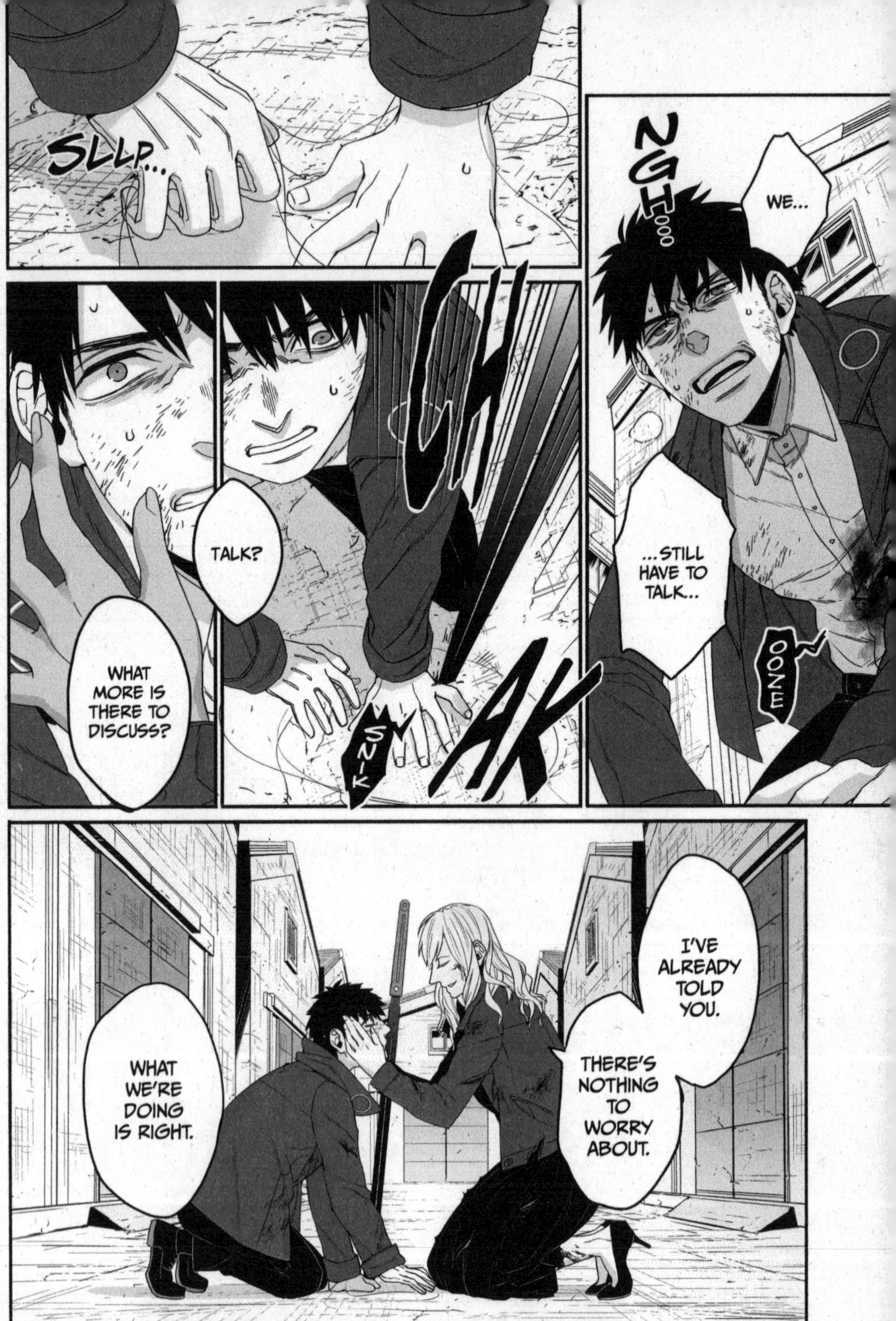
NGHooo
WE...
...STILL HAVE TO TALK...
OOZE
SLLP...
CHAK
SNIK
TALK?
WHAT MORE IS THERE TO DISCUSS?
I'VE ALREADY TOLD YOU.
THERE'S NOTHING TO WORRY ABOUT.
WHAT WE'RE DOING IS RIGHT.

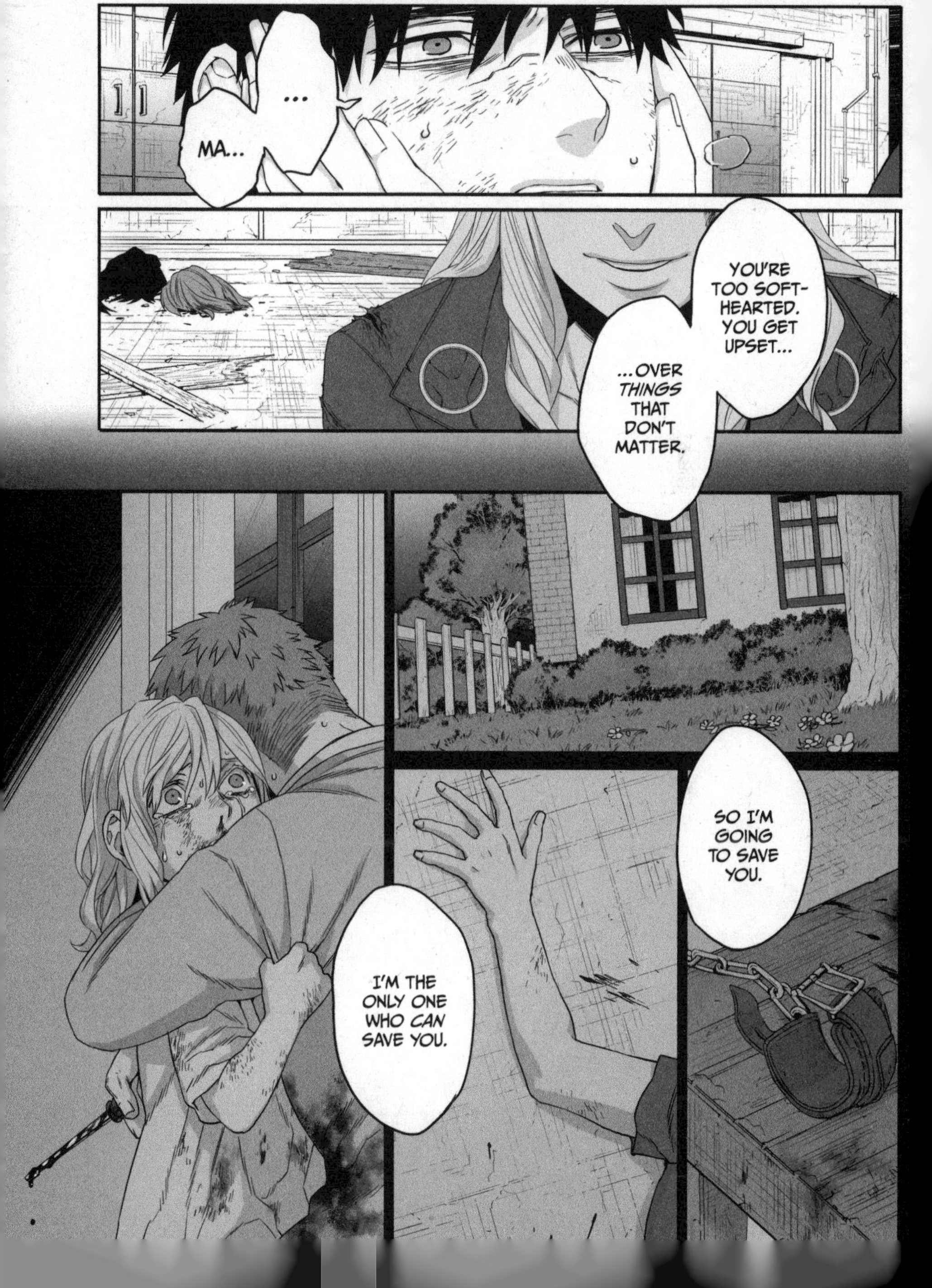
...
MA...
YOU'RE TOO SOFT-HEARTED. YOU GET UPSET...
...OVER THINGS THAT DON'T MATTER.
SO I'M GOING TO SAVE YOU.
I'M THE ONLY ONE WHO CAN SAVE YOU.

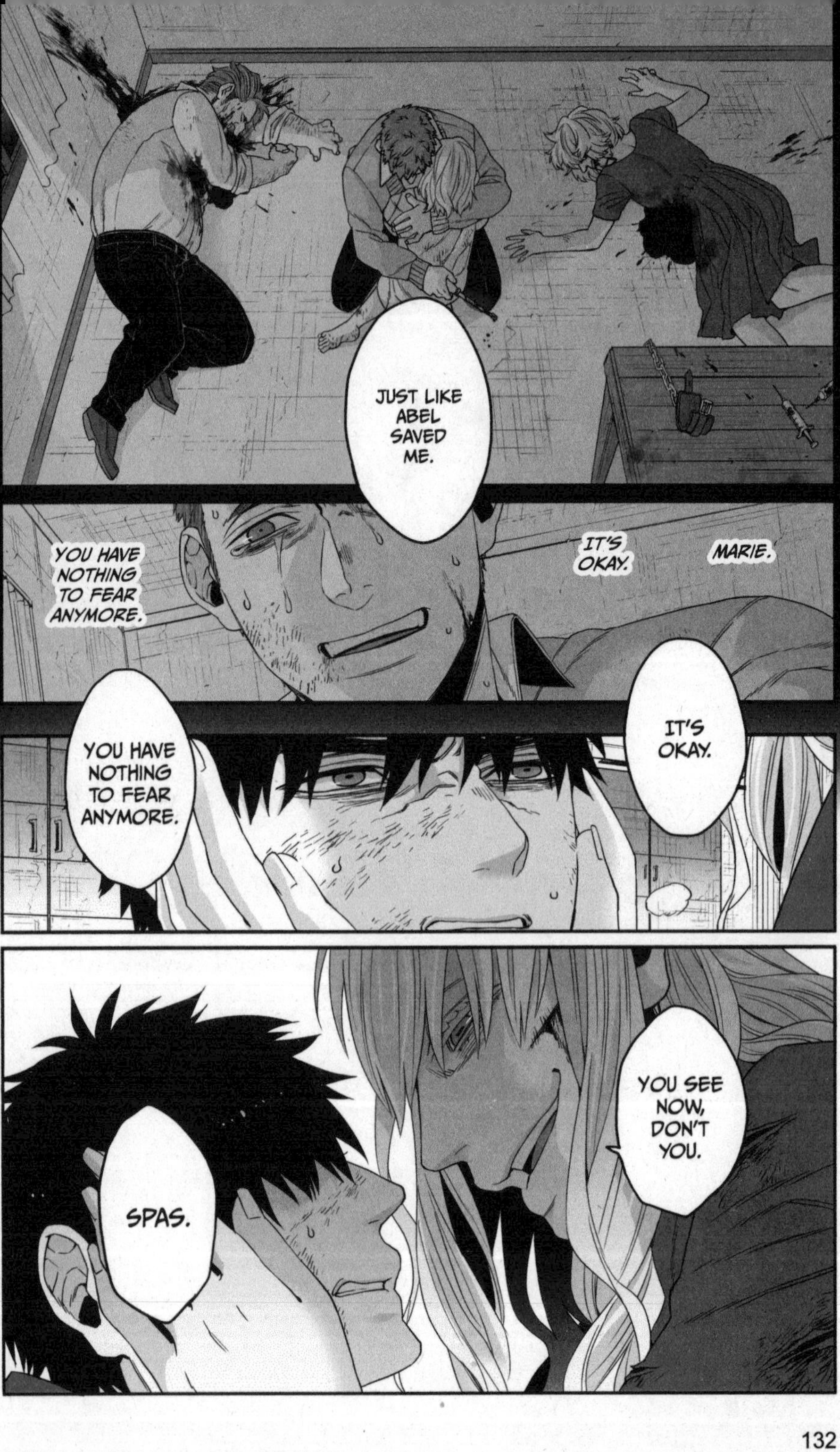
JUST LIKE ABEL SAVED ME.
MARIE.
IT'S OKAY.
YOU HAVE NOTHING TO FEAR ANYMORE.
IT'S OKAY.
YOU HAVE NOTHING TO FEAR ANYMORE.
YOU SEE NOW, DON'T YOU.
SPAS.

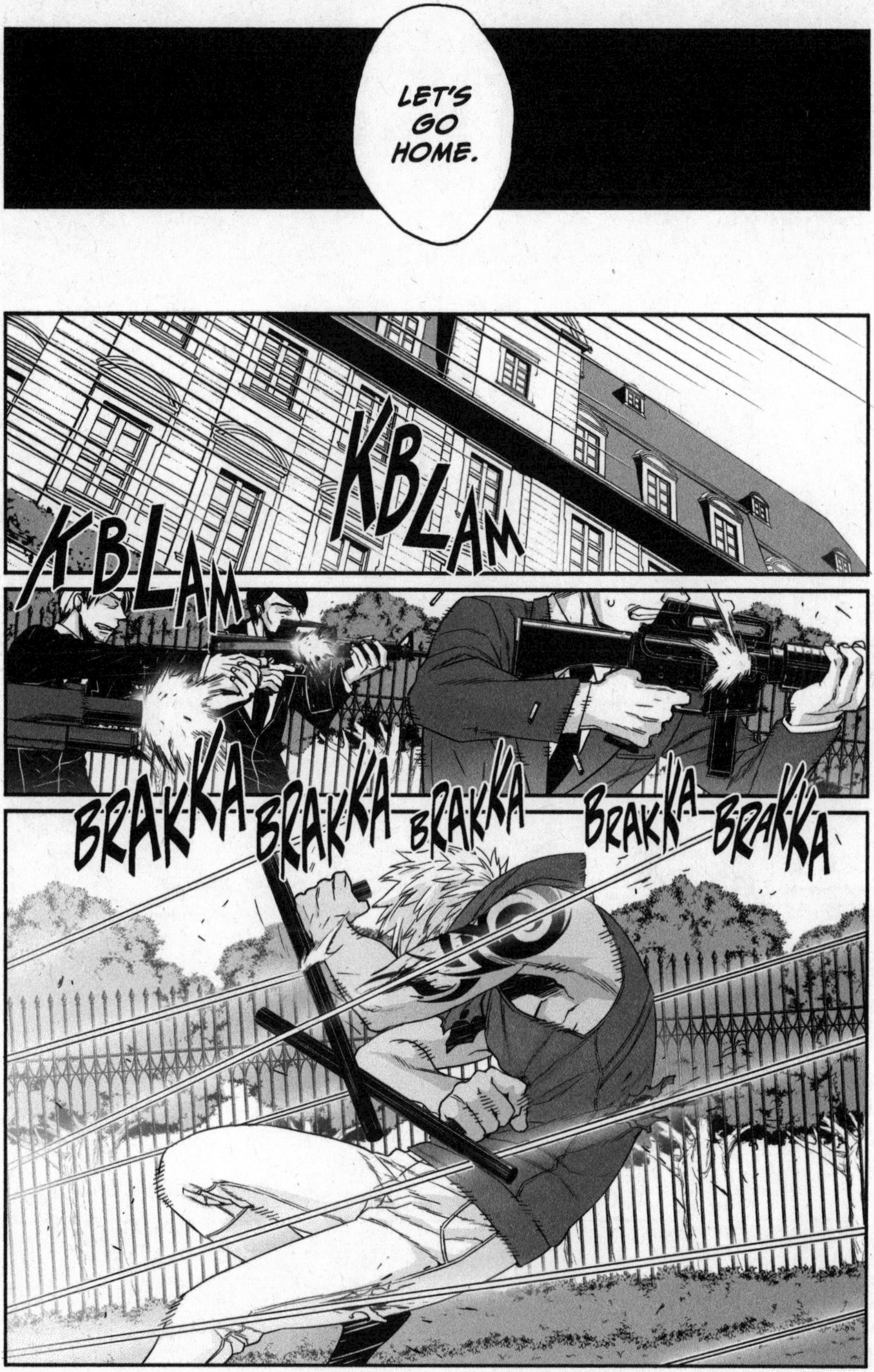
LET'S GO HOME.
KBLAM
KBLAM
BRAKKA
BRAKKA
BRAKKA
BRAKKA
BRAKKA

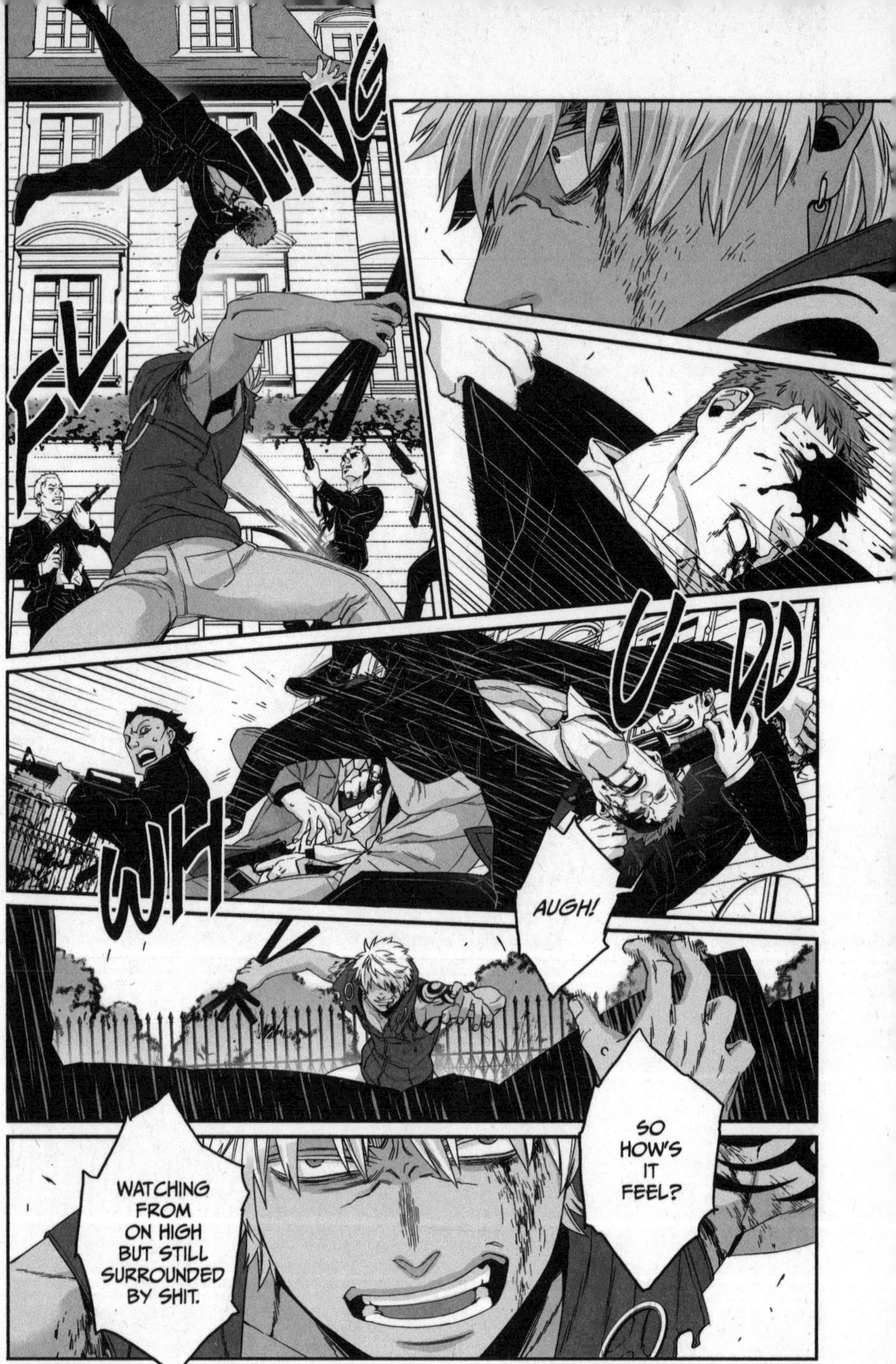
FLING
THUD
WHACK
AUGH!
SO HOW'S IT FEEL?
WATCHING FROM ON HIGH BUT STILL SURROUNDED BY SHIT.

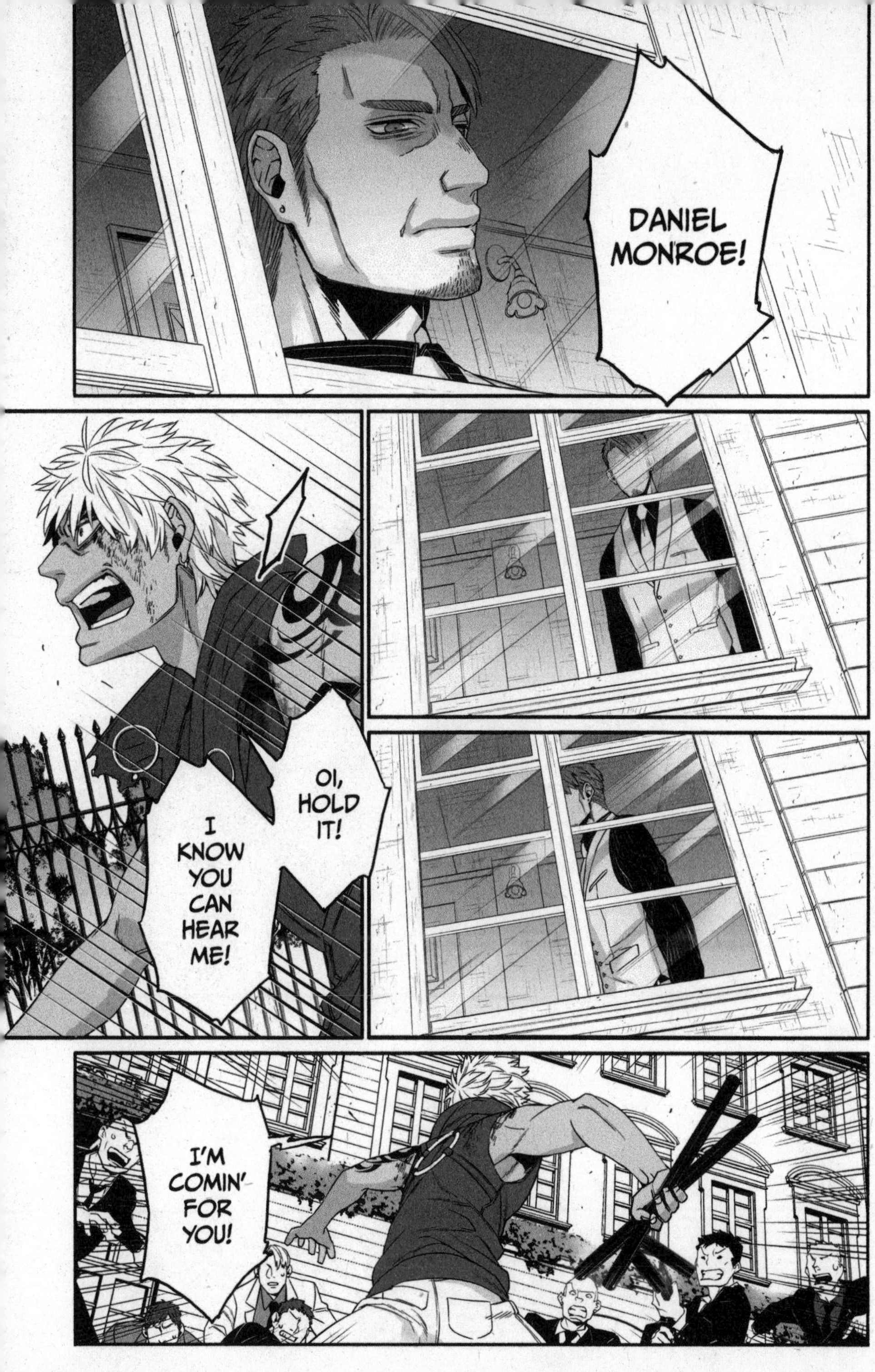
DANIEL MONROE!
OI, HOLD IT!
I KNOW YOU CAN HEAR ME!
I'M COMIN' FOR YOU!

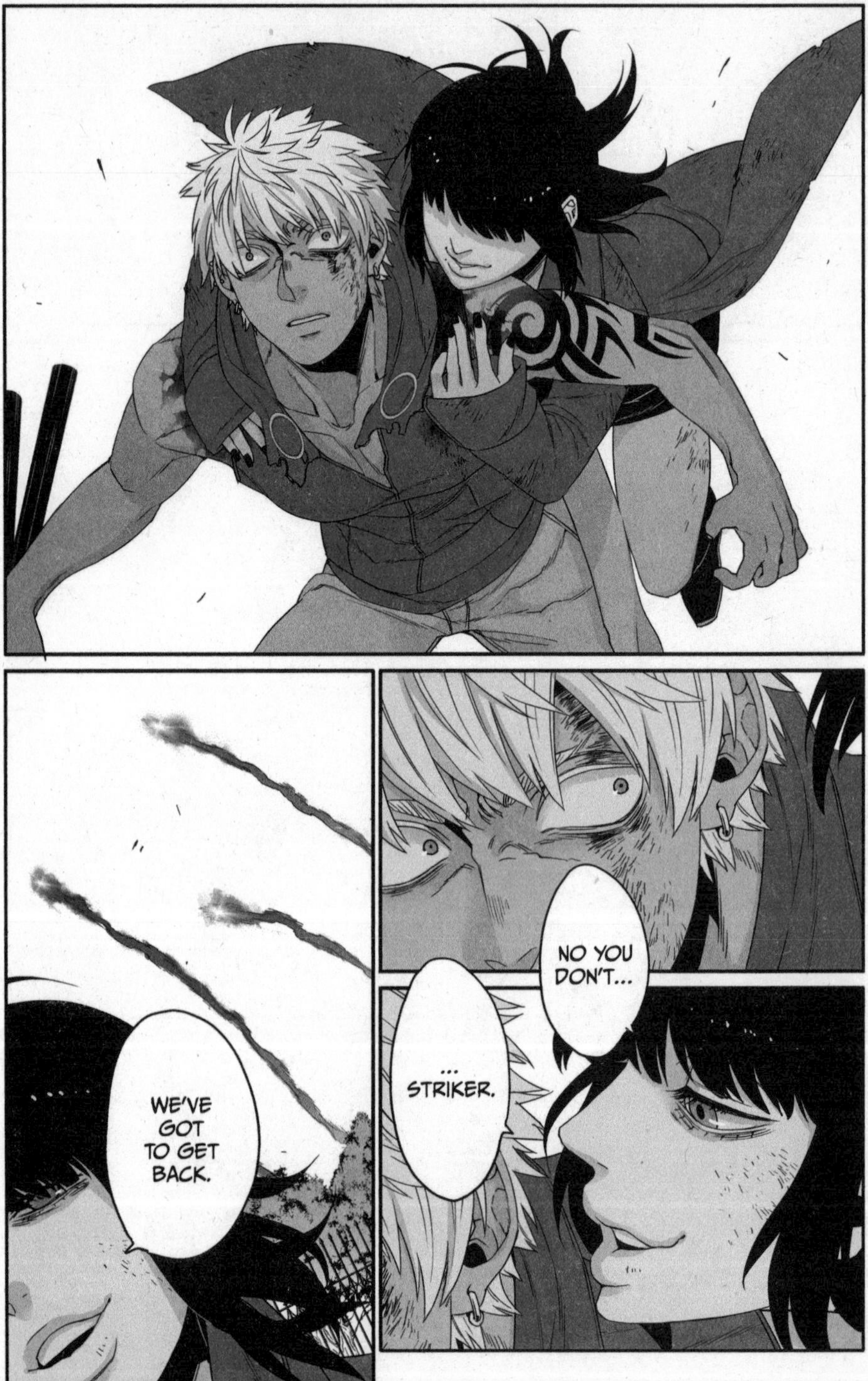
NO YOU DON'T...
... STRIKER.
WE'VE GOT TO GET BACK.

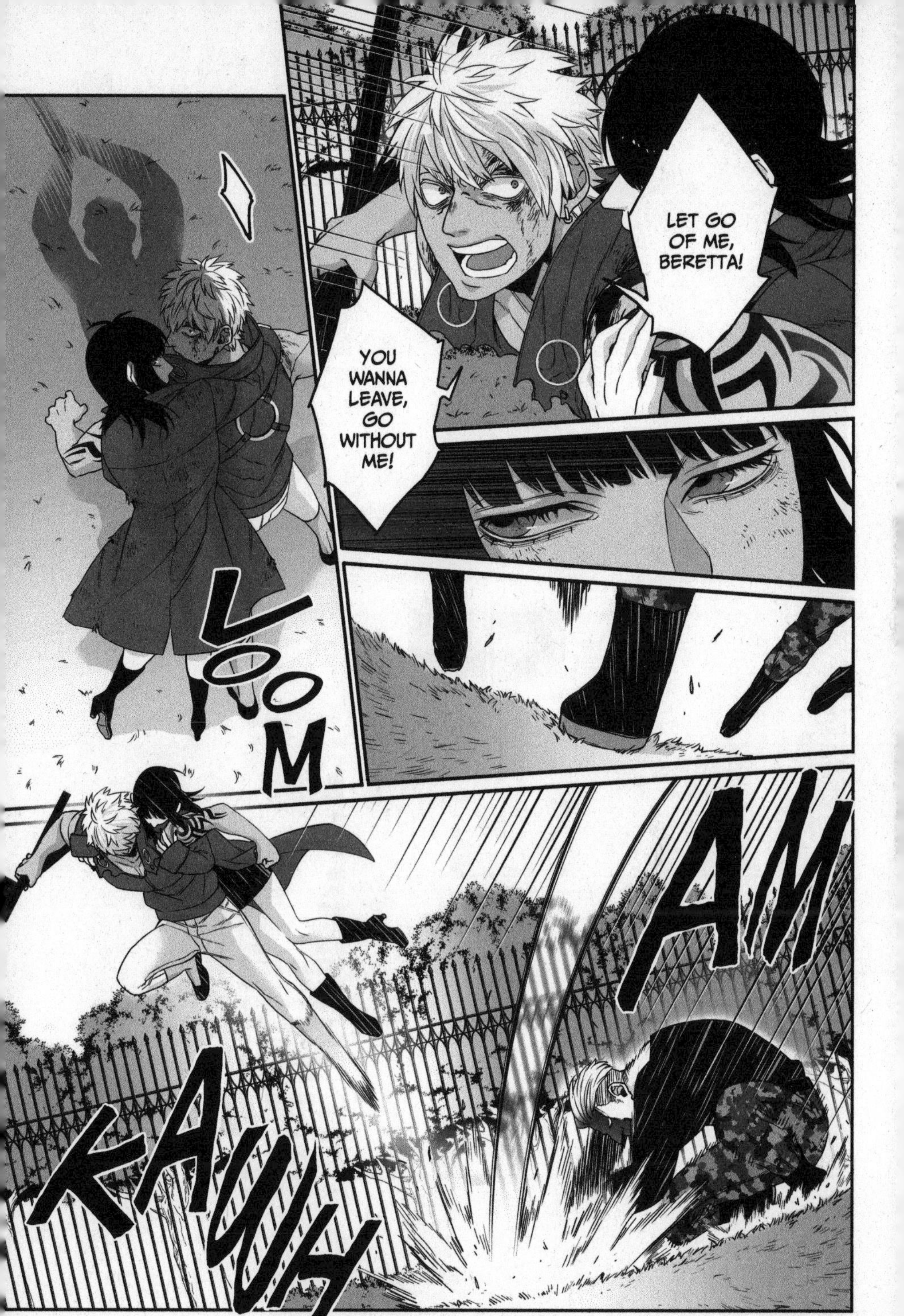
LET GO OF ME, BERETTA!
YOU WANNA LEAVE, GO WITHOUT ME!
VOOOM
KA
AM
KAUUH

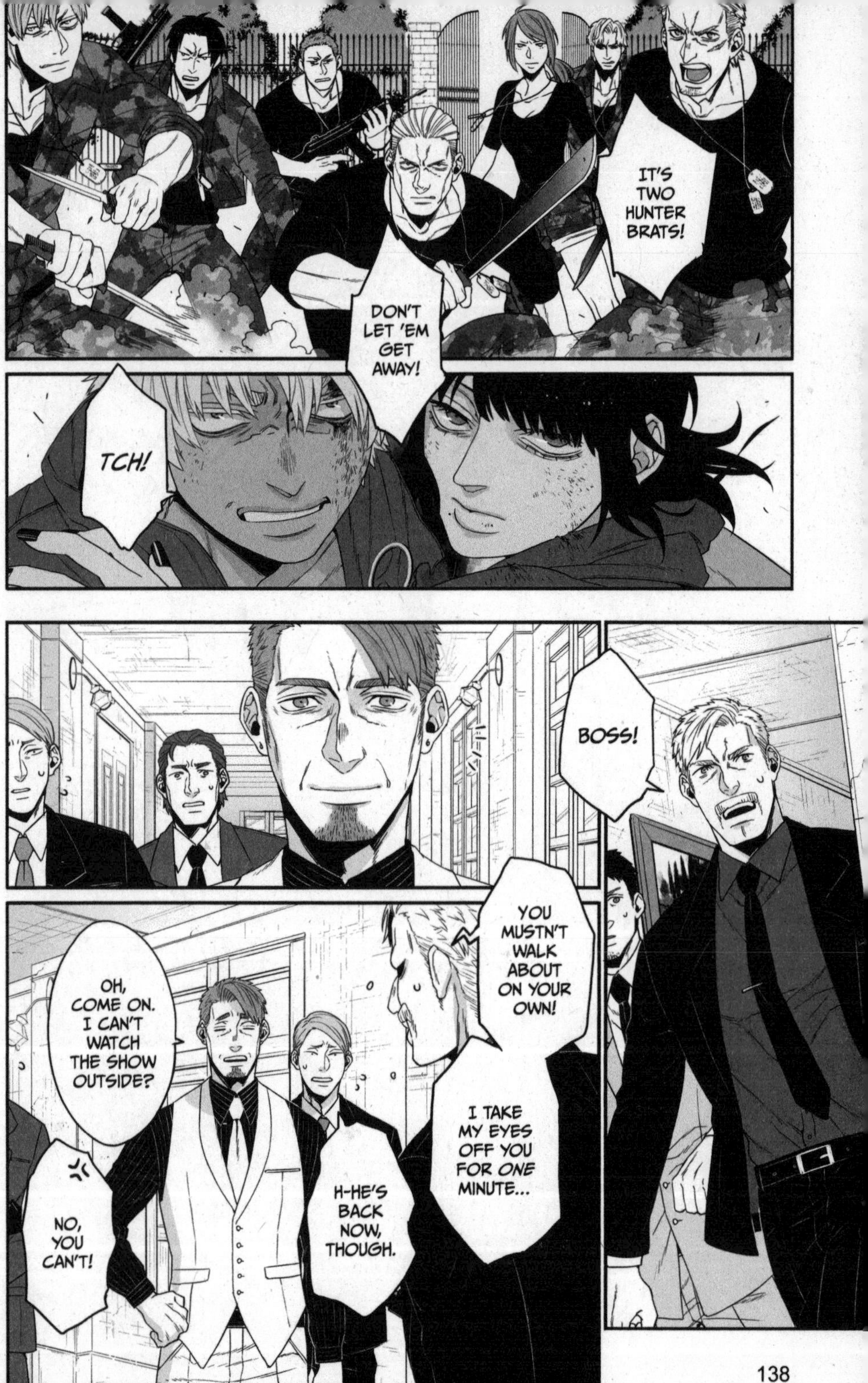
IT'S TWO HUNTER BRATS!
DON'T LET 'EM GET AWAY!
TCH!
BOSS!
YOU MUSTN'T WALK ABOUT ON YOUR OWN!
OH, COME ON. I CAN'T WATCH THE SHOW OUTSIDE?
I TAKE MY EYES OFF YOU FOR *ONE* MINUTE...
H-HE'S BACK NOW, THOUGH.
NO, YOU CAN'T!

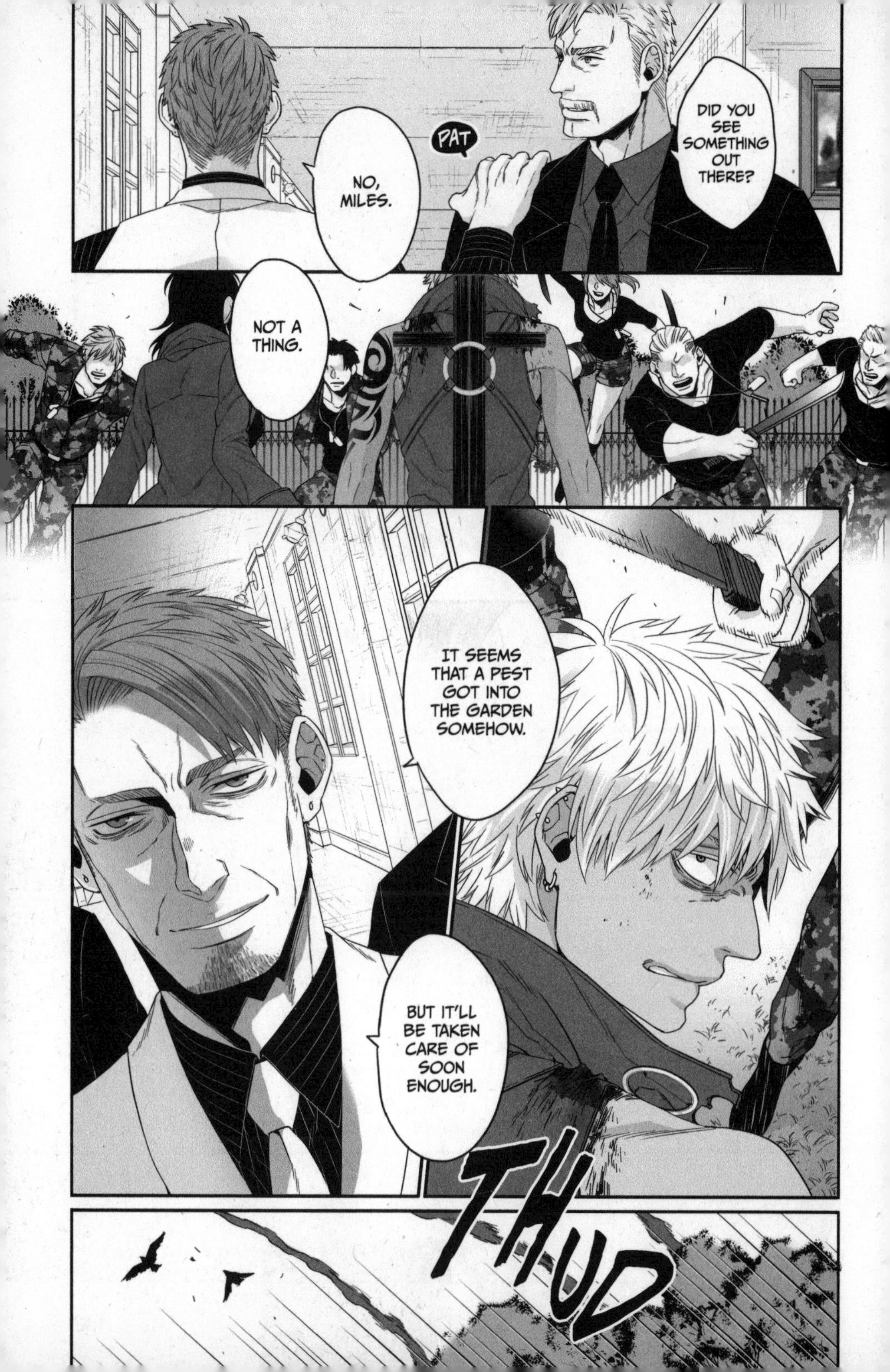
DID YOU SEE SOMETHING OUT THERE?
PAT
NO, MILES.
NOT A THING.
IT SEEMS THAT A PEST GOT INTO THE GARDEN SOMEHOW.
BUT IT'LL BE TAKEN CARE OF SOON ENOUGH.
THUD

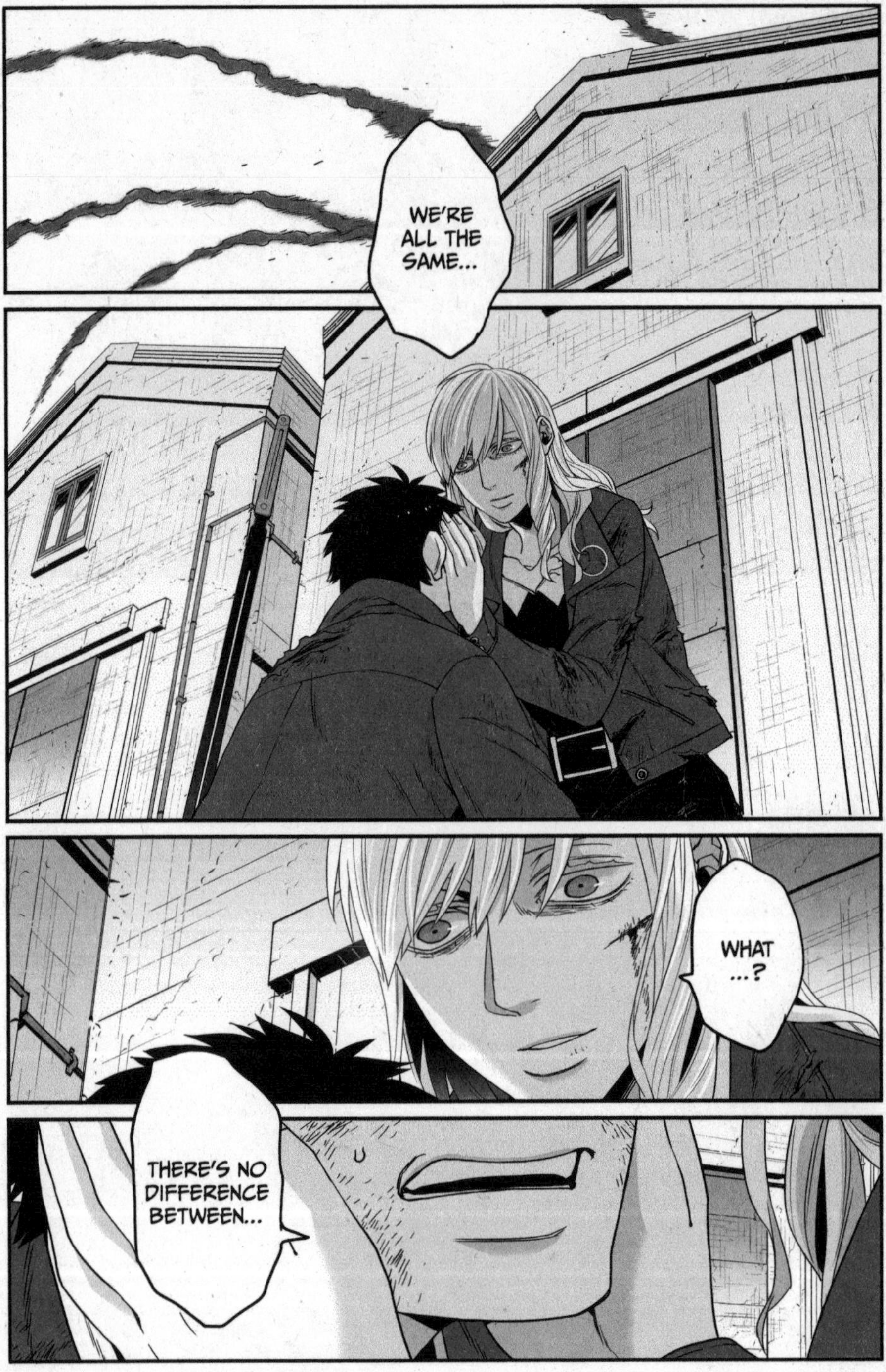
WE'RE ALL THE SAME...
WHAT ...?
THERE'S NO DIFFERENCE BETWEEN...

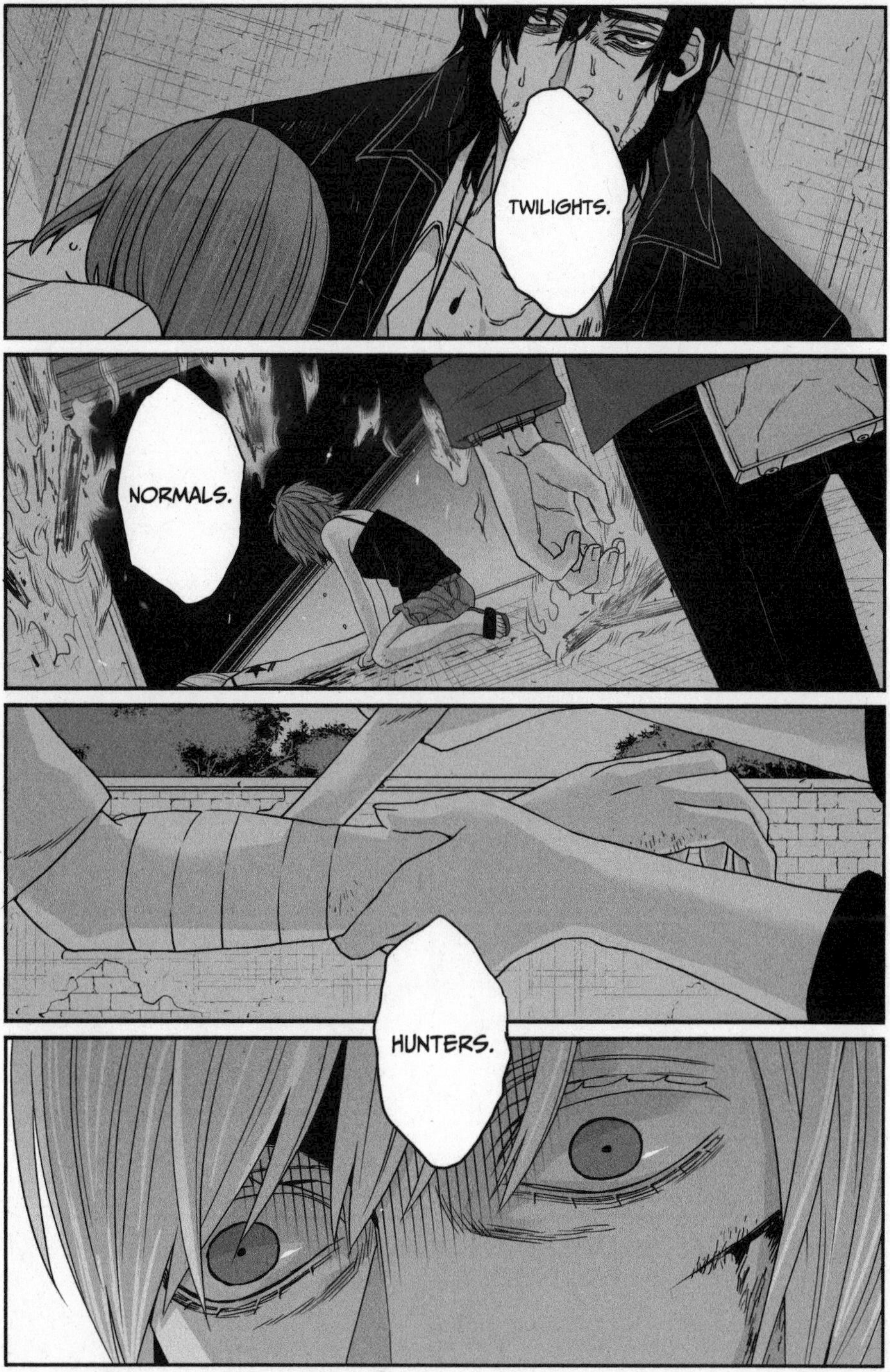
TWILIGHTS.
NORMALS.
HUNTERS.

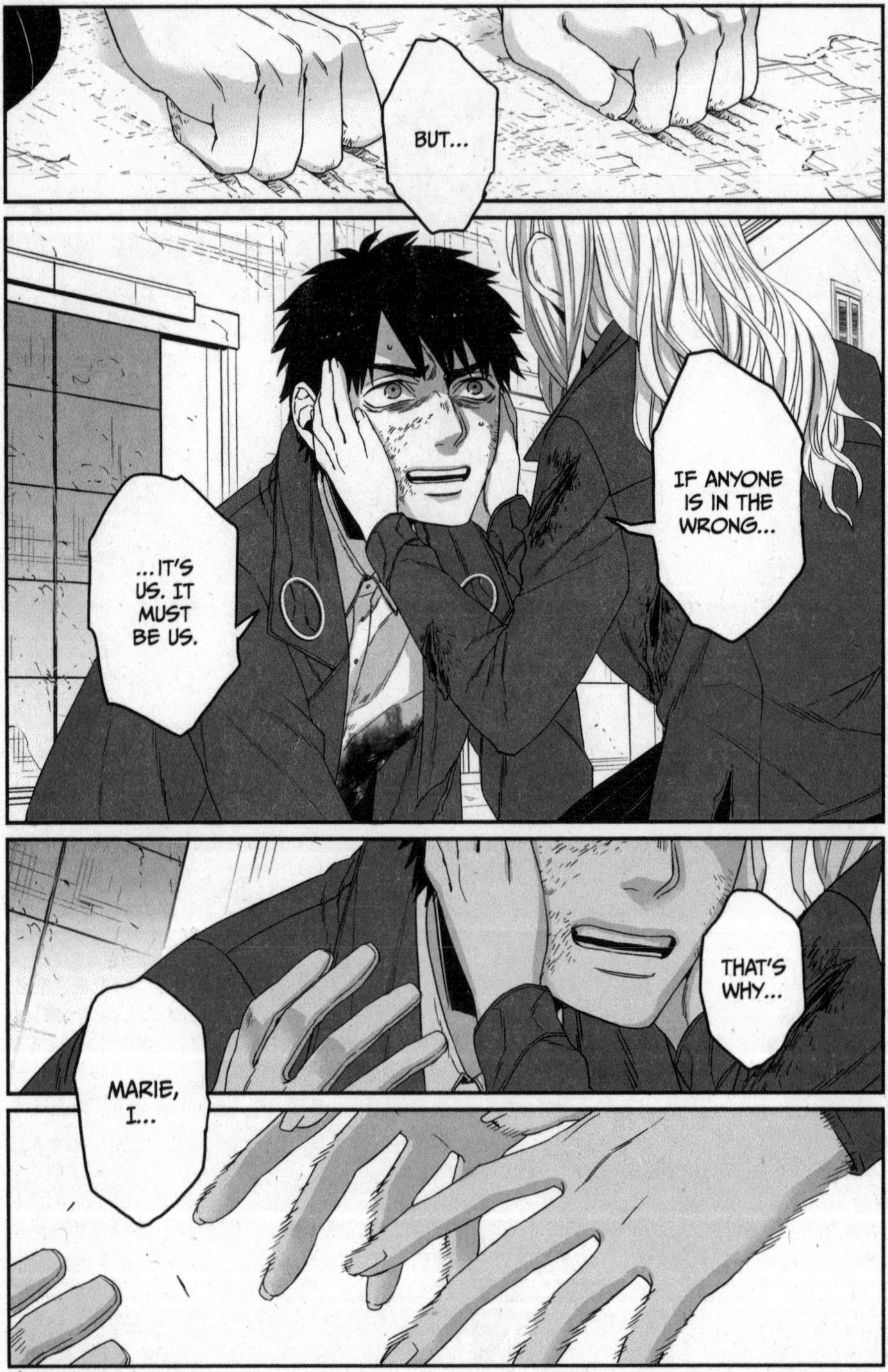
BUT...
IF ANYONE IS IN THE WRONG...
...IT'S US. IT MUST BE US.
THAT'S WHY...
MARIE, I...

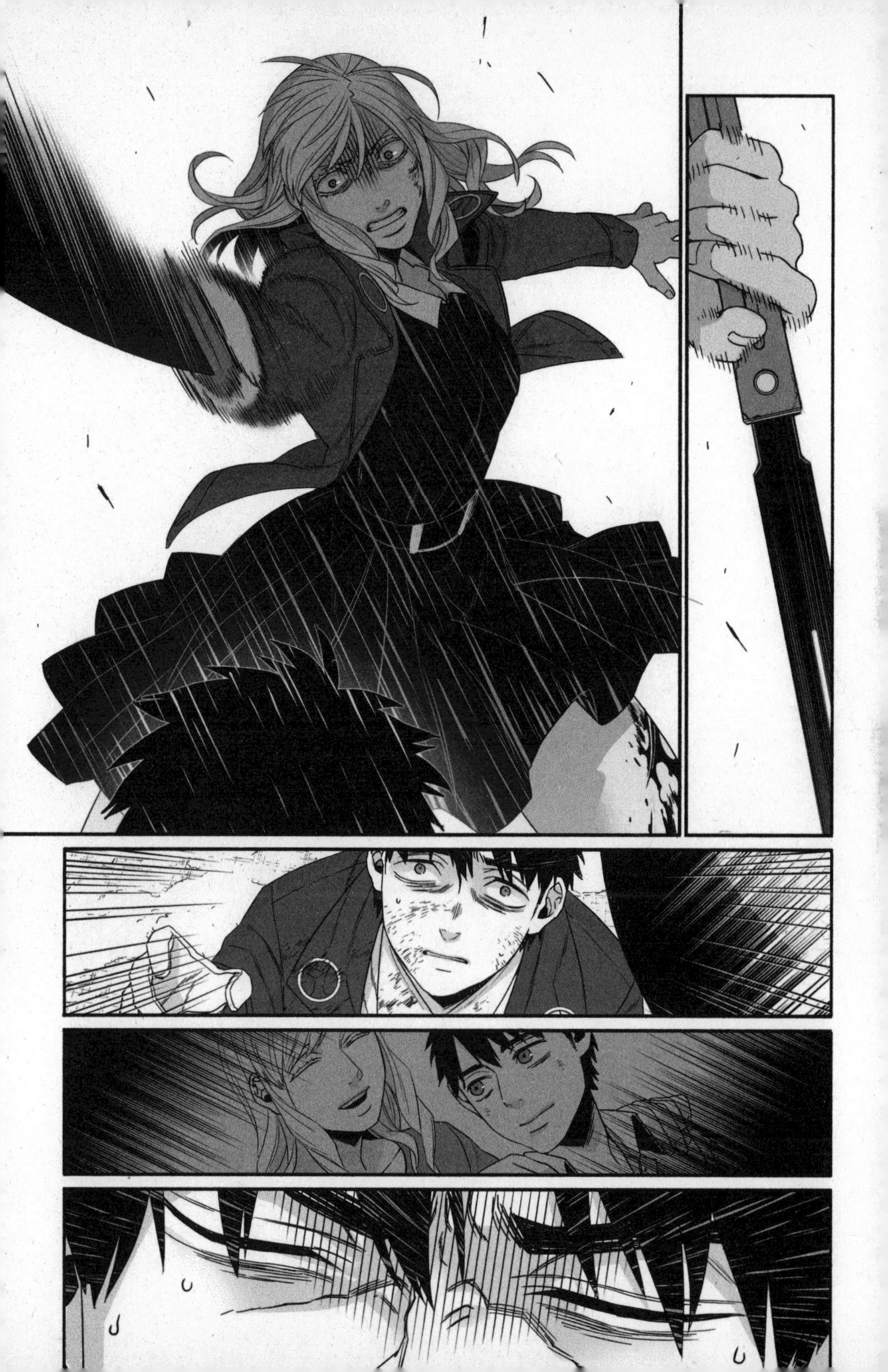

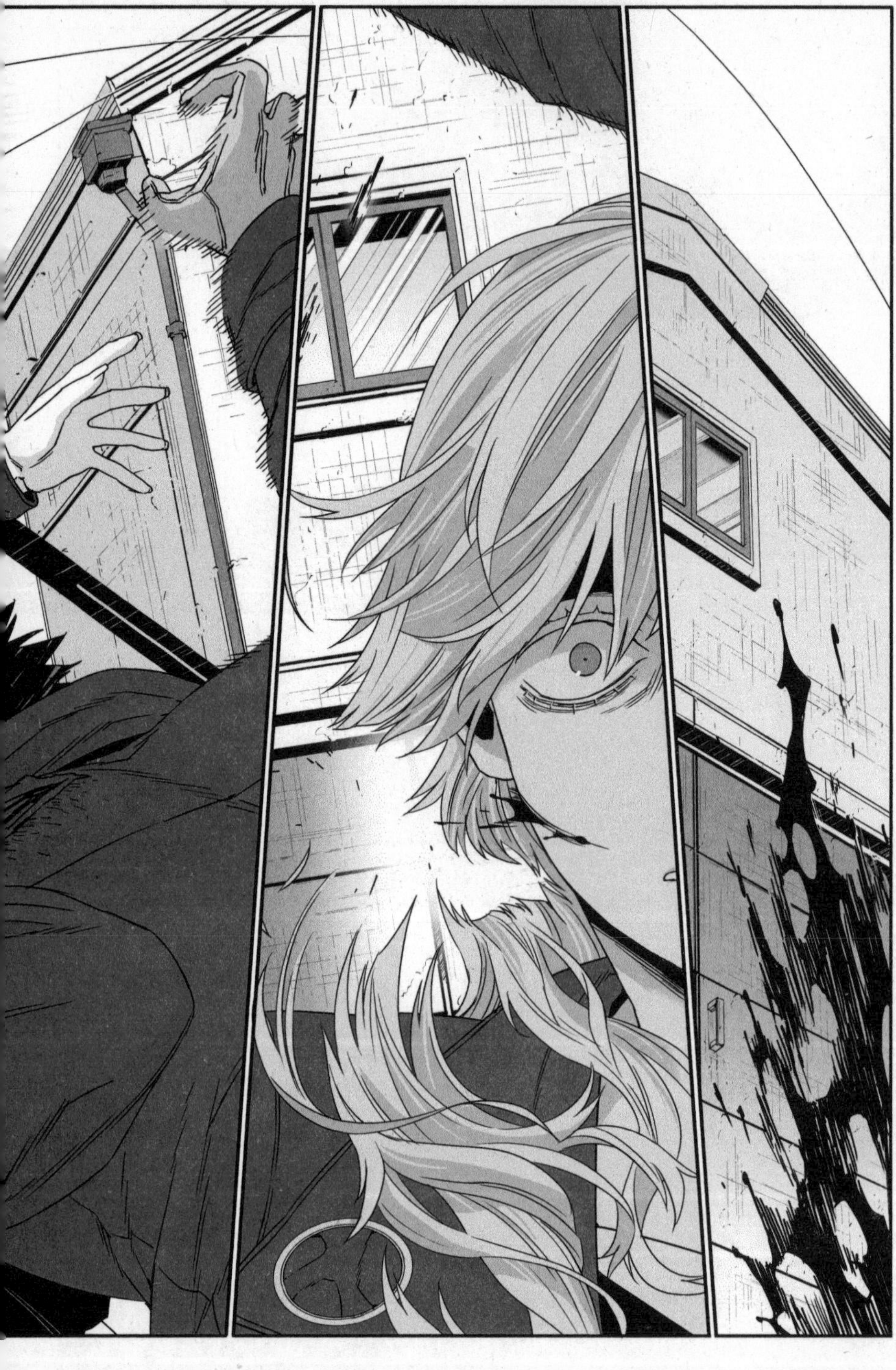

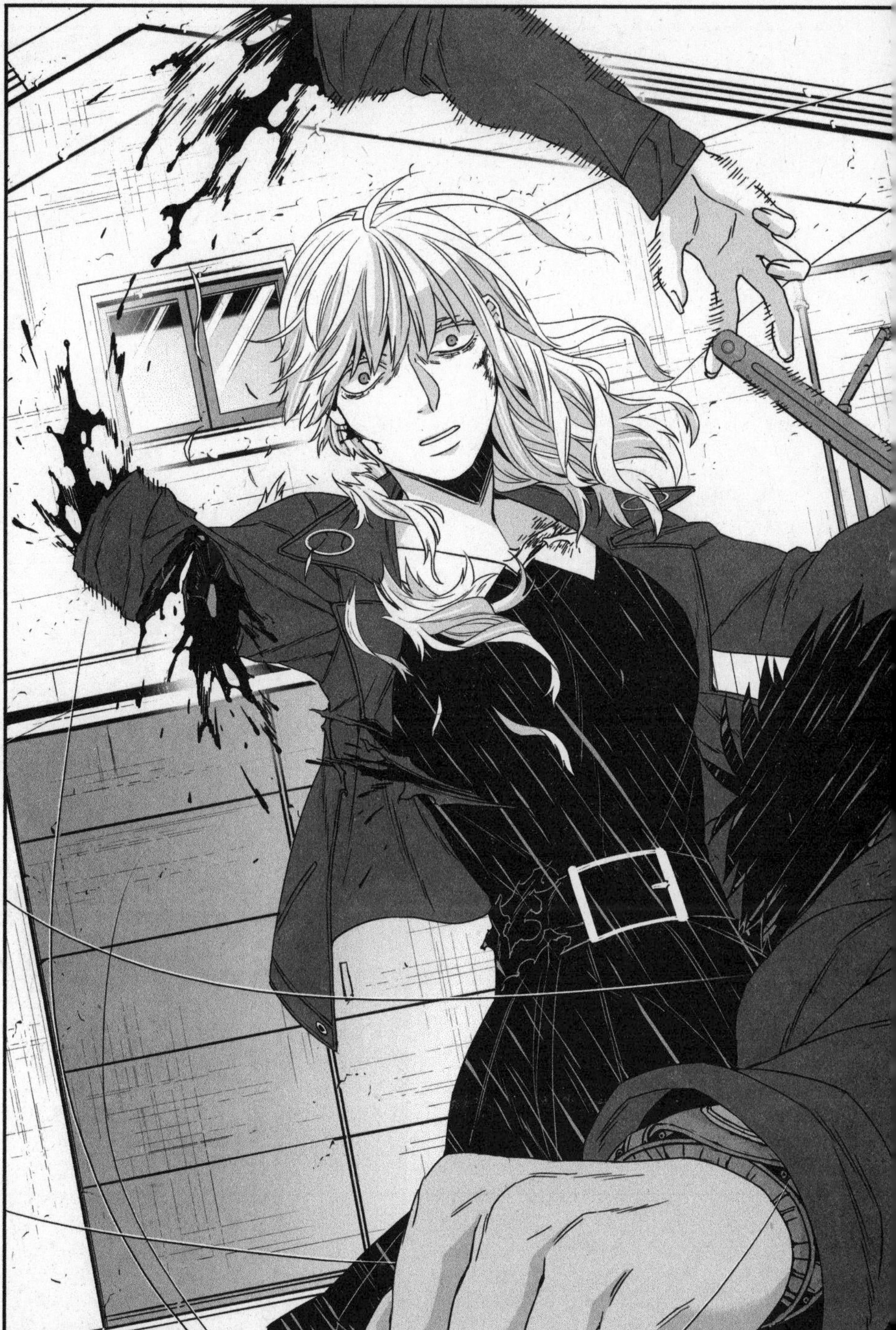

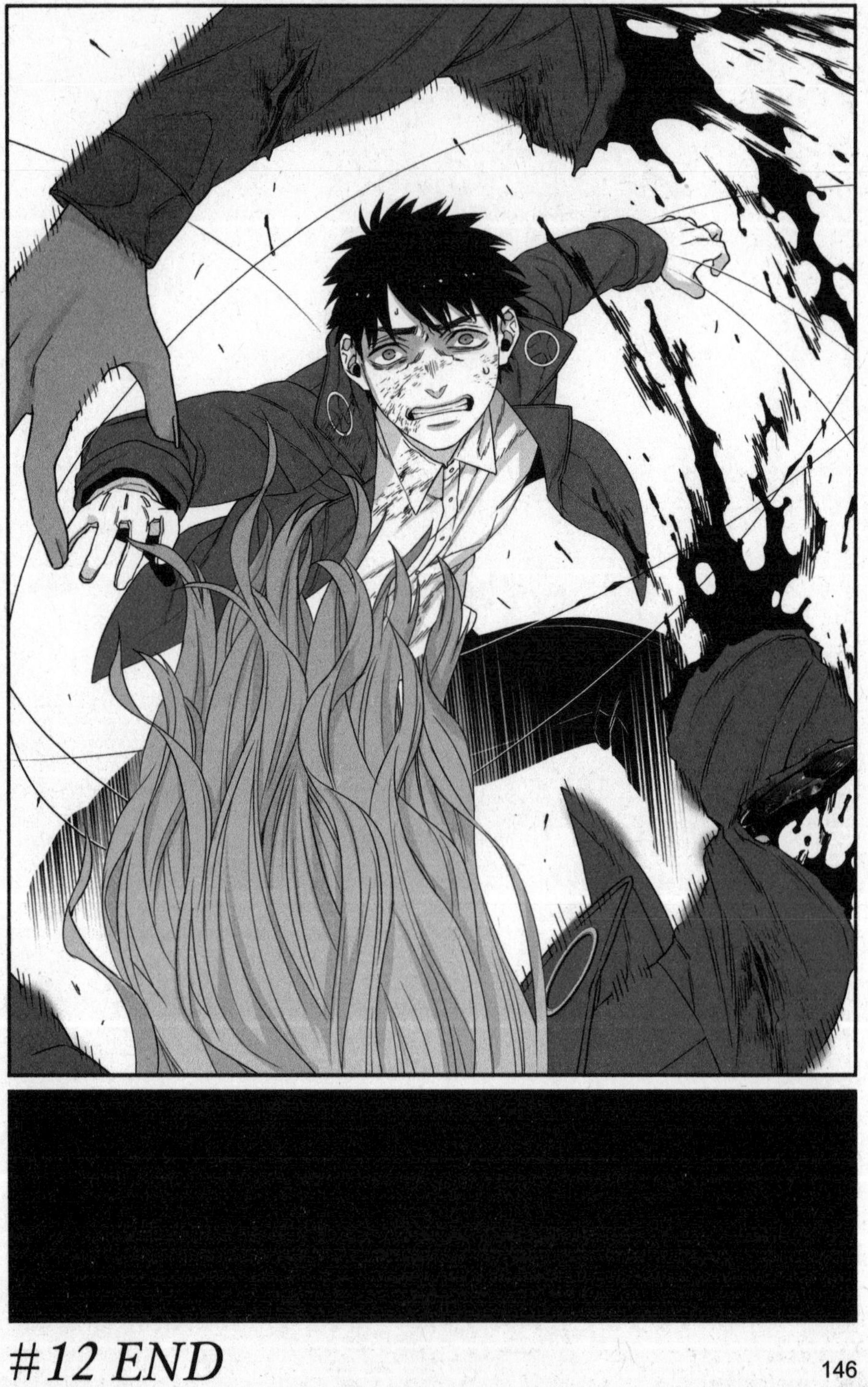

#12 END

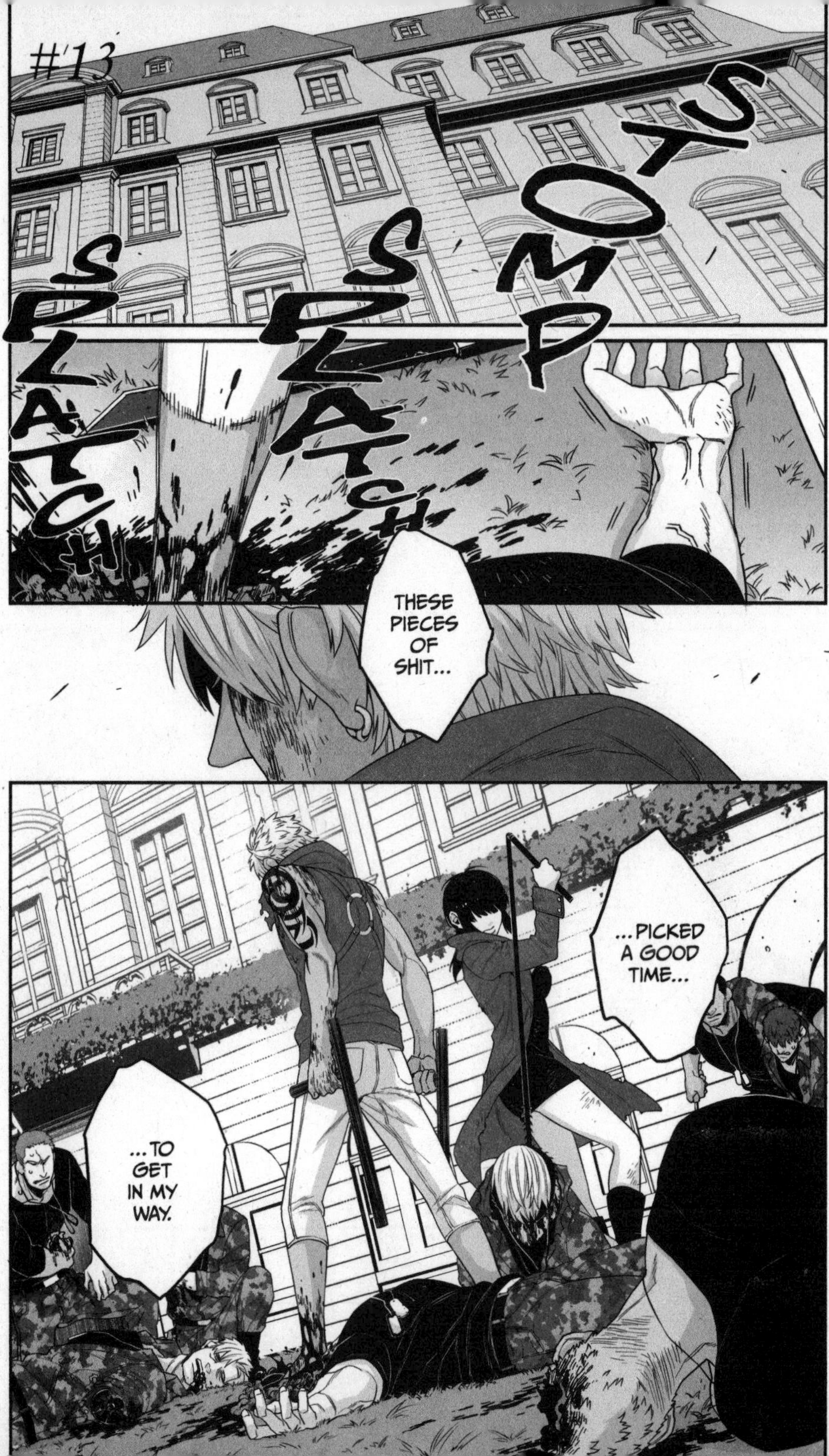
#13
STOMP
SPLATCH
SPLATCH
THESE PIECES OF SHIT...
...PICKED A GOOD TIME...
...TO GET IN MY WAY.

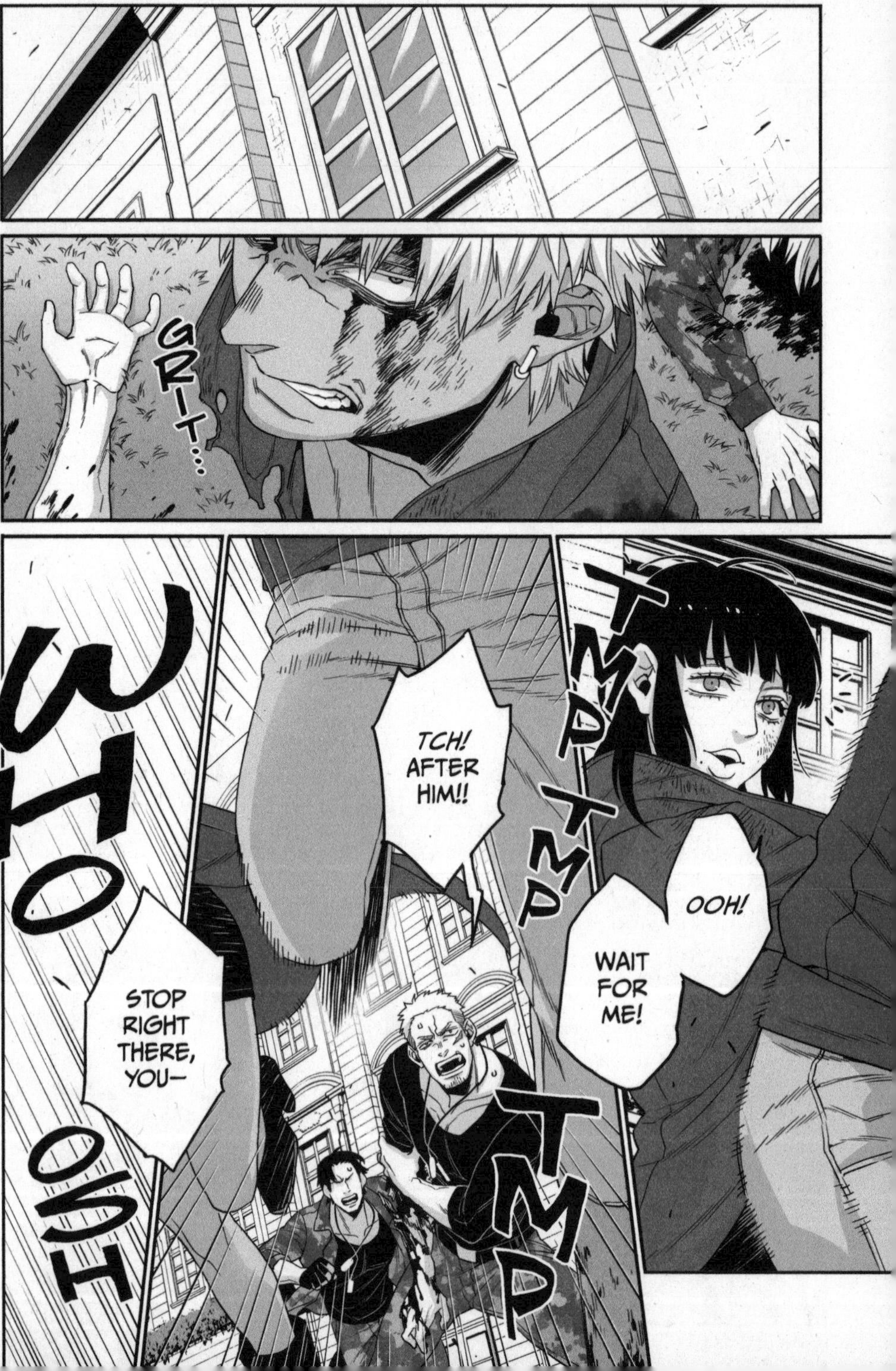
GRIT...
TMP TMP
OOH!
WAIT FOR ME!
TCH! AFTER HIM!!
TMP
STOP RIGHT THERE, YOU—
WHOOSH

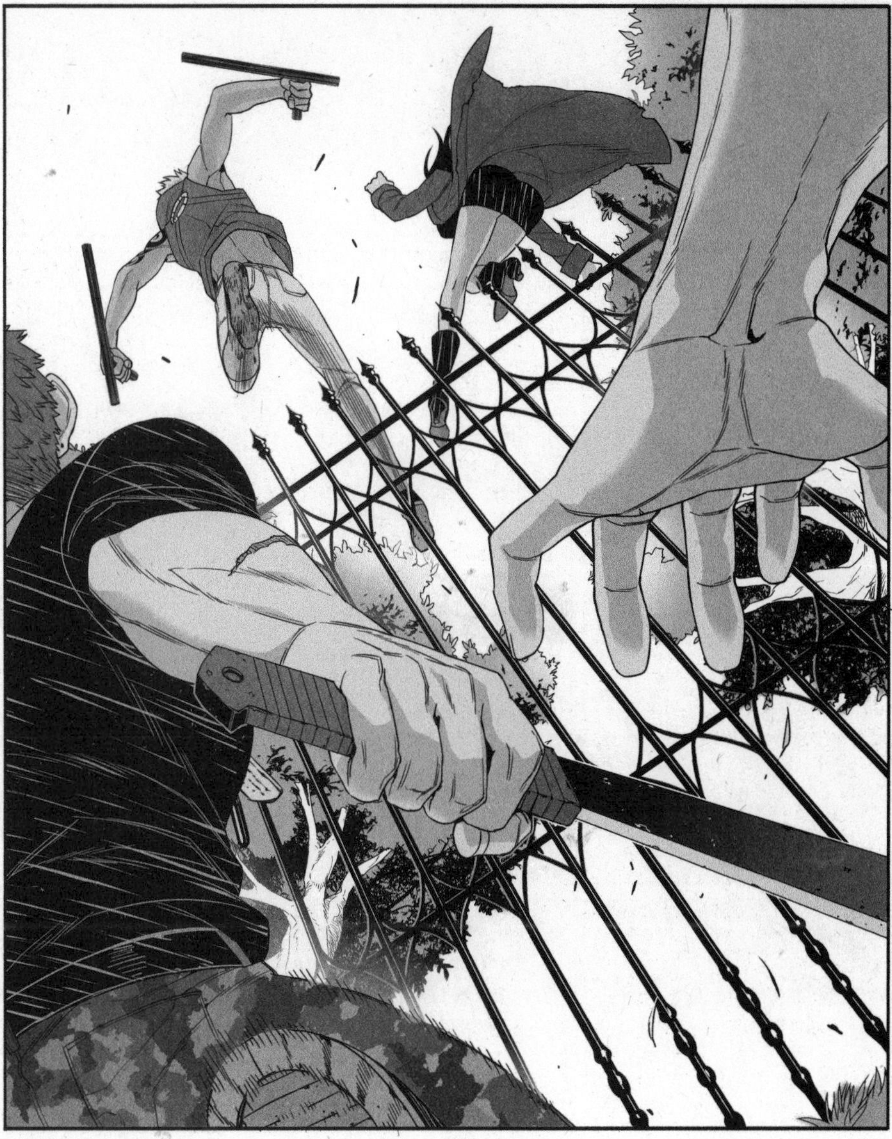

#13

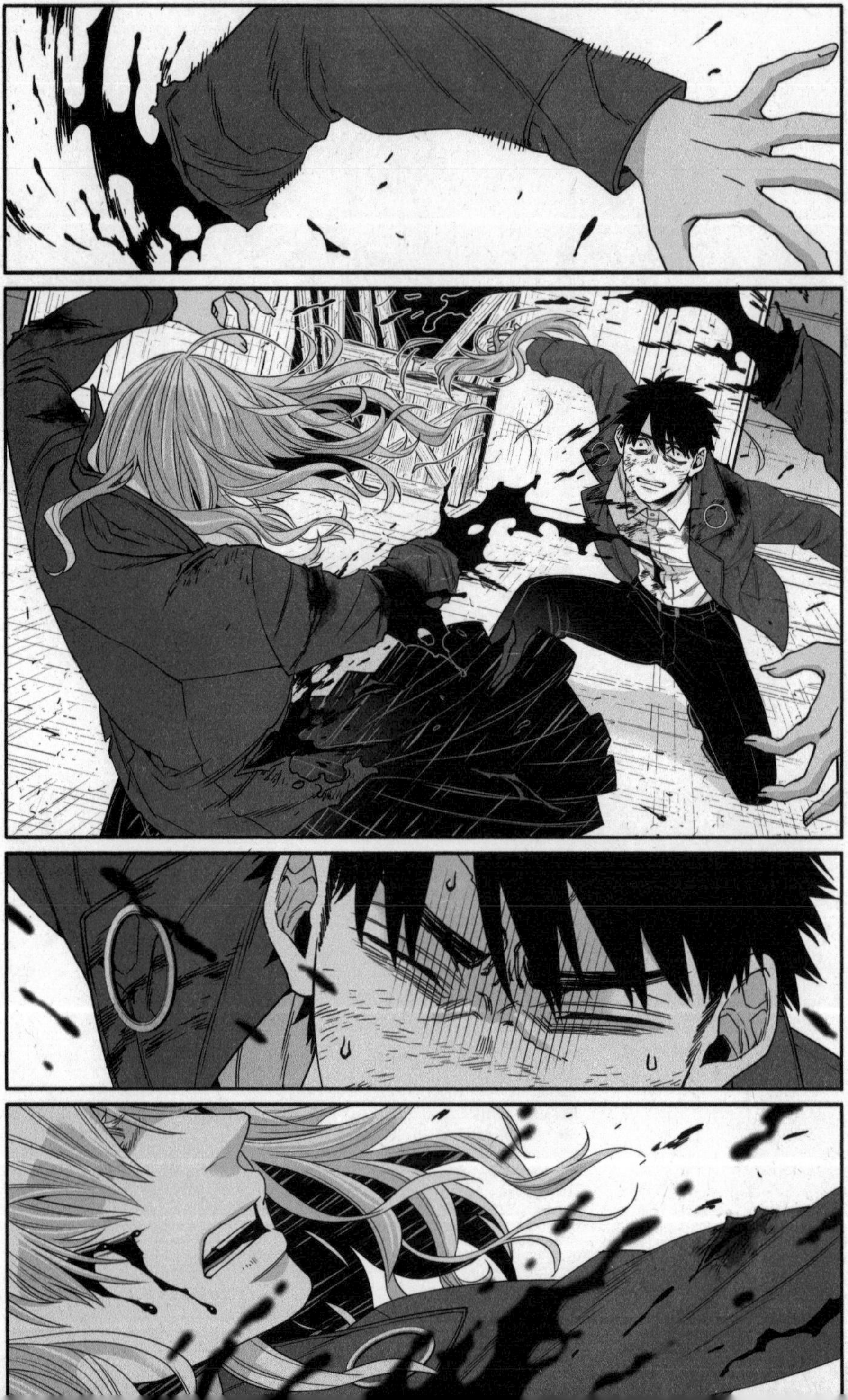

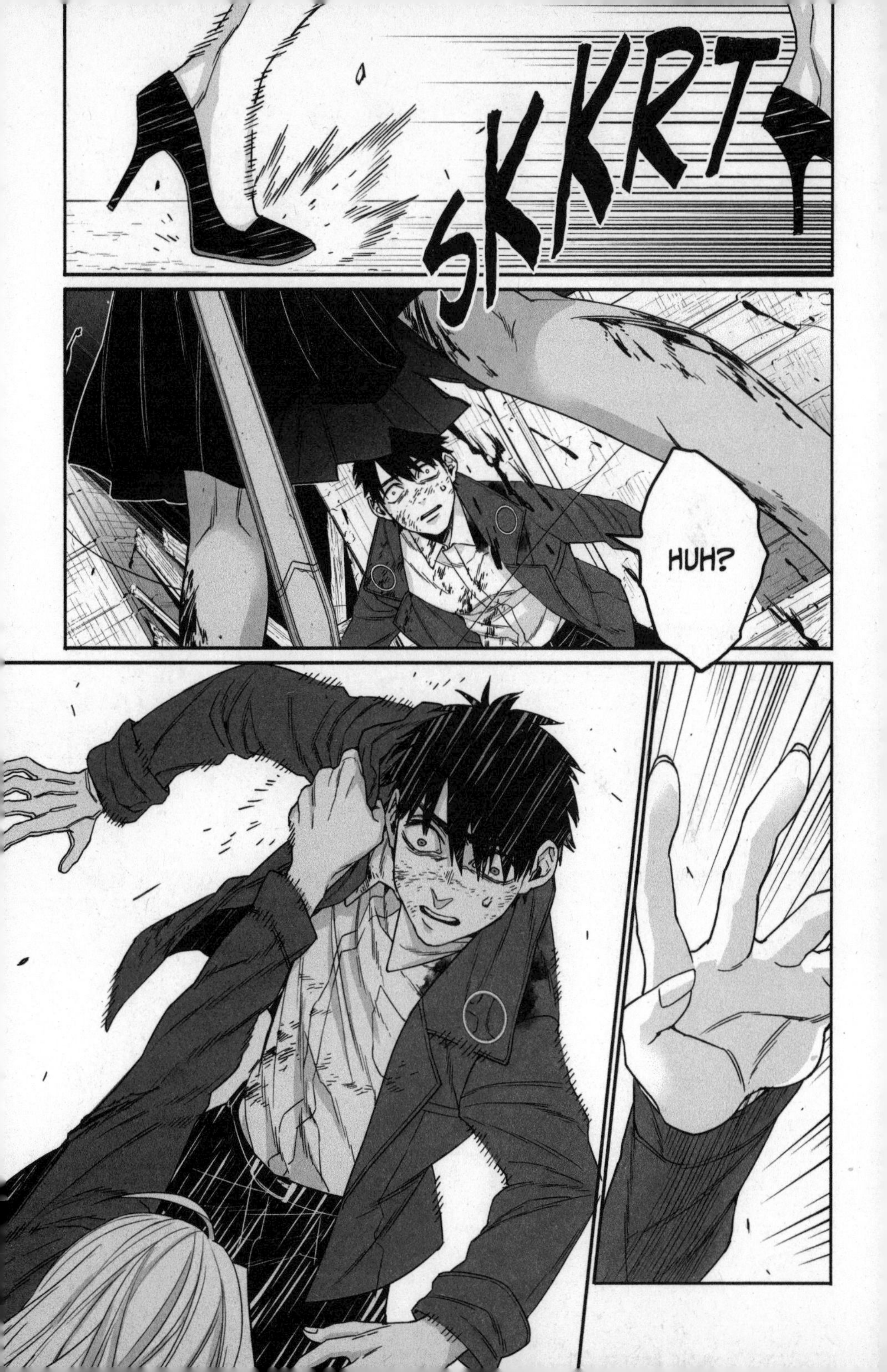
SKKRT
HUH?

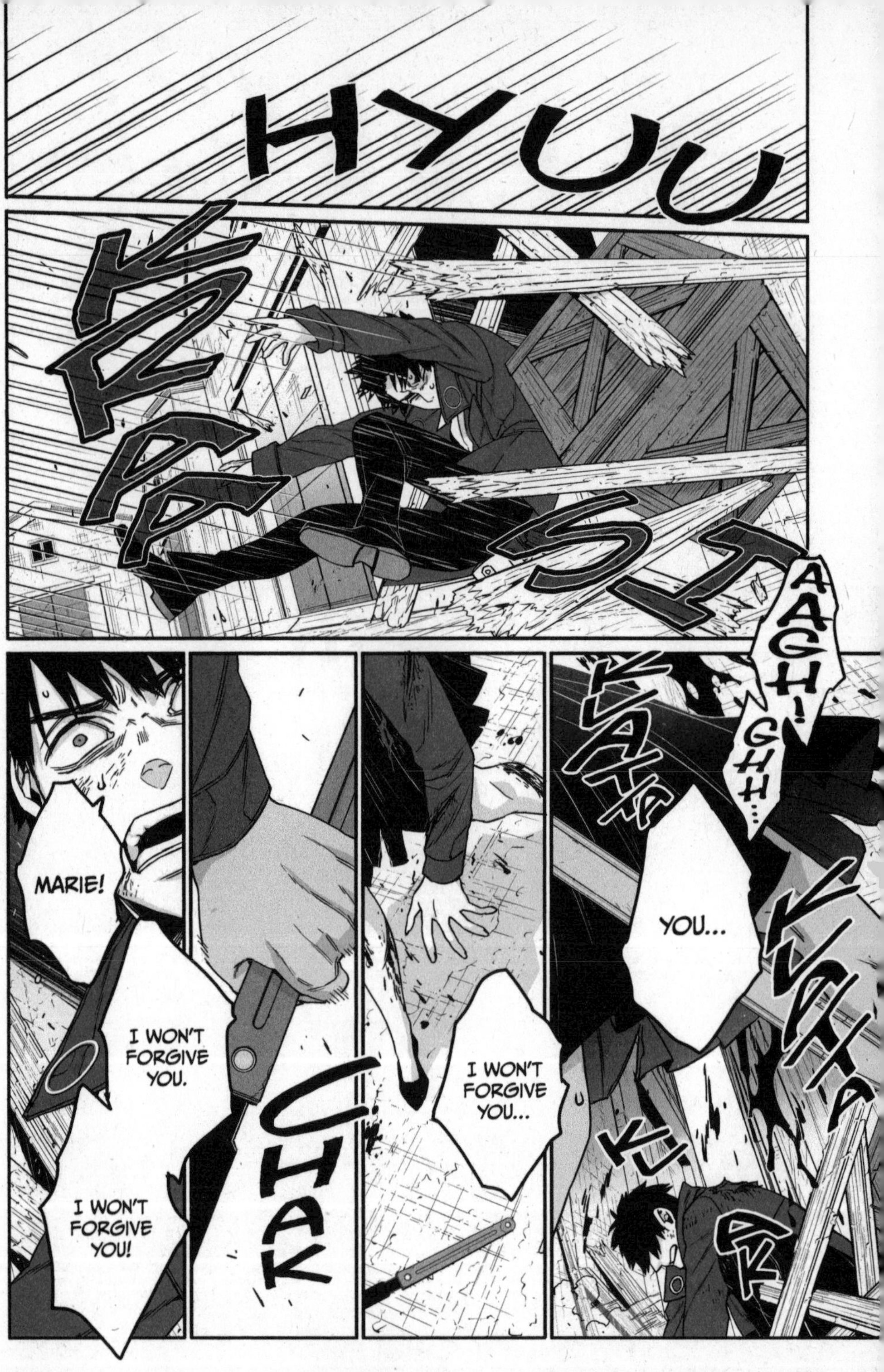
HYUU
AAGH!
GHH...
YOU...
KU
I WON'T FORGIVE YOU...
CHAK
MARIE!
I WON'T FORGIVE YOU.
I WON'T FORGIVE YOU!

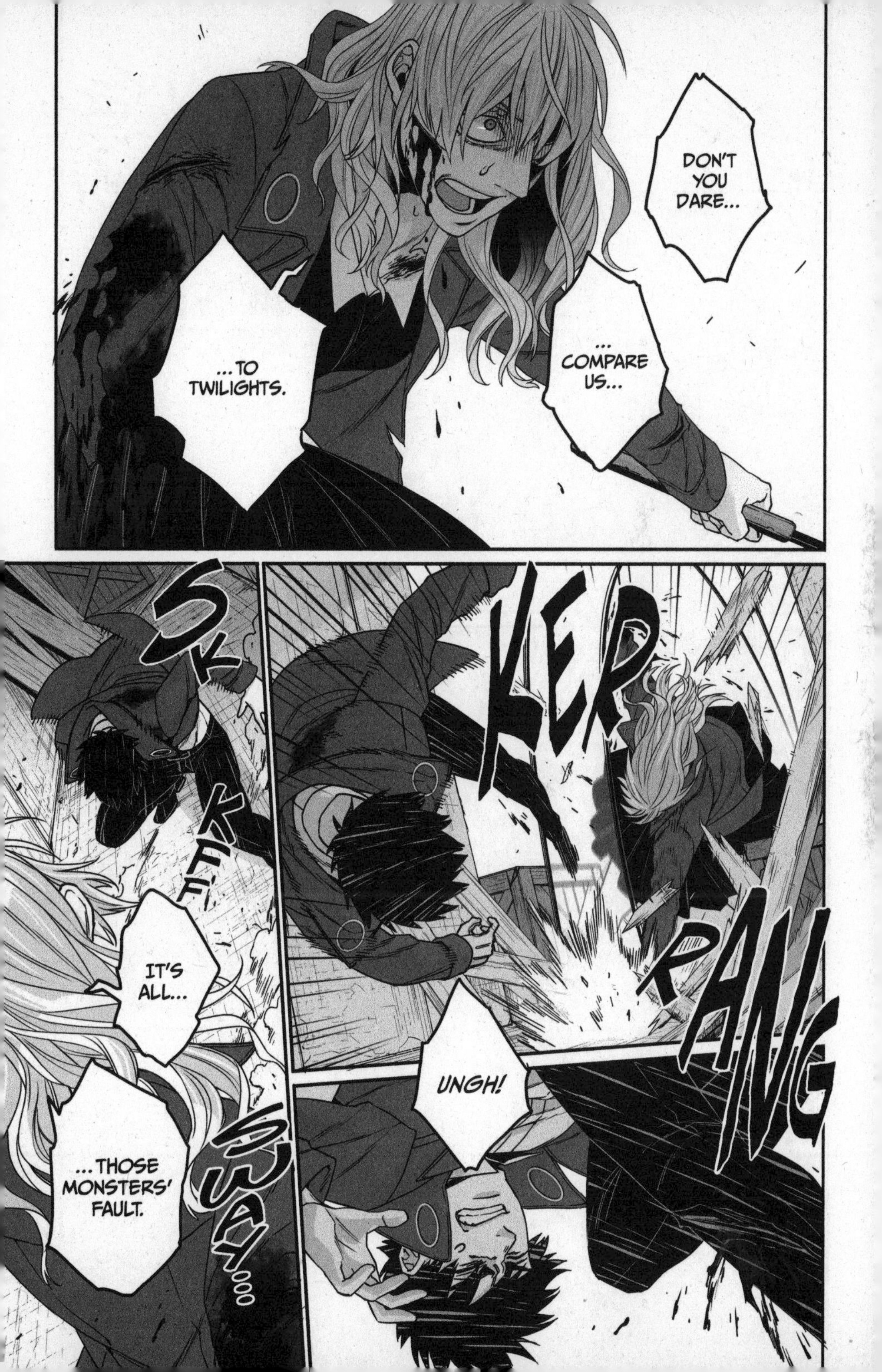
DON'T YOU DARE...
...COMPARE US...
...TO TWILIGHTS.
KERRANG
UNGH!
SKKFF
IT'S ALL...
...THOSE MONSTERS' FAULT.

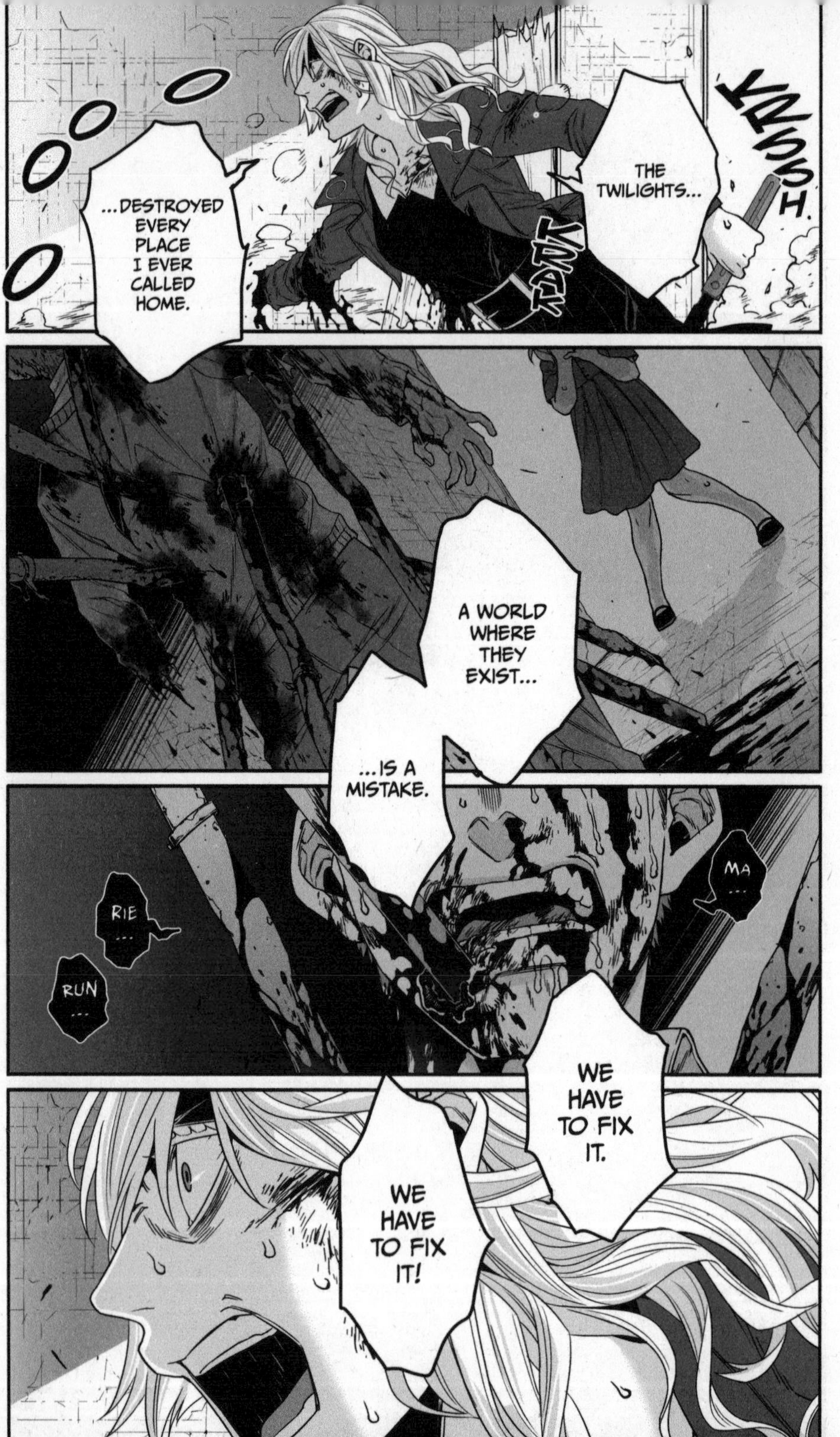
KRSSH.
THE TWILIGHTS...
KRAK
...DESTROYED EVERY PLACE I EVER CALLED HOME.
OOOOO
A WORLD WHERE THEY EXIST...
...IS A MISTAKE.
MA...
RIE...
RUN...
WE HAVE TO FIX IT.
WE HAVE TO FIX IT!

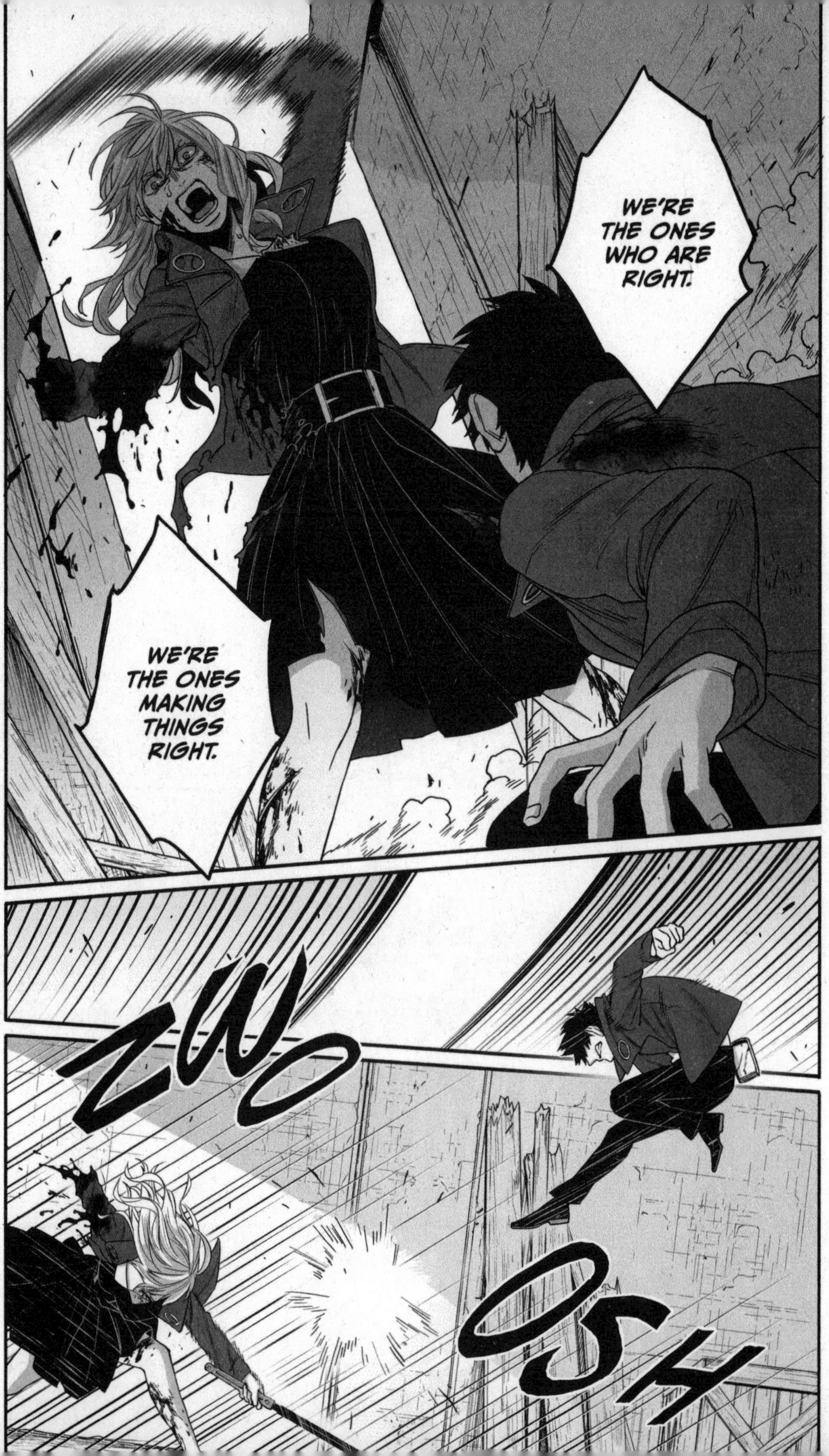
WE'RE THE ONES WHO ARE RIGHT.
WE'RE THE ONES MAKING THINGS RIGHT.
ZWOOSH

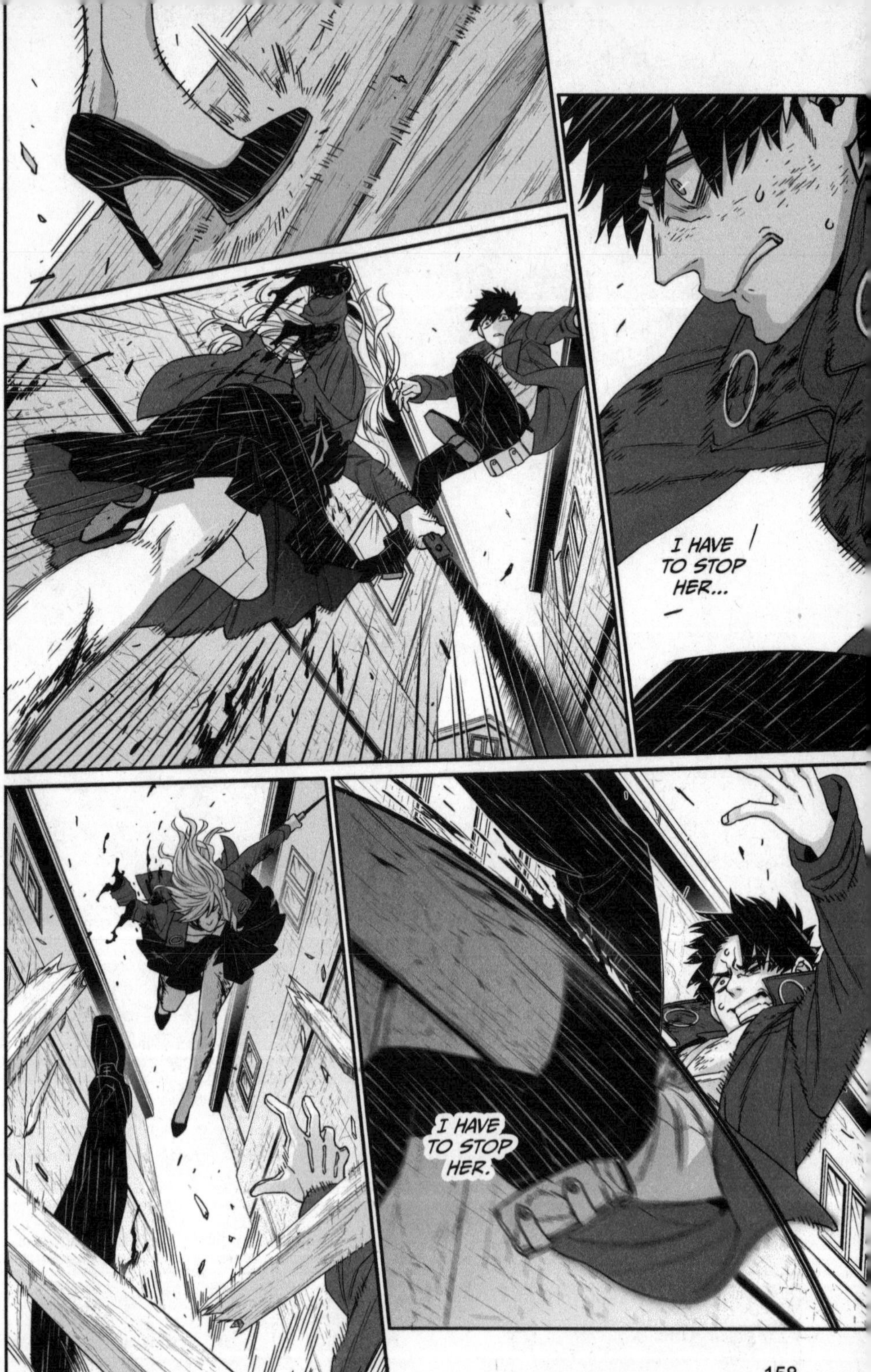
I HAVE TO STOP HER...
I HAVE TO STOP HER.

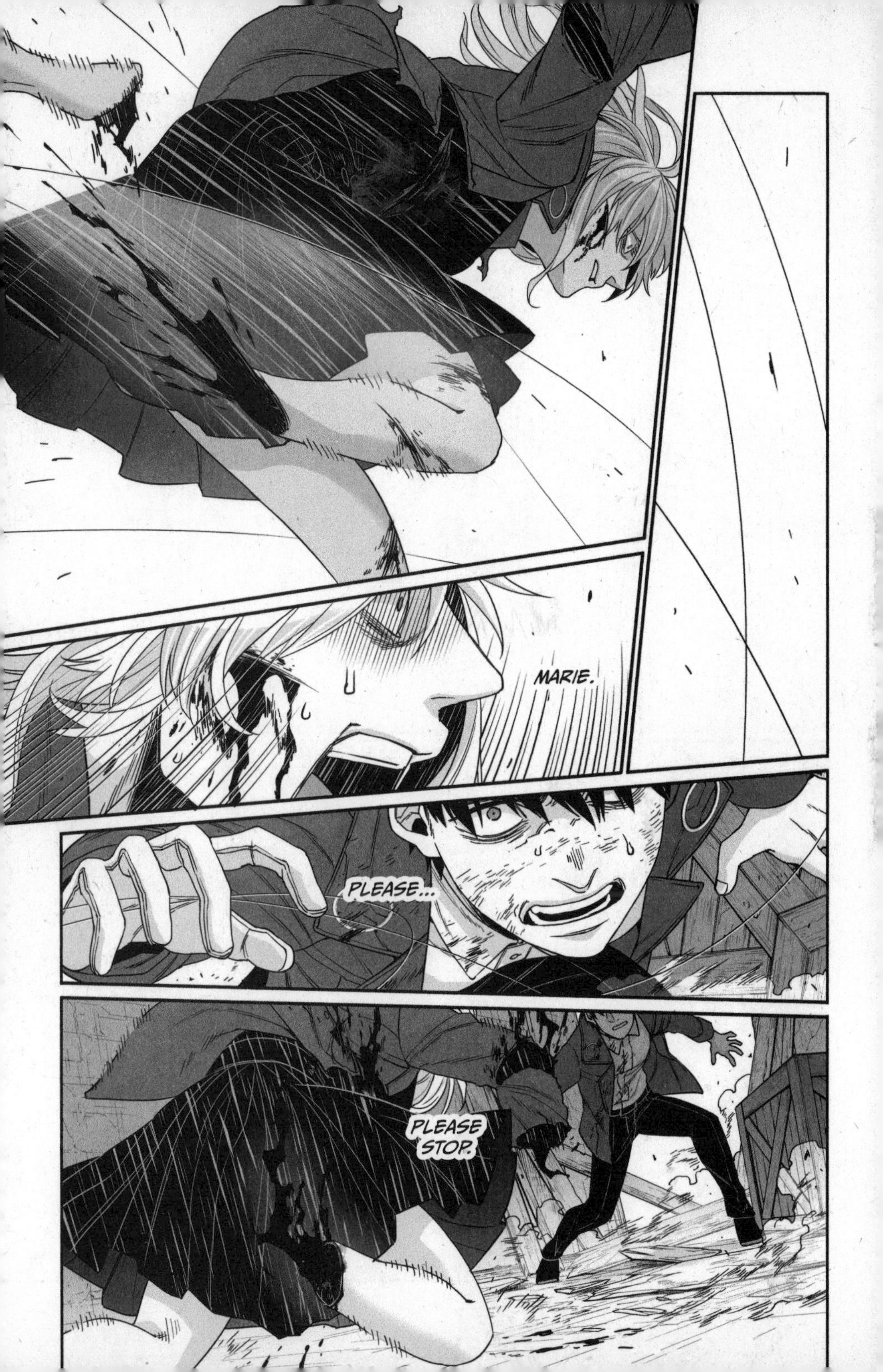
MARIE.
PLEASE...
PLEASE STOP.

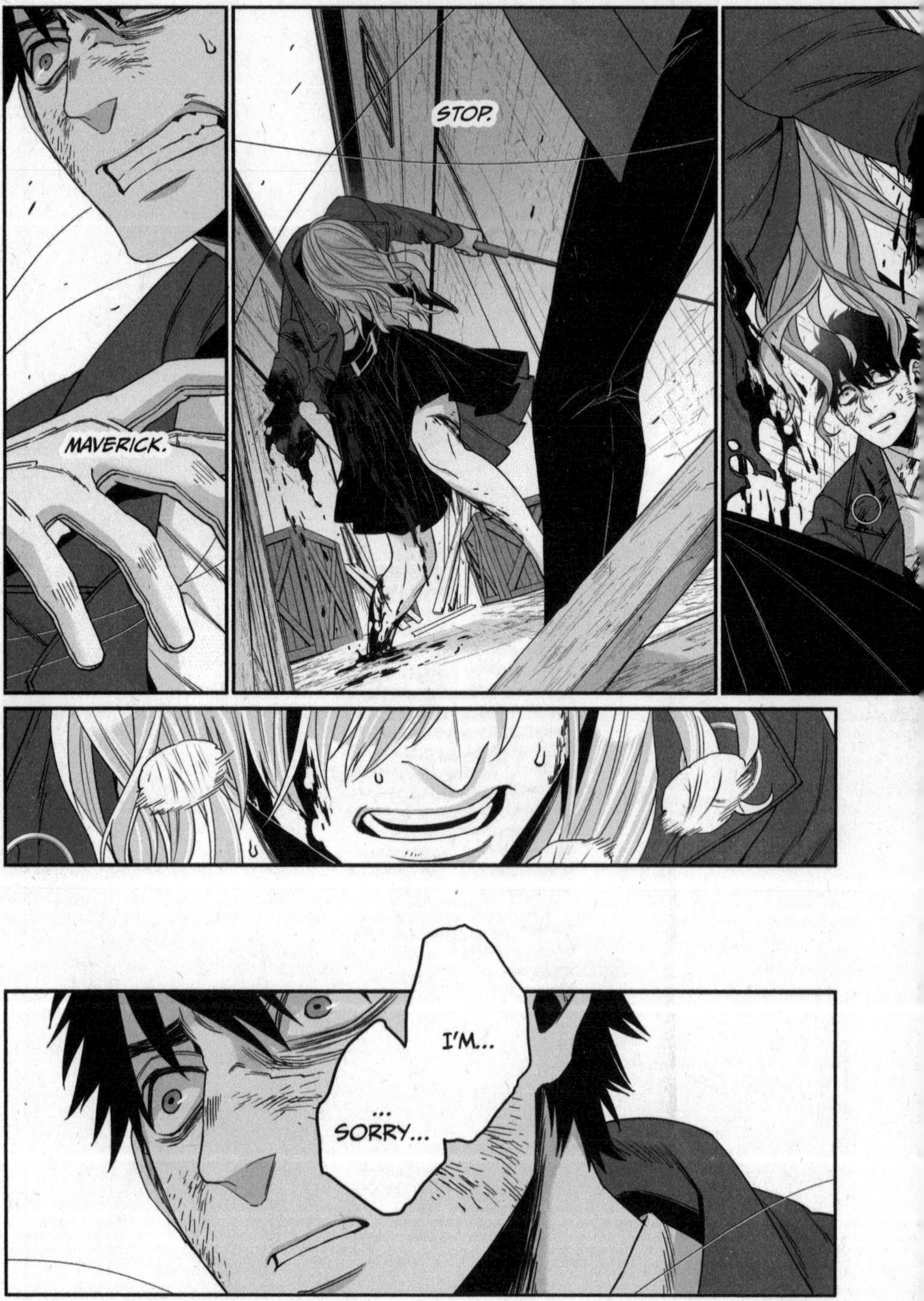
STOP.
MAVERICK.
I'M...
... SORRY...

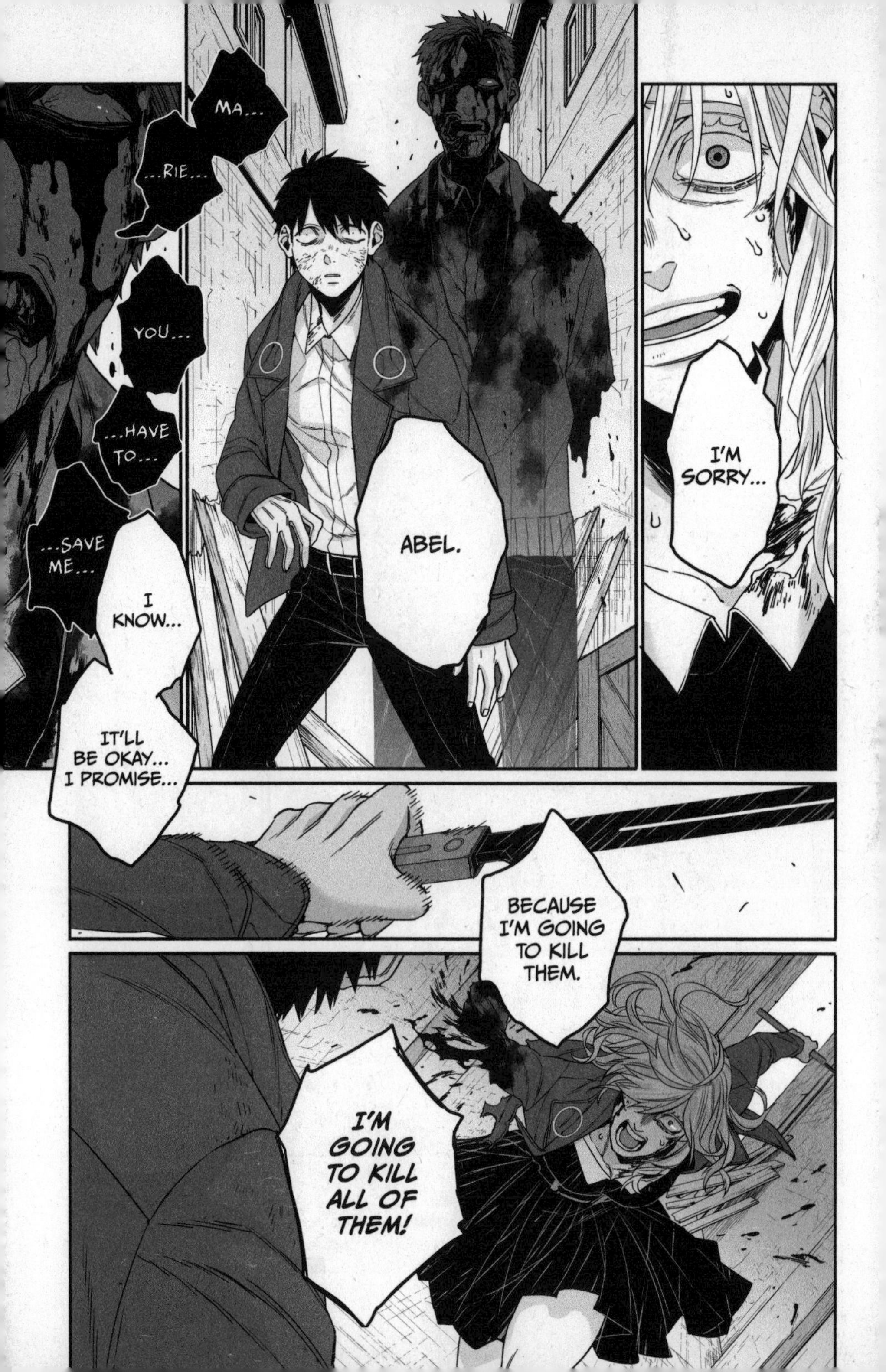
I'M SORRY...
ABEL.
MA...
...RIE...
YOU...
...HAVE TO...
...SAVE ME...
I KNOW...
IT'LL BE OKAY... I PROMISE...
BECAUSE I'M GOING TO KILL THEM.
I'M GOING TO KILL ALL OF THEM!

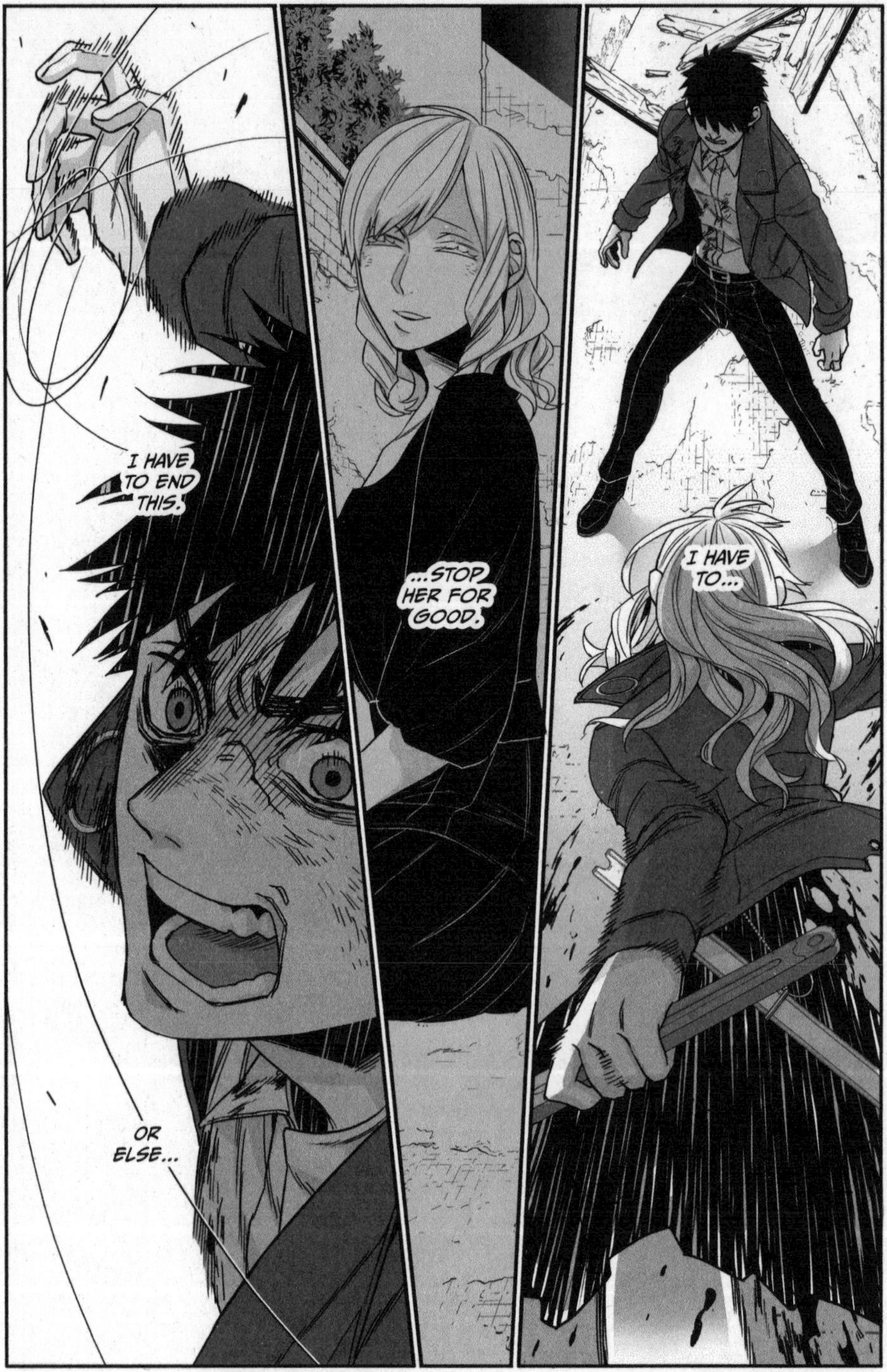
I HAVE TO...
...STOP HER FOR GOOD.
I HAVE TO END THIS.
OR ELSE...

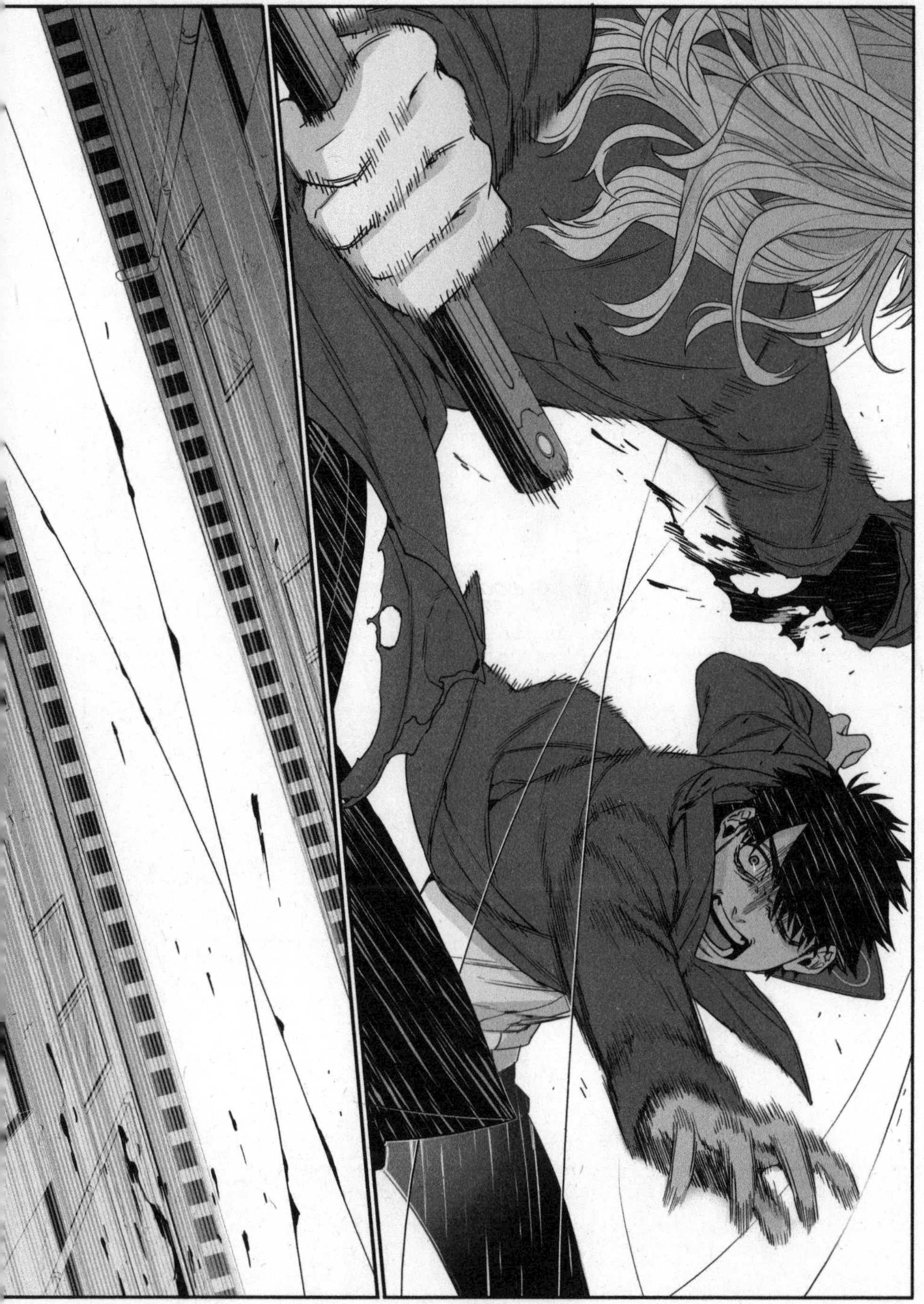

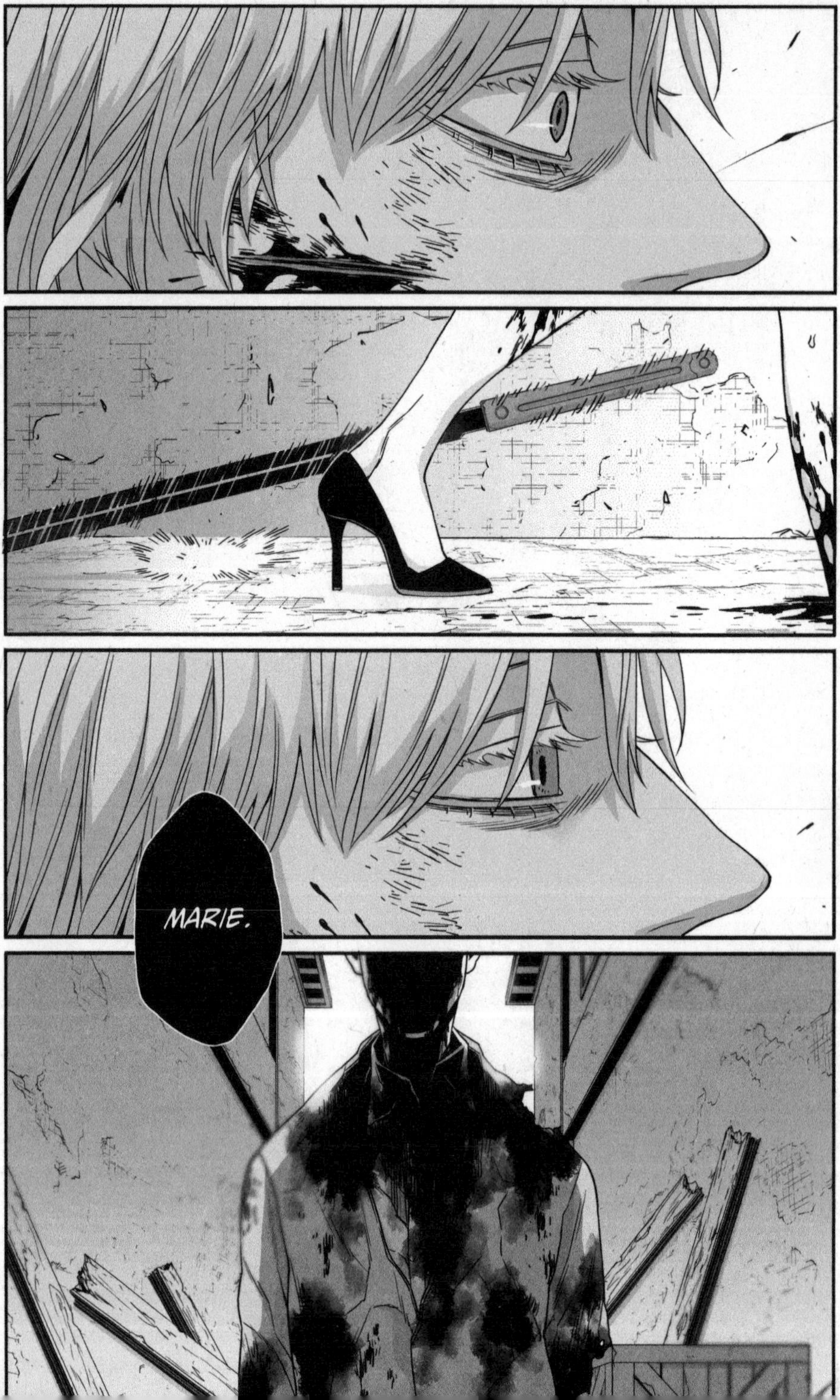
MARIE.

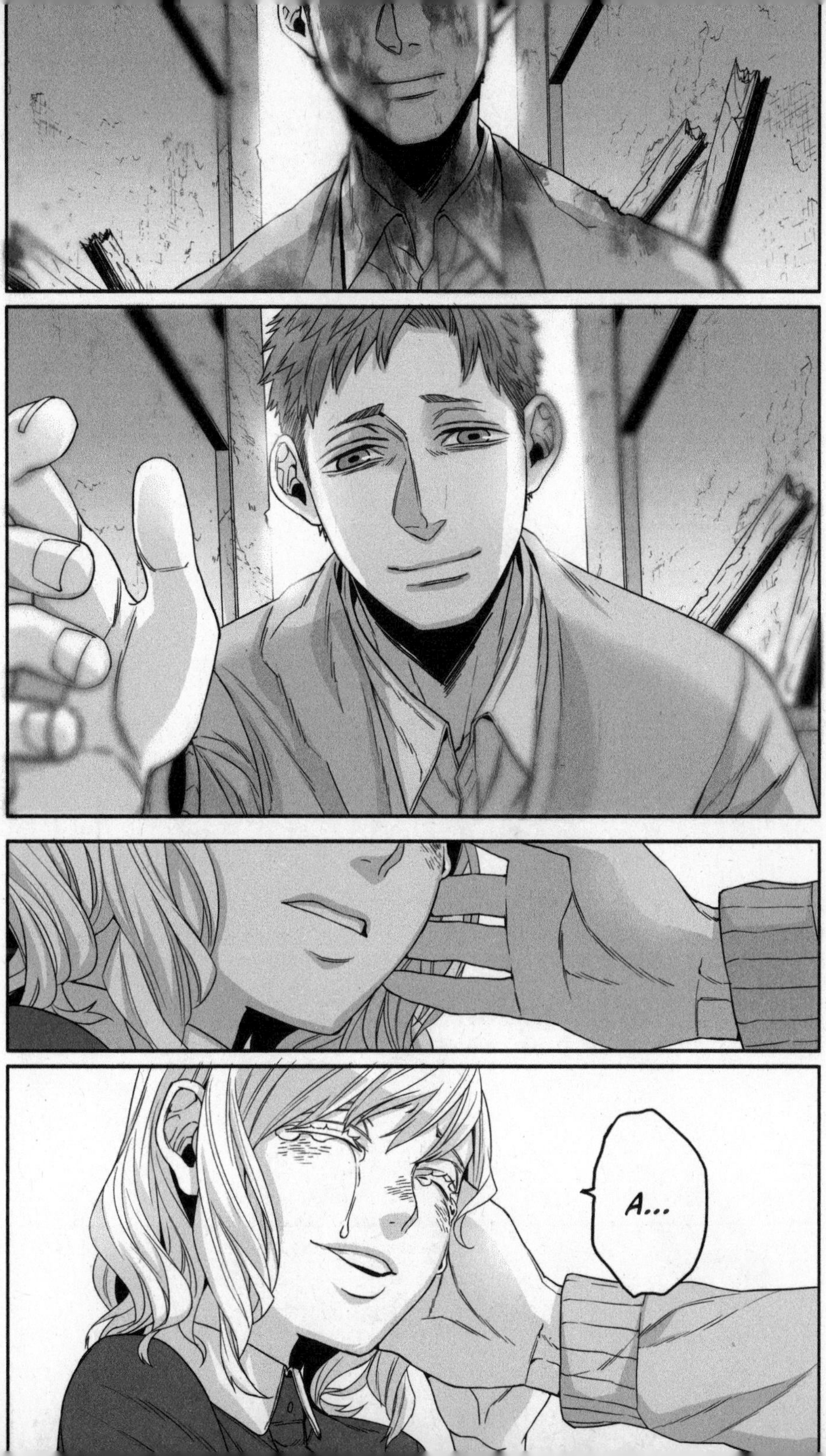
A...

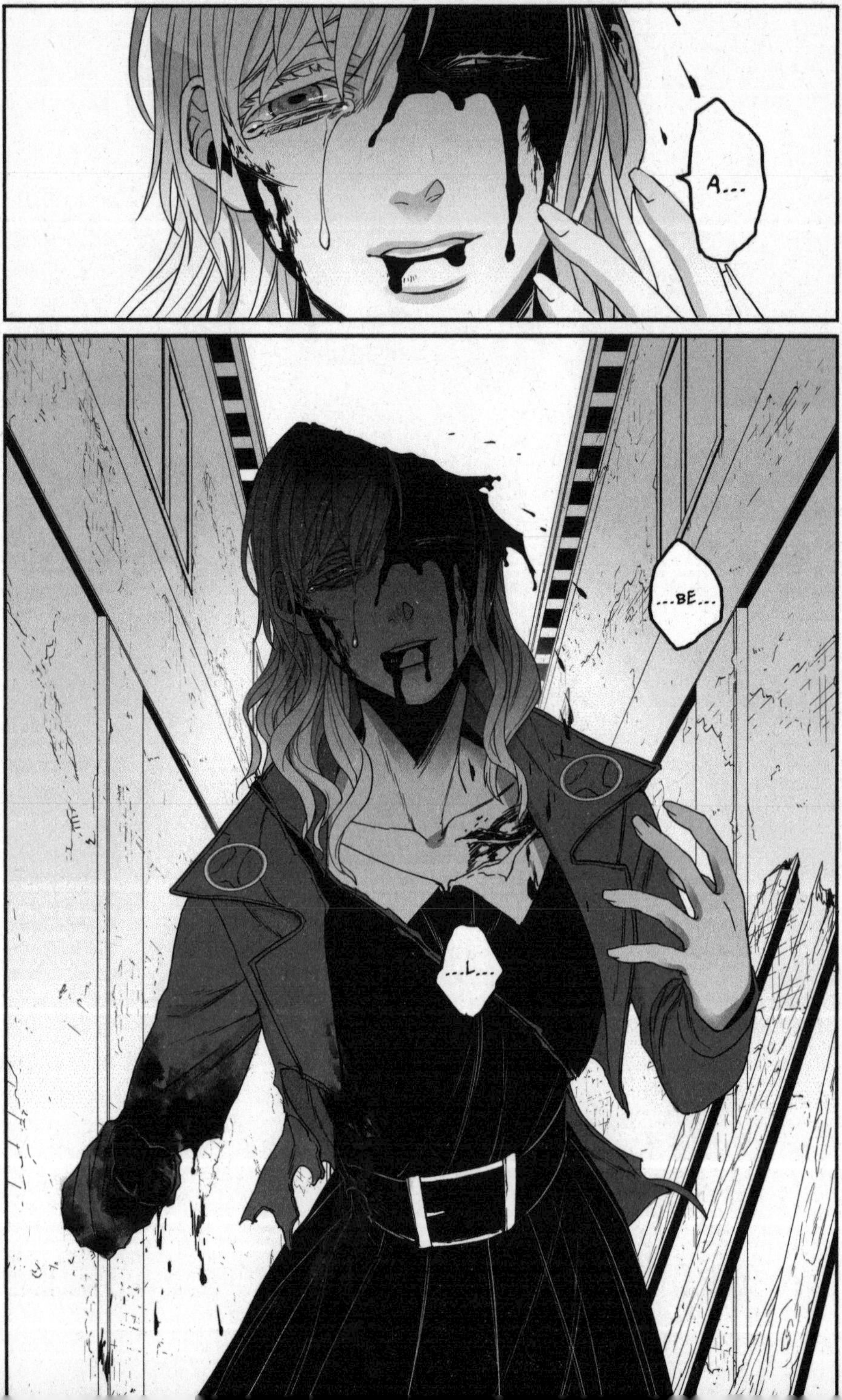
A...
...BE...
...L...

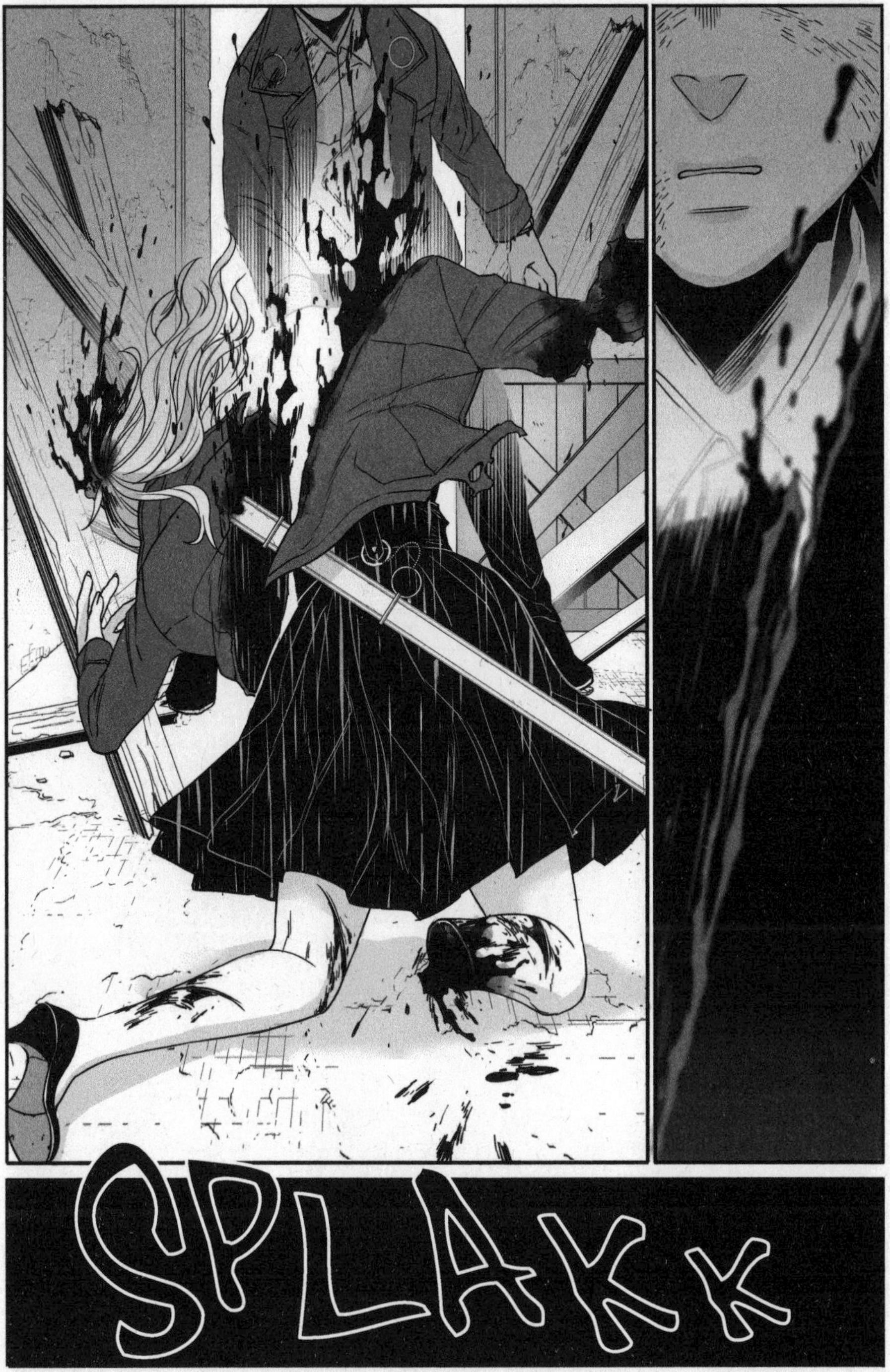
SPLAKK

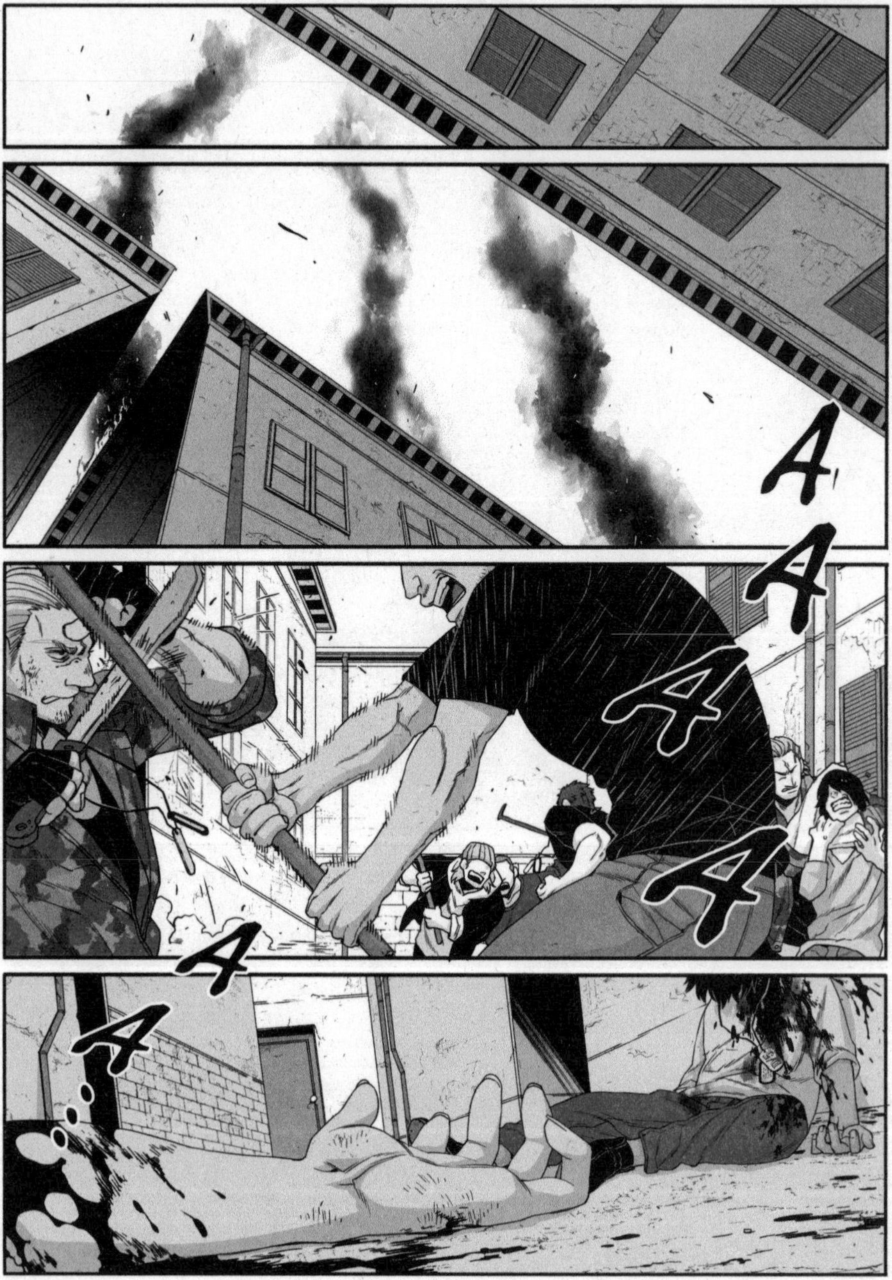
A
A
A
A
A
A
...

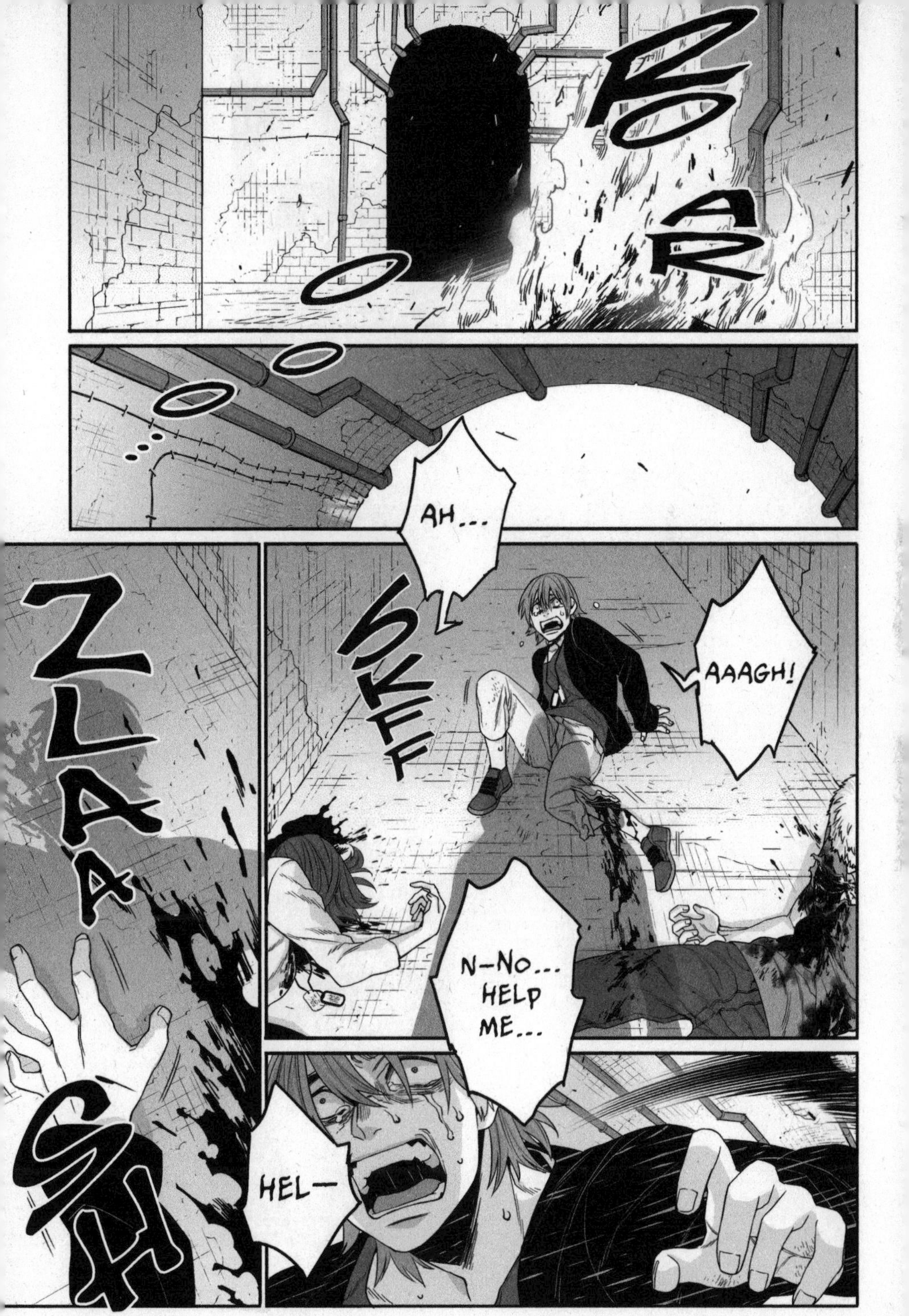
BOAR
OOO...
AH...
SKFF
AAAGH!
ZLAASH
N-NO... HELP ME...
HEL—

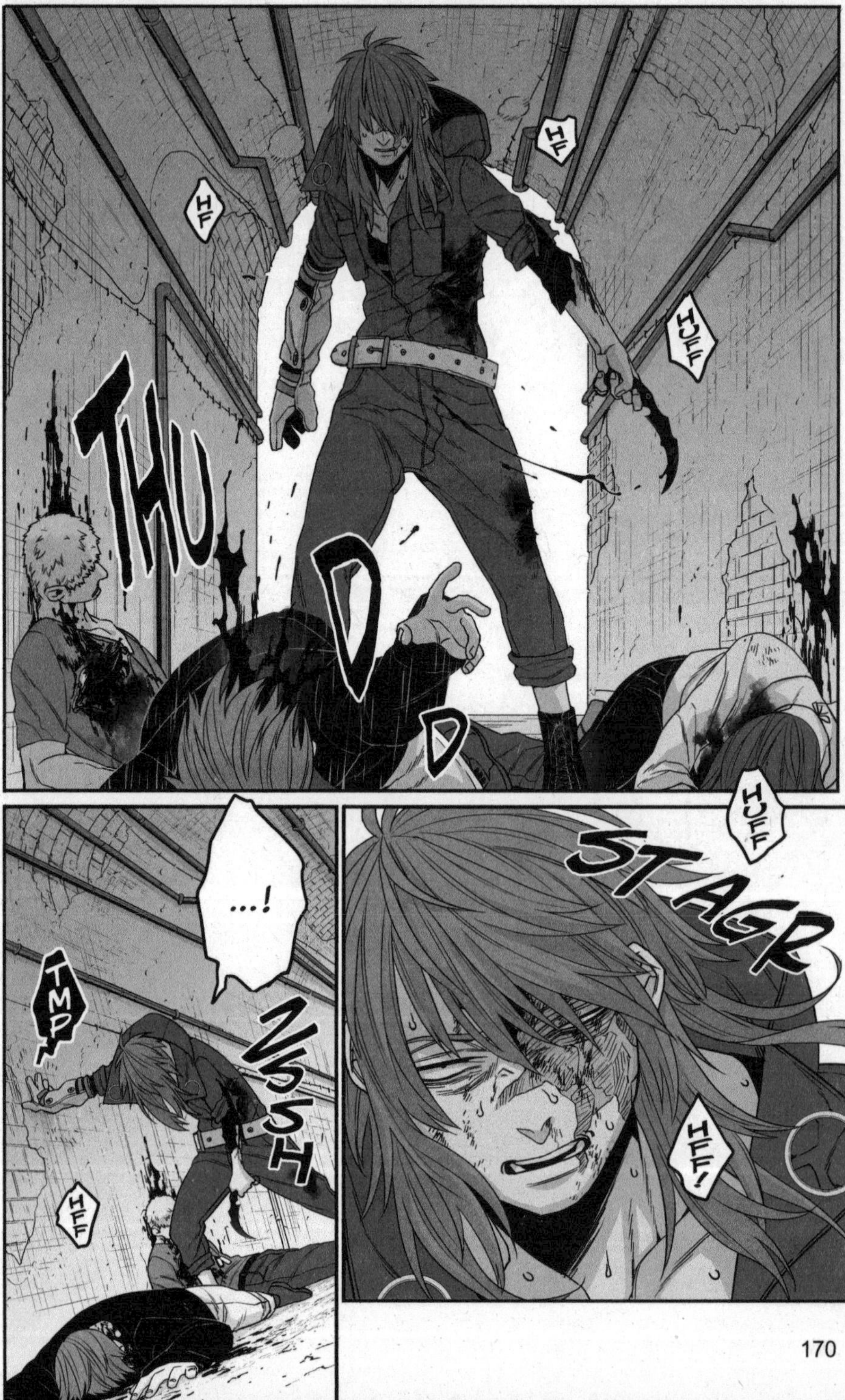
HF
HF
HUFF
THUD
D
HUFF
STAGR
HFF!
...!
TMP
ZSSH
HFF

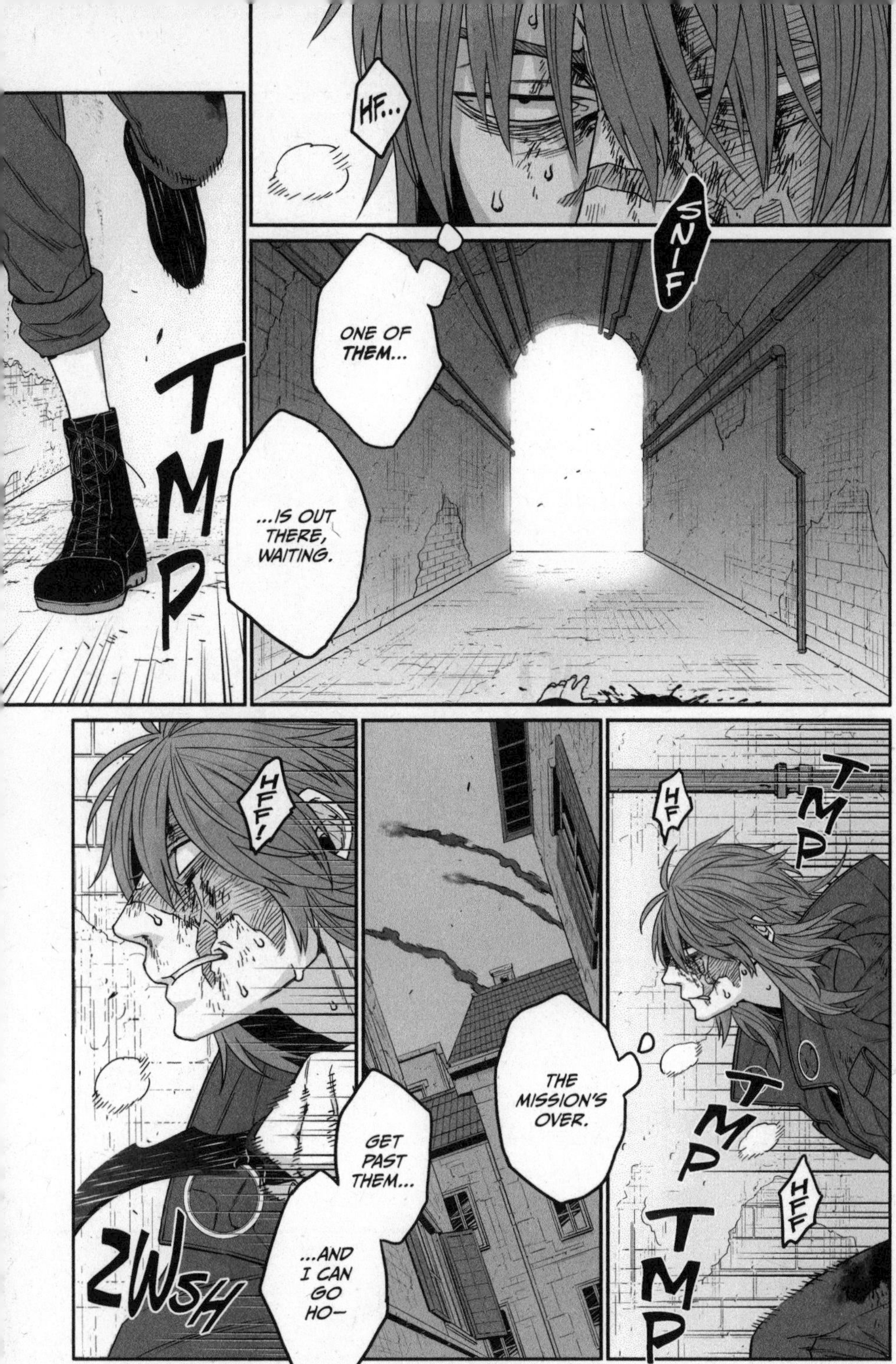
HF...
SNIF
TMP
ONE OF THEM...
...IS OUT THERE, WAITING.
TMP
HF
THE MISSION'S OVER.
TMP
HFF
TMP
GET PAST THEM...
...AND I CAN GO HO–
HFF!
ZWSH

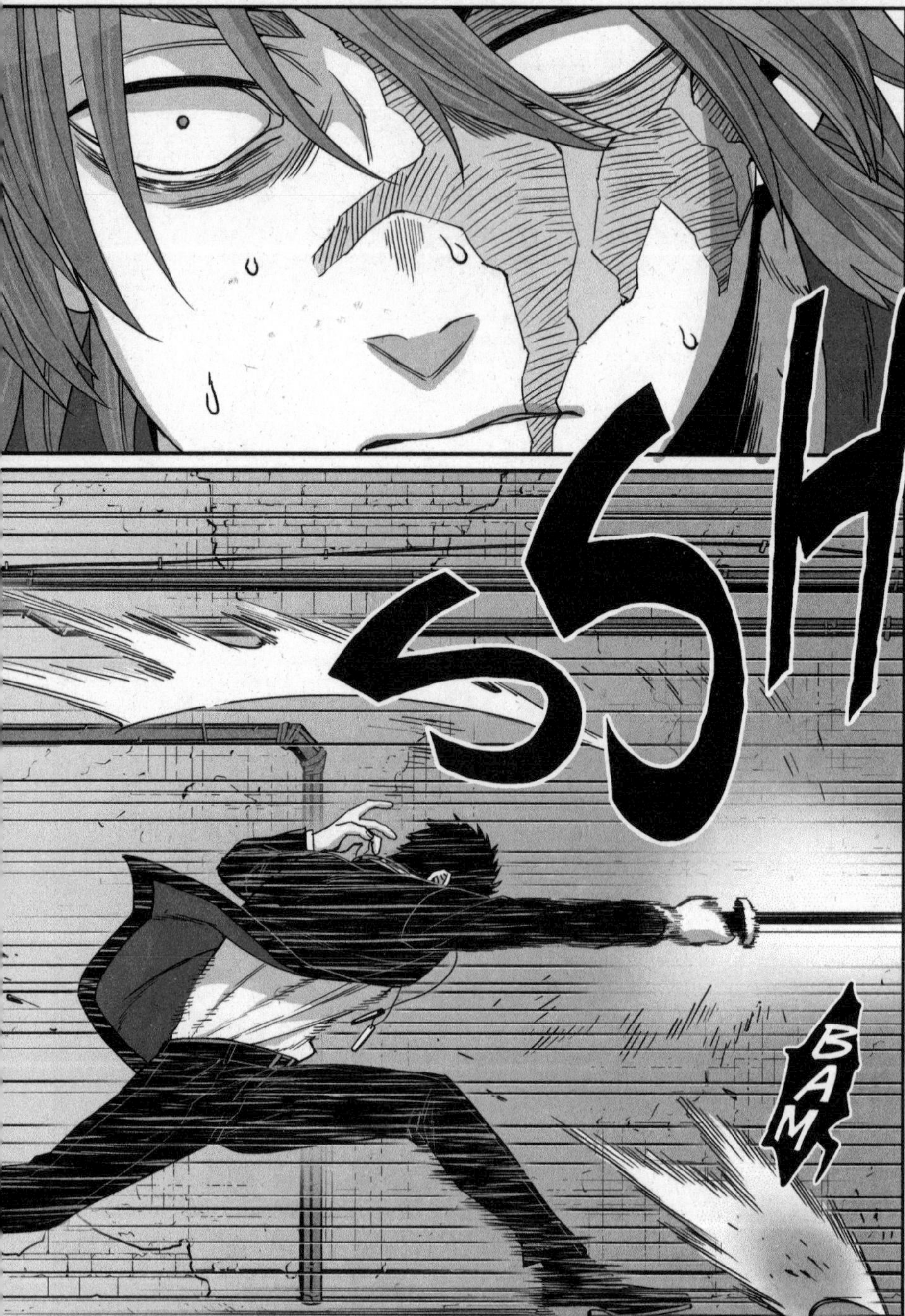
SSH
BAM

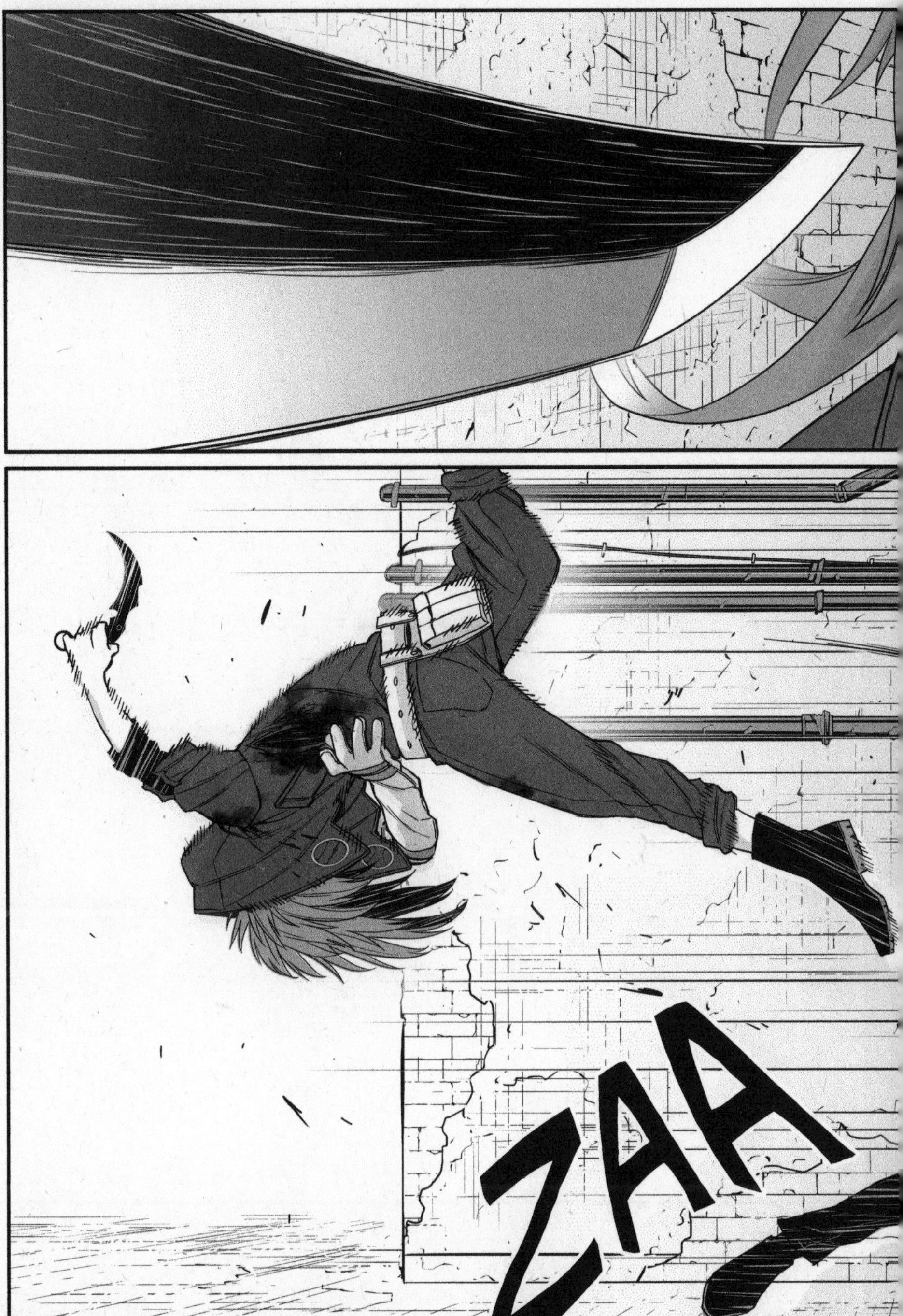
ZAA

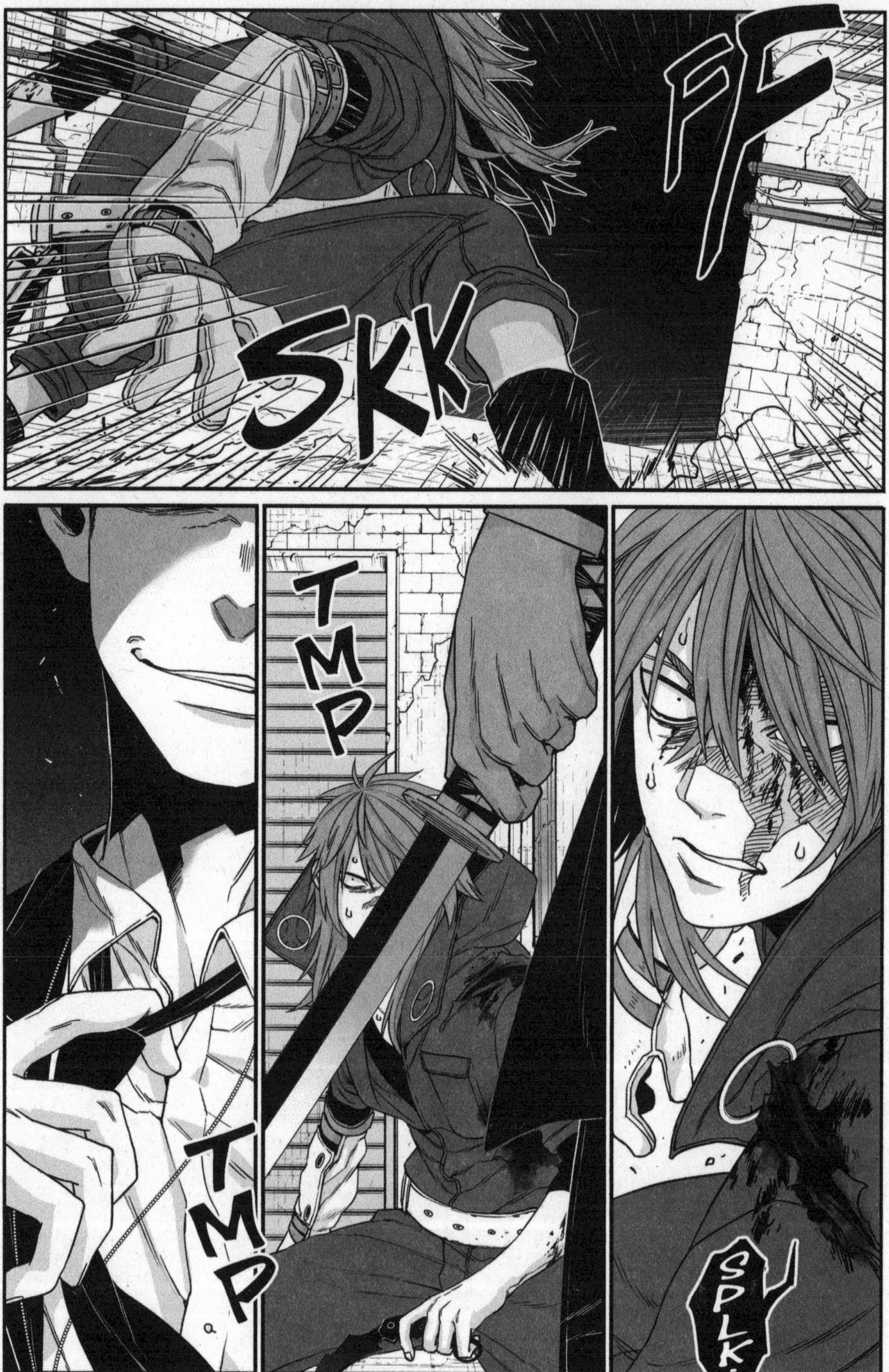
FF
SKK
TMP
TMP
SPLK...

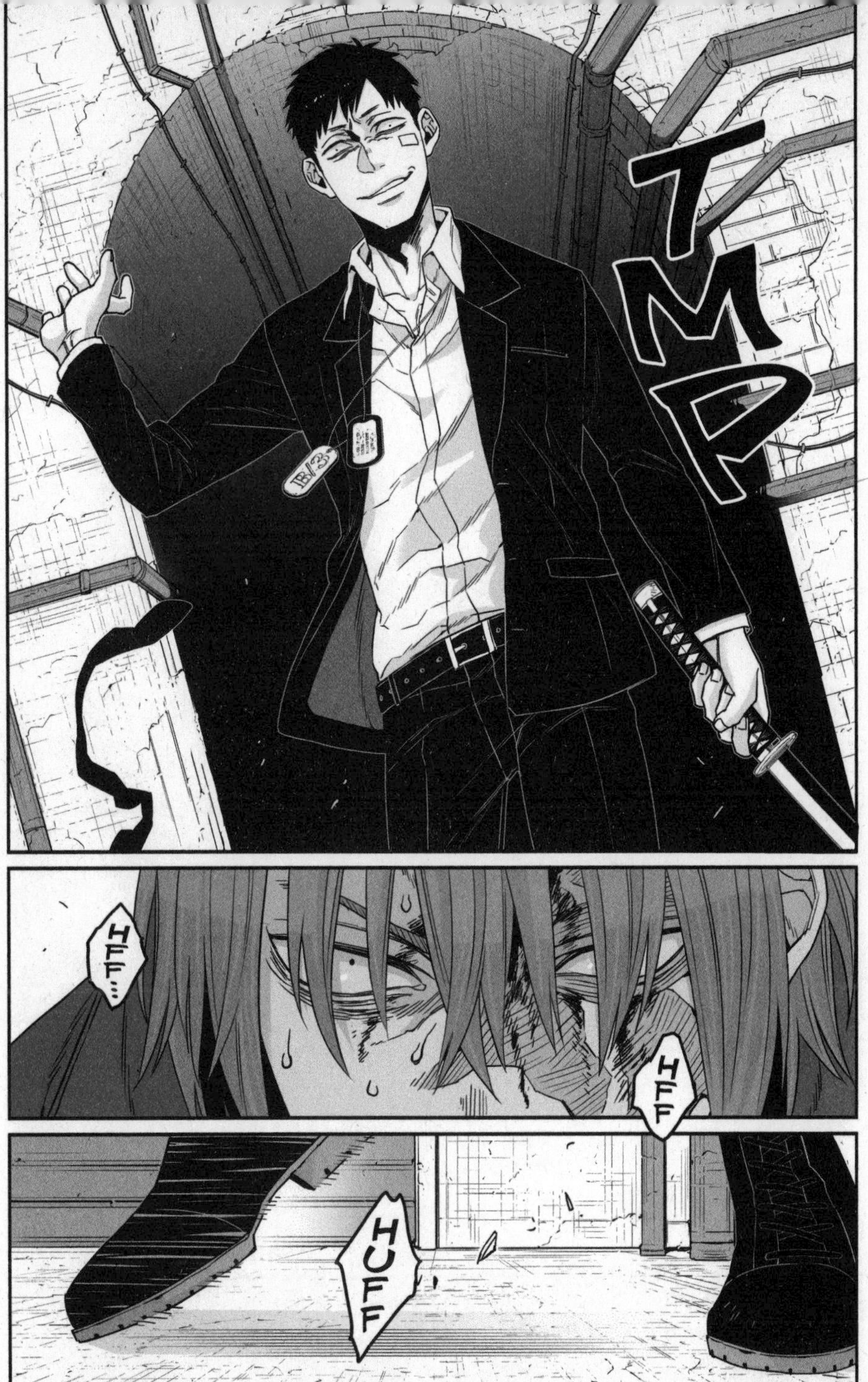
TMP
HFF...
HFF
HUFF

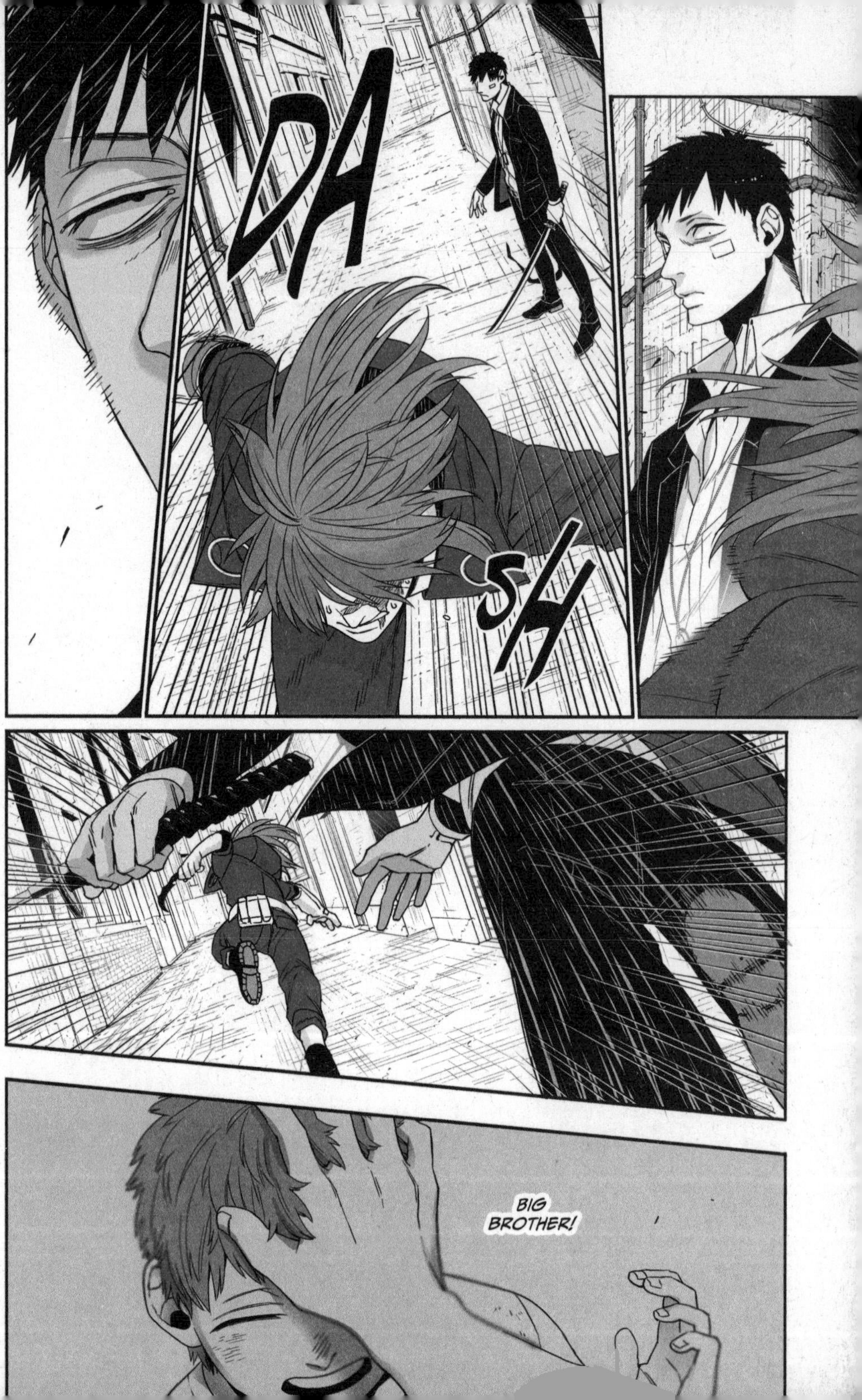
DA
SH
BIG BROTHER!

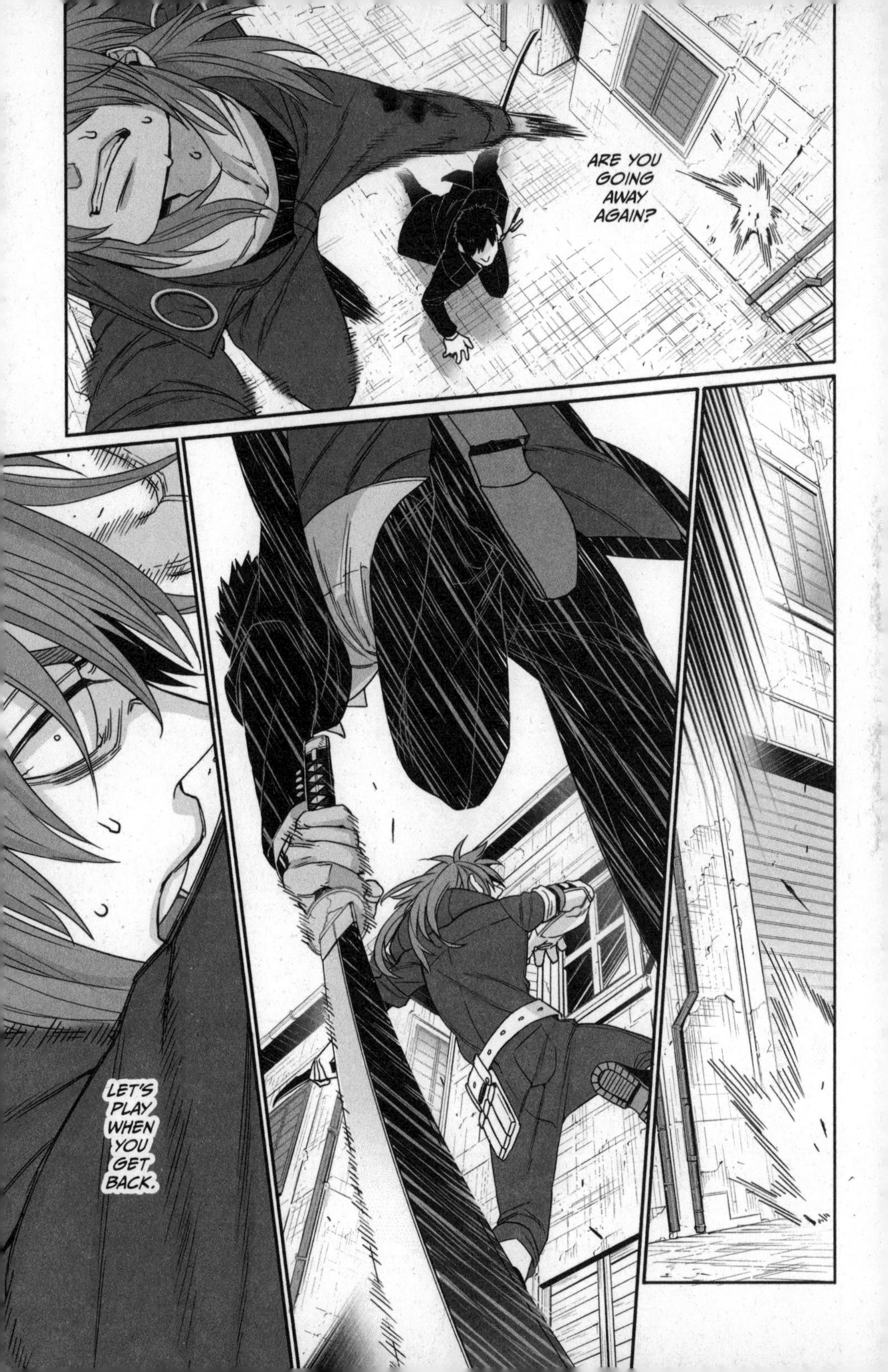
ARE YOU GOING AWAY AGAIN?
LET'S PLAY WHEN YOU GET BACK.

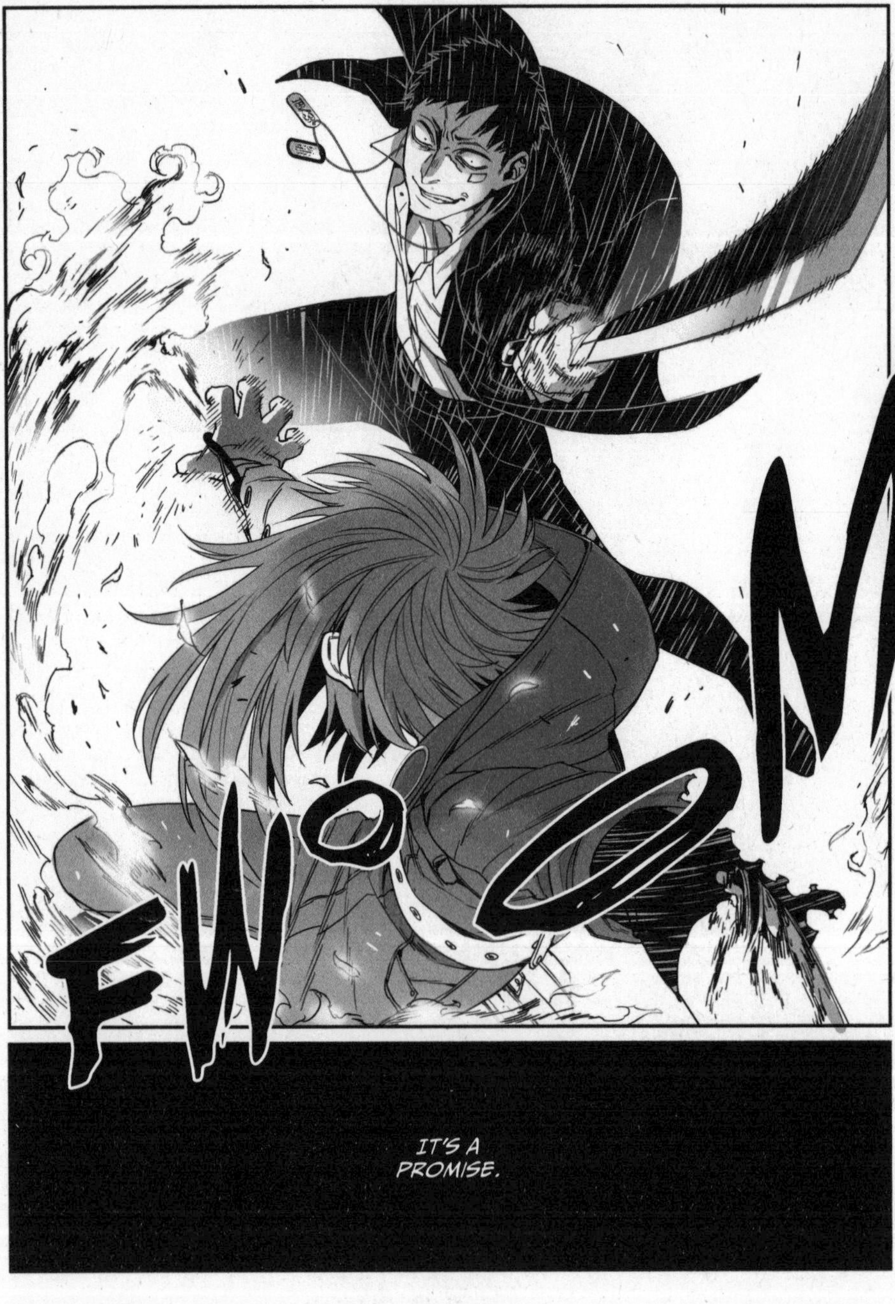
FWOOM
IT'S A PROMISE.

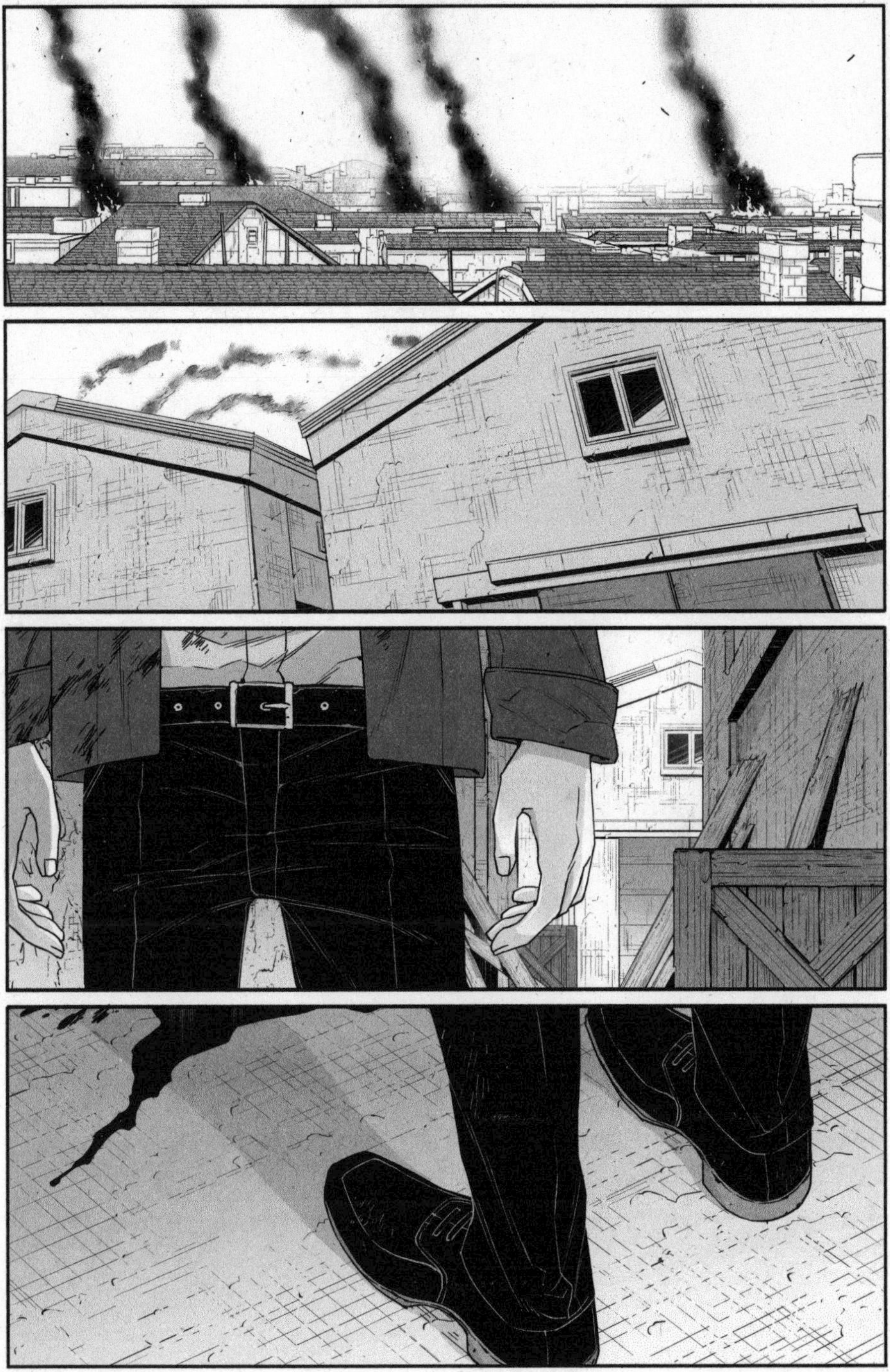

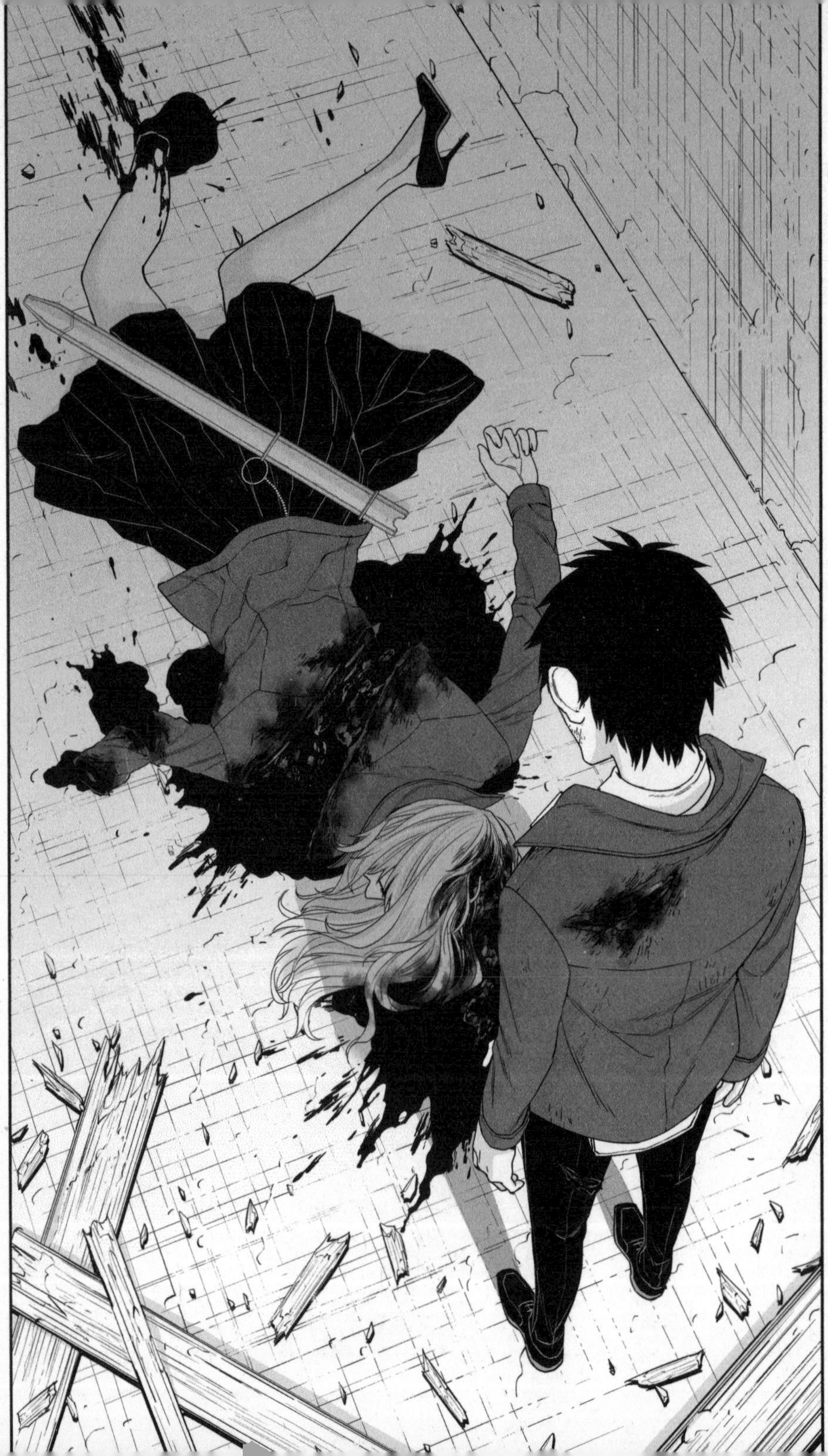

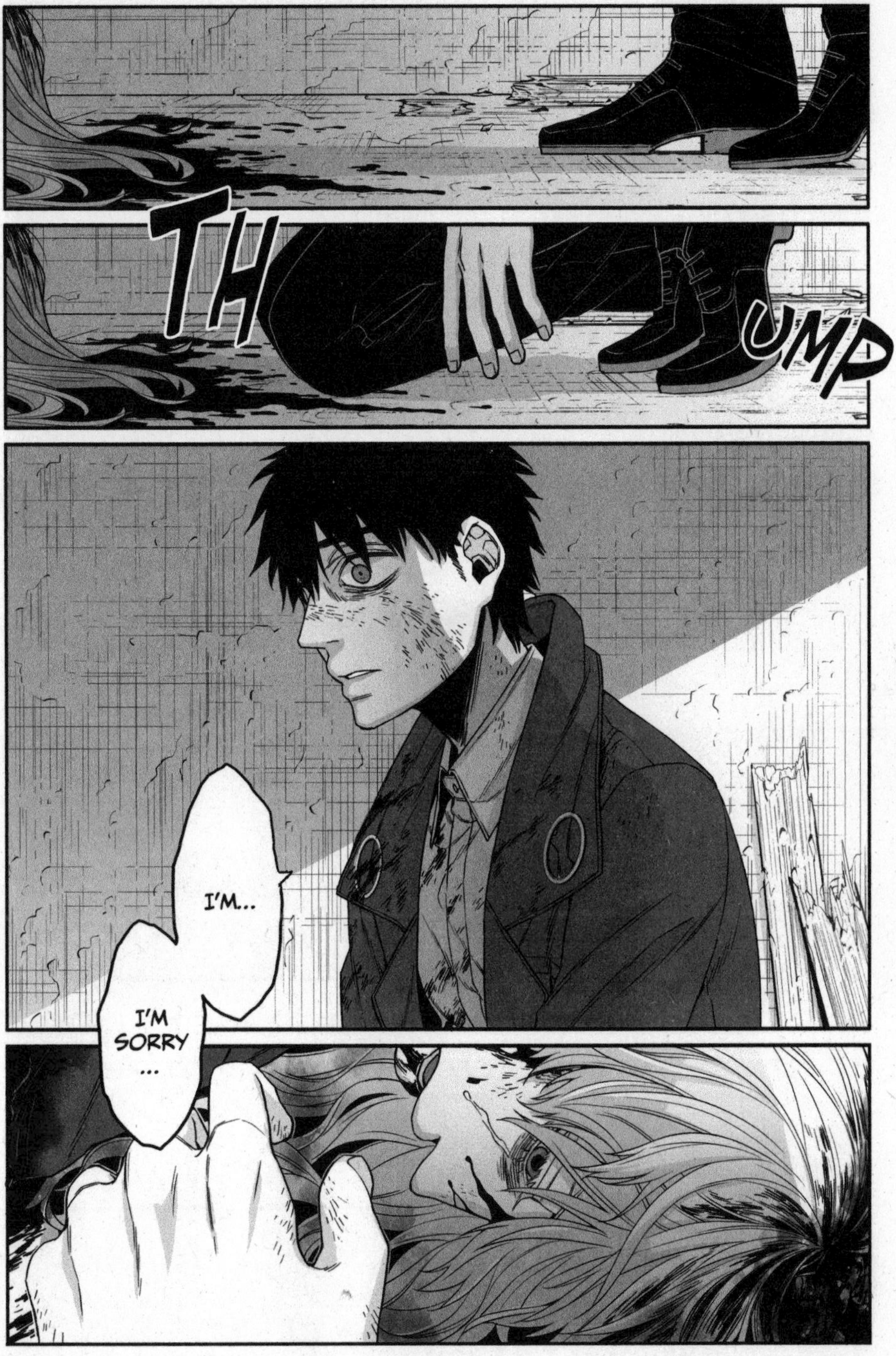
THUMP
I'M...
I'M SORRY ...

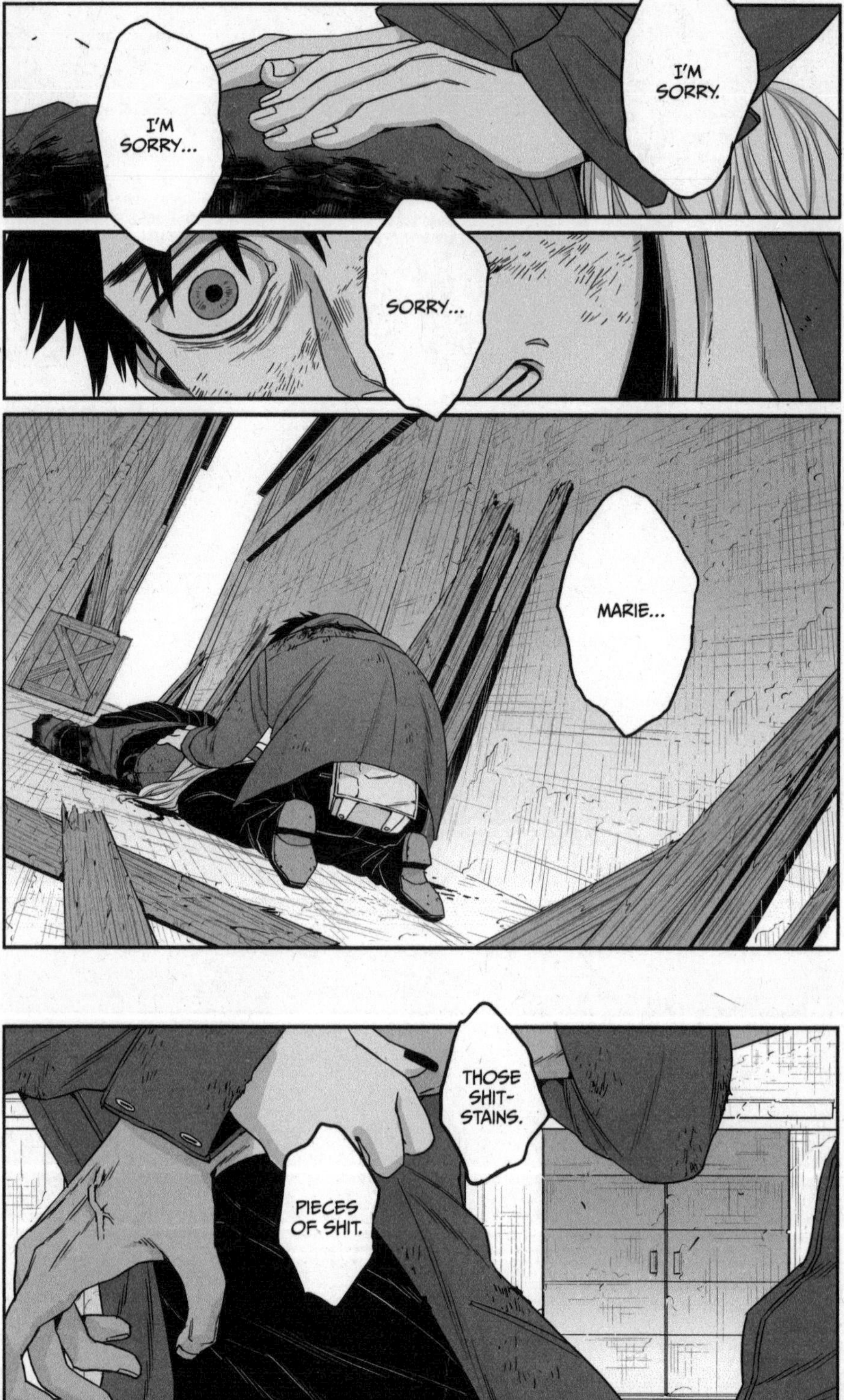
I'M SORRY.
I'M SORRY...
SORRY...
MARIE...
THOSE SHIT-STAINS.
PIECES OF SHIT.

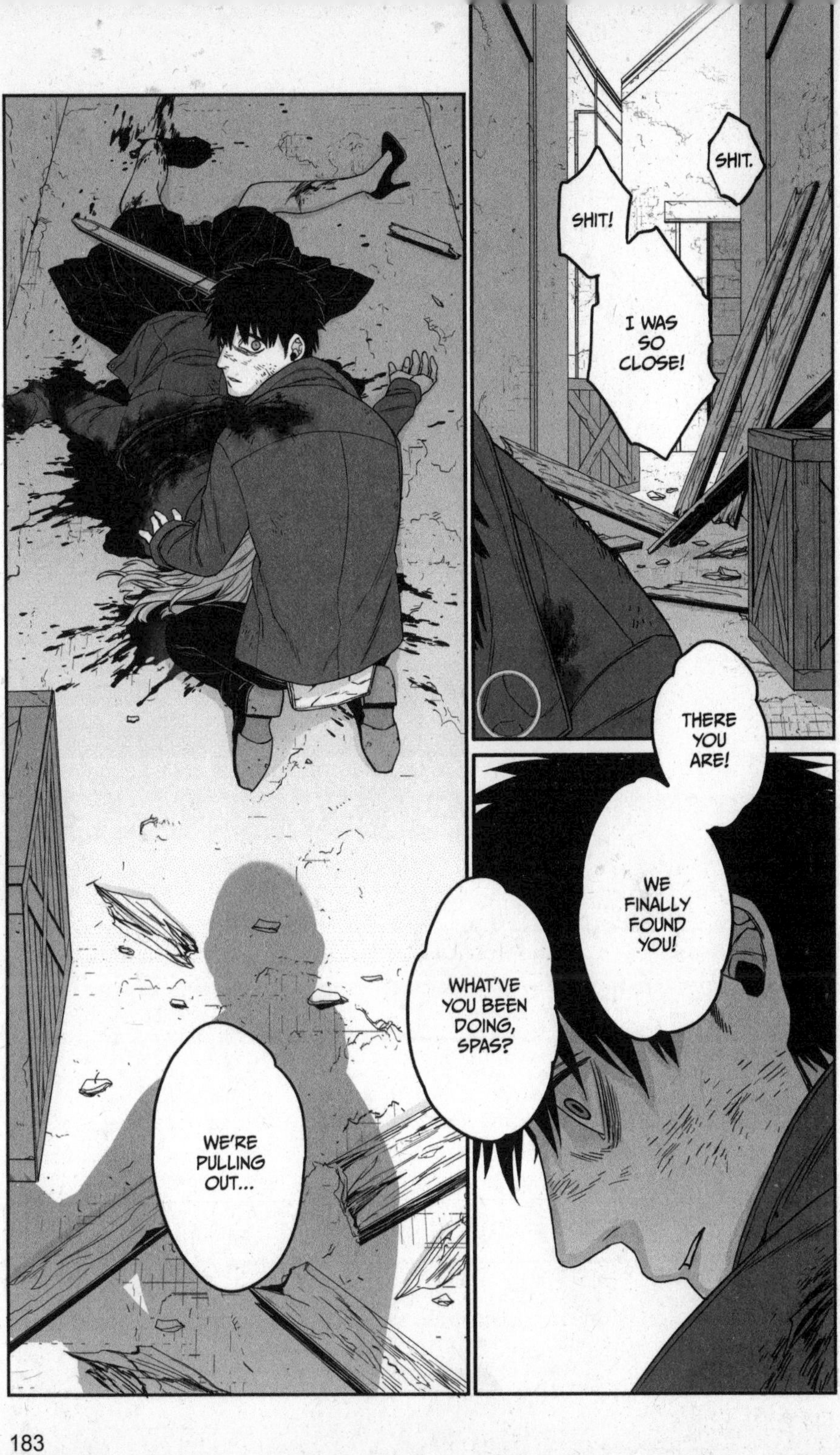
SHIT.
SHIT!
I WAS SO CLOSE!
THERE YOU ARE!
WE FINALLY FOUND YOU!
WHAT'VE YOU BEEN DOING, SPAS?
WE'RE PULLING OUT...

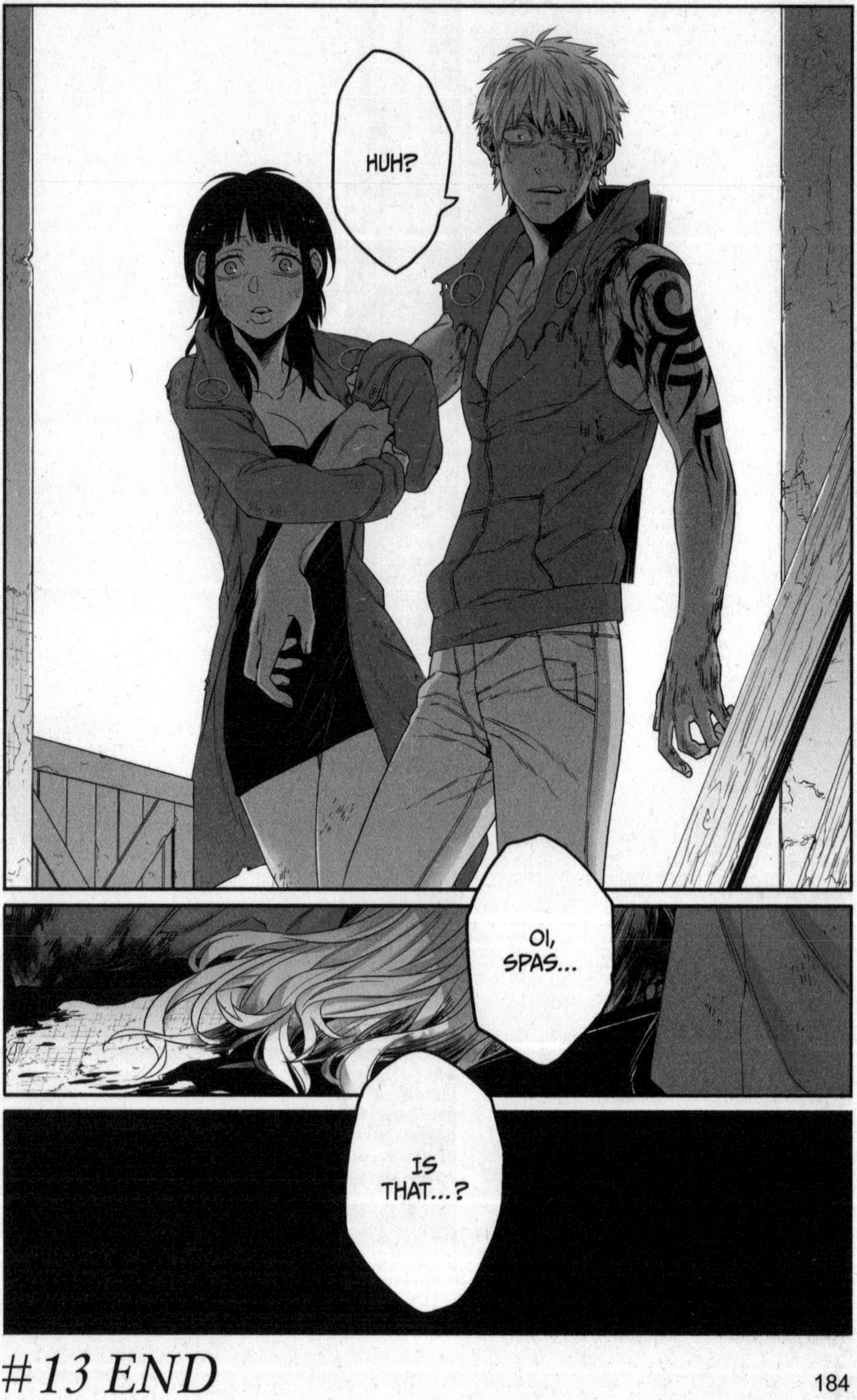
HUH?
OI, SPAS...
IS THAT...?

#13 END

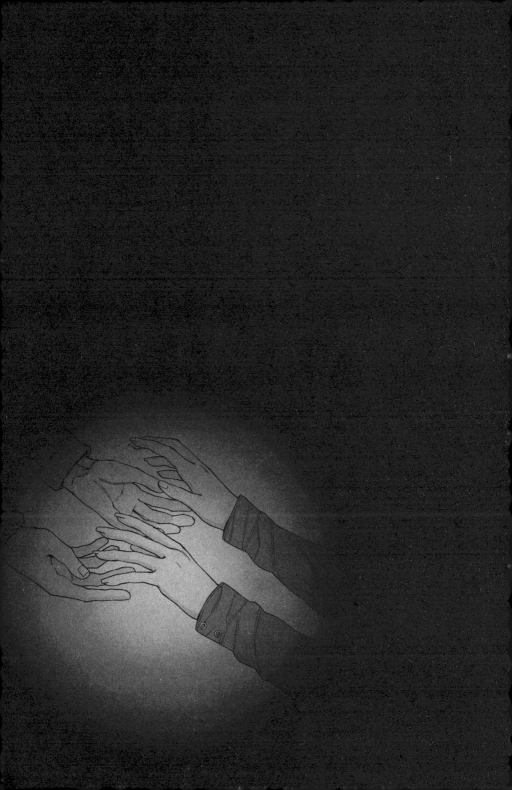

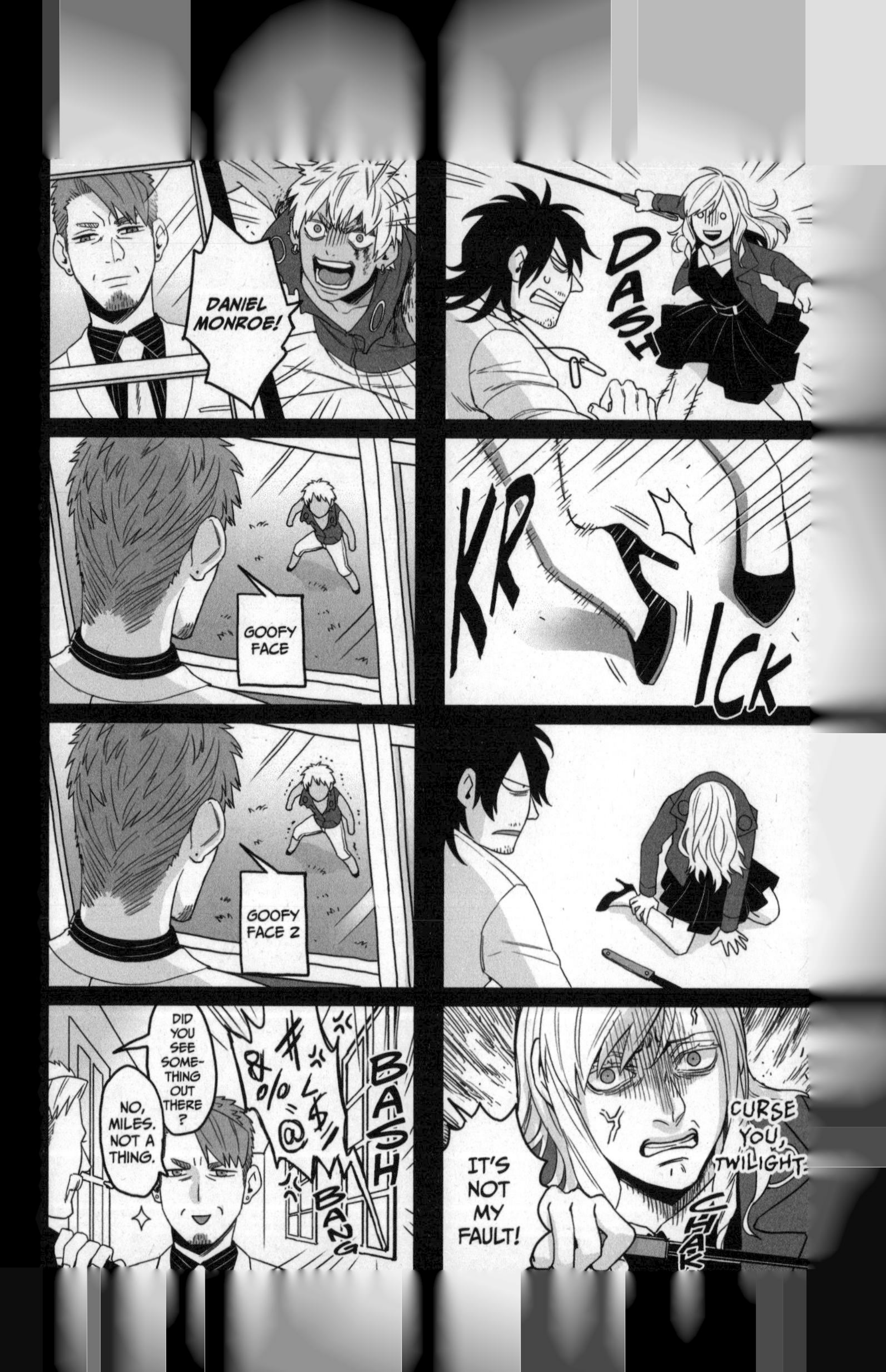

DASH
KRICK
CURSE YOU, TWILIGHT...
IT'S NOT MY FAULT!
CHAK
DANIEL MONROE!
GOOFY FACE
GOOFY FACE 2
DID YOU SEE SOME-THING OUT THERE?
NO, MILES. NOT A THING.
&%#$@
BASH
BANG

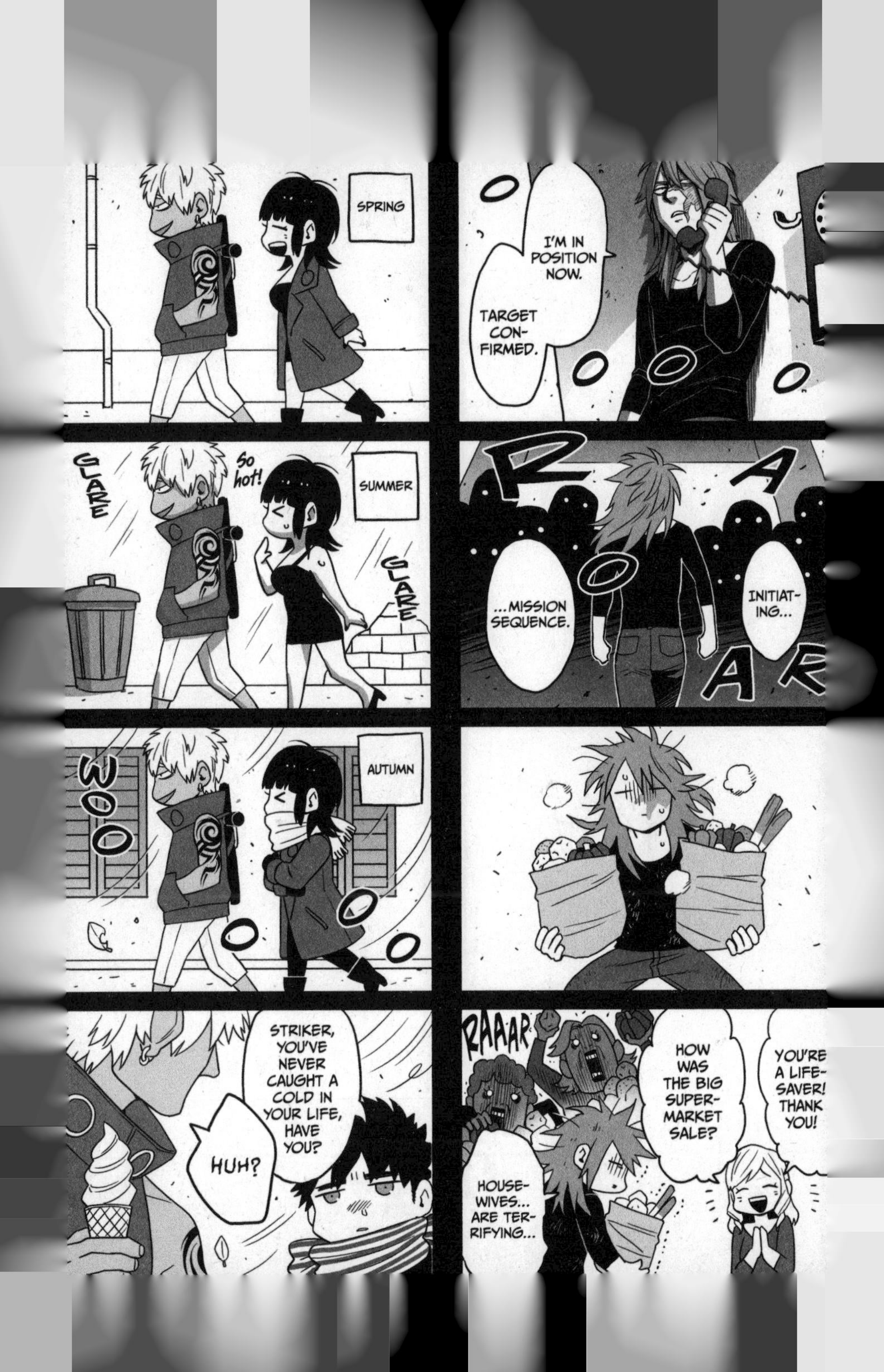
I'M IN POSITION NOW.
TARGET CON-FIRMED.
RAAAR
INITIATING...
...MISSION SEQUENCE.
RAAAR
YOU'RE A LIFE-SAVER! THANK YOU!
HOW WAS THE BIG SUPER-MARKET SALE?
HOUSE-WIVES... ARE TER-RIFYING...
SPRING
SUMMER
So hot!
GLARE
GLARE
AUTUMN
WOO
STRIKER, YOU'VE NEVER CAUGHT A COLD IN YOUR LIFE, HAVE YOU?
HUH?

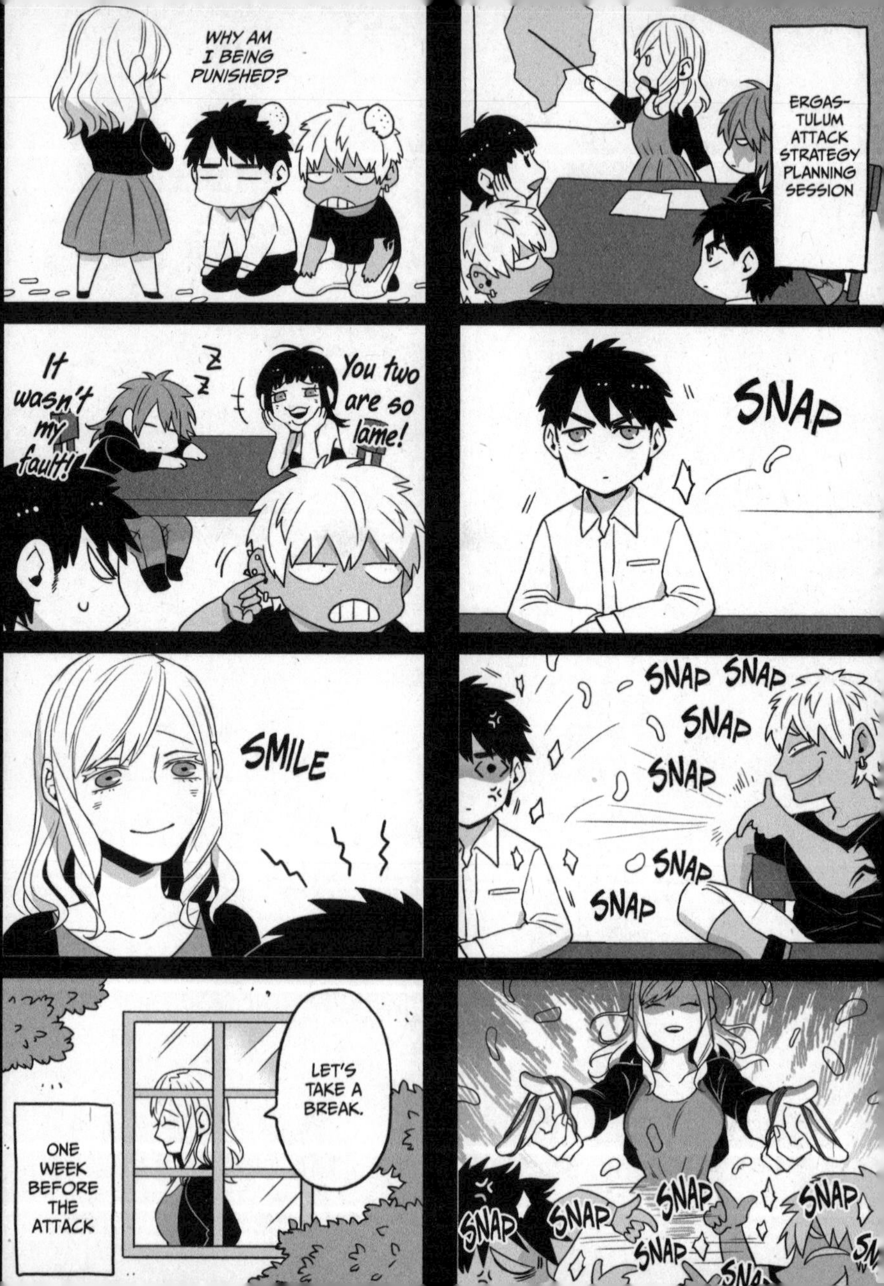
ERGASTULUM ATTACK STRATEGY PLANNING SESSION
SNAP
SNAP SNAP
SNAP
SNAP
SNAP
SNAP
SNAP
SNAP
SNAP
SNAP
SNAP
WHY AM I BEING PUNISHED?
It wasn't my fault!
You two are so lame!
SMILE
ONE WEEK BEFORE THE ATTACK
LET'S TAKE A BREAK.

Afterword

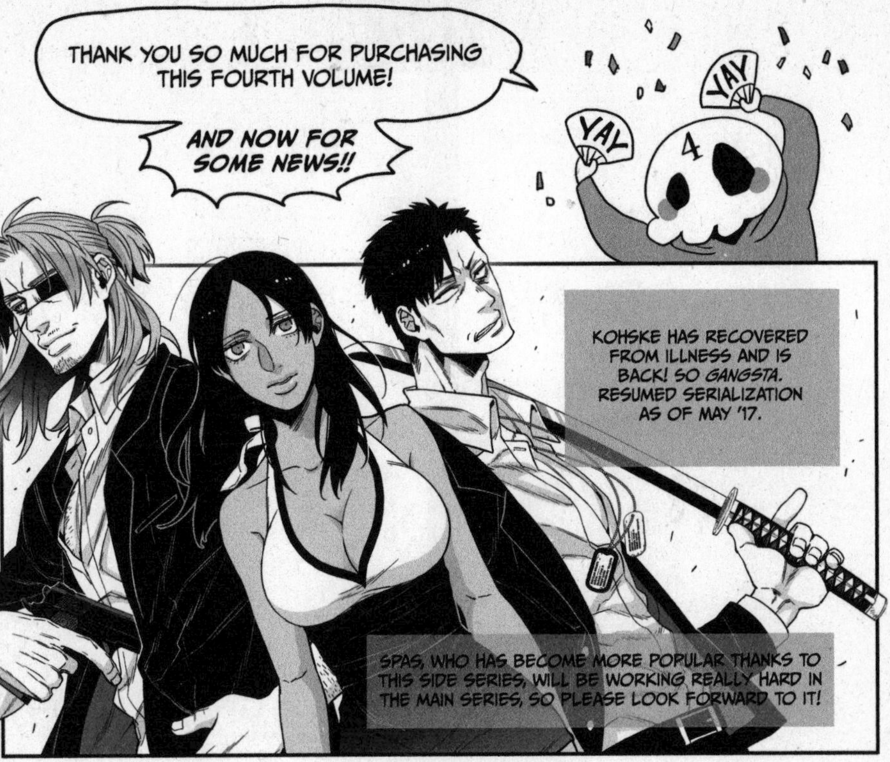

THANK YOU SO MUCH FOR PURCHASING THIS FOURTH VOLUME!
AND NOW FOR SOME NEWS!!
YAY
YAY
4
KOHSKE HAS RECOVERED FROM ILLNESS AND IS BACK! SO *GANGSTA.* RESUMED SERIALIZATION AS OF MAY '17.
SPAS, WHO HAS BECOME MORE POPULAR THANKS TO THIS SIDE SERIES, WILL BE WORKING REALLY HARD IN THE MAIN SERIES, SO PLEASE LOOK FORWARD TO IT!

SEE YOU NEXT VOLUME!

KOHSKE
ASSISTANT K / ASSISTANT M / ASSISTANT H
EDITOR H / DESIGNER ISHIKAWA
MOM / DAD / LITTLE BRO / MY DOG
AND TO EVERYONE WHO'S HELPED ME.

THANK YOU ALWAYS!

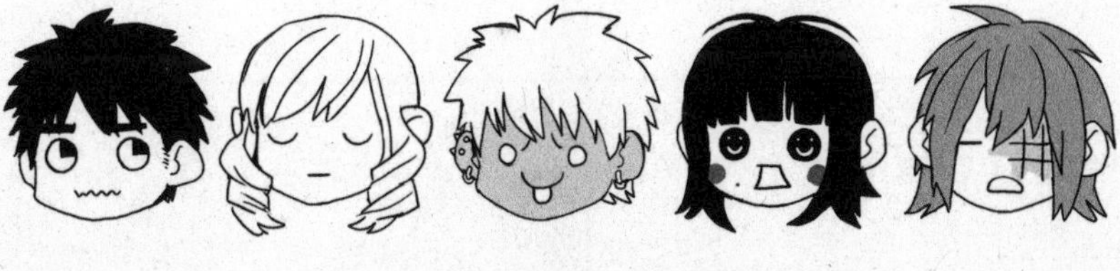

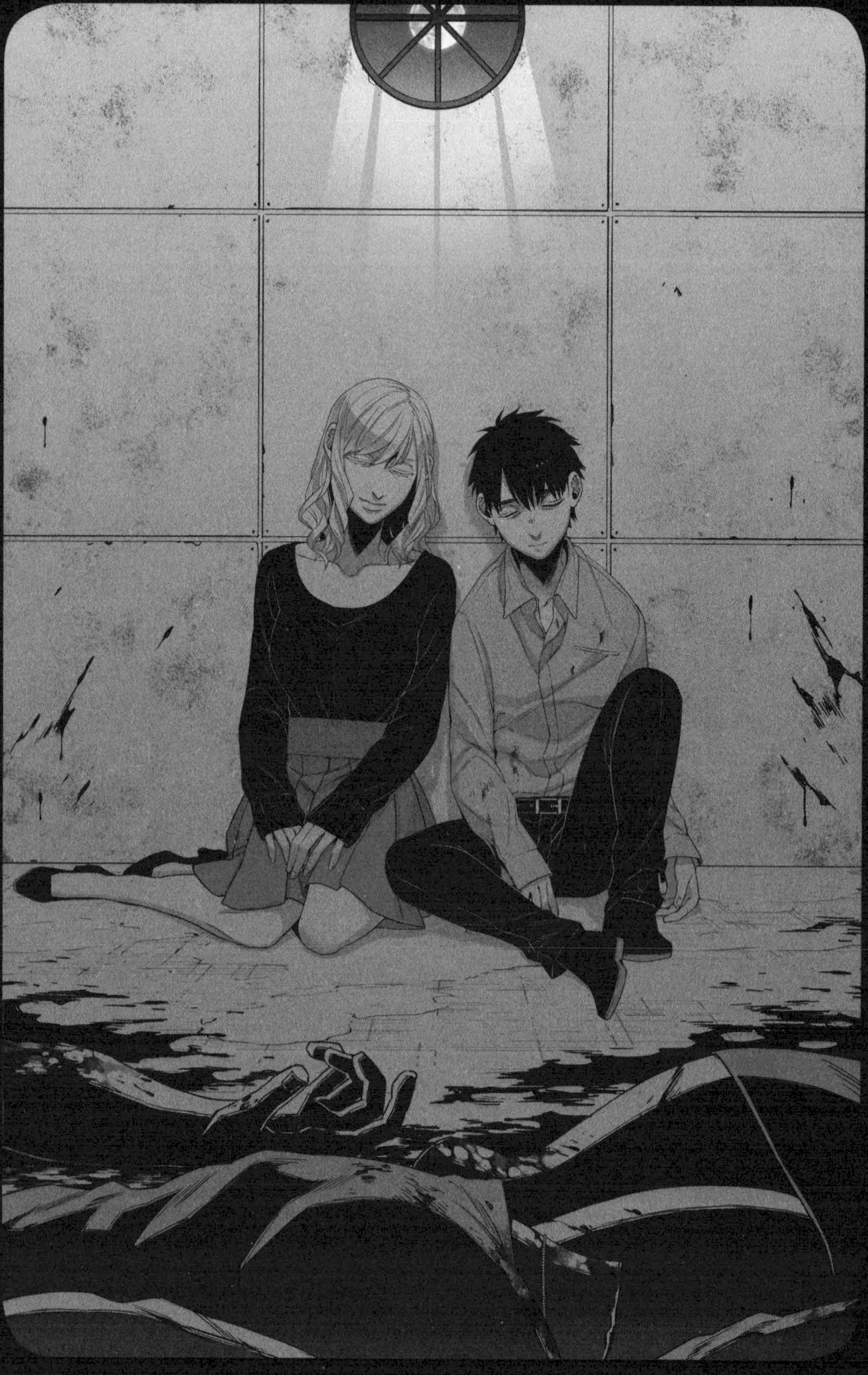

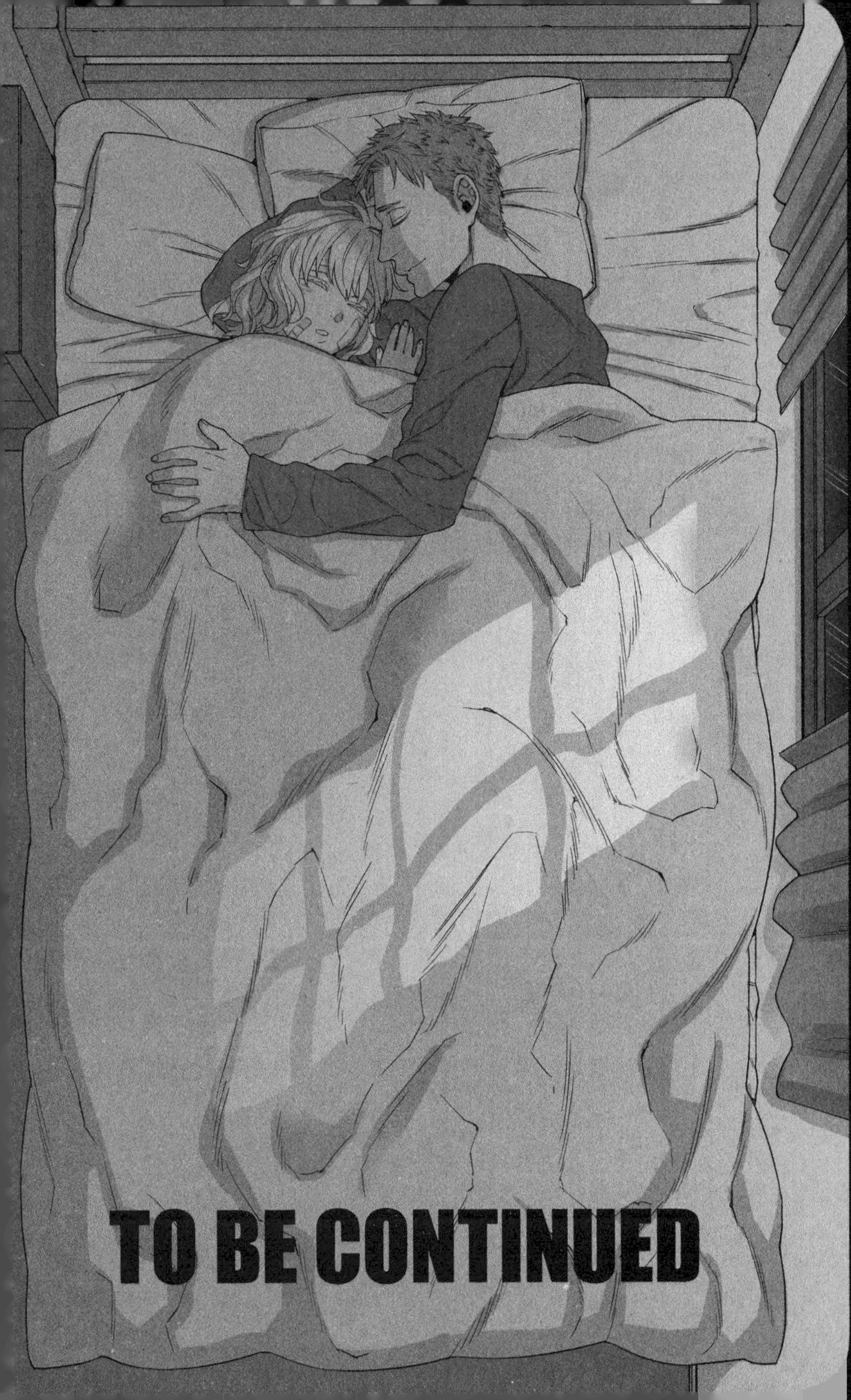
TO BE CONTINUED

GANGSTA:CURSED.
EP_MARCO ADRIANO

Gangsta:Cursed. Ep_Marco Adriano
Volume 4

VIZ Signature Edition

Story by Kohske
Art by Syuhei Kamo

Translation & Adaptation/Christine Schilling
Touch-up Art & Lettering/Eric Erbes
Cover & Graphic Design/Shawn Carrico
Editor/Leyla Aker

Printed in the U.S.A.

Published by VIZ Media, LLC
P.O. Box 77010
San Francisco, CA 94107

10 9 8 7 6 5 4 3 2 1
First printing, May 2018

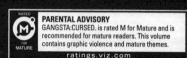

PARENTAL ADVISORY
GANGSTA:CURSED. is rated M for Mature and is
recommended for mature readers. This volume
contains graphic violence and mature themes.
ratings.viz.com

VIZSIGNATURE.COM